DISSENT IN AMERICA

To 1877

VOLUME I

Ralph F. Young

Temple University

PEARSON
Longman

New York   San Francisco   Boston
London   Toronto   Sydney   Tokyo   Singapore   Madrid
Mexico City   Munich   Paris   Cape Town   Hong Kong   Montreal

Vice President and Publisher: *Priscilla McGeehon*
Executive Marketing Manager: *Sue Westmoreland*
Senior Media Supplements Editor: *Kristi Olson*
Senior Media Editor: *Patrick McCarthy*
Production Manager: *Ellen MacElree*
Project Coordination, Text Design, and Electronic Page Makeup: *Stratford Publishing Services*
Cover Designer/Manager: *Wendy Ann Fredericks*
Cover Photo: *The Granger Collection, New York*
Photo Researcher: *Stratford Publishing Services*
Senior Manufacturing Buyer: *Dennis J. Para*
Printer and Binder: *Hamilton Printing Co.*
Cover Printer: *Phoenix Color Corps.*

Library of Congress Cataloging-in-Publication Data
Dissent in America / [edited by] Ralph F. Young.
         v.   cm.
       Contents: v. 1. To 1877. Pre-revolutionary roots, 1607–1760. Revolution and the birth of a
nation, 1760–1820. Questioning the nation, 1820–1860. War and Reconstruction, 1860–1877—
       ISBN 0-321-17976-5
       1. United States—Politics and government—Sources.   2. United States—Social
conditions—Sources.   3. Dissenters—United States—History—Sources.   4. Social
reformers—United States—History—Sources.   5. Democracy—United States—History—
Sources.   6. Social problems—United States—History—Sources.   I. Young, Ralph F.
   E183.D57 2004
   303.48'4' 0973—dc22   2004007552

Copyright © 2005 by Pearson Education, Inc.

Photo Credits
page 1: Photograph courtesy of Bettmann/Corbis.
page 49: Photograph courtesy of Terra Foundation for the Arts, Chicago.
page 125: Lowell Mill Girls: Photograph courtesy of American Textile History Museum. Henry
David Thoreau: From the collections of the Thoreau Society at the Thoreau Institute.
page 227: Photograph courtesy of the Florida State Archives.

Please visit us at http://www.ablongman.com

ISBN 0-321-17976-5

1 2 3 4 5 6 7 8 9 10—HT—07 06 05 04

To the memory of my parents,
Emily Mildred Young and Ralph Eric Young

CONTENTS

PREFACE

If a man does not keep pace with his companions, perhaps it is because he hears a different drummer. Let him step to the music which he hears, however measured or far away. *Henry David Thoreau*

You don't need a weatherman to know which way the wind blows. . . . *Bob Dylan*

———————————

Between 1955 and 1975, the United States underwent a profound change, from a nation that (somewhat naively and arrogantly) believed in its own myths to a nation that (somewhat naively and angrily) began to question those very myths.

For some citizens, the 1960s and the 5 years on either side of the decade were profoundly disturbing. For others, they were a breath of fresh air. For everyone, no matter what their perspective, it seemed that protest and dissent had reached a high-water mark. But the years that brought the Montgomery bus boycott, the lunch counter sit-ins, the Freedom Rides, the March on Washington, the Berkeley Free Speech Movement, the march on the Pentagon, Woodstock, Altamont, and Kent State, Allen Ginsberg, Malvina Reynolds, Joan Baez, Bob Dylan, Phil Ochs, Timothy Leary, Abbie Hoffman, Ella Baker, Malcolm X, Bobby Seale, Angela Davis, Betty Friedan, and Elizabeth Martinez, SDS, AIM, NOW, and the GLF were in no way an aberration; in no way were they contrary to American ideals and American principles. In fact, the political, cultural, and social upheavals of the 1960s were simply a culmination of the very spirit upon which this country was founded—the spirit of dissent.

All of a sudden, or so it seemed, civil rights activists, antiwar liberals, and songwriters took seriously the injunctions of John Locke and Thomas Jefferson that all of us were endowed with inalienable natural rights. They took seriously the lesson taught to every primary school pupil that the United States was the greatest country in the world because it stood for the inherent equality of *all* people. And yet when these same pupils, growing into adolescence and young adulthood, saw televised images of soldiers of the 101st Airborne (one of the first divisions to parachute into Normandy on June 6, 1944) protecting black teenagers as they entered Little Rock's Central High School in 1957, it suddenly dawned on many of them that the grand American values that they had been taught had simply not been realized. It was this blatant discrepancy between ideal and reality that had a huge impact on the escalation of dissent in the 1960s.

Between 1965 and 1967, while studying Puritanism as a graduate student at Michigan State University, I attended speeches by Martin Luther King Jr., Stokeley Carmichael, Timothy Leary, and (of all people) the führer of the American Nazi

Party, George Lincoln Rockwell, during their whirlwind visits to the campus. All four of these men, in their own way, dissented against the norms of American society and, to varying extents, the values of the "American way of life." Yet each man's convictions had historical antecedents. Martin Luther King Jr. adopted the words and ideas of Henry David Thoreau and Walter Rauschenbusch, Reinhold Niebuhr and Mahatma Gandhi, as well as the Bible and the Declaration of Independence, and applied them to America in the 1950s and 1960s. Stokeley Carmichael took Marcus Garvey's expressions of "black power" and "black is beautiful" and applied them to the African American experience as the civil rights movement was entering a more cynical phase in the late 1960s. Timothy Leary harked back to the visionaries and mystics of India and Tibet, to European Romanticism, and to the psychedelic experiences of North American Indian shamanism. George Lincoln Rockwell repeated the anti-Semitic, xenophobic sentiments that have persisted in America ever since the founding of the Grand Order of the Star Spangled Banner and the Know-Nothing Party in the nineteenth century.

What I heard in those speeches at Michigan State University was nothing new. Those who espouse radical (or reactionary) revolutionary (or counterrevolutionary) ideas are carrying on a tradition that began during the earliest days of settlement in the New World. In fact, theirs is a tradition that originated even before the foundation of the permanent English colonies that would eventually become the United States. For four centuries, dissent has played a central role in the American experience.

Acknowledgments

A number of my colleagues at Temple University graciously took time from their busy schedules to read and criticize portions of this book as it evolved. Gregory Urwin, Susan Klepp, Ruth Ost, Jim Hilty, Ken Kusmer, Richard Immerman, Vladislav Zubok, Herbert Ershkowitz, Howard Ohline, and David Farber all gave invaluable suggestions and pointed me in the direction of many important and neglected documents of dissent. Lively discussions with Jay Lockenour, Arthur Schmidt, Howard Spodek, Kathy Walker, Barbara Day-Hickman, Peter Gran, David Watt, Phil Evanson and Wilbert Jenkins were also important in honing my views as the book took shape.

Phyllis Cole of the Pennsylvania State University gave me important insights into the Transcendental movement. Barbara Winslow of Brooklyn College clarified many aspects of early feminism. David Wrobel of the University of Nevada, Las Vegas was instrumental in my thinking about this book from its inception and his advice has greatly improved the finished product. James Loewen offered valuable suggestions about the table of contents, and John Serembus and Craig Eisendrath challenged my thinking about the nature of dissent. Homer Yasui graciously offered expert advice on the Japanese American experience during World War II and furnished me with his brother Minoru's letters.

My students have, of course, influenced my thinking and my approach to dissent and protest. Justin Chapman, Shannon Delaney, Zachary Hanson-Hart, Evan

Hoffman, Courtney Mendillo, Barbara Saba, Adam Squire, Regina Szczesniak, Amanda Winalski, Stefanie Woolridge, and the rest of the students in Dissent in America are just a few of those I've taught over the years who have challenged me, inspired me, encouraged me, and made the classroom experience a sheer joy. Jonas Oesterle was especially helpful in enhancing my insights into contemporary protest music.

Terry Halbert's close reading of the manuscript, enthusiasm for the project, and personal encouragement greatly added to whatever value this work has. Even while in Helsinki, she went through the manuscript with the proverbial fine-tooth comb, tearing it apart and putting it back together again.

Without Ashley Dodge, my editor at Longman, this book would not exist. It was she who first recognized the importance of such a book and the central significance of dissent in American history. Without her insights, encouragement, challenging criticism, and valued friendship, this book would never have gotten off the ground. *Dissent in America* is as much hers as it is mine, for she knew its secret first.

Many others, in their own small ways, have contributed to this project. Thanks to Rafe for his tuna salad, tiramisu, and total zest for life; Norbert for his Vega banjo and Dutch bicycle; Istvan for his slivovitz and the story about that stormy night in Fairmount Park; the Radziwill clan for adopting me; Lucy for teaching loyalty; Vlad for his special horseradish vodka; Chris for being bothered enough to make all those telephone calls from Australia; Rachael for telling me to "go for it"; Tara Nevins for "No Place Like the Right Time"; Bruno et Marie-Camille for the fromage lessons; Annie for those quirky short stories; Tom for proving I really wasn't a computer Luddite; Don for all those all-night Michigan talkathons; Pat for the team-teaching suggestion; Peter for the never-ending supply of books and Jerry Garcia ties; Rich for the pesto; Darcie for all those e-mails; Leif for his bullet-proof vest; Beverly and Clare for that fiddle session; Len and Veronika for taking me under their collective wing; Gudrun for the seventeenth of January; Riley and Musette for their meditation lessons; Ann and Jessie for questioning my sanity; and Allen Ginsberg for playing his harmonium and singing Blake's "Tyger, Tyger Burning Bright" to me in my VW that day we were stuck in a traffic jam in Philadelphia.

Finally, I'd like to thank the following reviewers for their insightful comments: Martha Jane Brazy, University of South Alabama; Kathleen S. Carter, Hight Point University; Lauren Coodley, Napa Valley College; Edward J. Davies, University of Utah; Cole P. Dawson, Warner Pacific College; Mark D. Van Ells, City University of New York, Queens College; Rafaela Acvedo-Field, Mount San Antonio Community College; Tim Lehman, Rocky Mountain College; Johnny S. Moore, Radford University; Anne Paulet, Humboldt State University; Ann DeJesus Riley, Hartnell College; William B. Turner, St. Cloud State University; Jason Ward, Lee University; and Edmund F. Wehrle, Eastern Illinois University.

Ralph F. Young
Department of History
Temple University
ralph.young@temple.edu

ABOUT THE AUTHOR

Ralph Young is a history professor at Temple University in Philadelphia. He lived in England and Germany for ten years where he taught first at London University and later at Bremen Universität. He has done extensive research on seventeenth-century Puritanism, dissenters in the United States, and international terrorism.

Along with his scholarly research he has written novels on terrorism, one of which, *Crossfire,* won a Suntory Award for Suspense Fiction in Japan. At present, in addition to teaching the Dissent in America course at Temple University, he is developing a monograph on dissent in America, and, since September 2001, continuing to lead weekly teach-ins on the historical origins of current American foreign policy.

INTRODUCTION

Cautious, careful people, always casting about to preserve their reputation and social standing, never can bring about a reform. Those who are really in earnest must be willing to be anything or nothing in the world's estimation, and publicly and privately, in season and out, avow their sympathy with despised and persecuted ideas and their advocates, and bear the consequences. *Susan B. Anthony*

All we say to America is to be true to what you said on paper . . . Somewhere I read [*pause*] of the freedom of speech. Somewhere I read [*pause*] of the freedom of press. Somewhere I read [*pause*] that the greatness of America is the right to protest for right. *Martin Luther King, Jr.*

What Is Dissent?

A central aspect of a democratic society is the constitutional guarantee that all citizens possess freedom of speech, thought, and conscience. Throughout American history, individuals and groups of people, oftentimes vociferously, have expressed these freedoms by raising their voices in strident protest. These dissenters went against the grain, disagreeing with the majority view, and their actions have changed and formed our country.

Dissent has been expressed for many reasons and in many different forms. There have been those who sought more equality, more moral rectitude, and more freedom. Some dissenters criticized political issues, and others struggled against societal values and attitudes. There were also reactionaries who resisted change and wanted to maintain the privileges and supremacy of their class, race, or gender, and others simply strove to gain political power.

What is dissent? What makes a person a legitimate and thoughtful critic of our society? Are dissenters only those people who want to see a greater society? What is the difference between someone who wants to improve our society and someone who wants to destroy it? Are those who have purely selfish goals legitimate dissenters? Does dissent imply a broader, more inclusive worldview? Does dissent ever become treasonous? Is dissent patriotic or unpatriotic? Does dissent ultimately change society by offering new ideas and new perspectives, or does dissent merely confirm the status quo by providing a relatively harmless way of letting off steam?

When abolitionists demanded the end of slavery, antiabolitionists argued vehemently to preserve the institution. Do we regard defenders of slavery who considered their property rights superior to their slaves' human rights as "dissenters"?

Feminists sought suffrage and equality for women. Antifeminists sought to preserve male dominance and the subjugation of women. So who are the dissenters? *What* is dissent? Is dissent reserved for those with moral grievances whose chief desire is to persuade the United States to live up to its ideals and to ensure that the nation is truly a land where "all men are created equal"? Or is dissent a broader, more complex issue?

Ultimately, the definition of dissent has to be somewhat fluid, because the political/social/cultural/ideological mainstream of America has been fluid. Dissenters are not always responding to the same mainstream. Dissent against Puritanism is different from dissent against McCarthyism (despite the interesting parallels that historians have drawn between the two with respect to the theme of persecution and unfounded accusations). Anti-Puritan dissenters, such as Anne Hutchinson, were dissenting against the mainstream Puritan (religious/theological/theocratic) regimen. Anti-McCarthy spokespeople, such as Margaret Chase Smith, were dissenting against a politically intolerant mainstream. Hutchinson was protesting against the mainstream of her time, just as Senator Smith protested against the mainstream of hers and Martin Luther King Jr. fought against the racial mainstream of his. This kind of fluid view of dissent (i.e., the expression of antimainstream sentiments) means that even right-wing militia groups are also antimainstream dissenters.

However we define it, dissent has played a prominent and sometimes central role in American history. Indeed, in some ways dissent has been the fuel for the engine of progress. If we keep in mind the importance and, indeed, centrality of dissent and protest in the history of the United States, we begin to have a clearer view of our nation as it continues to define itself. In doing so, perhaps we inch closer to a personal historical awareness.

About the Documents

In tracing the theme of dissent as it weaves its way through the fabric of American history, the foremost difficulty is picking and choosing satisfactory samples that construct an accurate picture of American dissent. For every document chosen, scores of others could easily have been included in this book. Readers who further research any of the issues that seem intriguing or particularly stimulating will find the effort amply rewarded.

Some of the documents here are speeches, petitions, broadsides, posters, and songs that deal with various injustices. Other documents included are interviews, articles, recollections, and memoirs of events by the people involved, in which they retell their experiences in jail or on a protest march or simply their personal agonizing over how far to take their protest. Some of the documents were published at the time of the event; others were published years after the event. In scrutinizing the documents, keep in mind *who* is speaking, *what* that person's involvement is in the issue, and *to whom* the comments are addressed. Consider the person's race, class, and gender in reading the document. An African American, for example, writing about African American experience has a different point of view than either a sympathetic or antagonistic white person. Was the document created in an effort to influence people, or was it simply a neutral examination of the issue? Does the document reveal the writer's bias? The answers to these questions enable us to ascertain the accuracy of a particular document, determine how to interpret it, and assess its historical meaning.

It is also important, especially with the early Native American documents, to remember that many of them are speeches that were translated and transcribed by an English-speaking white Christian European who himself was not a neutral observer and therefore might not accurately reflect the sentiments of the speaker. Some of these transcriptions and memoirs were written years and even decades after the event and were therefore clouded by the passage of time.

Because there is not nearly enough space here to cover more than a few of the dissenters in American history, at the end of each section I provide a sampling of Web sites for further information and links about many of the dissenters. Remember that this book is *not* the definitive history of dissent. The documents I have chosen inevitably reflect my own view of dissent, and it is obvious that any other historian assembling such documents would choose alternative items. It is my modest hope that this book serves to illustrate that dissent has been a powerful and defining force throughout American history.

Note to Students

At the end of each section of *Dissent in America* is a list of Web resources. These are up-to-date as of publication, but be aware that these can change.

In using the Web as a research tool, the student must be acutely aware of the biases that most Web sites contain and make an effort to evaluate the accuracy and the authority of each site, as well as the evidence used to support any assertions that are made.

George Mason University has a site with links to many sources on American history that is invaluable for all students and teachers:

http://historymatters.gmu.edu

Another good overall source of links to many historical documents:

www.bedfordstmartins.com/doclinks

An excellent Web page at the George Mason University Web site called, "Making Sense of Evidence," contains a great deal of information on how to analyze primary sources and documents.

http://historymatters.gmu.edu/browse/makesense

For a list of suggested readings, visit the author's Web site at

http://oll.temple.edu/ryoung

PART ONE

Pre-Revolutionary Roots, 1607–1760

In the nineteenth century, artist Edwin Austin Abbey painted this stylized rendition of the trial of Anne Hutchinson. Notice how the artist casts more light on the embattled Hutchinson than on the authoritarian ministers and magistrates interrogating her.

Introduction: The Long Roots of Modern Dissent

An argument could be made that the history of the United States began in 1502, when Arthur Tudor, Prince of Wales, died at the age of 15. Or in 1517, when Luther tacked his Ninety-five Theses to the door of Wittenberg Cathedral. Or in 1553, when Mary Tudor began her reign by restoring the Catholic faith to England and initiating the martyrdom of the heretics. In a sense these sixteenth-century developments would eventually have a powerful impact on the founding of English colonies in the

New World, for these events led to a critical elevation of dissenting voices in the mother country and the eventual decision of many people, believing their differences were not being adequately addressed at home, to remove themselves to the American wilderness.

So dissent was endemic and pivotal in the political and intellectual history of the United States even before the idea of an independent nation in the New World had begun to take shape. Of course, a primary motive that propelled many colonists to leave their homelands and venture out into the unknown was economic. Enclosure, population growth, and increasing poverty had a huge impact. The economic motive cannot be in any way minimized, but understanding the complex texture and nuances of American history requires understanding the significant role dissent played. And it is important to appreciate the ironic fact that often those who raised voices of dissent and as a consequence were either demonized in their time as menaces to society or ignored as pathetic eccentrics became, to later generations, heroes and icons.

After Henry VII defeated Richard III at Bosworth Field in 1485 and consolidated the Tudor hold on the throne of England, he sought an alliance with one of England's chief rivals on the continent, Spain. To create this alliance, a marriage was arranged between Henry's son Arthur, the Prince of Wales, and Catherine of Aragon, the daughter of Ferdinand and Isabella. Within the year, at the age of 15, the ailing Arthur had died, and the accord with Spain was in jeopardy. After a good deal of diplomatic maneuvering, Henry VII convinced Pope Julius II to grant a special dispensation dissolving the marriage so that Catherine could be married off to Arthur's younger brother, Henry. When the marriage took place, the alliance with Spain became a reality. And it was Catherine of Aragon who was Henry VIII's queen when he succeeded his father in 1509.

On the continent, during the early sixteenth century, a young priest in Wittenberg, Martin Luther, began questioning many practices of the church. To help pay for the construction and artistic embellishment of St. Peter's Basilica and the Sistine Chapel, the pope had authorized the sale of indulgences, pluralism (by which a bishop could profit from holding more than one benefice), and other corrupt practices. To Luther, the sale of indulgences, which purportedly minimized the time a purchaser would have to spend in purgatory, gave the impression that believers could buy their way into heaven and that salvation came with a price. And so in 1517, after much prayer and contemplation, he tacked his Ninety-five Theses to the door of the cathedral in an effort to stimulate a debate that he hoped would lead the church to correct these abuses. Debate was not exactly what he got. The ensuing uproar got him excommunicated. He and his followers eventually formed the Lutheran church, and the Protestant Reformation was thereby launched. The primary problem these "protestors" presented to the church had to do with one of the central tenets of Luther's beliefs: that the only source of God's truth was Holy Scripture and therefore the Bible had authority, not the church hierarchy of pope, cardinals, archbishops, bishops, and priests. This undermining of the hierarchical structure of the church could not be allowed to go unchallenged. Luther, after his excommunication, was protected by numerous German princes who saw the political and economic advantages of emancipating themselves and their principalities from the strictures of the Vatican.

At first, one of the pope's most significant allies in his quarrel with Luther was England's Henry VIII. In fact, Henry issued a pamphlet, ghostwritten by Thomas More, that so vehemently attacked the Lutheran heresy that a grateful pope bestowed upon Henry and his heirs the title "Defender of the Faith." To this day, the English monarch retains this title, although it is now a different faith that is defended.

In the decade of the 1520s, the plot thickened, and a veritable soap opera emerged. Henry VIII, increasingly distraught that Catherine had not produced a male heir, began to question the legality and sanctity of his marriage to his brother's widow. Henry was concerned that if he died without a male heir, England would be plunged back into the chaos that it had known during the Wars of the Roses and that as a result another dynasty would attempt to place a male on the throne. Seeking to free himself of Catherine, he requested a dispensation from Pope Clement VII to dissolve the marriage. Normally, this would not pose any significant problem for the pope, but one of Clement VII's staunchest allies in the struggle against Lutheranism was Holy Roman Emperor Charles V—Catherine's nephew. Not wishing to alienate Charles V, the pope rejected Henry's request. Henry's response was to have Cardinal Wolsey, the archbishop of Canterbury, grant a divorce. Henry divorced Catherine and married Anne Boleyn, whereupon Clement VII excommunicated Henry and Cardinal Wolsey. England, because of Henry's actions, moved into the Protestant camp.

When, in 1533 Anne gave birth to a daughter, Henry was nearly beside himself. He made the decision to get rid of Anne and take yet another wife, who would presumably bear him a son. (Never, during any of this, did Henry consider *he* might be at fault! To him, it was the woman's fault, coupled with the fact that God was punishing him for having married his brother's widow.) Not wishing to go through another divorce, he had Anne tried on false charges of adultery. Found guilty of adultery (and therefore of treason), Anne was condemned to death. No sooner was she beheaded than Henry married Jane Seymour. His third wife eventually bore the desired son in 1538, but the infant Edward was sickly, and Jane died of complications from childbirth. Henry, not very good at being alone, went through another three wives (Anne of Cleves, divorced; Catherine Howard, beheaded; Catherine Paar, survived) before his death in 1547. His 9-year-old son succeeded him as Edward VI.

Under Edward's short reign, the Reformation in England was consolidated. Archbishop of Canterbury Thomas Cranmer introduced the *Book of Common Prayer* and established the requirements for the polity of the Church of England. However, upon Edward's death at the age of 16 in 1553, the new monarch, Mary Tudor, the Catholic daughter of Catherine of Aragon, restored Roman Catholicism as the true, rightful church of England. Under Mary, many Protestants, Thomas Cranmer included, were burnt at the stake for heresy. Thousands fled England for the safety of the continent, especially to such Protestant enclaves as Frankfurt and John Calvin's Geneva. When "Bloody" Mary died in 1558, she was succeeded by her half sister, Anne Boleyn's daughter, Elizabeth I. With the Elizabethan settlement, restoring Protestantism to England, many of the Marian exiles returned home. Their experience on the continent with Calvinism had radicalized them, and they soon demanded that Elizabeth purify the Church of England of its popish practices: vestments, crucifixes, and reading of prayers. Elizabeth turned a deaf ear to these "puritans," and thus throughout her long reign, radical dissenters and sects flourished.

In the early seventeenth century, with the Stuart accession, first of James I and then of Charles I, a number of these dissenters, discontented with the state of the church and despairing of ever accomplishing the total reformation they desired in England, began to abandon their homes and migrate first to Holland and eventually to Plymouth and Massachusetts Bay Colony. The "pilgrims" who settled in Plymouth in 1620 (after a sojourn of 12 years in Holland) were known as "separatists." They no longer wished to be associated with the Church of England, preferring instead complete separation. Those who settled in Massachusetts Bay Colony in the 1630s, however, were a different variety of Puritan. Although they were Independents ("non-separating puritans" according to scholar Perry Miller) who believed that each congregation was independent and should have complete authority to choose its own members and ministers, they had no intention of separating from the Church of England. To them, it was the true church. They believed that if they set up congregational churches in the New World, their brethren back home would use their example as a model to reform the Church of England. Governor John Winthrop's "citty upon a hill" would thus be a "beacon unto the world."

Many of those who left for New England had high hopes of bettering themselves both socially and economically, but pursuing the fruition of Reformation was what prompted many of the first settlers to risk crossing the Atlantic. What is confusing to the modern mind is that these Puritans, seeking toleration for their beliefs, seeking to create the ideal society, and seeking to set up the pure church, seemed to become themselves, in their new wilderness home, zealously intolerant of others. Remember, however, that they were products of their own age who never believed that all faiths should be tolerated, only *their* faith, which they deeply believed was the only true one. They were not seeking tolerance in the New World; they were seeking to practice what they knew in their hearts to be the true faith and polity. In Massachusetts Bay Colony, intolerance of opinions that undermined the basis of Congregational beliefs was perceived as absolutely necessary for the survival of the Holy Commonwealth, which such dissenters as Roger Williams, Anne Hutchinson, and Mary Dyer quickly discovered.

Colonies in which the economic motive took precedence over the religious also experienced outbreaks of dissent. In Virginia, Bacon's Rebellion in 1676 grew out of the grievances of settlers in the Piedmont region toward the colonial government in Williamsburg. Because such a large number of those who rose up in arms were indentured servants, the rebellion created so much anxiety about relying on indentured servants to solve the labor shortage in the colony that it added momentum to the growth of slavery in the Chesapeake region and established that slavery in the English colonies would be forever based on race. In Pennsylvania, the strong Quaker element led some to question the treatment of the Indians. William Penn himself insisted that Native Americans be dealt with fairly and that settlers had no right to take their land without compensation. Yet Penn's heirs moved away from his benevolent stance and allowed their hunger for land to dictate a far less humane relationship with the tribes. All throughout the colonies, Native Americans encountering the newcomers attempted with limited success to protest their treatment. Slaves, too, whose masters kept them illiterate and ignorant of such Enlightenment values as natural rights and liberty, tried as best they could to articulate their discontent. Women also were not afraid to struggle against the confines of a male-dominated society and to strive for more liberty than men were willing to concede. And 40 years before the American Revolution, a fledgling newspaper in New York that was brought to trial for libeling corrupt politicians argued successfully for freedom of the press in one of the most momentous court cases of the colonial period.

Roger Williams (c. 1603–1683)

From the moment Roger Williams arrived in the colonies, he ran headlong into the Massachusetts Bay authorities. He served for a time as teacher of the Salem church (many churches in New England had two ministers: the pastor and the teacher), but his form of Puritanism was considered too radical by the ministers and magistrates of the colony. Williams called for the complete separation of the New England churches from the Church of England. He also challenged the king's authority to grant a charter to the colonists and, in effect, to usurp Indian land. Finally, he argued for complete religious toleration. These views led to his banishment from the colony in 1635, whereupon he sought refuge among the Narragansett Indians. Eventually he purchased land from the Narragansetts and, in 1636, founded the colony of Providence in Rhode Island.

In 1644 he sailed to England to get a charter for the colony that would permit him to form a government. While in England, Williams published *The Bloudy Tenent of Persecution* in which he called for religious toleration of all faiths— including Jews and atheists—and the complete separation of church and state. The book is set up as a dialogue between the position of such Puritans as John Cotton and John Winthrop (*Truth*) and Williams's own view (*Peace*). He claimed that magistrates had no right to become involved in religious affairs, nor did they have the power to punish breaches of the Ten Commandments. What is Williams's reasoning in this argument for the separation of church and state? Is it to protect the state from the unwarranted influence of the church? Or vice versa? Or both? What authority does he use to support his argument in favor of toleration?

The Bloudy Tenent of Persecution: For the Cause of Conscience, Discussed in a Conference Between Truth and Peace, 1644

First, that the blood of so many hundred thousand souls of Protestants and Papists, spilt in the wars of present and former ages, for their respective consciences, is not required nor accepted by Jesus Christ the Prince of Peace.

SOURCE: Roger Williams, *The Bloudy Tenent of Persecution* (Providence, RI: Narragansett Club Publications, 1867) vol. III, 3–4, 58–59, 63, 138–139, 148, 170–171, 201, 247–250, 372–373, 424–425.

Secondly, pregnant scriptures and arguments are throughout the work proposed against the doctrine of persecution for cause of conscience.

Thirdly, satisfactory answers are given to scriptures, and objections produced by Mr. Calvin, Beza, Mr. Cotton, and the ministers of the New English churches and others former and later, tending to prove the doctrine of persecution for cause of conscience.

Fourthly, the doctrine of persecution for cause of conscience is proved guilty of all the blood of the souls crying for vengeance under the altar.

Fifthly, all civil states with their officers of justice in their respective constitutions and administrations are proved essentially civil, and therefore not judges, governors, or defenders of the spiritual or Christian state and worship.

Sixthly, it is the will and command of God that (since the coming of his Son the Lord Jesus) a permission of the most paganish, Jewish, Turkish, or antichristian consciences and worships, be granted to all men in all nations and countries; and they are only to be fought against with that sword which is only (in soul matters) able to conquer, to wit, the sword of God's Spirit, the Word of God.

Seventhly, the state of the Land of Israel, the kings and people thereof in peace and war, is proved figurative and ceremonial, and no pattern nor president for any kingdom or civil state in the world to follow.

Eighthly, God requireth not a uniformity of religion to be enacted and enforced in any civil state; which enforced uniformity (sooner or later) is the greatest occasion of civil war, ravishing of conscience, persecution of Christ Jesus in his servants, and of the hypocrisy and destruction of millions of souls.

Ninthly, in holding an enforced uniformity of religion in a civil state, we must necessarily disclaim our desires and hopes of the Jew's conversion to Christ.

Tenthly, an enforced uniformity of religion throughout a nation or civil state, confounds the civil and religious, denies the principles of Christianity and civility, and that Jesus Christ is come in the flesh.

Eleventhly, the permission of other consciences and worships than a state professeth only can (according to God) procure a firm and lasting peace (good assurance being taken according to the wisdom of the civil state for uniformity of civil obedience from all forts).

Twelfthly, lastly, true civility and Christianity may both flourish in a state or kingdom, notwithstanding the permission of divers and contrary consciences, either of Jew or Gentile. . . .

TRUTH. I acknowledge that to molest any person, Jew or Gentile, for either professing doctrine, or practicing worship merely religious or spiritual, it is to persecute him, and such a person (whatever his doctrine or practice be, true or false) suffereth persecution for conscience.

But withal I desire it may be well observed that this distinction is not full and complete: for beside this that a man may be persecuted because he holds or practices what he believes in conscience to be a truth (as Daniel did, for which he was cast into the lions' den, Dan. 6), and many thousands of Christians, because they durst not cease to preach and practice what they believed was by God commanded, as the Apostles answered (Acts 4 & 5), I say besides this a man may also be persecuted, because he dares not be constrained to yield obedience to such doctrines and worships as are by men invented and appointed. . . .

Dear TRUTH, I have two sad complaints:

First, the most sober of the witnesses, that dare to plead thy cause, how are they charged to be mine enemies, contentious, turbulent, seditious?

Secondly, thine enemies, though they speak and rail against thee, though they outrageously pursue, imprison, banish, kill thy faithful witnesses, yet how is all vermilion'd o'er for justice against the heretics? Yea, if they kindle coals, and blow the flames of devouring wars, that leave neither spiritual nor civil state, but burn up branch and root, yet how do all pretend an holy war? He that kills, and he that's killed, they both cry out: "It is for God, and for their conscience."

'Tis true, nor one nor other seldom dare to plead the mighty Prince Christ Jesus for their author, yet (both Protestant and Papist) pretend they have spoke with Moses and the Prophets who all, say they (before Christ came), allowed such holy persecutions, holy wars against the enemies of holy church.

TRUTH. Dear PEACE (to ease thy first complaint), 'tis true, thy dearest sons, most like their mother, peacekeeping, peacemaking sons of God, have borne and still must bear the blurs of troublers of Israel, and turners of the world upside down. And 'tis true again, what Solomon once spake: "The beginning of strife is as when one letteth out water, therefore (saith he) leave off contention before it be meddled with. This caveat should keep the banks and sluices firm and strong, that strife, like a breach of waters, break not in upon the sons of men."

Yet strife must be distinguished: It is necessary or unnecessary, godly or ungodly, Christian or unchristian, etc.

It is unnecessary, unlawful, dishonorable, ungodly, unchristian, in most cases in the world, for there is a possibility of keeping sweet peace in most cases, and, if it be possible, it is the express command of God that peace be kept (Rom. 13).

Again, it is necessary, honorable, godly, etc., with civil and earthly weapons to defend the innocent and to rescue the oppressed from the violent paws and jaws of oppressing persecuting Nimrods (Psal. 73; Job 29).

It is as necessary, yea more honorable, godly, and Christian, to fight the fight of faith, with religious and spiritual artillery, and to contend earnestly for the faith of Jesus, once delivered to the saints against all opposers, and the gates of earth and hell, men or devils, yea against Paul himself, or an angel from heaven, if he bring any other faith or doctrine. . . .

PEACE. I add that a civil sword (as woeful experience in all ages has proved) is so far from bringing or helping forward an opposite in religion to repentance that magistrates sin grievously against the work of God and blood of souls by such proceedings. Because as (commonly) the sufferings of false and antichristian teachers harden their followers, who being blind, by this means are occasioned to tumble into the ditch of hell after their blind leaders, with more inflamed zeal of lying confidence. So, secondly, violence and a sword of steel begets such an impression in the sufferers that certainly they conclude (as indeed that religion cannot be true which needs such instruments of violence to uphold it so) that persecutors are far from soft and gentle commiseration of the blindness of others. . . .

For (to keep to the similitude which the Spirit useth, for instance) to batter down a stronghold, high wall, fort, tower, or castle, men bring not a first and second admonition, and after obstinacy, excommunication, which are spiritual weapons concerning them that be in the church: nor exhortation to repent and be baptized, to believe in the Lord Jesus, etc., which are proper weapons to them that be without, etc. But to take a stronghold, men bring cannons, culverins, saker, bullets, powder, muskets, swords, pikes, etc., and these to this end are weapons effectual and proportionable.

On the other side, to batter down idolatry, false worship, heresy, schism, blindness, hardness, out of the soul and spirit, it is vain, improper, and unsuitable to bring those weapons which are used by persecutors, stocks, whips, prisons, swords, gibbets, stakes, etc. (where these seem to prevail with some cities or kingdoms, a stronger force sets up again, what a weaker pull'd down), but against these spiritual strongholds in the souls of men, spiritual artillery and weapons are proper, which are mighty through God to subdue and bring under the very thought to obedience, or else to bind fast the soul with chains of darkness, and lock it up in the prison of unbelief and hardness to eternity. . . .

PEACE. I pray descend now to the second evil which you observe in the answerer's position, viz., that it would be evil to tolerate notorious evildoers, seducing teachers, etc.

TRUTH. I say the evil is that he most improperly and confusedly joins and couples seducing teachers with scandalous livers.

PEACE. But is it not true that the world is full of seducing teachers, and is it not true that seducing teachers are notorious evildoers?

TRUTH. I answer, far be it from me to deny either, and yet in two things I shall discover the great evil of this joining and coupling seducing teachers, and scandalous livers as one adequate or proper object of the magistrate's care and work to suppress and punish.

First, it is not an homogeneal [homogeneous] (as we speak) but an hetergeneal [heterogeneous] commixture or joining together of things most different in kinds and natures, as if they were both of one consideration. . . .

TRUTH. I answer, in granting with Brentius [Lutheran theologian Johann Brenz] that man hath not power to make laws to bind conscience, he overthrows such his tenent and practice as restrain men from their worship, according to their conscience and belief, and constrain them to such worships (though it be out of a pretense that they are convinced) which their own souls tell them they have no satisfaction nor faith in.

Secondly, whereas he affirms that men may make laws to see the laws of God observed.

I answer, God needeth not the help of a material sword of steel to assist the sword of the Spirit in the affairs of conscience, to those men, those magistrates, yea that commonwealth which makes such magistrates, must needs have power and authority from Christ Jesus to fit judge and to determine in all the great controversies concerning doctrine, discipline, government, etc.

And then I ask whether upon this ground it must not evidently follow that:

Either there is no lawful common earth nor civil state of men in the world, which is not qualified with this spiritual discerning (and then also that the very commonweal hath more light concerning the church of Christ than the church itself).

Or, that the commonweal and magistrates thereof must judge and punish as they are persuaded in their own belief and conscience (be their conscience paganish,

Turkish, or antichristian) what is this but to confound heaven and earth together, and not only to take away the being of Christianity out of the world, but to take away all civility, and the world out of the world, and to lay all upon heaps of confusion? . . .

PEACE. The fourth head is the proper means of both these powers to attain their ends.

First, the proper means whereby the civil power may and should attain its end are only political, and principally these five.

First, the erecting and establishing what form of civil government may seem in wisdom most meet, according to general rules of the world, and state of the people.

Secondly, the making, publishing, and establishing of wholesome civil laws, not only such as concern civil justice, but also the free passage of true religion; for outward civil peace ariseth and is maintained from them both, from the latter as well as from the former.

Civil peace cannot stand entire, where religion is corrupted (2 Chron. 15. 3. 5. 6; and Judges 8). And yet such laws, though conversant about religion, may still be counted civil laws, as, on the contrary, an oath cloth still remain religious though conversant about civil matters.

Thirdly, election and appointment of civil officers to see execution to those laws.

Fourthly, civil punishments and rewards of transgressors and observers of these laws.

Fifthly, taking up arms against the enemies of civil peace.

Secondly, the means whereby the church may and should attain her ends are only ecclesiastical, which are chiefly five.

First, setting up that form of church government only of which Christ hath given them a pattern in his Word.

Secondly, acknowledging and admitting of no lawgiver in the church but Christ and the publishing of His laws.

Thirdly, electing and ordaining of such officers only, as Christ hath appointed in his Word.

Fourthly, to receive into their fellowship them that are approved and inflicting spiritual censures against them that offend.

Fifthly, prayer and patience in suffering any evil from them that be without, who disturb their peace.

So that magistrates, as magistrates, have no power of setting up the form of church government, electing church officers, punishing with church censures, but to see that the church does her duty herein. And on the other side, the churches as churches, have no power (though as members of the commonweal they may have power) of erecting or altering forms of civil government, electing of civil officers, inflicting civil punishments (no not on persons excommunicate) as by deposing magistrates from their civil authority, or withdrawing the hearts of the people against them, to their laws, no more than to discharge wives, or children, or servants, from due obedience to their husbands, parents, or masters; or by taking up arms against their magistrates, though he persecute them for conscience: for though members of churches who are public officers also of the civil state may suppress by force the violence of usurpers, as Iehoiada did Athaliah, yet this they do not as members of the church but as officers of the civil state.

TRUTH. Here are divers considerable passages which I shall briefly examine, so far as concerns our controversy.

First, whereas they say that the civil power may erect and establish what form of civil government may seem in wisdom most meet, I acknowledge the proposition to be most true, both in itself and also considered with the end of it, that a civil government is an ordinance of God, to conserve the civil peace of people, so far as concerns their bodies and goods, as formerly hath been said.

But from this grant I infer (as before hath been touched) that the sovereign, original, and foundation of civil power lies in the people (whom they must needs mean by the civil power distinct from the government set up). And, if so, that a people may erect and establish what form of government seems to them most meet for their civil condition; it is evident that such governments as are by them erected and established have no more power, nor for no longer time, than the civil power or people consenting and agreeing shall betrust them with. This is clear not only in reason but in the experience of all commonweals, where the people are not deprived of their natural freedom by the power of tyrants.

And, if so, that the magistrates receive their power of governing the church from the people, undeniably it follows that a people, as a people, naturally consider (of what nature or nation soever in Europe, Asia, Africa, or America), have fundamentally and originally, as men, a power to govern the church, to see her do her duty, to correct her, to redress, reform, establish, etc. And if this be not to pull God and Christ and Spirit out of heaven, and subject them unto natural, sinful, inconstant men, and so consequently to Satan himself, by whom all peoples naturally are guided, let heaven and earth judge. . . .

PEACE. Some will here ask: What may the magistrate then lawfully do with his civil horn or power in matters of religion?

TRUTH. His horn not being the horn of that unicorn or rhinoceros, the power of the Lord Jesus in spiritual cases, his sword not the two-edged sword of the spirit, the word of God (hanging not about the loins or side, but at the lips, and proceeding out of the mouth of his ministers) but of an humane and civil nature and constitution, it must consequently be of a humane and civil operation, for who knows not that operation follows constitution; And therefore I shall end this passage with this consideration:

The civil magistrate either respecteth that religion and worship which his conscience is persuaded is true, and upon which he ventures his soul; or else that and those which he is persuaded are false.

Concerning the first, if that which the magistrate believeth to be true, be true, I say he owes a threefold duty unto it:

First, approbation and countenance, a reverent esteem and honorable testimony, according to Isa. 49, and Revel. 21, with a tender respect of truth, and the professors of it.

Secondly, personal submission of his own soul to the power of the Lord Jesus in that spiritual government and kingdom, according to Matt. 18 and 1 Cor. 5.

Thirdly, protection of such true professors of Christ, whether apart, or met together, as also of their estates from violence and injury, according to Rom. 13.

Now, secondly, if it be a false religion (unto which the civil magistrate dare not adjoin, yet) he owes:

First, permission (for approbation he owes not what is evil) and this according to Matthew 13.30 for public peace and quiet's sake.

Secondly, he owes protection to the persons of his subjects (though of a false worship), that no injury be offered either to the persons or goods of any. . . .

The God of Peace, the God of Truth will shortly seal this truth, and confirm this witness, and make it evident to the whole world, that the doctrine of persecution for cause of conscience, is most evidently and lamentably contrary to the doctrine of Christ Jesus the Prince of Peace. Amen.

Anne Hutchinson (1591–1643)

Anne Hutchinson is one of the most controversial figures in colonial American history. She was an extraordinary woman who led weekly in-depth discussions about the sermons delivered the previous Sunday by Boston ministers John Cotton and John Wilson. Partly because she had stepped out of the submissive role of her gender and partly because she began accusing John Wilson of preaching the "popish" doctrine of a covenant of works (salvation could be achieved through individual effort and not through faith alone), she was brought to trial. During the trial, she asserted that she was in direct communication with God. To Puritans, who believed that only scripture reveals God's truth, this was the heresy of antinomianism. If the final authority of scripture was supplanted by direct communication with God, then what was to prevent any individual, even a murderer, from saying that God had told him to dispatch his victim? This would lead to the breakdown of law. As a result, Anne Hutchinson was banished.

What, according to the trial transcript, is the chief reason for Anne Hutchinson's banishment? How significant is the fact that she is a woman?

Excerpt from the Trial of Anne Hutchinson, 1637

Mr. Winthrop, governor: Mrs. Hutchinson, you are called here as one of those that have troubled the peace of the commonwealth and the churches here; you are known to be a woman that hath had a great share in the promoting and divulging of those opinions that are causes of this trouble, and . . . you have spoken divers things as we have been informed very prejudicial to the honour of the churches and ministers thereof, and you have maintained a meeting and an

Source: Thomas Hutchinson, *History of the Colony and Province of Massachusetts* (Boston, 1767).

assembly in your house that hath been condemned by the general assembly as a thing not tolerable nor comely in the sight of God nor fitting for your sex, and notwithstanding that was cried down you have continued the same, therefore we have thought good to send for you to understand how things are, that if you be in an erroneous way we may reduce you that so you may become a profitable member here among us, otherwise if you be obstinate in your course that then the court may take such course that you may trouble us no further, therefore I would intreat you to express whether you do not hold and assent in practice to those opinions and factions that have been handled in court already, that is to say, whether you do not justify Mr. Wheelwright's sermon and the petition.

MRS. HUTCHINSON: I am called here to answer before you but I hear no things laid to my charge.

GOV: I have told you some already and more I can tell you.

MRS. H: Name one Sir.

GOV: Have I not named some already?

MRS. H: What have I said or done?

GOV: Why for your doings, this you did harbour and countenance those that are parties in this faction that you have heard of.

MRS. H: That's matter of conscience, Sir.

GOV: Your conscience you must keep or it must be kept for you.

MRS. H: Must not I then entertain the saints because I must keep my conscience.

GOV: Say that one brother should commit felony or treason and come to his other brother's house, if he knows him guilty and conceals him he is guilty of the same. It is his conscience to entertain him, but if his conscience comes into act in giving countenance and entertainment to him that hath broken the law he is guilty too. So if you do countenance those that are transgressors of the law you are in the same fact.

MRS. H: What law do they transgress?

GOV: The law of God and of the state.

MRS. H: In what particular?

GOV: Why in this among the rest, whereas the Lord doth say honour thy father and thy mother.

MRS. H: Ey Sir in the Lord.

GOV: This honour you have broke in giving countenance to them.

MRS. H: In entertaining those did I entertain them against any act (for there is the thing) or what God hath appointed?

GOV: You knew that Mr. Wheelwright did preach this sermon and those that countenance him in this do break a law.

MRS. H: What law have I broken?

GOV: Why the fifth commandment.

MRS. H: I deny that for he saith in the Lord. . . .

GOV: You have councelled them.

MRS. H: Wherein?

GOV: Why in entertaining them.

MRS. H: What breach of law is that Sir?

Gov: Why dishonouring of parents.

Mrs. H: But put the case Sir that I do fear the Lord and my parents, may not I entertain them that fear the Lord because my parents will not give me leave?

Gov: If they be the fathers of the commonwealth, and they of another religion, if you entertain them then you dishonour your parents and are justly punishable.

Mrs. H: If I entertain them, as they have dishonoured their parents I do.

Gov: No but you by countenancing them above others put honor upon them.

Mrs. H: I may put honor upon them as the children of God and as they do honor the Lord.

Gov: We do not mean to discourse with those of your sex but only this; you do adhere unto them and do endeavour to set forward this faction and so you do dishonour us.

Mrs. H: I do acknowledge no such thing neither do I think that I ever put any dishonour upon you.

Gov: Why do you keep such a meeting at your house as you do every week upon a set day?

Mrs. H: It is lawful for me so to do, as it is all your practices and can you find a warrant for yourself and condemn me for the same thing? The ground of my taking it up was, when I first came to this land because I did not go to such meetings as those were, it was presently reported that I did not allow of such meetings but held them unlawful and therefore in that regard they said I was proud and did despise all ordinances, upon that a friend came unto me and told me of it and I to prevent such aspersions took it up, but it was in practice before I came therefore I was not the first.

Gov: For this, that you appeal to our practice you need no confutation. If your meeting had answered to the former it had not been offensive, but I will say that there was no meeting of women alone, but your meeting is of another sort for there are sometimes men among you.

Mrs. H: There was never any man with us.

Gov: Well, admit there was no man at your meeting and that you was sorry for it, there is no warrant for your doings, and by what warrant do you continue such a course?

Mrs. H: I conceive there lies a clear rule in Titus, that the elder women should instruct the younger [Titus 2:3–5] and then I must have a time wherein I must do it. . . .

Gov: But suppose that a hundred men come unto you to be instructed will you forbear to instruct them?

Mrs. H: As far as I conceive I cross a rule in it.

Gov: Very well and do you not so here?

Mrs. H: No Sir for my ground is they are men.

Gov: Men and women all is one for that, but suppose that a man should come and say Mrs. Hutchinson I hear that you are a woman that God hath given his grace unto and you have knowledge in the word of God I pray instruct me a little, ought you not to instruct this man?

Mrs. H: I think I may.—Do you think it not lawful for me to teach women and why do you call me to teach the court?

Gov: We do not call you to teach the court but to lay open yourself. . . .

Gov: Your course is not to be suffered for, besides that we find such a course as this to be greatly prejudicial to the state, besides the occasion that it is to seduce many honest persons that are called to those meetings and your opinions being known to be different from the word of God may seduce many simple souls that resort unto you, besides that the occasion which hath come of late hath come from none but such as have frequented your meetings, so that now they are flown off from magistrates and ministers and this since they have come to you, and besides that it will not well stand with the Commonwealth that families should be neglected for so many neighbours and dames and so much time spent, we see no rule of God for this, we see not that any should have authority to set up any other exercises besides what authority hath already set up and so what hurt comes of this you will be guilty of and we for suffering you.

Mrs. H: Sir I do not believe that to be so.

Gov: Well, we see how it is we must therefore put it away from you, or restrain you from maintaining this course.

Mrs. H: If you have a rule for it from God's word you may.

Gov: We are your judges, and not you ours and we must compel you to it.

Mrs. H: If it please you by authority to put it down I will freely let you for I am subject to your authority. . . .

Mr. Dudley, Dep. Gov: Here hath been much spoken concerning Mrs. Hutchinson's meetings and among other answers she saith that men come not there, I would ask you this one question then, whether never any man was at your meeting?

Gov: There are two meetings kept at their house.

Dep. Gov: How is there two meetings?

Mrs. H: Ey Sir, I shall I not equivocate, there is a meeting of men and women and there is a meeting only for women.

Dep. Gov: Are they both constant?

Mrs. H: No, but upon occasions they are deferred.

Mr. Endicot: Who teaches in the men's meetings none but men, do not women sometimes?

Mrs. H: Never as I heard, not one.

Dep. Gov: I would go a little higher with Mrs. Hutchinson. About three years ago we were all in peace. Mrs. Hutchinson from that time she came hath made a disturbance, and some that came over with her in the ship did inform me what she was as soon as she was landed. I being then in place dealt with the pastor and teacher of Boston and desired them to enquire of her, and then I was satisfied that she held nothing different from us, but within half a year after, she had vented divers of her strange opinions and had made parties in the country, and at length it comes that Mr. Cotton and Mr. Vane were of her judgment, but Mr. Cotton cleared himself that he was not of that mind, but now it appears by this woman's meeting that Mrs. Hutchinson hath so forestalled the minds of many by their resort to her meeting that now she hath a potent party in the country. Now if all these things have endangered us as from that foundation and if she in particular hath disparaged all our ministers in the land that they have preached a covenant of works, and only Mr. Cotton a covenant of grace, why this is not to be suffered, and therefore being driven to the foundation and it being found that Mrs. Hutchinson is she that hath depraved all the ministers and hath been the cause of what is fallen out, why we must take away the foundation and the building will fall.

Mrs. H: I pray Sir prove it that I said they preached nothing but a covenant of works.

Dep. Gov: Nothing but a covenant of works, why a Jesuit may preach truth sometimes.

Mrs. H: Did I ever say they preached a covenant of works then?

Dep. Gov: If they do not preach a covenant of grace clearly, then they preach a covenant of works.

Mrs. H: No Sir, one may preach a covenant of grace more clearly than another, so I said. . . .

D. Gov: I will make it plain that you did say that the ministers did preach a covenant of works.

Mrs. H: I deny that. . . .

D. Gov: What do I do charging of you if you deny what is so fully proved.

Gov: Here are six undeniable ministers who say it is true and yet you deny that you did say that they did preach a covenant of works and that they were not able ministers of the gospel, and it appears plainly that you have spoken it, and whereas you say that it was drawn from you in a way of friendship, you did profess then that it was out of conscience that you spake and said. The fear of man is a snare wherefore should I be afraid, I will speak plainly and freely.

Mrs. H: That I absolutely deny, for the first question was thus answered by me to them. They thought that I did conceive there was a difference between them and Mr. Cotton. At the first I was somewhat reserved, then said Mr. Peters I pray answer the question directly as fully and as plainly as you desire we should tell you our minds. Mrs. Hutchinson we come for plain dealing and telling you our hearts. Then I said I would deal as plainly as I could, and whereas they say I said they were under a covenant of works and in the state of the apostles why these two speeches cross one another. I might say they might preach a covenant of works as did the apostles, but to preach a covenant of works and to be under a covenant of works is another business.

Dep. Gov: There have been six witnesses to prove this and yet you deny it.

Mrs. H: I deny that these were the first words that were spoken.

Gov: You make the case worse, for you clearly shew that the ground of your opening your mind was not to satisfy them but to satisfy your own conscience. . . .

Mrs. H: I acknowledge using the words of the apostle to the Corinthians unto him, that they that were ministers of the letter and not the spirit did preach a covenant of works. . . .

Gov: Let us state the case and then we may know what to do. That which is laid to Mrs. Hutchinson's charge is this, that she hath traduced the magistrates and ministers of this jurisdiction, that she hath said the ministers preached a covenant of works and Mr. Cotton a covenant of grace, and that they were not able ministers of the gospel, and she excuses it that she made it a private conference and with a promise of secrecy, &c. now this is charged upon her, and they therefore sent for her seeing she made it her table talk, and then she said the fear of man was a snare and therefore she would not be affeared of them. . . .

MRS. H: If you please to give me leave I shall give you the ground of what I know to be true. Being much troubled to see the falseness of the constitution of the church of England, I had like to have turned separatist; whereupon I kept a day of solemn humiliation and pondering of the thing; this scripture was brought unto me—he that denies Jesus Christ to be come in the flesh is antichrist—This I considered of and in considering found that the papists did not deny him to‧ be come in the flesh nor we did not deny him—who then was antichrist? . . . The Lord knows that I could not open scripture; he must by his prophetical office open it unto me. . . . I bless the Lord, he hath let me see which was the clear ministry and which the wrong. Since that time I confess I have been more choice and he hath let me to distinguish between the voice of my beloved and the voice of Moses, the voice of John Baptist and the voice of antichrist, for all those voices are spoken of in scripture. Now if you do condemn me for speaking what in my conscience I know to be truth I must commit myself unto the Lord.

MR. NOWELL: How do you know that that was the spirit?

MRS. H: How did Abraham know that it was God that bid him offer his son, being a breach of the sixth commandment?

DEP. GOV: By an immediate voice.

MRS. H: So to me by an immediate revelation.

DEP. GOV: How! an immediate revelation.

MRS. H: By the voice of his own spirit to my soul. I will give you another scripture, Jer. 46. 27, 28—out of which the Lord shewed me what he would do for me and the rest of his servants.—But after he was pleased to reveal himself to me. . . . Ever since that time I have been confident of what he hath revealed unto me. . . . Therefore I desire you to look to it, for you see this scripture fulfilled this day and therefore I desire you that as you tender the Lord and the church and commonwealth to consider and look what you do. You have power over my body but the Lord Jesus hath power over my body and soul, and assure yourselves thus much, you do as much as in you lies to put the Lord Jesus Christ from you, and if you go on in this course you begin you will bring a curse upon you and your posterity, and the mouth of the Lord hath spoken it. . . .

GOV: The court hath already declared themselves satisfied concerning the things you hear, and concerning the troublesomeness of her spirit and the danger of her course amongst us, which is not to be suffered. Therefore if it be the mind of the court that Mrs. Hutchinson for these things that appear before us is unfit for our society, and if it be the mind of the court that she shall be banished out of our liberties and imprisoned till she be sent away, let them hold up their hands. . . .

GOV: Mrs. Hutchinson, the sentence of the court you hear is that you are banished from out of our jurisdiction as being a woman not fit for our society, and are to be imprisoned till the court shall send you away.

MRS. H: I desire to know wherefore I am banished?

GOV: Say no more, the court knows wherefore and is satisfied.

Alice Tilly (1594–c. 1660)

Petitions in colonial Massachusetts were not happily received by those in authority, and there are even cases on record in which petitioners were penalized for having submitted their complaints. Still, people did petition the General Court when they felt they wanted to protest a decision that had been handed down. When John Wheelwright was banished, a group of men petitioned the General Court; others protested Governor John Winthrop's role in resolving the Hingham militia election by signing a petition. In 1649, when midwife Alice Tilly was convicted, a group of nearly 300 women (and some men) filed a total of six petitions protesting her sentence. The court records are no longer extant, and it is not known precisely what Alice Tilly's offense was, but we do have the petitions, and we do know that the petitioners were successful in their effort to secure Alice Tilly's release so that she could continue to perform her midwife services in the colony. This is the earliest known example of collective political action by women in the English colonies and indicates that reproductive issues were significant long before Margaret Sanger's twentieth-century birth control movement.

The last four of the six petitions are reprinted here. What do these petitions reveal about the lives of women in seventeenth-century Massachusetts? The petitioners had enough faith in the justice of their cause to sign their names to these petitions. What does this say about the power, or lack of power, of women?

Petitions for the Release of Alice Tilly, 1649

PETITION 3: FROM THE WOMEN OF DORCHESTER, CIRCA EARLY MAY 1649

Alice Tilly the wife of William Tilly a professed servant of Jesus Christ both in old england and new: as we have heard and by experience doe finde that shee hath ben a woeman of singular use in the place from whence shee came {and here allso} and wee bless the Lord for her life and for the experience wee have had of her not in ordynary cases but in extraordynary cases: but wee have ben informed here of late that she hath ben a hard hearted woeman and that many woemen and children doe die under her hands which doth much redound to her discreddit and the disheart-eninge of our woemen amongst us—and we have heard that shee is much oppressed by the reports that goe about on her but wee whose names are her under Written

SOURCE: Mary Beth Norton, "The Ablest Midwife That Wee Knowe in the Land": Mistress Alice Tilly and the Women of Boston and Dorchester, 1649–1650, *William and Mary Quarterly*, Third Series, 55, 1 (Jan. 1998), 105–134.

with the consent of a greate many more doe earnestly pray unto god to undertake for her in a way of his owne: to cleare her name that she {may} have free passage in her callinge to the good of us and of our children from Dorchester.

PETITION 4: TO THE COURT OF ASSISTANTS FROM BOSTON WOMEN, CIRCA MID-MAY 1649

To the honored Maiistrates Now assembled at Boston & elcewhere the humble Petition of us whose names are hereunto subscribed as alsoe in the name & with the Consent of many others Humbly sheweth.

That whereas wee yor Worships humble Petitioners did put up a petition unto your Worships in the behalfe of our approued midwife namely Mrs Tilly wee which are but fewe of many, whoe if need require; shall come and speake in her halfe; whoe hath through the goodnes of God bin carried through such difficulties in her calling that none of those whoe are her accusers could Doe but have either sent for her or left the work undone.

And as the honored Deputie Governor namely Mr Dudly Esquire did say tht shee was the ablest midwife inthe land; and as wee conceiue all the rest of the honored Maijstrats consented thereunto being silent in the thing; But whereas the honord Magistrates and many men more can speake but by hearesay; wee and many more of us can speake by experience and some by hearesay and whoe have bin eyewitnesses tht have bin with her in times of distrese.

Therefore our humble Petition unto yor Worships with one consent of us whose names are hereunto subscribed and in the behalfe of many others is that your Worships would bee pleased so farre to Grattify yor Worships most humble Petitioners as to vouchsafe unto us the liberty of our midwife for whome wee are bound in conscience to supplycate knowing the present need tht some of us have of her and alsoe knowing the sad events tht haue falne out both before her liberty was detained and since where she hath not had to doe and some of us heare and some of us know which make us affrayd to putt our selves into the hands of any besides our midwife tht wee haue had experience of, and of the blesseing of god uppon her endeauors and to say plainely wee realy in or conscience doe Judge her to bee the ablest midwife {that wee knowe} in the land and wee think wee canne make it appeare if {need} require.

Now the lord Guid yor worships tht you may heare the cryes of mothers, and of children yet unborne tht soe yor worships may bee moued thereby to Grant unto us yor Humble petitioners the liberty of our midwife for otherwise wee are like to Doe without seing her her husband hath inioyned her that shee should not goe forth to any uppon bayle only to a few whome shee was ingaged unto before hee went.

And Soe Humbly expecting a gratious Answere which if you grant wee shall for euer bee bound to bee thankfull to God and remaine yors in the Lord.

PETITION 5: TO THE GENERAL COURT FROM THE WOMEN OF DORCHESTER, CIRCA MAY 1650

To our honored Gouernour Deputie Gouernor And to the rest of the magistrates or any other whom it may concerne.

The humble petition of those whose names are vnder written.

Whereas Mris Tillie now of Boston a woman well knowne to be of good use in the Countrey amonge women in that practice she is often Called unto & imployed aboute yet nothwithstanding hath had great Discoragments of late tymes in that practice & her husband also for wch Cause he thinks and we doe heare & are informed, to remove himselfe & her also, unto the place whereunto he belongs, unless {her} innocencie may be cleared her Discoragments are well knowne we are informed that we feare most, is her removall, which if it should soe bee, yor poore petitioners shall be verie much grieved, & sadded, in our spirits, haveinge had such good experience of her, both of her skills, & redines, & paynfulnes, helpfulnes, & Courage, and all this through the blessings of god on her indeavours that yor poore Petitioners may blesse god that ever we knewe her & have bine partakers of her help {as some of us have} even in such tymes as in the eye of sence or reason nothinge but Death was to be expected some of us have had Experience of her a longe tyme & all of us in tymes of our needs & therefore we doe Judge her able & fitt for that place & Callinge.

May it therefor please yor Honored selves whom it may concerne to take her cause into yor greate wise & Juditious considerations that soe if possiblie may be Innocencie may be cleared that neyther her husband nor her selfe may be grieved & may not have such thoughts of removinge but be willinge to give up to this worke of god amongst which wilbe heart reioycing unto us & many more in the Country about us and as sad her removall from us this not doubtinge of yor wisedomes care about the accomplishinge of our humble desires herein we shall humbly pray for yor worships prosperitie & remaine thankfully obliged unto your worships.

PETITION 6: TO THE GENERAL COURT FROM THE WOMEN OF BOSTON, BEFORE MAY 22, 1650

To the right worpll John Endicott Esq Governour, Tho: Dudley Esq Deputy Governor with the rest of the worpll Court.

The humble Petition of divers women in Boston.

Humbly sheweth, tht whereas yor Petitioners having had manifolde experiences of the skill & ability (through the good hand of God) of an usefull instrument, who by providence is become a prisoner to yor Worpps (namely Alice Tilly wife to Wm Tilly) by hauing the black side of her actions presented to yor Worpps, & therein seuerall crimes written on her forehead, wch peradventure God nor her owne conscience may lay to her charge, further then this speaking dispensation, to take her off an ouer-much selfe conceitednes in what shee hath received, tht shee may remember tht shee hath all upon the accompt of receipt, wch yr Petitioners hope shall bee, as pray itt may bee the effect thereof.

Wherefore yor humble Petitioners though in all humility, yett in childlike boldnes, to & wth yor worpps, whose care wee believe, is as for our good, so for the posterity to succeede out of wch care (wee as hope so) desire tht yor Worpps will please to comiserate the condition of so many of yor poore trembling Petitioners, whose burdens wee doubt nott, butt will move yor compassions, as in answering some who have gone before us in this way of petitioning; so to orselues wth as much fauour as clemency may afford, ouerlooking the line of justice, so farre as will stand wth good conscience & Honor, wherein wee dare nott assume aboue or line to direct, butt leave the composure thereof to God & the wisedome given of God to you, who wee doubt nott butt will direct yor worpps therein, so as tht his owne honour may bee preserved, the security of yor children, yea those of the weakest sexe provided for, & the humble requests of yor poore petitioners granted, in opening the door of free liberty to or wonted way of instrumentall helpfullnes by her, of whom or expereinces are greatt, & necessityes greater.

Yor fauours herein given forth will more oblige yor Petitioners, who shall how euer count themselues bound to pray for you, & all of God sett ouer us, while wee shall remaine (though weake yett) true hearted well wishers, & endeauourers of the publick good of those churches & Comon wealth God hath cast us in.

William Dyer (1609–1672) and Mary Dyer (c. 1611–1660)

Mary Dyer was a follower of Anne Hutchinson during the Antinomian controversy. When Hutchinson was banished, Mary Dyer went with her to Rhode Island. Later, in the 1650s, Dyer went back to England, where she became a Quaker. Returning to Boston in 1657, she began proselytizing for Quakerism. She was imprisoned in 1657 and then again in 1659. When she was released, she was banished from Massachusetts Bay Colony and told that she would be executed if she ever returned. In October 1659 she did go back, was sentenced to death, and, while awaiting her turn on the gallows as two Quaker men (Marmaduke Stephenson and William Robinson) were hanged at her side, she was reprieved and again banished. In May 1660 she visited Boston a final time, knowing exactly what lay in store for her. She was hanged on June first.

Following are two letters from William Dyer pleading for his wife's release, as well as two prison letters of Mary Dyer's. Why, according to her husband, is Mary Dyer illegally incarcerated? What is Mary Dyer protesting?

Petitions and Letters, 1660

WILLIAM DYER'S LETTER TO THE BOSTON MAGISTRATES, 1659

Gentlemen:

Having received some letters from my wife, I am given to understand of her commitment to close prison to a place (according to description) not unlike Bishop Bonner's rooms. . . . It is a sad condition, in executing such cruelties towards their fellow creatures and sufferers. . . . Had you no commiseration of a tender soul that being wett to the skin, you cause her to thrust into a room whereon was nothing to sitt or lye down upon but dust. . . . had your dogg been wett you would have offered it the liberty of a chimney corner to dry itself, or had your hoggs been pend in a sty, you would have offered them some dry straw, or else you would have wanted mercy to your beast, but alas Christians now with you are used worse [than] hoggs or doggs . . . oh merciless cruelties.

You have done more in persecution in one year than the worst bishops did in seven, and now to add more towards a tender woman . . . that gave you no just cause against her for did she come to your meeting to disturb them as you call itt, or did she come to reprehend the magistrates? [She] only came to visit her friends in prison and when dispatching that her intent of returning to her family as she declared in her [statement] the next day to the Governor, therefore it is you that disturbed her, else why was she not let alone. [What] house entered she to molest or what did she, that like a malefactor she must be hauled to [prison] or what law did she transgress? She was about a business justifiable before God and all good men.

The worst of men, the bishops themselves, denied not the visitation and release of friends to their prisoners, which myself hath often experienced by visiting Mr. Prine, Mr. Smart and other eminent [men] yea when he was commanded close in the towne, I had resort once or twice a week and [I was] never fetched before authority to ask me wherefore I came to the towne, or Kings bench, or Gatehouse . . . had there not been more adventurours tender hearted professors than yo'selves many of them you call godly ministers and others might have perished . . . if that course you take had been in use with them, as to send for a person and ask them whe'fore they came thither. What hath not people in America the same liberty as beasts and birds to pass the land or air without examination?

Have you a law that says the light in M. Dyre is not M. Dyre's rule, if you have for that or any the fornamed a law, she may be made a transfresso', for words and your mittimus hold good, but if not, then have you imprisoned her and punisht her without law and against the Law of god and man . . . behold my wife without law and against Law is imprison' and punished and so higly condemned for saying the light is the Rule! It is not your light within your rule by which you make and act such lawes for ye have no rule of Gods word in the Bible to make a law titled Quakers nor have you any order from the Supreme State of England to make such lawes. Therefore, it must be your light within you is your rule and you walk by. . . . Remember what Jesus Christ said, 'if the light that be in you is darkness, how great is that darkness.'

SOURCE: Horatio Rogers, *Mary Dyer of Rhode Island The Quaker Martyr That Was Hanged on Boston Common, June 1, 1660* (Norwood, MA, 1896).

[illegible] . . . conscience, the first and next words after appearance is 'You are a Quaker' see the steppes you follow and let their misry be your warning; and then if answer be not made according to the ruling will; away with them to the Cobhole or new Prison, or House of Correction. . . . And now Gentlemen consider their ends, and believe it, itt was certaine the Bishops ruine suddenly followed after their hott persuanes of some godly people by them called Puritans . . . especially when they proceeded to suck the blood of Mr. Prine, Mr. Burton and Dr. Bostwicks eares, only them three and butt three, and they were as odious to them as the Quakers are to you.

What witness or legal testimony was taken that my wife Mary Dyre was a Quaker, if not before God and man how can you clear yourselves and seat of justice, from cruelty persecution ye as so fair as in you lies murder as to her and to myself and family oppression and tiranny. The God of trust knows all this. The God of truth knows all this. This is the sum and totals of a law title Quakers: that she is guilty of a breach of a tittled Quakers is as strange, that she is lawfully convicted of 2 witnesses is not hear of, that she must be banished by law tittled Quakers being not convicted by law but considered by surmise and condemned to close prison by Mr. Bellingham's suggestion is so absurd and ridiculous, the meanest pupil in law will hiss at such proceeds in Old Lawyers . . . is your law tittled Quakers Felony or Treason, that vehement suspicion render them capable of suffering. . . . If you be men I suppose your fundamental lawes is that noe person shall be imprisoned or molested but upon the breach of a law, yett behold my wife without law and against law is imprisoned and punished.

My wife writes me word and information, ye she had been above a fortnight and had not trode on the ground, but saw it out your window; what inhumanity is this, had you never wives of your own, or ever any tender affection to a woman, deal so with a woman, what has nature forgotten if refreshment be debarred?

I have written thus plainly to you, being exceedingly sensible of the unjust molestations and detaining of my deare yokefellow, mine and my familyes want of her will crye loud in yo' eares together with her sufferings of your part but I questions not mercy favor and comfort from the most high of her owne soule, that at present my self and family bea by you deprived of the comfort and refreshment we might have enjoyed by her [presence].

her husband
W. Dyre
Newport this 30 August 1659

MARY DYER'S FIRST LETTER WRITTEN FROM PRISON, 1659

Whereas I am by many charged with the Guiltiness of my own Blood: if you mean in my Coming to Boston, I am therein clear, and justified by the Lord, in whose Will I came, who will require my Blood of you, be sure, who have made a Law to take away the Lives of the Innocent Servants of God, if they come among you who are called by you, 'Cursed Quakers,' altho I say, and am a Living Witness for them and the Lord, that he hath blessed them, and sent them unto you: Therefore, be not found Fighters against God, but let my Counsel and Request be accepted with you, To repeal all such Laws, that the Truth and Servants of the Lord, may have free Passage among you and you be kept from shedding innocent Blood, which I know there are many among you would not do, if they knew it so to be: Nor can the Enemy that stirreth you up thus to destroy this holy Seed, in any Measure contervail, the great Damage that you will by thus doing procure: Therefeore, seeing the Lord hath not hid it from me, it lyeth upon me, in Love to your Souls, thus to persuade you: I have no Self Ends, the Lord knoweth, for if my Life were freely granted by you, it would not avail me, nor could I expect it of you, so long as I shall daily hear and see, of the Sufferings of these People, my dear Brethren and Seed, with whom my Life is bound up, as I have done these two Years, and not it is like to increase, even unto Death, for no evil Doing, but Coming among you: Was ever the like laws heard of, among a People that profess Christ come in the Flesh? And have such no other Weapons, but such Laws, to fight with against spiritual Wickedness with all, as you call it? Wo is me for you! Of whom take you Counsel! Search with the light of Christ in you, and it will show you of whom, as it hath done me, and many more, who have been disobedient and deceived, as now you are, which Light, as you come into, and obey what is made manifest to you therein, you will not repent, that you were kept from shedding Blood, tho be a Woman: It's not my own Life I seek (for I chose rather to suffer with the People of God, than to enjoy the Pleasures of Egypt) but the Life of the Seed, which I know the Lord hath blessed, and therefore seeks the Enemy thus vehemently the Life thereof to destroy, as in all ages he ever did: Oh! hearken not unto him, I beseech you, for the Seed's Sake, which is One in all, and is dear in the Sight of God; which they that touch, Touch the Apple of his Eye, and cannot escape his Wrath; whereof I having felt, cannot but persuade all men that I have to do withal, especially you who name the Name of Christ, to depart from such Iniquity, as shedding BLOOD, even of the SAINTS of the Most High. Therefore let my Request have as much Acceptance with you, if you be Christians as Esther had with Ahasuerus whose relation is short of that that's between Christians and my Request is the same that her's was: and he said not, that he had made a Law, and it would be dishonourable for him to revoke it: but when he understood that these People were so prized by her, and so nearly concerned her (as in Truth these are to me) as you may see what he did for her: Therefore I leave these Lines with you, appealing to the faithful and true Witness of God, which is One in all Consciences, before whom we must all appear; with whom I shall eternally rest, in Everlasting Joy and Peace, whether you will hear or forebear: With him is my Reward, with whom to live is my Joy, and to die is my Gain, tho' I had not had your forty-eight Hours Warning, for the Preparation of the Death of Mary Dyar.

And know this also, that if through the Enmity you shall declare yourselves worse than Ahasueras, and confirm your Law, tho' it were but the taking away the Life of one of us, That the Lord will overthrow both your Law and you, by his righteous Judgments and Plagues poured justly upon you who now whilst you are warned thereof, and tenderly sought unto, may avoid the one, by removing the other; If you neither hear nor obey the Lord nor his Servants, yet will he send more of his Servants among you, so that your End shall be frustrated, that think to restrain them, you call 'Cursed Quakers' from coming among you, by any Thing you can do to them; yea, verily, he hath a Seed here among you, for whom we have suffered all this while, and yet suffer:

whom the Lord of the Harvest will send forth more Labourers to gather (out of the Mouths of the Devourers of all sorts) into his Fold, where he will lead them into fresh Pastures, even the Paths of Righteousness, for his Name's Sake: Oh! let non of you put this Day far from you, which verily in the light of the Lord I see approaching, even to many in and about Boston, which is the bitterest and darkest professing Place, and so to continue as long as you have done, that ever I heard of; let the time past therefore suffice, for such a Profession as bring forth such Fruits as these Laws are, In Love and in the Spirit of Meekness, I again beseech you, for I have no Enmity to the Persons of any; but you shall know, that God will not be mocked, but what you sow, that shall you reap from him, that will render to everyone according to the Deeds done in the Body, whether Good or Evil, Even so be it, saith

Mary Dyar

MARY DYER'S SECOND LETTER WRITTEN FROM PRISON, 1659, AFTER THE HANGING OF STEPHENSON & ROBINSON

Once more the General Court, Assembled in Boston, speaks Mary Dyar, even as before: My life is not accepted, neither availeth me, in Comparison of the Lives and Liberty of the Truth and Servants of the Living God, for which in the Bowels of Love and Meekness I sought you; yet nevertheless, with wicked Hands have you put two of them to Death, which makes me to feel, that the Mercies of the Wicked is Cruelty. I rather chuse to die than to live, as from you, as Guilty of their innocent Blood. Therefore, seeing my Request is hindered, I leave you to the Righteous Judge and Searcher of all Hearts, who, with the pure measure of Light he hath given to every Man to profit withal, will in his due time let you see whose Servants you are, and of whom you have taken Counsel, which desire you to search into: But all his counsel hath been slighted, and, you would none of his reproofs. Read your Portion, Prov. 1:24 to 32. 'For verily the Night cometh on you apace, wherein no Man can Work, in which you shall assuredly fall to your own Master, in Obedience to the Lord, whom I serve with my Spirit, and to pity to your Souls, which you neither know nor pity: I can do no less than once more to warn you, to put away the Evil of your Doings, and Kiss the Son, the Light in you before his wrath be kindled in you; for where it is, nothing without you can help or deliver you out of his hand at all; and if these things be not so, then say, There hath been no prophet from the Lord sent amongst you: yet it is his Pleasure, by Things that are not, to bring to naught Things that are.'

When I heard your last Order read, it was a disturbance unto me, that was so freely Offering up my life to him that give it me, and sent me hither to do, which Obedience being his own Work, he gloriously accompanied with his Presence, and Peace, and Love in me, in which I rested from my labour, till by your Order, and the People, I was so far disturbed, that I could not retain anymore of the words thereof, than that I should return to Prison, and there remain Forty and Eight hours; to which I submitted, finding nothing from the Lord to the contrary, that I may know what his Pleasure and Counsel is concerning me, on whom I wait therefore, for he is my Life, and the length of my Days, and as I said before, I came at his command, and go at His command.

Mary Dyar

WILLIAM DYER'S LETTER PETITIONING THE BOSTON MAGISTRATES TO SPARE MARY DYER'S LIFE

Honor S',

It is not little greif of mind, and sadness of hart that I am necessitated to be so bold as to supplicate you' Honor self w' the Honorable Assembly of yo' Generall Courte to extend yo' mercy and favo' once agen to me and my children, little did I dream that I shuld have had occasion to petition you in a matter of this nature, but so it is that throw the devine prouidence and yo' benignity my sonn obtayned so much pitty and mercy att yo' hands as to enjoy the life of his mother, now my supplication yo' Hono' is to begg affectioinately, the life of my deare wife, tis true I have not seen her aboue this half yeare and therefor cannot tell how in the frame of her spiritt she was moved thus againe to runn so great a Hazard to herself, and perplexity to me and mine and all her friends and well wishers; so itt is from Shelter Island about by Pequid Marragansett and to the Towne of Prouidence she secretly and speedyly journyed, and as secretly from thence came to yo' jurisdiction, unhappy journy may I say, and woe to theat generatcon say I that gives occasion thus of grief and troble (to those that desire to be quiett) by helping one another (as I may say) to Hazard their lives for I know not watt end or to what purpose; If her zeale be so greatt as thus to adventure, oh lett your favoure and pitty surmount itt and save her life. Let not yo' forwanted Compassion bee conquared by her inconsiderate maddnesse, and how greatly will yo' renowne be spread if by so conquering yo' become victorious, what shall I say more, I know yo' are all sensible of my condition, and lett the reflect bee, and you will see whatt my peticon is and what will give me and mine peace, oh Lett mercies wings once more sore above justice ballance, and then whilst I live shall I exalt yo' goodness butt other wayes twill be a languishing sorrow, yea so great that I shuld gladly suffer thie blow att once much rather: I shall forebear to troble yo' Hn' with words neythe am I in capacity to expatiate myself at present; I only say that yo'selves have been and are or may bee husbands to wife or wiues, so am I: yea to once most dearely beloved: oh do not you deprive me of her, but I pray give her me once agen and I shall bee so much obleiged for ever, that I shall endeavor continually to utter my thanks and render you Love and Honor most renowned: pitty me, I begg itt with teares, and rest you.

> Most humbly suppliant
> W. Dyre
> Portsmouth 27 of [May] 1660

Nathaniel Bacon (1647–1676)

Bacon's Rebellion in 1676 was the result of a series of economic problems and the rising costs of real estate in colonial Virginia. New settlers arriving in the colony and servants finishing their indentures could not afford the more desirable plots of land in the settled areas. As a result, they began moving to the backcountry, where they came into conflict with the Indians. A number of frontiersmen, under the leadership of Nathaniel Bacon, began wantonly attacking Indians. When the governor, Sir William Berkeley, attempting to restore peace, reprimanded Bacon for his attacks on the Indians, many settlers took Bacon's side and became critical of the governor. To them, it appeared that Berkeley was siding with the Indians. In July, Bacon and his followers marched on the colonial capital at Jamestown, where he demanded to be given a commission, granting him official authority to fight the Indians. Berkeley relented and, in essence, abdicated power. On July 30, Bacon issued a "Declaration in the Name of the People" in which he cataloged his grievances. For the next two months, Bacon held power in the capital, but when Berkeley tried to regain control, Bacon, on September 19, burned Jamestown to the ground. In October, Bacon suddenly became ill with dysentery and died. The rebellion was over.

In the past, many historians viewed Bacon's Rebellion as a precursor to the American Revolution. More recently, historians have emphasized the power struggle between the Virginia tidewater elite and the backcountry people. Does Bacon's Rebellion anticipate the grievances that would surface again a century later during the deterioration of relations between the colonies and the mother country? How important are anti-Indian beliefs and the racist attitudes of the settlers in this crisis?

Declaration in the Name of the People, July 30, 1676

THE DECLARACON OF THE PEOPLE

1. For haveing upon specious pretenses of publiqe works raised greate unjust taxes upon the Comonality for the advancement of private favorites and other sinister ends, but noe visible effects in any measure adequate, For not haveing dureing this long time of his Gouvernement in any measure advanced this hopefull Colony either by fortificacons Townes or Trade.

SOURCE: Nathaniel Bacon, "The declaration of the people against Sir William Berkeley, and present governors of Virginia," 1676. In Edward D. Neill, *Virginia Carolorum: The Colony Under the Rule of Charles the First and Second, A.D. 1625–1685* (Albany, NY: 1886), 361–365.

2. For haveing abused and rendred contemptable the Magistrates of Justice, by advanceing to places of Judicature, scandalous and Ignorant favorites.

3. For haveing wronged his Majesties prerogative and interest, by assumeing Monopoly of the Beaver trade, and for haveing in that unjust gaine betrayed and sold his Majesties Country and the lives of his loyall subjects, to the barbarous heathen.

4. For haveing, protected, favoured, and Imboldned the Indians against his Majesties loyall subjects, never contriveing, requireing, or appointing any due or proper meanes of sattisfaction for theire many Invasions, robbories, and murthers comitted upon us.

5. For haveing when the Army of English, was just upon the track of those Indians, who now in all places burne, spoyle, murther and when we might with ease have distroyed them: who then were in open hostillity, for then haveing expressly countermanded, and sent back our Army, by passing his word for the peaceable demeanour of the said Indians, who imediately prosecuted theire evill intentions, comitting horred murthers and robberies in all places, being protected by the said ingagement and word past of him the said Sir William Berkeley, haveing ruined and laid desolate a greate part of his Majesties Country, and have now drawne themselves into such obscure and remote places, and are by theire success soe imboldned and confirmed, by theire confederacy soe strengthned that the cryes of blood are in all places, and the terror, and constimation of the people soe greate, are now become, not onely a difficult, but a very formidable enimy, who might att first with ease have beene distroyed.

6. And lately when upon the loud outcryes of blood the Assembly had with all care raised and framed an Army for the preventing of further mischeife and safeguard of this his Majesties Colony.

7. For haveing with onely the privacy of some few favorites, without acquainting the people, onely by the alteracon of a figure, forged a Comission, by we know not what hand, not onely without, but even against the consent of the people, for the raiseing and effecting civill warr and distruction, which being happily and without blood shed prevented, for haveing the second time attempted the same, thereby calling downe our forces from the defence of the fronteeres and most weekely exposed places.

8. For the prevencon of civill mischeife and ruin amongst ourselves, whilst the barbarous enimy in all places did invade, murther and spoyle us, his majesties most faithfull subjects.

Of this and the aforesaid Articles we accuse Sir William Berkeley as guilty of each and every one of the same, and as one who hath traiterously attempted, violated and Injured his Majesties interest here, by a loss of a greate part of this his Colony and many of his faithfull loyall subjects, by him betrayed and in a barbarous and shamefull manner expoased to the Incursions and murther of the heathen,

And we doe further declare these the ensueing persons in this list, to have beene his wicked and pernicious councellours Confederates, aiders, and assisters against the Comonality in these our Civill comotions.

Sir Henry Chichley
Lieut. Coll. Christopher Wormeley
William Sherwood
John Page Clerke
John Cluffe Clerke
John West
Hubert Farrell
Thomas Reade
Matthew Kempe
Joseph Bridger

William Claiburne Junior
Thomas Hawkins
Phillip Ludwell
Robert Beverley
Richard Lee
Thomas Ballard
William Cole
Richard Whitacre
Nicholas Spencer

And we doe further demand that the said Sir William Berkeley with all the persons in this list be forthwith delivered up or surrender themselves within fower days after the notice hereof, Or otherwise we declare as followeth.

That in whatsoever place, howse, or ship, any of the said persons shall reside, be hidd, or protected, we declaire the owners, Masters or Inhabitants of the said places, to be confederates and trayters to the people and the estates of them is alsoe of all the aforesaid persons to be confiscated, and this we the Comons of Virginia doe declare, desiering a firme union amongst our selves that we may joyntly and with one accord defend our selves against the common Enimy, and lett not the faults of the guilty be the reproach of the inocent, or the faults or crimes of the oppressours devide and separate us who have suffered by theire oppressions.

These are therefore in his majesties name to command you forthwith to seize the persons above mentioned as Trayters to the King and Country and them to bring to Midle plantacon, and there to secure them untill further order, and in case of opposition, if you want any further assistance you are forthwith to demand itt in the name of the people in all the Counties of Virginia.

Nathaniel Bacon
Generall by Consent of the people.

Letter from an Anonymous Slave

This recently discovered letter by an anonymous slave is a petition to the Bishop of London to influence King George I to grant freedom. Though the letter failed to receive a response from the bishop, it is an important early example of the efforts made by some slaves to protest their condition by appealing to the powers that be.

Why does the writer compare the plight of the slaves with that of the Children of Israel? Why does he or she emphasize the desire that their children be educated according to Christian doctrine? Who does the author consider unjustly enslaved?

Release Us Out of This Cruell Bondegg

AUGUST THE FORTH 1723

to the Right Raverrand father in god my Lord arch Bishop of Lonnd. . . .

this coms to sattesfie your honoour that there is in this Land of verjennia a Sort of people that is Calld molatters which are Baptised and brouaht up in the way of the Christian faith and followes the ways and Rulles of the Chrch of England and sum of them has white fathars and sum white mothers and there is in this Land a Law or act which keeps and makes them and there seed Slaves forever. . . .

wee your humbell and poore partishinners doo begg Sir your aid and assisttancce in this one thing . . . which is that your honour will by the help of our Sufvering Lord King George and the Rest of the Rullers will Releese us out of this Cruell Bondegg. . . .

wee are commandded to keep holey the Sabbath day and wee doo hardly know when it comes for our task mastrs are has hard with us as the Egyptions was with the Chilldann of Issarall. . . . wee are kept out of the Church and matrimony is deenied us and to be plain they doo Look no more upon us then if wee ware dogs which I hope when these Strange lines comes to your Lord Ships hands will be Looket in to. . . .

And Sir wee your humble perticners do humblly beg . . . that our childarn may be broatt up in the way of the Christtian faith and our desire is that they may be Larnd the Lords prayer the creed and the ten commandements and that they may appeare Every Lord's day att Church before the Curatt to bee Exammond for our desire is that godllines Shoulld be abbound amongs us and wee desire that our Childarn be putt to Scool and Larnd to Reed through the Bybell.

My Riting is varfy bad. . . . I am but a poore Slave that writt itt and has no other time butt Sunday and hardly that att Sumtimes. . . . wee dare nott Subscribe any mans name to this for feare of our masters for if they knew that wee have sent home to your honour wee Should goo neare to Swing upon the gallass tree.

Native American Voices, 1609–1752

The indigenous people of the New World faced a grave crisis with European settlement. From their first encounters with Columbus and the Spanish, their culture was profoundly threatened. The Indian population dropped so

-----

SOURCE: Thomas N. Ingersoll, "'Releese Us Out of This Cruell Bondegg': An Appeal from Virginia in 1723," *William and Mary Quarterly*, Third Series, 51 (October 1994), 776–782.

precipitously through disease and murderous onslaughts that the results might as well be labeled genocide, although not all that befell them was intentional. The term *dissent* does not adequately describe Native American resistance or the valiant attempt to preserve their disappearing way of life. Though they expressed their grievances against the conquerors in petitions and speeches, few such documents have survived. The reason for this is twofold: Much of their resistance and protest took the form of warfare, and the Indian tradition is primarily an oral one. Few of their speeches or petitions, especially in the sixteenth through nineteenth centuries, were written down. Those that were often were transcribed by Europeans who rarely understood the nuances and subtleties of the Indian perspective or who intentionally distorted what the Indians wanted to express. Furthermore, many of the documents that have survived were written down years and even decades after the event and so must be read with additional skepticism. Yet documents from the colonial period do exist and shed some light on the Native American point of view.

What common themes and grievances can you identify in these documents?

Powhatan

One of the most familiar tales about colonial America is the story that the Jamestown settlers would never have survived the winter of 1607 and 1608 without the aid of the Powhatan Indians. Even with that help, only half the settlers were still alive by the spring of 1608. But deep-seated English distrust and belligerence toward the Indians elicited distrust of the settlers from the Powhatan tribe. By 1609, tensions between the two groups erupted into open warfare. In 1612, after his return to England, Captain John Smith published an account of the Jamestown colony in which he recorded the following speech by the Indian chief Powhatan.

What, according to Powhatan, is the best way to resolve their differences? Why does the chief use irony to express his resentment at the way the tribe is treated by the English? Why do you think the English would not seek a peaceful resolution?

Speech to John Smith, 1609

Captaine Smith, you may understand that I having seene the death of all my people thrice, and not any one living of these three generations but my selfe; I know the difference of Peace and Warre better than any in my Country. But now I am old and

Source: Philip L. Barbour, ed., *The Complete Works of Captain John Smith* (Chapel Hill: University of North Carolina Press, 1986), vol. I, 247.

ere long must die, my brethren, namely Opitchapam, Opechancanough, and Kekataugh, my two sisters, and their two daughters, are distinctly each other successors. I wish their experience no lesse then mine, and your love to them no lesse then mine to you. But this bruit from Nandsamund, that you are come to destroy my Country, so much affrighteth all my people as they dare not visit you. What will it availe you to take that by force you may quickly have by love, or to destroy them that provide you food. What can you get by warre, when we can hide our provisions and fly to the woods? Whereby you must famish by wronging us your friends. And why are you thus jealous of our loves seeing us unarmed, and both doe, and are willing still to feede you, with that you cannot get but by our labours? Thinke you I am so simple, not to know it is better to eate good meate, lye well, and sleepe quietly with my women and children, laugh and be merry with you, have copper, hatchets, or what I want being your friend: then be forced to flie from all, to lie cold in the woods, feede upon Acornes, rootes, and such trash, and be so hunted by you, that I can neither rest, eate, nor sleepe; but my tyred men must watch, and if a twig but breake, every one cryeth there commeth Captaine Smith: then must I fly I know not whether: and thus with miserable feare, end my miserable life leaving my pleasures to such youths as you, which through your rash unadvisednesse may quickly as miserably end, for want of that, you never know where to finde. Let this therefore assure you of our loves, and every yeare our friendly trade shall furnish you with Corne; and now also, if you would come in friendly manner to see us, and not thus with your guns and swords as to invade your foes.

Garangula

Garangula, an Onondaga, met with the governor of New France in 1684 on the shores of Lake Ontario, and after listening to the Frenchman's bullying attempt to coerce his people, replied in a fashion that made it clear that the Five Nations of the Iroquois were not to be intimidated. Garangula's eloquent comments reveal both his pride in the Iroquois and his scathing contempt for the French and the English. The result was a reversal for the French; Governor La Barre and he signed a treaty obliging the French to leave the next day.

What does Garangula imply will happen if the French break the peace treaty?

Speech to Governor La Barre of New France, 1684

Yonnondio [La Barre], I Honour you, and the Warriors that are with me all likewise honour you. Your interpreter has finished your Speech; I now begin mine. My words make haste to reach your Ears; hearken to them.

SOURCE: Cadwallader Colden, *History of the Five Indian Nations,* part 1 (London, 1727), 53–55.

Yonnondio, You must have believed, when you left Quebeck, that the Sun had burnt up all the Forests which render our Country Unaccessible to the French, or that the Lakes had so far overflown the Banks that they had surrounded our Castles, and that it was impossible for us to get out of them. Yes, Yonnondio, surely you must have thought so, and the Curiosity of seeing so great a Country burnt up, or under Water, has brought you so far. Now you are undeceived, since that I and my Warriors are come to assure you that the Sennekas, Cayugas, Onnondagas, Oneydoes and Mohawks are yet alive. I thank you, in their Name, for bringing back into their Country the Calumet which your Predecessor received from their hands. It was happy for you that you left under ground that Murdering Hatchet which has been so often dyed in the Blood of the French. Hear Yonnondio, I do not Sleep, I have my eyes Open, and the Sun which enlightens me discovers to me a great Captain at the head of a Company of Soldiers, who speaks as if he were Dreaming. He says that he only came to the Lake to smoke on the great Calumet with the Onnondagas. But Garangula says that he sees the Contrary, that it was to knock them on the head, if Sickness had not weakned the Arms of the French.

I see Yonnondio Raving in a Camp of sick men, whose lives the Great Spirit has saved by Inflicting this Sickness on them. Hear Yonnondio, Our Women had taken their Clubs, our Children and Old Men had carried their Bows and Arrows into the heart of your Camp, if our Warriors had not disarmed them, and retained them when your Messenger, Ohguesse appeared in our Castle. It is done, and I have said it.

Hear, Yonnondio, we plundered none of the French but those that carried Guns, Powder and Ball to the Twihtwies [The Miami] and Chictaghicks [The Illinois], because those Arms might have cost us our Lives. Herein we follow the example of the Jesuits, who stove all the Barrels of Rum brought to our Castle, lest the Drunken Indians should knock them on the Head. Our Warriors have not Bevers enough to pay for all those Arms that they have taken, and our Old Men are not afraid of the War. *This Belt Preserves my Words.*

We carried the English into our Lakes to traffick there with the Utawawas [The Ottawa] and Quatoghies [The Huron] as the Adirondacks [The Algonkin] brought the French to our Castles to carry on a Trade which the English say is theirs. We are born free. We neither depend on Yonnondio nor Corlaer [the Governor of New York].

We may go where we please, and carry with us whom we please, and buy and sell what we please. If your Allies be your Slaves, use them as such. Command them to receive no other but your people. *This Belt Preserves my Words.*

We knockt the Twihtwies and Chictaghicks on the head because they had cut down the Trees of Peace which were the Limits of our Country. They had hunted Bever on our Lands. They have acted contrary to the Custom of all Indians; for they left none of the Bevers alive, they kill'd both Male and Female. They brought the Satanas [The Shawnees] into their Country to take part with them, and Arm'd them, after they had concerted ill Designs against us. We have done less than either the English or French, that have usurp'd the Lands of so many Indian Nations, and chased them from their own Country. *This Belt Preserves my Words.*

Hear Yonnondio, What I say is the Voice of all the Five Nations. Hear what they Answer, Open your Ears to what they Speak. The Sennekas, Cayugas, Onnondagas,

Oneydoes, and Mohawks say, That when they buried the Hatchet at Cadarackui (in the presence of your Predecessor) in the middle of the Fort, they planted the Tree of Peace in the same place, to be there carefully preserved, that in a place of a Retreat for Soldiers, that Fort might be a Rendevouze of Merchants; that in place of Arms and Munitions of War, Bevers and Merchandize should only enter there.

Hear, Yonnondio, Take care for the future, that so great a Number of Soldiers as appear here do not choak the Tree of Peace planted in so small a Fort. It will be a great Loss, if after it had so easily taken root, you should stop its growth and prevent its covering your Country and ours with its Branches. I assure you, in the Name of the Five Nations, That our Warriors shall dance to the Calumet of Peace under its leaves, and shall remain quiet on their Mats, and shall never dig up the Hatchet till their Brethren, Yonnondio, or Corlaer, shall, either joyntly or separately endeavour to attack the Country which the Great Spirit has given to our Ancestors. *This Belt preserves my Words; and this other, the Authority which the Five Nations have given me.*

Stung Serpent

In 1723, war broke out in Mississippi between the French and the Natchez. One of the Indians, Stung Serpent, suddenly ended his friendship with Antoine Simon Le Page du Pratz, a Frenchman who had been living among the Natchez for 5 years. Disconcerted, du Pratz wanted to know the reason Stung Serpent had suddenly turned on him. The Indian's response, recorded by Le Page du Pratz years later in his *History of Louisiana*, was probably a sentiment shared by many Native Americans in the eighteenth century.

What did the French bring to the Indians that could be viewed as positive?

Reply to Antoine Simon Le Page du Pratz, 1723

"Why," continued he, with an air of displeasure, "did the French come into our country? We did not go to seek them: they asked for land of us, because their country was too little for all the men that were in it. We told them they might take land where they pleased, there was enough for them and for us; that it was good the same sun should enlighten us both, and that we would walk as friends in the same path; and that we would give them of our provisions, assist them to build, and to labour in their fields. We have done so; is not this true? What occasion then had we for Frenchmen? Before they came, did we not live better than we do, seeing we deprive ourselves of a part of our corn, our game, and fish, to give a part to them? In what respect, then, had we occasion for them? Was it for their guns? The bows and arrows

SOURCE: Le Page du Pratz, *The History of Louisiana* (London, 1774), reprinted by J. S. W. Harmanson (New Orleans, 1947), 41.

which we used, were sufficient to make us live well. Was it for their white, blue, and red blankets? We can do well enough with buffalo skins, which are warmer; our women wrought feather-blankets for the winter, and mulberry-mantles for the summer; which indeed were not so beautiful; but our women were more laborious and less vain than they are now. In fine, before the arrival of the French, we lived like men who can be satisfied with what they have; whereas at this day we are like slaves, who are not suffered to do as they please."

Loron Sauguaarum

The following is a rare narrative, from the Indian point of view, of the negotiations that led to the Casco Bay Treaty of 1727, in which the British claimed the Indians had relinquished their sovereignty. Loron Sauguaarum, a Penobscot, was one of the delegates negotiating with the English.

What does his account reveal about actual and potential English-Indian misunderstanding?

Negotiations for the Casco Bay Treaty, 1727

I, Panaouamskeyen, do inform ye—ye who are scattered all over the earth take notice—of what has passed between me and the English in negotiating the peace that I have just concluded with them. It is from the bottom of my heart that I inform you; and, as a proof that I tell you nothing but the truth, I wish to speak to you in my own tongue.

My reason for informing you, myself, is the diversity and contrariety of the interpretations I receive of the English writing in which the articles of Peace are drawn up that we have just mutually agreed to. These writings appear to contain things that are not, so that the Englishman himself disavows them in my presence, when he reads and interprets them to me himself.

I begin then by informing you; and shall speak to you only of the principal and most important matter.

First, that I did not commence the negotiation for a peace, or settlement, but he, it was, who first spoke to me on the subject, and I did not give him any answer until he addressed me a third time. I first went to Fort St. George to hear his propositions, and afterwards to Boston, whither he invited me on the same business.

We were two that went Boston: I, Laurance Sagouarrab, and John Ehennekouit. On arriving there I did indeed salute him in the usual mode at the first interview, but I was not the first to speak to him. I only answered what he said to me, and such was the course I observed throughout the whole of our interview.

He began by asking me, what brought me hither? I did not give him for answer—

SOURCE: E. B. O'Callaghan, ed., *Documents Relative to the Colonial History of the State of New York,* 15 vols. (Albany: Weed, Parsons & Co., 1855), vol. 9, 966–967.

I am come to ask your pardon; nor, I come to acknowledge you as my conqueror; nor, I come to make my submission to you; nor, I come to receive your commands. All the answer I made was that I was come on his invitation to me to hear the propositions for a settlement that he wished to submit to me.

Wherefore do we kill one another? he again asked me. 'Tis true that, in reply, I said to him—You are right. But I did not say to him, I acknowledge myself the cause of it, nor I condemn myself for having made war on him.

He next said to me—Propose what must be done to make us friends. 'Tis true that thereupon I answered him—It is rather for you to do that. And my reason for giving him that answer is, that having himself spoken to me of an arrangement, I did not doubt but he would make me some advantageous proposals. But I did not tell him that I would submit in every respect to his orders.

Thereupon, he said to me—Let us observe the treaties concluded by our Fathers, and renew the ancient friendship which existed between us. I made him no answer thereunto; much less, I repeat, did I, become his subject, or give him my land, or acknowledge his King as my King. This I never did, and he never proposed it to me. I say, he never said to me—Give thyself and thy land to me, nor acknowledge my King for thy King, as thy ancestors formerly did.

He again said to me—But do you not recognize the King of England as King over all his states? To which I answered—Yes, I recognize him King of all his lands; but I rejoined, do not hence infer that I acknowledge thy King as my King, and King of my lands. Here lies my distinction—my Indian distinction. God hath willed that I have no King, and that I be master of my lands in common.

He again asked me—Do you not admit that I am at least master of the lands I have purchased? I answered him thereupon, that I admit nothing, and that I knew not what he had reference to.

He again said to me—If, hereafter, any one desire to disturb the negotiation of the peace we are at present engaged about, we will join together to arrest him. I again consented to that. But I did not say to him, and do not understand that he said to me, that we should go in company to attack such person, or that we should form a joint league, offensive and defensive, or that I should unite my Brethren to his. I said to him only, and I understand him to say to me, that if any one wished to disturb our negotiation of Peace, we would both endeavor to pacify him by fair words, and to that end would direct all our efforts.

He again said to me—In order that the peace we would negotiate be permanent, should any private quarrel arise hereafter between Indians and Englishmen, they must not take justice into their own hands, nor do any thing, the one to the other. It shall be the business of us Chiefs to decide. I again agreed with him on that article, but I did not understand that he alone should be judge. I understood only that he should judge his people, and that I would judge mine.

Finally he said to me—There's our peace concluded; we have regulated every thing.

I replied that nothing had been yet concluded, and that it was necessary that our acts should be approved in a general assembly. For the present, an armistice is sufficient. I again said to him—I now go to inform all my relatives of what has passed between us, and will afterwards come and report to you what they'll say to me. Then he agreed in opinion with me.

Such was my negotiation on my first visit to Boston.

As for any act of grace, or amnesty, accorded to me by the Englishman, on the part of his King, it is what I have no knowledge of, and what the Englishman never spoke to me about, and what I never asked him for.

On my second visit to Boston we were four: I, Laurence Sagourrab, Alexis, Francois Xavier and Migounambe. I went there merely to tell the English that all my nation approved the cessation of hostilities, and the negotiation of peace, and even then we agreed on the time and place of meeting to discuss it. That place was Caskebay, and the time after Corpus Christi.

Two conferences were held at Caskebay. Nothing was done at these two conferences except to read the articles above reported. Every thing I agreed to was approved and ratified, and on these conditions was the peace concluded. One point only did I regulate at Caskebay. This was to permit the Englishman to keep a store at St. Georges; but a store only, and not to build any other house, nor erect a fort there, and I did not give him the land.

These are the principal matters that I wished to communicate to you who are spread all over the earth. What I tell you now is the truth. If, then, any one should produce any writing that makes me speak otherwise, pay no attention to it, for I know not what I am made to say in another language, but I know well what I say in my own. And in testimony that I say things as they are, I have signed the present minute which I wish to be authentic and to remain for ever.

Leni Lenape

Although William Penn strove at all times to deal fairly with the Leni Lenape (Delaware) Indians, even paying the large sum of £1200 for title to the land on which he built his colony, his descendants did not share the same ethical principles. In the 1730s, his son Thomas produced a 1686 deed, purportedly drawn up between his father and several Delaware chiefs, giving the colonists the rights to all the land "as far as a man can go in a day and a half" and from there to the Delaware River and along its length. To prepare for the implementation of this "treaty," the colonists cleared a trail. Instead of having one man walk as far as he could in a day and a half, three runners set out on the expedition. At the point where the third runner fell exhausted (65 miles distant), the colonists marked their new boundary, in effect taking from the Indians most of the territory of eastern Pennsylvania up to the Lehigh Valley.

In 1740, several Delaware chiefs petitioned the magistrates of Pennsylvania to remove the colonists who had settled on these lands. Notice how the Indians have adopted a method of framing a petition along lines that would easily be understood by the English.

Grievance Against the "Walking Purchase," 1740

TO MR. JEREMIAH LANGHORNE, 1740

To Mr. Jeremiah Langhorne & all Magistrates of Pennsilvania:

We pray that You would take Notice of the Great Wrong We Receive in Our Lands, here are about 100 families Settled On it for what Reason they Cant tell. They tell them *that Thomas Penn has sold them the Land Which We think must be Very Strange that T. Penn Should Sell him that which was never his for We never Sold him this Land.* The Case was this. That When We Were With Penn to treat as usual with his Father, He keep begging & plagueing us to Give him some Land & Never gives us leave to treat upon any thing till he Wearies us Out of Our Lives but What should We give Penn any Land for We never had any thing from him but honest Dealings & Civility. If he lets us alone We will let him alone. The Lands we do Own to be Ours, Begin, at the Mouth of Tohickon Runs up along the said Branch to the Head Springs thence up With a strait line [to] Patquating thence with a strait Line to the Blew Mountain thence to a Place called Mohaining thence along a Mountain called Neshameek thence along the Great Swamp to a Branch of Delaware River So along Delaware River to the Place where it first began. All this is Our own Land Except Some tracts We have disposed off. The Tract of Durham The tract of Nicholas Depuis The Tract of Old Weiser. We have Sold *But for the Rest We have Never sold & We Desire Thomas Penn Would take these People off from their Land in Peace that we May not be at the trouble to drive them off for the Land WE Will hold fast With both Our hands not in privately but in Open View of all the Countrey & all Our Friends & Relations That is the Eastern Indians & Our Uncles the five Nations & the Mohikkons & the Twitways Shawanahs Shawekelou Tuskeroroes & the Takkesaw the last. These all shall be by & hear us Speak & We Shall Stand at Our Uncles Breast When We Shall Speak.* Now Gentlemen & all others We Desire some of Your Assistance in this Affair for We have lived in Brotherly Friend Ship So We Desire to Continue the same if So be We can be Righted any Manner of Ways So We Remainz

Your Friends

Atiwaneto

In 1752, Phineas Stevens attempted to negotiate a treaty between the colony of Massachusetts and the Abenaki. At a conference in Montreal, the Abenaki spokesman Atiwaneto made it clear that his tribe did not trust the colonists and that they would resist any further pressure to give up their land.

According to Atiwaneto, who would be at fault if hostilities broke out between the colonists and the Indians? How does Atiwaneto attempt to intimidate the English settlers?

SOURCE: Donald H. Kent, ed., *Pennsylvania Indian Treaties, 1737–1756* (Frederick, MD: University Publications of America, 1984), 24, 45–46.

Remarks to Phineas Stevens, 1752

Propositions of the Abenakis of St. Francis to Captain Phineas Stevents, delegate from the Governor of Boston, in presence of the Baron de Longueuil. Governor of Montreal, Commandant of Canada and of the Iroquois of the Sault Saint Louis and of the Lake of the Two Mountains, 5th of July, 1752.

Brother, We speak to you as if we spoke to your Governor of Boston. We hear on all sides that this Governor and the Bostonians say that the Abenakis are bad people. 'Tis in vain that we are taxed with having a bad heart; it is you, brother, that always attack us; your mouth is of sugar but your heart of gall; in truth, the moment you begin we are on our guard.

Brothers, We tell you that we seek not war, we ask nothing better than to be quiet, and it depends, Brothers, only on you English, to have peace with us.

We have not yet sold the lands we inhabit, we wish to keep the possession of them. Our elders have been willing to tolerate you, brothers Englishmen, on the seaboard as far as Sawakwato, as that has been so decided, we wish it to be so.

But we will not cede one single inch of the lands we inhabit beyond what has been decided formerly by our fathers.

You have the sea for your share from the place where you reside; you can trade there. But we expressly forbid you to kill a single beaver, or to take a single stick of timber on the lands we inhabit. If you want timber we'll sell you some, but you shall not take it without our permission.

Brothers, Who hath authorized you to have those lands surveyed ? We request our brother, the Governor of Boston, to have these Surveyors punished, as we cannot imagine that they have acted by his authority.

Brother, You are therefore masters of the peace that we are to have with you. On condition that you will not encroach on those lands we will be at peace, as the King of France is with the King of Great Britain.

By a Belt. I repeat to you, Brothers, by this Belt, that it depends on yourselves to be at peace with the Abenakis.

Our Father who is here present has nothing to do with what we say to you; we speak to you of our own accord, and in the name of all our allies. We regard our Father, in this instance, only as a witness of our words.

We acknowledge no other boundaries of yours than your settlements whereon you have built, and we will not, under any pretext whatsoever, that you pass beyond them. The lands we possess have been given us by the Master of Life. We acknowledge to hold only from him.

We are entirely free. We are allies of the King of France, from whom we have received the Faith and all sorts of assistance in our necessities. We love that monarch, and we are strongly attached to his interests.

Let us have an answer to the propositions we address you, as soon as possible. Take this message in writing to give to your Governor. We also shall keep a copy of it to use in case of need.

SOURCE: E. B. O'Callaghan, ed., *Documents Relative to the Colonial History of the State of New York*, 15 vols. (Albany: Weed, Parsons & Co., 1853–1887), Vol. X., 252–254.

Without stirring a step it is easy for your Governor to transmit his answer to us; he will have merely to address it to our Father who will have the goodness to send it to us.

Mashpee

This petition is an example of an attempt by an Indian tribe to protest their treatment at the hands of English colonists. The petition did result in the Mashpee (who had converted to Christianity) being granted self-government, and for several years they were satisfied that their grievance had been heard. However, their satisfaction was short-lived, for when the American Revolution came to an end, their right to self-government was removed.

Petition to the Massachusetts General Court, 1752

Barnstable, June 11, 1752

Oh! Our honorable gentlemen and kind gentlemen in Boston in Massachusetts Bay, here in New England, the great ones who oversee the colony in Boston, gentlemen. Oh!, Oh!, gentlemen, hear us now, Oh! ye, us poor Indians. We do not clearly have thorough understanding and wisdom. Therefore we now beseech you, Oh!, Boston gentlemen. Oh! Hear our weeping, and hear our beseeching of you, Oh!, and answer this beseeching of you by us, Oh!, gentlemen of Boston, us poor Indians in Mashpee in Barnstable County.

Now we beseech you, what can we do with regard to our land, which was conveyed to you by these former sachems of ours. What they conveyed to you was this piece of land. This was conveyed to us by Indian sachems. Our former Indian sachems were called Sachem Wuttammohkin and Sachem Quettatsett, in Barnstable County, the Mashpee Indian place. This Indian land, this was conveyed to us by these former sachems of ours. We shall not give it away, nor shall it be sold, nor shall it be lent, but we shall always use it as long as we live, we together with all our children, and our children's children, and our descendants, and together with all their descendants. They shall always use it as long as Christian Indians live. We shall use it forever and ever. Unless we all peacefully agree to give it away or to sell it. But as of now not one of all of us Indians has yet agreed to give away, or sell, or lend this Indian land, or marsh, or wood. Fairly, then, it is this: we state frankly we have never conveyed them away.

But now clearly we Indians say this to all you gentlemen of ours in Boston: We poor Indians in Mashpee, in Barnstable County, we truly are much troubled by these English neighbors of ours being on this land of ours, and in our marsh and trees. Against our will these Englishmen take away from us what was our land. They parcel it out to each

SOURCE: Ives Goddard and Kathleen J. Bragdon, *Native Writings in Massachusetts* (Philadelphia: American Philosophical Society, 1988), 373.

other, and the marsh along with it, against our will. And as for our streams, they do not allow us peacefully to be when we peacefully go fishing. They beat us greatly, and they have houses on our land against our will. Truly we think it is this: We poor Indians soon shall not have any place to reside, together with our poor children, because these Englishmen trouble us very much in this place of ours in Mashpee, Barnstable County.

Therefore now, Oh! you kind gentlemen in Boston, in Massachusetts Bay, now we beseech you: defend us, and they would not trouble us any more on our land.

John Peter Zenger (1697–1746)

John Peter Zenger began publishing one of the first newspapers in New York in 1733. *The Journal*, edited by James Alexander, was very critical of Governor William Cosby, a notoriously corrupt appointee of the Crown. It was common knowledge that Cosby had rigged elections, bribed judges and legislators, and dipped into the public treasury. When *The Journal* ran several articles calling for freedom of the press and condemning the governor's actions, Cosby seized the newspaper and had Zenger arrested for libel. In the eighteenth century, all that had to be proved at the trial to convict Zenger of libel was that he had published the articles. Even though the articles dealt with facts, truth—according to British law—was not considered a defense against libel. Philadelphia lawyer Andrew Hamilton, however, argued that truth *was* a defense: "If libel is understood in the unlimited sense urged by the attorney general, there is scarce a writing I know that may not be called a libel or scarce a person safe from being called to account as a libeler. Moses, meek as he was, libeled Cain—and who is it that not libeled the devil?" Zenger's acquittal was a precedent-setting victory for freedom of the press.

The following articles appeared in *The Journal* in November 1733 and led to Zenger's eventual arrest and trial. Much of the argument echoes John Locke's *Second Treatise of Government*, one of the philosophical cornerstones for the revolution to come. What is the distinction between an absolute monarchy and a limited monarchy? Why is freedom of the press essential to a free society?

Articles from *The New York Weekly Journal*, 1733

NOVEMBER 12, 1733

The liberty of the press is a subject of the greatest importance, and in which every individual is as much concerned as he is in any other part of liberty: Therefore it will not be improper to communicate to the public the sentiments of a late excellent

SOURCE: *The New York Weekly Journal*, November 12 and 19, 1733.

writer upon this point. Such is the elegance and perspicuity of his writings, such the inimitable force of his reasoning, that it will be difficult to say anything new that he has not said, or not to say that much worse which he has said.

There are two sorts of monarchies, an absolute and a limited one. In the first, the liberty of the press can never be maintained, it is inconsistent with it; for what absolute monarch would suffer any subject to animadvert on his actions when it is in his power to declare the crime and to nominate the punishment? This would make it very dangerous to exercise such a liberty. Besides the object against which those pens must be directed is their sovereign, the sole supreme magistrate; for there being no law in those monarchies but the will of the prince, it makes it necessary for his ministers to consult his pleasure before anything, can be undertaken: He is therefore properly chargeable with the grievances of his subjects, and what the minister there acts being in obedience to the prince, he ought not to incur the hatred of the people; for it would be hard to impute that to him for a crime which is the fruit of his allegiance, and for refusing which he might incur the penalties of treason. Besides, in an absolute monarchy, the will of the prince being the law, a liberty of the press to complain of grievances would be complaining against the law and the constitution, to which they have submitted or have been obliged to submit; and therefore, in one sense, may be said to deserve punishment; so that under an absolute monarchy, I say, such a liberty is inconsistent with the constitution, having no proper subject to politics on which it might be exercised, and if exercised would incur a certain penalty.

But in a limited monarchy, as England is, our laws are known, fixed, and established. They are the straight rule and sure guide to direct the king, the ministers, and other his subjects: And therefore an offense against the laws is such an offense against the constitution as ought to receive a proper adequate punishment; the several constituents of the government, the ministry, and all subordinate magistrates, having their certain, known, and limited sphere in which they move; one part may certainly err, misbehave, and become criminal, without involving the rest or any of them in the crime or punishment.

But some of these may be criminal, yet above punishment, which surely cannot be denied, since most reigns have furnished us with too many instances of powerful and wicked ministers, some of whom by their power have absolutely escaped punishment, and the rest, who met their fate, are likewise instances of this power as much to the purpose; for it was manifest in them that their power had long protected them, their crimes having, often long preceded their much desired and deserved punishment and reward.

That might overcomes right, or which is the same thing, that might preserves and defends men from punishment, is a proverb established and confirmed by time and experience, the surest discoverers of truth and certainty. It is this therefore which makes the liberty of the press in a limited monarchy and in all its colonies and plantations proper, convenient, and necessary, or indeed it is rather incorporated and interwoven with our very constitution; for if such an overgrown criminal, or an impudent monster in iniquity, cannot immediately be come at by ordinary Justice, let him yet receive the lash of satire, let the glaring truths of his ill administration, if possible, awaken his conscience, and if he has no conscience, rouse his fear by showing him his deserts, sting him with the dread of punishment, cover him with shame, and render his actions odious to all honest minds. These methods may in time, and by watching and exposing his actions, make him at least more cautious, and perhaps at last bring down the great haughty and secure criminal within the reach and grasp of ordinary justice. This advantage therefore of exposing the exorbitant crimes of wicked ministers under a limited monarchy makes the liberty of the press not only consistent with, but a necessary part of, the constitution itself.

It is indeed urged that the liberty of the press ought to be restrained because not only the actions of evil ministers may be exposed, but the character of good ones traduced. Admit it in the strongest light that calumny and lies would prevail and blast the character of a great and good minister; yet that is a less evil than the advantages we reap from the liberty of the press, as it is a curb, a bridle, a terror, a shame, and restraint to evil ministers; and it may be the only punishment, especially for a time. But when did calumnies and lies ever destroy the character of one good minister? Their benign influences are known, tasted, and felt by everybody: Or if their characters have been clouded for a time, yet they have generally shined forth in greater luster: Truth will always prevail over falsehood.

The facts exposed are not to be believed because said or published; but it draws people's attention, directs their view, and fixes the eye in a proper position that everyone may judge for himself whether those facts are true or not. People will recollect, enquire and search, before they condemn; and therefore very few good ministers can be hurt by falsehood, but many wicked ones by seasonable truth: But however the mischief that a few may possibly, but improbably, suffer by the freedom of the press is not to be put in competition with the danger which the KING and the people may suffer by a shameful, cowardly silence under the tyranny of an insolent, rapacious, infamous minister.

NOVEMBER 19, 1733 (THE REMAINDER OF THE LETTER CONCERNING THE LIBERTY OF THE PRESS BEGUN IN OUR LAST [ISSUE].)

Inconveniences are rather to be endured than that we should suffer an entire and total destruction. Who would not lose a leg to save his neck? And who would not endanger his hand to guard his heart? The loss of liberty in general would soon follow the suppression of the liberty of the press; for as it is an essential branch of liberty, so perhaps it is the best preservation of the whole. Even a restraint of the press would have a fatal influence. No nation ancient or modern ever lost the liberty of freely speaking, writing, or publishing their sentiments but forthwith lost their liberty in general and became slaves. LIBERTY and SLAVERY! how amiable is one! how odious and abominable the other! Liberty is universal redemption, joy, and happiness; but servitude is absolute reprobation and everlasting perdition in politics.

All the venal supporters of wicked ministers are aware of the great use of the liberty of the press in a limited free monarchy: They know how vain it would be to attack it openly, and therefore endeavor to puzzle the case with words, inconsistencies, and nonsense; but if the opinion of the most numerous, unprejudiced and impartial part of mankind is an argument of truth, the liberty of the press has that as well as reason on its side. I believe every honest Briton of whatever denomination, who loves his country, if left to his own free and unbiased judgment is a friend to the liberty of the press and an enemy to any restraint upon it. Surely all the independent whigs, to a man, are of this opinion. By an Independent Whig, I mean one whose principles lead him to be firmly attached to the present happy establishment, both in church and state, and whose fidelity to the royal family is so staunch and riveted as not to be called in question, tho' his mind is not overswayed, or rather necessitated, by the extraordinary weight of lucrative posts or pensions. The dread of infamy hath certainly been of great use to the cause of virtue, and is a stronger curb upon the passions and appetites of some men than any other consideration moral or religious. Whenever, therefore, the talent of satire is made use of to restrain men by the fear of shame from immoral actions, which either do or do not fall under the cognizance of the law, it is properly, and justly, and commendably applied: On the contrary, to condemn all satire is in effect the same thing as countenancing vice by screening it from reproach and the just indignation of mankind. The use of satire was of great service to the patriot whigs in the reign of King Charles and King James the second, as well as in that of Queen Anne. They asserted the freedom of writing against wicked ministers; and tho' they knew it would signify nothing to accuse them publicly whilst they were in the zenith of their power, they made use of satire to prepare the way and alarm the people against their designs. If men in power were always men of integrity, we might venture to trust them with the direction of the press, and there would be no occasion to plead against the restraint of it; but as they have vices like their fellows, so it very often happens that the best intended and the most valuable writings are the objects of their resentment, because opposite to their own tempers or designs. In short, I think, every man of common sense will judge that he is an enemy to his king and country who pleads for any restraint upon the press; but by the press, when nonsense, inconsistencies, or personal reflections are writ, if despised, they die of course; if truth, solid arguments, and elegant, just sentiments are published, they should meet with applause rather than censure; if sense and nonsense are blended, then, by the free use of the press, which is open to all, the inconsistencies of the writer may be made apparent; but to grant a liberty only for praise, flattery, and panegyric, with a restraint on everything which happens to be offensive and disagreeable to those who are at any time in power, is absurd, servile, and ridiculous; upon which, I beg leave to quote one observation of the ingenious Mr. Gordon, in his excellent discourses upon Tacitus. "In truth," says he, where no liberty is allowed to speak of governors besides that of praising them, their praises will be little believed; their tenderness and aversion to have their conduct examined will be apt to prompt people to think their conduct guilty or weak, to suspect their management and designs to be worse perhaps than they are, and to become turbulent and seditious, rather than be forced to be silent. . . .

Eighteenth-Century Runaway Women

According to English law, married women were *femes covert*; that is, their identity was "covered" by their husbands. Legally they did not exist.[1] Their property (including whatever wages they might earn and even the clothes they wore) belonged to their husbands, and it was their duty to serve and obey them. Husbands had complete control over their wives. They had the legal right to beat them, when necessary, to enforce that control. It was illegal for women to run away, but, because it was virtually impossible to obtain a divorce, many wives did just that.

These advertisements, published in the *Pennsylvania Gazette* in the mid-eighteenth century, are an intriguing glimpse into marital relations in colonial America. Husbands who advertised that they would not pay their runaway wives' debts were hoping to starve their wives into submission, shame them for unfeminine behavior, or finally be rid of them. Abused women, however, frequently asserted themselves and presented their own side by responding to advertisements with their own in the same paper, thus revealing that women were far from the submissive, docile creatures that many scholars have assumed them to be. And so it seems that feminist stirrings were already brewing in the pre-Revolutionary period.

What do these notices reveal about a woman's rights within a marriage? What were the differences between the letter of the law and the actual behavior of some husbands and wives? How did these women define a good marriage? What were the practical difficulties that might have kept many women from eloping in protest over bad marriages?

Advertisements from the *Pennsylvania Gazette*, 1742–1748

March 25, 1742:

Whereas ELIZABETH DUNLAP, Wife of JAMES DUNLAP of Piles Grove, Salem County in the Province of New-Jersey, hath lately eloped from the said James Dunlap her Husband. These are therefore to forwarn and forbid any Person to trust said Elizabeth for any Goods or other things whatsoever for that her said Husband will pay no Debt or Debts contracted by her after the Date hereof. . . .

---

[1]Women could not legally make contracts. If there was a divorce, husbands had automatic custody over the children. If a wife was injured and the husband sued the responsible party to recover money damages, the recovery belonged to him, not to her.

Source: *Runaway Women: Elopements and Other Miscreant Deeds As Advertised in the* Pennsylvania Gazette, *1728–1789 (Together with a Few Abused Wives and Unfortunate Children)*, compiled by Judith Ann Highley Meier (Apollo, PA: Closson Press, 1993), 5, 6, 11, 13.

June 17, 1742:

Whereas JAMES DUNLAP, of Piles Grove, in the County of Salem, in the province of New-Jersey, by an advertisement lately inserted in the American Weekly Mercury and in the Pennsylvania Gazette, did publish the elopement of ELIZABETH DUNLAP his Wife, and forewarned all Persons to trust her for any goods or other things, etc.

These are therefore to certify all Persons whom it may concern, that the contents of the said advertisement as to the elopement of the said Elizabeth is utterly false, for the said Elizabeth never eloped from the said James Dunlap her Husband, but was obliged in safety of her life to leave her said Husband because of his threats and cruel abuse for several years past repeatedly offered and done to her, and that she went no farther than to her Father's House in said county, where she has resided ever since her departure from her said Husband, and still continues to reside. And the same James Dunlap having a considerable estate in lands in said county, which the said Elizabeth is informed he intends to sell as soon as he can, she therefore thought proper to give this notice to any Person or Persons that may offer to buy, that she will not join in the sale of any part of said lands, but that she intends to claim her thirds (or right of dower) of and in all the lands the said James Dunlap has been seized and possessed of since their intermarriage, whosoever may purchase the same.

Elizabeth Dunlap.

July 31, 1746:

Whereas MARY, the Wife of JOHN FENBY, Porter, hath eloped from her said Husband without any cause; this is to forwarn all Persons not to trust her on his Account; for he will pay no Debts she shall contract from the Date hereof.

August 7, 1746:

Whereas JOHN, the Husband of MARY FENBY, hath advertis'd her in this Paper, as eloped from him, &c., tho' 'tis well known, they parted by Consent, and agreed to divide their Goods in a Manner which he has not yet been so just as fully to comply with, but detains her Bed and Wedding Ring: And as she neither has, nor desires to run him in Debt, believing her own Credit to be full as good as his; so she desires no one would trust him on her Account, for neither will she pay any Debts of his contracting.

MARY FENBY

June 9, 1748:

Whereas JANE, the wife of PETER HENRY DORSIUS, of Philadelphia county, the daugher of DERRICK HOGELAND of Bucks county, hath eloped from her said husband; this is to desire all persons not to trust her on his account, for he will pay no debts of her contracting, from the date hereof.

June 16, 1748:

Whereas PETER HENRY DORSIUS hath in the last Gazette advertised his wife JANE, as eloped from him, &c. This is to certify whom it may concern, that after a long series of ill usage patiently borne by the said Jane, and after a course of intemperance and extravagance, for which he has been suspended the exercise of his ministerial office in the Dutch Congregation in Southampton; when he had squandered most of his substance, sold and spent great part of his houshold goods, and was about to sell the remainder; tho' he had before in his sober hours, by Direction of a Magistrate made them over for the use of his Family; when he had for several Days abandoned his Dwelling, and left his wife and their children nothing to subsist on, her father found himself at length under a necessity to take her and them into his care and protection, and accordingly fetch'd them home to his own house, which he would not otherwise have done, having besides a large Family of his own to provide for.

DERRICK HOGELAND

WEB RESOURCES FOR PART ONE

SITES FEATURING A NUMBER OF THE DISSENTERS IN PART ONE

Roger Williams
www.rogerwilliams.org/biography.htm
http://en2.wikipedia.org/wiki/Roger_Williams

Anne Hutchinson
www.annehutchinson.com/
www.piney.com/ColAnnHutchTrial.html

Mary Dyer
www.geocities.com/Heartland/Valley/2822/marydyer.html

Nathaniel Bacon
www.nps.gov/colo/Jthanout/BacRebel.html
www.ls.net/~newriver/va/bacon.htm

Indians in the Seventeenth and Eighteenth Centuries
www.tngenweb.org/cessions/colonial.html

John Peter Zenger
www.law.umkc.edu/faculty/projects/ftrials/zenger/zenger.html

OTHER DISSENTING VOICES OF THE TIME

Robert Child in New England

For information on Robert Child and his plea for religious toleration in 1640s New England, see:

www.law.du.edu/russell/lh/alh/docs/childremonstrance.html
http://puritanism.online.fr/puritanism/child.html

Jacob Leisler in New York

For biographical information on the man who led a rebellion in New York in 1689, see:

www.nyu.edu/leisler/

Protestant Associators in Maryland

A site about the 1688 revolt of Protestants against the Catholic proprietors of Maryland:

www.combs-families.org/combs/records/md/1689/sayer.htm

Sam Davies dissenting against the Virginia religious establishment

For information on Sam Davies and his attempt to disestablish the Anglican Church in Virginia, see:

www.pastwords.net/pw222.html

PART TWO

Revolution and the Birth of a Nation, 1760–1820

A portrait of Judith Sargent Murray (1751–1820) by John Singleton Copley, circa 1772, painted 18 years before the publication of her "On the Equality of the Sexes." This landmark essay, calling for equal educational opportunities for all women, had a profound influence on the early feminist movement.

Introduction: The Republic Takes Shape

The history of the seventeenth century is a history of settlement, diversification, expansion, and conflict, the impact of which led to unanticipated repercussions by the eighteenth century. As English settlers expanded farther into what they saw as a wilderness, there were increasing and deadly confrontations between them and the native peoples who encountered them. But clashes also intensified between the nations that were struggling for control of the North American continent. Conflicts between the French and the British were contested on both sides of the Atlantic, and because of their global context, these wars, in a sense, can be viewed as the first world wars. In the 1690s, King William's War (War of the League of Augsburg in Europe) was a struggle between the British and French. From 1702 to 1713, Queen Anne's War (War of the Spanish Succession in Europe, where the French were allied with the Spanish) broke out; in the colonies, it was simply a continuation of the previous conflict between the English and French for control of the Hudson River, Acadia, and New Brunswick. The struggle resumed in the 1740s as King George's War (War of the Austrian Succession in Europe, where the Prussians joined with the British, and the Austrians and Spanish with the French). In the 1750s, deeply entrenched tensions were further exacerbated when the French began to expand into the Ohio River valley and built Fort Duquesne at the confluence of the Monongahela and Allegheny rivers. In 1754, the young Virginia militia captain, George Washington, was sent to dislodge the French from this fort. The resulting skirmish, leading to Washington's hasty retreat, marked the outbreak of the French and Indian War (Seven Years' War in Europe). This war was truly a world war, and when the Peace of Paris was finally signed in 1763, the world had changed irrevocably. France relinquished all its possessions in continental North America; Britain had emerged as the most powerful nation in Europe, with its empire extending from North America to India; and the throne of England was occupied by the first English-speaking Hanoverian, *our* last king, George III.

During this volatile period, the writings of John Locke, David Hume, Montesquieu, Voltaire, and other Enlightenment philosophers were spreading rapidly through the Western world. In the American colonies, educated people increasingly discussed the notions of natural rights and the nature of government. Locke's ideas especially found fertile soil in a society that had begun to think of the government in London after the Glorious Revolution as a distant and negligent institution out of touch with its colonial subjects. But it was at the end of the French and Indian War, as Parliament and the new king, in an effort to recoup the costs of the war and reestablish London's control over the American colonies, that these ideas about the nature of freedom and equality took hold in a way that was simply unimaginable to British subjects at midcentury.

The colonists' protests against the new taxes imposed by Parliament led, in little more than a decade, directly to the American Revolution. The Sons of Liberty, Committees of Correspondence, the Boston Massacre, the Boston Tea Party, and the Intolerable Acts had their impact on the eventual separation of the colonies from the mother country. Loyalists, on the other hand, facing increasing discrimination and violence against themselves and their property, raised their voices in defense of the Crown. The words *liberty* and *equality* were so bandied about, so popularized, and so contagious that even groups to whom the words had never been applied also began to yearn for their attainment. When southern planters resisted the "slavery" they believed Parliament was trying to impose on them, their bondsmen were inspired to hope that freedom from tyranny might belong to them, too. Even before

Jefferson wrote "all men are created equal," many women had begun to question their subordination.

When the Revolution ended, although slavery was abolished in several northern states and women's educational opportunities expanded, little else was accomplished for women and poor white men, and nothing at all for slaves in the South. And as far as the Indian people were concerned, the impact of the Revolution was devastating. No longer were the English a force to slow down the westward expansion of the settlers, nor were the French and Spanish available as allies. In fact, the American Revolution might rightfully be regarded as phase one of an uncompleted revolution. The subsequent history of the United States has arguably been the gradual (and often violently disputed) unfolding of the Jeffersonian concept, so that today it encompasses far more people than it did in 1776. Although equality is central to the American canon, in reality we are still struggling to defend that principle. The Revolution is an ongoing process that has still not come to fruition.

Even as the American nation took shape in the ensuing decades, many people and groups dissented against the authority of the new powers that be. Women arguing for their rights, Quakers like Anthony Benezet and John Woolman as well as countless slaves demanding abolition, free blacks protesting racism and segregation in the north, Indians petitioning the government for fair treatment, the Shaysite rebellion against the taxes imposed by the Massachusetts legislature, Anti-Federalists deeply distrustful of a strong central government, farmers in western Pennsylvania denouncing the excise tax, Republicans condemning the Alien and Sedition Acts, New Englanders and pro-British Federalists vehemently protesting the U.S. entry into the War of 1812, Philadelphia blacks protesting the underlying racism of the American Colonization Society's strategy of emancipating the slaves and sending them back to Africa—all were dissenting voices raised during this critical era in American history.

John Woolman (1720–1772)

John Woolman lived his Quaker ideals to the fullest. He believed that all living beings were interconnected, that there was divinity in all, and that it was necessary for all people to be aware of this connection. "I was convinced in my mind," he wrote in his *Journal*, "that true religion consisted in an inward life, wherein the heart doth love and reverence God the Creator, and learns to exercise true justice and goodness, not only toward all men, but also toward the brute creatures." Such a philosophy convinced him that slavery was wrong, and during his brief life he was not afraid to express this view even to his fellow Quakers, many of whom owned slaves. As he went about the country, he never let up in arguing against slavery, both in speeches and in print. Eventually his influence led the Society of Friends in Philadelphia to deny membership to anyone who owned slaves.

The following excerpts are from "Considerations on Keeping Negroes, Part Second," one of the several essays he wrote on the subject. Much of the essay is a demolition of the biblical argument slaveholders used to defend slavery: God's curse on Ham and his descendants and the familiar injunction that servants should obey their masters. What other arguments does Woolman use?

"Considerations on Keeping Negroes, Part Second," 1762

As some in most religious Societies amongst the English are concerned in importing or purchasing the inhabitants of Africa as slaves, and as the professors of Christianity of several other nations do the like, the circumstances tend to make people less apt to examine the practice so closely as they would if such a thing had not been, but was now proposed to be entered upon. It is, however, our duty and what concerns us individually as creatures accountable to our Creator, to employ rightly the understanding which he hath given us in humbly endevouring to be aquainted with his will concerning us and with the nature and tendency of those things which we practice. For as justice remains to be justice, so many people of reputation in the world joining with wrong things do not excuse others in joining with them nor make the consequence of their proceedings less dreadful in the final issue than it would be otherwise.

It looks to me that the slave trade was founded and hath generally been carried on in a wrong spirit, that the effects of it are detrimental to the real prosperity of our

SOURCE: Phillips P. Moulton, ed., *The Journal and Major Essays of John Woolman* (New York: Oxford University Press, 1971), 211–237 passim.

country, and will be more so except we cease from the common motives of keeping them and treat them in future agreeable to Truth and pure justice.

Negroes may be imported who, for their cruelty to their countrymen and the evil disposition of their minds, may be unfit at liberty; and if we, as lovers of righteousness, undertake the management of them, we should have a full and clear knowledge of their crimes and those circumstances which might operate in their favor; but the difficulty of obtaining this is so great that we have great reason to be cautious therein. But should it plainly appear that absolute subjection were a condition the most proper for the person who is purchased, yet the innocent children ought not to be made slaves because their parents sinned.

Placing on men the ignominious title SLAVE, dressing them in uncomely garments, keeping them to servile labour in which they are often dirty tends gradually to fix a notion in the mind that they are a sort of people below us in nature, and leads us to consider them as such in all our conclusions about them. And, moreover, a person which in our esteem is mean and contemptible, if their language or behavior toward us is unseemly or disrespectful, it excites wrath more powerfully than the like conduct in one we accounted our equal or superior, and where this happens to be the case it disqualifies for candid judgement; for it is unfit for a person to sit as judge in a case where his own personal resentments are stirred up, and as members of society in a well-framed government we are mutually dependent. Present interest incites to duty and makes each man attentive to the convenience of others; but he whose wants are supplied without feeling any obligation to make equal returns to his benefactor, his irregular appetites find as open field for motion, and he is in danger of growing hard and inattentive to their convenience who labour for his support, and so loses that disposition in which alone men are fit to govern.

The English government hath been commended by candid foreigners for the disuse of racks and tortures, so much practiced in some states; but this multiplying slaves now leads to it. For where people exact hard labour of others without a suitable reward and are resolved to continue in that way, severity to such who oppose them becomes the consequence; and several Negro criminals among the English in America have been executed in a lingering, painful way, very terrifying to others.

It is a happy case to set out right and persevere in the same way. A wrong beginning leads into many difficulties, for to support one evil, another becomes customary. Two produces more, and the further men proceed in this way the greater their dangers, their doubts and fears, and the more painful and perplexing are their circumstances, so that such who are true friends to the real and lasting interest of our country and candidly consider the tendency of things cannot but feel some concern on this account. . . .

Seed sown with the tears of a confined oppressed people, harvest cut down by an overborne discontented reaper, makes bread less sweet to the taste of an honest man, than that which is the produce or just reward of such voluntary action which is one proper part of the business of human creatures. . . .

He who reverently observes that goodness manifested by our gracious Creator toward the various species of beings in this world, will see that in our frame and constitution is clearly shown that innocent men capable to manage for themselves were not intended to be slaves.

A person lately travelling amongst the Negroes near Senegal hath this remark: "Which way soever I turned my eyes on this pleasant spot, I beheld a perfect image of pure nature: an agreeable solitude bounded on every side by charming landscapes, the rural situation of cottages in the midst of trees, the ease and indolence of the Negroes reclined under the shade of their spreading foliage, the simplicity of their dress and manners—the whole revived in my mind the idea of our first parents, and I seemed to contemplate the world in its primitive state."—M. Adanson, page 55.

Some Negroes in these parts who have had an agreeable education have manifested a brightness of understanding equal to many of us. A remark of this kind we find in Bosman, page 328: "The Negroes of Fida," saith he, "are so accurately quick in their merchandise accounts that they easily reckon as justly and quickly in their heads only, as we with the assistance of pen and ink, though the sum amounts to several thousands."

Through the force of long custom it appears needful to speak in relation to colour. Suppose a white child born of parents of the meanest sort who died and left him an infant falls into the hands of a person who endeavours to keep him a slave. Some men would account him an unjust man in doing so, who yet appear easy while many black people of honest lives and good abilities are enslaved in a manner more shocking than the case here supposed. This is owing chiefly to the idea of slavery being connected with the black colour and liberty with the white. And where false ideas are twisted into our minds, it is with difficulty we get fairly disentangled. . . .

Selfishness being indulged clouds the understanding; and where selfish men for a long time proceed on their way without opposition, the deceivableness of unrighteousness gets so rooted in their intellects that a candid examination of things relating to self-interest is prevented; and in this circumstance some who would not agree to make a slave of a person whose colour is like their own, appear easy in making slaves of others of a different colour, though their understandings and morals are equal to the generality of men of their own colour.

The colour of a man avails nothing in matters of right and equity. Consider colour in relation to treaties. By such, disputes betwixt nations are sometimes settled. And should the Father of us all so dispose things that treaties with black men should sometimes be necessary, how then would it appear amongst the princes and ambassadors to insist on the prerogative of the white colour? Whence is it that men who believe in a righteous Omnipotent Being, to whom all nations stand equally related and are equally accountable, remain so easy in it, but for that the ideas of Negroes and slaves are so interwoven in the mind that they do not discuss this matter with that candour and freedom of thought which the case justly calls for? . . .

Many are desirous of purchasing and keeping slaves that they may live in some measure comfortable to those customs of the times which have in them a tincture of luxury; for when we in the least degree depart from that use of the creatures which the Creator of all things intended for them, there luxury begins.

And if we consider this way of life seriously, we shall see there is nothing in it sufficient to induce a wise man to choose it before a plain, simple way of living. If we examine stately buildings and equipage, delicious foods, superfine clothes, silks, and linens; if we consider the splendor of choice metal fastened upon raiment, and the most showy inventions of men; it will yet appear that the humble-minded man who is contented with the true use of houses, food, and garments, and cheerfully exerciseth himself agreeable to his station in civil society to earn them, acts more reasonably and discovers more soundness of understanding in his conduct than such who lay heavy burdens on others to support themselves in a luxurious way of living. . . .

Should we consider ourselves present as spectators when cruel Negroes privately catch innocent children who are employed in the fields, hear their lamentable cries under the most terrifying apprehensions, or should we look upon it as happening in our own families—having our children carried off by savages—we must needs own that such proceedings are contrary to the nature of Christianity. Should we meditate on the wars which are greatly increased by this trade and on that affliction which many thousands live in, through apprehensions of being taken or slain; on the terror and amazement that villages are in when surrounded by these troops of enterprisers; on the great pain and misery of groaning, dying men who get wounded in those skirmishes; we shall necessarily see that it is impossible to be parties in such a trade on the motives of gain and retain our innocence.

Should we consider the case of multitudes of those people who in a fruitful soil and hot climate with a little labour raise grain, roots, and pulse to eat, spin and weave cotton, and fasten together the large feathers of fowls to cover their nakedness, many of whom in much simplicity live inoffensive in their cottages and take great comfort in raising up children; should we contemplate on their circumstances when suddenly attacked and labour to understand their inexpressible anguish of soul who survive the conflict; should we think of inoffensive women who fled at the alarm and at their return saw that village, in which they and their acquaintance were raised up and had pleasantly spent their youthful days, now lying in gloomy desolation, some shocked at finding the mangled bodies of their near friends amongst the slain, others bemoaning the absence of a brother, a sister, a child, or a whole family of children, who by cruel men are bound and carried to market, to be sold without the least hopes of seeing them again; add to this the afflicted condition of these poor captives who are separated from family connections and all the comforts arising from friendship and acquaintance, carried amongst a people of a strange language, to be parted from their fellow captives, put to labour in a manner more servile and wearisome than what they were used to, with many sorrowful circumstances attending their slavery—and we must necessarily see that it belongs not to the followers of Christ to be parties in such a trade on the motives of outward gain.

Though there were wars and desolations among the Negroes before the Europeans began to trade there for slaves, yet now the calamities are greatly increased, so many thousands being annually brought from thence and we by purchasing them with views of self-interest are become parties with them and accessory to that increase.

In this case, we are not joining against an enemy who is fomenting discords on our continent and using all possible means to make slaves of us and our children, but against a people who have not injured us. If those who were spoiled and wronged should at length make slaves of their oppressors and continue slavery to their posterity, it would look rigorous to candid men. But to act that part toward a people when neither they nor their fathers have injured us, hath something in it extraordinary, and requires our serious attention. . . .

Negroes are our fellow creatures and their present condition amongst us requires our serious consideration. We know not the time when those scales in which mountains are weighed may turn. The parent of mankind is gracious. His care is over his smallest creatures, and a multitude of men escape not his notice; and though many of them are trodden down and despised, yet he remembers them. He seeth their affliction and looketh upon the spreading, increasing exaltation of the oppressor. He turns the channels of power, humbles the most haughty people, and gives deliverance to the oppressed at such periods as are consistent with his infinite justice and goodness. And wherever gain is preferred to equity and wrong things publicly encouraged, to that degree that wickedness takes root and spreads wide amongst the inhabitants of a country, there is real cause for sorrow to all such whose love to mankind stands on a true principle and wisely consider the end and event of things.

John Killbuck

After the French and Indian War, the British, in an effort to prevent war from breaking out again, issued the Proclamation Line of 1763. This line followed the crest of the Appalachian Mountains dividing the colonies on the east from Indian territory on the west. If the colonists, it was reasoned, were prevented from trespassing on and taking over Indian lands, peace would be stabilized, and England would then not have to defend the colonists in another costly war. However, the Proclamation Line did nothing to impede the continual westward expansion of the colonists. In 1768, the Fort Stanwix Treaty shifted the line farther west to the bank of the Ohio River. In 1771, chiefs from several tribes met with the governors of Virginia, Maryland, and Pennsylvania, and one of the Delaware chieftains, John Killbuck, gave the following speech in which he expressed their deep alarm at white encroachment.

Once again, we see that Native Americans have learned enough about European institutions that they appeal to the governors to use their authority and implement the laws governing the settlers. What will be the consequence if the governors do not enforce these laws? What does Killbuck's speech reveal about the settlers' relations with each other?

Speech to the Governors of Pennsylvania, Maryland, and Virginia, December 4, 1771

Brethren, in former times our forefathers and yours lived in great friendship together and often met to strengthen the chain of their friendship. As your people grew numerous we made room for them and came over the Great Mountains to

---

SOURCE: Public Record Office, C.O. 5/90:5; also Library of Congress transcript; reprinted in K.G. Davies, ed., *Documents of the American Revolution* (Shannon: Irish University Press, 1977–1981), 3:254–255.

Ohio. And some time ago when you were at war with the French your soldiers came into this country, drove the French away and built forts. Soon after a number of your people came over the Great Mountains and settled on our lands. We complained of their encroachments into our country, and, brethren, you either could not or would not remove them. As we did not choose to have any disputes with our brethren, the English, we agreed to make a line and the Six Nations at Fort Stanwix three years ago sold the King all the lands on the east side of the Ohio down to the Cherokee River, which lands were the property of our confederacy, and gave a deed to Sir William Johnson as he desired. Since that time great numbers more of your people have come over the Great Mountains and settled throughout this country. And we are sorry to tell you that several quarrels have happened between your people and ours, in which people have been killed on both sides, and that we now see the nations round us and your people ready to embroil in a quarrel, which gives our nation great concern, as we on our parts want to live in friendship with you, as you have always told us you have laws to govern your people by (but we do not see that you have). Therefore, brethren, unless you can fall upon some method of governing your people who live between the Great Mountains and the Ohio River and who are now very numerous, it will be out of the Indians' power to govern their young men, for we assure you the black clouds begin to gather fast in this country. And if something is not soon done those clouds will deprive us of seeing the sun. We desire you to give the greatest attention to what we now tell you as it comes from our hearts and a desire we have to live in peace and friendship with our brethren the English. And therefore it grieves us to see some of the nations about us and your people ready to strike each other. We find your people are very fond of our rich land. We see them quarrelling every day about land and burning one another's houses. So that we do not know how soon they may come over the River Ohio and drive us from our villages, nor do we see you brethren take any care to stop them. It's now several years since we have met together in council, which all nations are surprised and concerned at. What is the reason you kindled a fire at Ohio for us to meet you (which we did and talked friendly together) that you have let your fire go out for some years past? This makes all nations jealous about us as we also frequently hear of our brethren the English meeting with Cherokees and with the Six Nations to strengthen their friendship, which gives us cause to think you are forming some bad designs against us who lives between the Ohio and Lakes. I have now told you everything that is in my heart and desire you will write what I have said and send it to the Great King. A belt. Killbuck, speaker.

Samuel Adams (1722–1803)

Samuel Adams, a failure at almost every business venture he ever attempted, was elected to the Massachusetts General Court in 1765, and from this point on he became one of the boldest of the political propagandists opposing Parliament's colonial policies during the decade leading up to the American

Revolution. He was a member of the Sons of Liberty and organized Committees of Correspondence to disseminate news of British "atrocities" like the Boston Massacre throughout all 13 colonies. Though the British soldiers who fired on the unruly mob in March 1770 were acting in self-defense, Adams spread news throughout the land that it was an unprovoked massacre. Two years later, Samuel Adams issued a report of the Committee of Correspondence enumerating the rights of the colonists.

In what ways does the report echo John Locke's *Second Treatise of Government* and anticipate the Declaration of Independence? Why are Roman Catholics excluded from toleration?

The Rights of the Colonists—The Report of the Committee of Correspondence to the Boston Town Meeting, November 20, 1772

. . . I^{ST.} NATURAL RIGHTS OF THE COLONISTS AS MEN.

Among the natural rights of the Colonists are these: First, a right to Life; Secondly, to Liberty; Thirdly, to Property; together with the right to support and defend them in the best manner they can. These are evident branches of, rather than deductions from, the duty of self-preservation, commonly called the first law of nature.

All men have a right to remain in a state of nature as long as they please; and in case of intolerable oppression, civil or religious, to leave the society they belong to, and enter into another.

When men enter into society, it is by voluntary consent; and they have a right to demand and insist upon the performance of such conditions and previous limitations as form an equitable original compact.

Every natural right not expressly given up, or, from the nature of a social compact, necessarily ceded, remains.

All positive and civil laws should conform, as far as possible, to the law of natural reason and equity.

As neither reason requires nor religion permits the contrary, every man living in or out of a state of civil society has a right peaceably and quietly to worship God according to the dictates of his conscience.

"Just and true liberty, equal and impartial liberty," in matters spiritual and temporal, is a thing that all men are clearly entitled to by the eternal and immutable laws of God and nature, as well as by the law of nations and all well-grounded municipal laws, which must have their foundation in the former.

In regard to religion, mutual toleration in the different professions thereof is what all good and candid minds in all ages have ever practised, and, both by precept

---

SOURCE: Harry Alonzo Cushing, ed., *The Writings of Samuel Adams* (New York: G. P. Putnam's Sons, 1906), vol. II, 350–359. Some punctuation and capitalization have been modernized.

and example, inculcated on mankind. And it is now generally agreed among Christians that this spirit of toleration, in the fullest extent consistent with the being of civil society, is the chief characteristical mark of the Church. Insomuch that Mr. Locke has asserted and proved, beyond the possibility of contradiction on any solid ground, that such toleration ought to be extended to all whose doctrines are not subversive of society. The only sects which he thinks ought to be, and which by all wise laws are excluded from such toleration, are those who teach doctrines subversive of the civil government under which they live. The Roman Catholics or Papists are excluded by reason of such doctrines as these, that princes excommunicated may be deposed, and those that they call heretics may be destroyed without mercy; besides their recognizing the Pope in so absolute a manner, in subversion of government, by introducing, as far as possible into the states under whose protection they enjoy life, liberty, and property, that solecism in politics, imperium in imperio, leading directly to the worst anarchy and confusion, civil discord, war, and bloodshed.

The natural liberty of man, by entering into society, is abridged or restrained, so far only as is necessary for the great end of society, the best good of the whole.

In the state of nature every man is, under God, judge and sole judge of his own rights and of the injuries done him. By entering into society he agrees to an arbiter or indifferent judge between him and his neighbors; but he no more renounces his original right than by taking a cause out of the ordinary course of law, and leaving the decision to referees or indifferent arbitrators. In the last case, he must pay the referees for time and trouble. He should also be willing to pay his just quota for the support of government, the law, and the constitution; the end of which is to furnish indifferent and impartial judges in all cases that may happen, whether civil, ecclesiastical, marine, or military.

"The natural liberty of man is to be free from any superior power on earth, and not to be under the will or legislative authority of man, but only to have the law of nature for his rule."

In the state of nature men may, as the patriarchs did, employ hired servants for the defence of their lives, liberties, and property; and they should pay them reasonable wages. Government was instituted for the purposes of common defence, and those who hold the reins of government have an equitable, natural right to an honorable support from the same principle that "the laborer is worthy of his hire." But then the same community which they serve ought to be the assessors of their pay. Governors have no right to seek and take what they please; by this, instead of being content with the station assigned them, that of honorable servants of the society, they would soon become absolute masters, despots, and tyrants. Hence, as a private man has a right to say what wages he will give in his private affairs, so has a community to determine what they will give and grant of their substance for the administration of public affairs. And, in both cases, more are ready to offer their service at the proposed and stipulated price than are able and willing to perform their duty.

In short, it is the greatest absurdity to suppose it in the power of one, or any number of men, at the entering into society, to renounce their essential natural rights, or the means of preserving those rights; when the grand end of civil government, from the very nature of its institution, is for the support, protection, and defence of those very rights; the principal of which, as is before observed, are Life, Liberty, and Property. If men, through fear, fraud, or mistake, should in terms renounce or give up any essential natural right, the eternal law of reason and the grand end of society would absolutely vacate such renunciation. The right to freedom being the gift of God Almighty, it is not in the power of man to alienate this gift and voluntarily become a slave.

2^{D.} THE RIGHTS OF THE COLONISTS AS CHRISTIANS.

These may be best understood by reading and carefully studying the institutes of the great Law Giver and Head of the Christian Church, which are to be found clearly written and promulgated in the New Testament.

By the act of the British Parliament, commonly called the Toleration Act, every subject in England, except Papists, &c., was restored to, and re-established in, his natural right to worship God according to the dictates of his own conscience. And, by the charter of this Province, it is granted, ordained, and established (that is, declared as an original right) that there shall be liberty of conscience allowed in the worship of God to all Christians, except Papists, inhabiting, or which shall inhabit or be resident within, such Province or Territory. Magna Charta itself is in substance but a constrained declaration or proclamation and promulgation in the name of the King, Lords, and Commons, of the sense the latter had of their original, inherent, indefeasible natural rights, as also those of free citizens equally perdurable with the other. That great author, that great jurist, and even that court writer, Mr. Justice Blackstone, holds that this recognition was justly obtained of King John, sword in hand. And peradventure it must be one day, sword in hand, again rescued and preserved from total destruction and oblivion.

3^{D.} THE RIGHTS OF THE COLONISTS AS SUBJECTS.

A commonwealth or state is a body politic, or civil society of men, united together to promote their mutual safety and prosperity by means of their union.

The absolute rights of Englishmen and all freemen, in or out of civil society, are principally personal security, personal liberty, and private property.

All persons born in the British American Colonies are, by the laws of God and nature and by the common law of England, exclusive of all charters from the Crown, well entitled, and by acts of the British Parliament are declared to be entitled, to all the natural, essential, inherent, and inseparable rights, liberties, and privileges of subjects born in Great Britain or within the realm. Among those rights are the following, which no man, or body of men, consistently with their own rights as men and citizens, or members of society, can for themselves give up or take away from others.

First, "The first fundamental, positive law of all common wealths or states is the establishing the legislative power. As the first fundamental natural law, also, which is to govern even the legislative power itself, is the preservation of the society."

Secondly, The Legislative has no right to absolute, arbitrary power over the lives and fortunes of the people; nor can mortals assume a prerogative not only too high for men, but for angels, and therefore reserved for the exercise of the Deity alone.

"The Legislative cannot justly assume to itself a power to rule by extempore arbitrary decrees; but it is bound to see that justice is dispensed, and that the rights of the subjects be decided by promulgated, standing, and known laws, and authorized independent judges"; that is, independent, as far as possible, of Prince and people. "There should be one rule of justice for rich and poor, for the favorite at court, and the countryman at the plough."

Thirdly, The supreme power cannot justly take from any man any part of his property, without his consent in person or by his representative.

These are some of the first principles of natural law and justice, and the great barriers of all free states and of the British Constitution in particular. It is utterly irreconcilable to these principles and to many other fundamental maxims of the common law, common sense, and reason that a British House of Commons should have a right at pleasure to give and grant the property of the Colonists. (That the Colonists are well entitled to all the essential rights, liberties, and privileges of men and freemen born in Britain is manifest not only from the Colony charters in general, but acts of the British Parliament.) The statute of the 13th of Geo. 2, C. 7, naturalizes even foreigners after seven years' residence. The words of the Massachusetts charter are these: "And further, our will and pleasure is, and we do hereby for us, our heirs, and successors, grant, establish, and ordain, that all and every of the subjects of us, our heirs, and successors, which shall go to, and inhabit within our said Province or Territory, and every of their children, which shall happen to be born there or on the seas in going thither or returning from thence, shall have and enjoy all liberties and immunities of free and natural subjects within any of the dominions of us, our heirs, and successors, to all intents, constructions, and purposes whatsoever as if they and every one of them were born within this our realm of England." Now what liberty can there be where property is taken away without consent? Can it be said with any color of truth and justice, that this continent of three thousand miles in length, and of a breadth as yet unexplored, in which, however, it is supposed there are five millions of people, has the least voice, vote, or influence in the British Parliament? Have they all together any more weight or power to return a single member to that House of Commons who have not inadvertently, but deliberately, assumed a power to dispose of their lives, liberties, and properties, than to choose an Emperor of China? Had the Colonists a right to return members to the British Parliament, it would only be hurtful; as, from their local situation and circumstances, it is impossible they should ever be truly and properly represented there. The inhabitants of this country, in all probability, in a few years, will be more numerous than those of Great Britain and Ireland together; yet it is absurdly expected by the promoters of the present measures that these, with their posterity to all generations, should be easy, while their property shall be disposed of by a House of Commons at three thousand miles' distance from them, and who cannot be supposed to have the least care or concern for their real interest; who have not only no natural care for their interest, but must be in effect bribed against it, as every burden they lay on the Colonists is so much saved or gained to themselves. Hitherto, many of the Colonists have been free from quit rents; but if the breath of a British House of Commons can originate an act for taking away all our money, our lands will go next, or be subject to rack rents from haughty and relentless landlords, who will ride at ease, while we are trodden in the dirt. The Colonists have been branded with the odious names of traitors and rebels only for complaining of their grievances. How long such treatment will or ought to be borne, is submitted.

Revolutionary Women

Women in the period before the Revolution were often just as forceful as men in their protests against London's policies. In 1768, Hannah Griffiths published a poem in which she proclaimed that women were ready to boycott British goods and wear only clothing made out of American homespun cloth to protest the taxes that British prime ministers George Grenville and Charles Townshend levied on sugar, tea, paint, and glass.

A few years later, after the December 1773 Boston Tea Party, Parliament passed the Coercive Acts (dubbed the Intolerable Acts by the colonists), which, among other penalties, closed the port of Boston. Response was swift and vocal. Around the colonies, people showed their solidarity with Boston through demonstrations and protests. Once again, women were not shy about making their dissenting voices heard. In Edenton, North Carolina, in October 1774, 51 women signed a pledge not to drink tea or wear English-made clothing: "We, the Ladys of Edenton, do hereby solemnly engage not to conform to the Pernicious Custom of Drinking Tea" and "We, the aforesaid Ladys will not promote ye wear of any manufacturer from England until such time that all acts which tend to enslave our Native country shall be repealed."

Do the women believe that their boycott would have a significant impact on the British government?

Hannah Griffiths, Poem, 1768

THE FEMALE PATRIOTS. ADDRESS'D TO THE DAUGHTERS OF LIBERTY IN AMERICA. BY THE SAME, 1768

Since the Men from a Party, or fear of a Frown,
Are kept by a Sugar-Plumb, quietly down.
Supinely asleep, & depriv'd of their Sight
Are strip'd of their Freedom, & rob'd of their Right.
If the Sons (so degenerate) the Blessing despise,
Let the Daugthers of Liberty, nobly arise,
And tho' we've no Voice, but a negative here.
The use of the Taxables, let us forebear,
(Then Merchants import till yr. Stores are all full
May the Buyers be few & yr. Traffick be dull.)
Stand firmly resolved & bid Grenville to see

SOURCE: Catherine La Courreye Blecki and Karin A. Wulf, eds. *Milcah Martha Moore's Book, A Commonplace Book from Revolutionary America,* (University Park: Pennsylvania State University Press, 1997), 172–173.

That rather than Freedom, we'll part with our Tea
And well as we love the dear Draught when a dry,
As American Patriots,—our Taste we deny,
Sylvania's, gay Meadows, can richly afford,
To pamper our Fancy, or furnish our Board,
And Paper sufficient (at home) still we have,
To assure the Wise-acre, we will not sign Slave.
When this Homespun shall fail, to remonstrate our Grief
We can speak with the Tongue or scratch on a Leaf.
Refuse all their Colours, tho richest of Dye,
The juice of a Berry—our Paint can supply,
To humour our Fancy—& as for our Houses,
They'll do without painting as well as our Spouses,
While to keep out the Cold of a keen winter Morn
We can screen the Northwest, with a well polish'd Horn,
And trust me a Woman by honest Invention
Might give this State Doctor a Dose of Prevention.
Join mutual in this, & but small as it seems
We may Jostle a Grenville & puzzle his Schemes
But a motive more worthy our patriot Pen,
Thus acting—we point out their Duty to Men,
And should the bound Pensioners, tell us to hush
We can throw back the Satire by biding them blush.

by Hannah Griffiths

Ladies of Edenton, North Carolina, Agreement, 1774–1775

MORNING CHRONICLE AND LONDON ADVERTISER, JANUARY 16, 1775

The provincial deputies of North Carolina having resolved not to drink any more tea nor wear any more British cloth, etc., many ladies of this province have determined to give a memorable proof of their patriotism, and have accordingly entered into the following honorable and spirited association. I send it to you to show your fair countrywomen how zealously and faithfully American ladies follow the laudable example of their husbands, and what opposition your *matchless* ministers may expect to receive from a people, thus firmly united against them:

EDENTON, NORTH CAROLINA, OCTOBER 25 (1774)

As we cannot be indifferent on any occasion that appears nearly to affect the peace and happiness of our country, and as it has been thought necessary, for the public

---

SOURCE: Richard Dillard, *The Historic Tea Party of Edenton, October 25, 1774* (Raleigh: Capital Printing, 1901).

good, to enter into several particular resolves by a meeting of members deputed from the whole province, it is a duty which we owe, not only to our near and dear connections, who have concurred in them, but to ourselves, who are essentially interested in their welfare, to do everything, as far as lies in our power, to testify our sincere adherence to the same; and we do therefore accordingly subscribe this paper as a witness of our fixed intention and solemn determination to do so:

Abagail Charlton,
Elizabeth Creacy,
Anne Johnstone,
Mary Woolard,
Jean Blair,
Frances Hall,
Mary Creacy,
Mary Blount,
Margaret Cathcart,
Jane Wellwood,
Penelope Dawson,
Susanna Vail,
Elizabeth Vail,
Elizabeth Vail,
J. Johnstone,
Elizabeth Patterson
Margaret Pearson,

Sarah Beasley,
Grace Clayton,
Mary Jones,
Mary Creacy,
Anne Hall,
Sarah Littlejohn,
Sarah Hoskins,
M. Payne,
Elizabeth Cricket,
Lydia Bonner,
Anne Horniblow,
Marion Wells,
Sarah Mathews,
Elizabeth Roberts,
Rebecca Bondfield,
Sarah Howcott,
Elizabeth P. Ormond,

Sarah Valentine,
Mary Bonner,
Mary Ramsey,
Lydia Bennett,
Tresia Cunningham,
Anne Haughton,
Elizabeth Roberts,
Ruth Benbury,
Penelope Barker,
Mary Littledle,
Elizabeth Johnstone,
Elizabeth Green,
Sarah Howe,
Mary Hunter,
Anne Anderson,
Elizabeth Bearsley,
Elizabeth Roberts.

The Second Continental Congress

In response to the Coercive Acts, delegates from 12 of the colonies met in Philadelphia in September 1774 to set a course of action. Radicals called for resistance, moderates for reconciliation. After much debate they implemented a policy of nonimportation of goods from England. When they adjourned they agreed to meet again the following year. By the time they reassembled in May 1775, hostilities had broken out at Lexington and Concord. The delegates therefore found it necessary to shift their focus from their original purpose and discuss the question of war. Though still not wishing to break irrevocably with the mother country, they issued a declaration justifying the colonists' resort to arms.

Why, according to the delegates, is it necessary to issue this statement? What is the basis for colonial discontent with London? Do they see themselves as Americans or loyal British subjects? What is their most potent argument? Is armed resistance justified?

A Declaration by the Representatives of the United Colonies of North America, Now Met in General Congress at Philadelphia, Setting Forth the Causes and Necessity of Their Taking Up Arms, 1775

If it was possible for men, who exercise their reason, to believe, that the Divine Author of our existence intended a part of the human race to hold an absolute property in, and an unbounded power over others, marked out by his infinite goodness and wisdom, as the objects of a legal domination never rightfully resistible, however severe and oppressive, the inhabitants of these colonies might at least require from the Parliament of Great Britain some evidence that this dreadful authority over them has been granted to that body. But a reverence for our great Creator, principles of humanity, and the dictates of common sense must convince all those who reflect upon the subject that government was instituted to promote the welfare of mankind and ought to be administered for the attainment of that end. The legislature of Great Britain, however, stimulated by an inordinate passion for a power, not only unjustifiable, but which they know to be peculiarly reprobated by the very constitution of that kingdom, and desperate of success in any mode of contest, where regard should be had to truth, law, or right, have at length, deserting those, attempted to effect their cruel and impolitic purpose of enslaving these colonies by violence, and have thereby rendered it necessary for us to close with their last appeal from reason to arms.

Yet, however blinded that assembly may be, by their intemperate rage for unlimited domination, so to slight justice and the opinion of mankind, we esteem ourselves bound, by obligations of respect to the rest of the world, to make known the justice of our cause.

Our forefathers, inhabitants of the island of Great Britain, left their native land to seek on these shores a residence for civil and religious freedom. At the expense of their blood, at the hazard of their fortunes, without the least charge to the country from which they removed, by unceasing labor, and an unconquerable spirit, they effected settlements in the distant and inhospitable wilds of America, then filled with numerous and warlike nations of barbarians. Societies or governments, vested with perfect legislatures, were formed under charters from the crown, and a harmonious intercourse was established between the colonies and the kingdom from which they derived their origin. The mutual benefits of this union became in a short time so extraordinary as to excite astonishment. It is universally confessed that the amazing increase of the wealth, strength, and navigation of the realm arose from this source; and the minister, who so wisely and successfully directed the measures of Great Britain in the late war, publicly declared that these colonies enabled her to triumph over her enemies.

Toward the conclusion of that war, it pleased our sovereign to make a change in his counsels. From that fatal moment, the affairs of the British Empire began to fall into confusion, and gradually sliding from the summit of glorious prosperity, to

Source: *Journals of the Continental Congress, 1774–1789*, II, 140–157.

which they had been advanced by the virtues and abilities of one man, are at length distracted by the convulsions that now shake it to its deepest foundations. The new ministry finding the brave foes of Britain, though frequently defeated, yet still contending, took up the unfortunate idea of granting them a hasty peace and of then subduing her faithful friends.

These devoted colonies were judged to be in such a state, as to present victories without bloodshed, and all the easy emoluments of statutable plunder. The uninterrupted tenor of their peaceable and respectful behavior from the beginning of colonization, their dutiful, zealous, and useful services during the war, though so recently and amply acknowledged in the most honorable manner by His Majesty, by the late king, and by Parliament, could not save them from the meditated innovations.

Parliament was influenced to adopt the pernicious project, and assuming a new power over them, have, in the course of eleven years, given such decisive specimens of the spirit and consequences attending this power, as to leave no doubt concerning the effects of acquiescence under it. They have undertaken to give and grant our money without our consent, though we have ever exercised an exclusive right to dispose of our own property; statutes have been passed for extending the jurisdiction of courts of admiralty and vice-admiralty beyond their ancient limits; for depriving us of the accustomed and inestimable privilege of trial by jury, in cases affecting both life and property; for suspending the legislature of one of the colonies; for interdicting all commerce to the capital of another; and for altering fundamentally the form of government established by charter and secured by acts of its own legislature solemnly confirmed by the crown; for exempting the "murderers" of colonists from legal trial and, in effect, from punishment; for erecting in a neighboring province, acquired by the joint arms of Great Britain and America, a despotism dangerous to our very existence; and for quartering soldiers upon the colonists in time of profound peace. It has also been resolved in Parliament that colonists charged with committing certain offenses shall be transported to England to be tried.

But why should we enumerate our injuries in detail? By one statute it is declared, that Parliament can "of right make laws to bind us IN ALL CASES WHATSOEVER." What is to defend us against so enormous, so unlimited a power? Not a single man of those who assume it is chosen by us or is subject to our control or influence; but, on the contrary, they are all of them exempt from the operation of such laws, and an American revenue, if not diverted from the ostensible purposes for which it is raised, would actually lighten their own burdens in proportion as they increase ours. We saw the misery to which such despotism would reduce us. We for ten years incessantly and ineffectually besieged the throne as supplicants; we reasoned, we remonstrated with Parliament, in the most mild and decent language. But administration, sensible that we should regard these oppressive measures as freemen ought to do, sent over fleets and armies to enforce them. The indignation of the Americans was roused, it is true; but it was the indignation of a virtuous, loyal, and affectionate people. A Congress of Delegates from the United Colonies was assembled at Philadelphia, on the fifth day of last September. We resolved again to offer a humble and dutiful petition to the king, and also addressed our fellow-subjects of Great Britain. We have pursued every temperate, every respectful, measure:

we have even proceeded to break off our commercial intercourse with our fellow-subjects, as the last peaceable admonition, that our attachment to no nation upon earth should supplant our attachment to liberty. This, we flattered ourselves, was the ultimate step of the controversy. But subsequent events have shown how vain was this hope of finding moderation in our enemies.

Several threatening expressions against the colonies were inserted in His Majesty's speech; our petition, though we were told it was a decent one, and that His Majesty had been pleased to receive it graciously, and to promise laying it before his Parliament, was huddled into both houses amongst a bundle of American papers, and there neglected. The Lords and Commons in their address, in the month of February, said, that "a rebellion at that time actually existed within the province of Massachusetts Bay; and that those concerned in it, had been countenanced and encouraged by unlawful combinations and engagements, entered into by His Majesty's subjects in several of the other colonies; and therefore they besought His Majesty, that he would take the most effectual measures to enforce due obedience to the laws and authority of the supreme legislature."

Soon after, the commercial intercourse of whole colonies, with foreign countries, and with each other, was cut off by an act of Parliament; by another, several of them were entirely prohibited from the fisheries in the seas near their coasts, on which they always depended for their sustenance; and large reinforcements of ships and troops were immediately sent over to General Gage.

Fruitless were all the entreaties, arguments, and eloquence of an illustrious band of the most distinguished Peers, and Commoners, who nobly and strenuously asserted the justice of our cause, to stay, or even to mitigate the heedless fury with which these accumulated and unexampled outrages were hurried on. Equally fruitless was the interference of the city of London, of Bristol, and many other respectable towns in our favor. Parliament adopted an insidious maneuver calculated to divide us, to establish a perpetual auction of taxations where colony should bid against colony, all of them uninformed what ransom would redeem their lives; and thus to extort from us, at the point of the bayonet, the unknown sums that should be sufficient to gratify, if possible to gratify, ministerial rapacity, with the miserable indulgence left to us of raising, in our own mode, the prescribed tribute. What terms more rigid and humiliating could have been dictated by remorseless victors to conquered enemies? In our circumstances to accept them would be to deserve them.

Soon after the intelligence of these proceedings arrived on this continent, General Gage, who in the course of the last year had taken possession of the town of Boston, in the province of Massachusetts Bay, and still occupied it as a garrison, on the 19th day of April, sent out from that place a large detachment of his army, who made an unprovoked assault on the inhabitants of the said province, at the town of Lexington, as appears by the affidavits of a great number of persons, some of whom were officers and soldiers of that detachment, murdered eight of the inhabitants, and wounded many others. From thence the troops proceeded in warlike array to the town of Concord, where they set upon another party of the inhabitants of the same province, killing several and wounding more, until compelled to retreat by the country people suddenly assembled to repel this cruel aggression. Hostilities, thus commenced by the British troops, have been since prosecuted by them without regard to faith or reputation. The inhabitants of Boston being confined within that town by the General, their Governor, and having, in order to procure their dismission, entered into a treaty with him, it was stipulated that the said inhabitants, having deposited their arms with their own magistrates, should have liberty to depart, taking with them their other effects. They accordingly delivered up their arms, but in open violation of honor, in defiance of the obligation of treaties, which even savage nations esteemed sacred, the Governor ordered the arms deposited as aforesaid, that they might be preserved for their owners, to be seized by a body of soldiers; detained the greatest part of the inhabitants in the town, and compelled the few who were permitted to retire to leave their most valuable effects behind.

By this perfidy wives are separated from their husbands, children from their parents, the aged and the sick from their relations and friends, who wish to attend and comfort them; and those who have been used to live in plenty and even elegance are reduced to deplorable distress.

The General, further emulating his ministerial masters, by a proclamation bearing date on the 12th day of June, after venting the grossest falsehoods and calumnies against the good people of these colonies, proceeds to "declare them all, either by name or description, to be rebels and traitors, to supersede the course of the common law, and instead thereof to publish and order the use and exercise of the law martial." His troops have butchered our countrymen, have wantonly burned Charles-Town, besides a considerable number of houses in other places; our ships and vessels are seized; the necessary supplies of provisions are intercepted, and he is exerting his utmost power to spread destruction and devastation around him.

We have received certain intelligence that General Carleton, the Governor of Canada, is instigating the people of that province and the Indians to fall upon us; and we have but too much reason to apprehend that schemes have been formed to excite domestic enemies against us. In brief, a part of these colonies now feels, and all of them are sure of feeling, as far as the vengeance of administration can inflict them, the complicated calamities of fire, sword, and famine. We are reduced to the alternative of choosing an unconditional submission to the tyranny of irritated ministers, or resistance by force. The latter is our choice. We have counted the cost of this contest and find nothing so dreadful as voluntary slavery. Honor, justice, and humanity forbid us tamely to surrender that freedom which we received from our gallant ancestors, and which our innocent posterity have a right to receive from us. We cannot endure the infamy and guilt of resigning succeeding generations to that wretchedness which inevitably awaits them, if we basely entail hereditary bondage upon them.

Our cause is just. Our union is perfect. Our internal resources are great, and, if necessary, foreign assistance is undoubtedly attainable. We gratefully acknowledge, as signal instances of the Divine favor toward us, that his Providence would not permit us to be called into this severe controversy, until we were grown up to our present strength, had been previously exercised in warlike operation, and possessed of the means of defending ourselves. With hearts fortified with these animating reflections, we most solemnly, before God and the world, declare that, exerting the utmost energy of those powers which our beneficent Creator hath graciously bestowed upon us, the arms we have been compelled by our enemies to assume we will, in defiance of every hazard, with unabating firmness and perseverance, employ for the preservation of our liberties; being with our [one] mind resolved to die free men rather than live slaves.

Lest this declaration should disquiet the minds of our friends and fellow-subjects in any part of the Empire, we assure them that we mean not to dissolve that union which has so long and so happily subsisted between us, and which we sincerely wish to see restored. Necessity has not yet driven us into that desperate measure, or induced us to excite any other nation to war against them. We have not raised armies with ambitious designs of separating from Great Britain establishing independent states. We fight not for glory or for conquest. We exhibit to mankind the remarkable spectacle of a people attacked by unprovoked enemies, without any imputation or even suspicion of offense. They boast of their privileges and civilization and yet proffer no milder conditions than servitude or death.

In our own native land, in defense of the freedom that is our birthright, and which we ever enjoyed till the late violation of it—for the protection of our property, acquired solely by the honest industry of our forefathers and ourselves, against violence actually offered, we have taken up arms. We shall lay them down when hostilities shall cease on the part of the aggressors, and all danger of their being renewed shall be removed, and not before.

With a humble confidence in the mercies of the supreme and impartial Judge and Ruler of the universe, we most devoutly implore his divine goodness to protect us happily through this great conflict, to dispose our adversaries to reconciliation on reasonable terms, and thereby to relieve the Empire from the calamities of civil war.

By order of Congress,

JOHN HANCOCK,
President

Attested,

CHARLES THOMSON,
Secretary

PHILADELPHIA, July 6th, 1775

Thomas Paine (1737–1809)

After only a year in the colonies, radical thinker Thomas Paine was dismayed and irritated that the colonists had not formally declared their independence from Great Britain, even after hostilities had broken out in April 1775 at Lexington and Concord. In January 1776, Paine published *Common Sense*, in which he urged the colonists that the only sensible thing to do was to separate entirely from the mother country. This brief pamphlet (selling 120,000 copies in its first 3 months) had an enormous impact on colonial opinion, and by July the Second Continental Congress had issued the Declaration of Independence.

On what grounds did Paine base his argument for independence? What was Paine's view of monarchy? Representative government? Did he appeal to reason or emotion?

Common Sense, 1776

In the following pages I offer nothing more than simple facts, plain arguments, and common sense; and have no other preliminaries to settle with the reader, than that he will divest himself of prejudice and prepossession, and suffer his reason and his feelings to determine for themselves; that he will put on, or rather that he will not put off, the true character of a man, and generously enlarge his views beyond the present day.

Volumes have been written on the subject of the struggle between England and America. Men of all ranks have embarked in the controversy, from different motives, and with various designs; but all have been ineffectual, and the period of debate is closed. Arms, as the last resource, decide the contest; the appeal was the choice of the king, and the continent hath accepted the challenge. . . .

The sun never shined on a cause of greater worth. 'Tis not the affair of a city, a country, a province, or a kingdom, but of a continent of at least one eighth part of the habitable globe. 'Tis not the concern of a day, a year, or an age; posterity are virtually involved in the contest, and will be more or less affected, even to the end of time, by the proceedings now. Now is the seed time of continental union, faith and honor. The least fracture now will be like a name engraved with the point of a pin on the tender rind of a young oak; The wound will enlarge with the tree, and posterity read it in full grown characters.

By referring the matter from argument to arms, a new area for politics is struck; a new method of thinking hath arisen. All plans, proposals, &c. prior to the nineteenth of April, i. e. to the commencement of hostilities, are like the almanacs of the last year; which, though proper then, are superseded and useless now. Whatever was advanced by the advocates on either side of the question then, terminated in one and the same point, viz. a union with Great Britain; the only difference between the parties was the method of effecting it; the one proposing force, the other friendship; but it hath so far happened that the first hath failed, and the second hath withdrawn her influence.

As much hath been said of the advantages of reconciliation, which, like an agreeable dream, hath passed away and left us as we were, it is but right, that we should examine the contrary side of the argument, and inquire into some of the

Source: [Thomas Paine] *Common Sense, Addressed to the Inhabitants of America* (Philadelphia, 1776), 29–60 *passim.*

many material injuries which these colonies sustain, and always will sustain, by being connected with, and dependant on Great Britain. To examine that connection and dependance, on the principles of nature and common sense, to see what we have to trust to, if separated, and what we are to expect, if dependant.

I have heard it asserted by some, that as America hath flourished under her former connection with Great Britain, that the same connection is necessary towards her future happiness, and will always have the same effect. Nothing can be more fallacious than this kind of argument. We may as well assert, that because a child has thrived upon milk, that it is never to have meat; or that the first twenty years of our lives is to become a precedent for the next twenty. But even this is admitting more than is true, for I answer roundly, that America would have flourished as much, and probably much more, had no European power had any thing to do with her. The commerce by which she hath enriched herself are the necessaries of life, and will always have a market while eating is the custom of Europe.

But she has protected us, say some. That she hath engrossed us is true, and defended the continent at our expense as well as her own is admitted, and she would have defended Turkey from the same motive, viz. the sake of trade and dominion.

Alas, we have been long led away by ancient prejudices and made large sacrifices to superstition. We have boasted the protection of Great Britain, without considering, that her motive was interest not attachment; that she did not protect us from our enemies on our account, but from her enemies on her own account, from those who had no quarrel with us on any other account, and who will always be our enemies on the same account. Let Britain wave her pretensions to the continent, or the continent throw off the dependance, and we should be at peace with France and Spain were they at war with Britain. The miseries of Hanover last war ought to warn us against connections. It hath lately been asserted in parliament, that the colonies have no relation to each other but through the parent country, i. e. that Pennsylvania and the Jerseys, and so on for the rest, are sister colonies by the way of England; this is certainly a very roundabout way of proving relation ship, but it is the nearest and only true way of proving enemyship, if I may so call it. France and Spain never were, nor perhaps ever will be our enemies as Americans, but as our being the subjects of Great Britain.

But Britain is the parent country, say some. Then the more shame upon her conduct. Even brutes do not devour their young; nor savages make war upon their families; wherefore the assertion, if true, turns to her reproach; but it happens not to be true, or only partly so, and the phrase Parent or mother country hath been jesuitically adopted by the king and his parasites, with a low papistical design of gaining an unfair bias on the credulous weakness of our minds. Europe, and not England, is the parent country of America. This new world hath been the asylum for the persecuted lovers off civil and religious liberty from every part of Europe. Hither have they fled, not from the tender embraces of the mother, but from the cruelty of the monster; and it is so far true of England, that the same tyranny which drove the first emigrants from home pursues their descendants still. . . .

Much hath been said of the united strength of Britain and the colonies, that in conjunction they might bid defiance to the world. But this is mere presumption; the fate of war is uncertain, neither do the expressions mean anything; for this continent would never suffer itself to be drained of inhabitants to support the British arms in either Asia, Africa, or Europe.

Besides, what have we to do with setting the world at defiance? Our plan is commerce, and that, well attended to, will secure us the peace and friendship of all Europe; because it is the interest of all Europe to have America a free port. Her trade will always be a protection, and her barrenness of gold and silver secure her from invaders.

I challenge the warmest advocate for reconciliation, to show, a single advantage that this continent can reap, by being connected with Great Britain. I repeat the challenge, not a single advantage is derived. Our corn will fetch its price in any market in Europe, and our imported goods must be paid for buy them where we will.

But the injuries and disadvantages we sustain by that connection, are without number; and our duty to mankind at large, as well as to ourselves, instruct us to renounce the alliance: Because, any submission to, or dependance on Great Britain, tends directly to involve this continent in European wars and quarrels; and sets us at variance with nations, who would otherwise seek our friendship, and against whom, we have neither anger nor complaint. As Europe is our market for trade, we ought to form no partial connection with any part of it. It is the true interest of America to steer clear of European contentions, which she never can do, while by her dependance on Britain, she is made the make-weight in the scale of British politics.

Europe is too thickly planted with kingdoms to be long at peace, and whenever a war breaks out between England and any foreign power, the trade of America goes to ruin, because of her connection with Britain. The next war may not turn out like the past, and should it not, the advocates for reconciliation now will be wishing for separation then, because, neutrality in that case, would be a safer convoy than a man of war. Every thing that is right or natural pleads for separation. The blood of the slain, the weeping voice of nature cries, 'TIS TIME TO PART. Even the distance at which the Almighty hath placed England and America, is a strong and natural proof, that the authority of the one, over the other, was never the design of Heaven. The time likewise at which the continent was discovered, adds weight to the argument, and the manner in which it was peopled increases the force of it. The reformation was preceded by the discovery of America, as if the Almighty graciously meant to open a sanctuary to the persecuted in future years, when home should afford neither friendship nor safety.

The authority of Great Britain over this continent, is a form of government, which sooner or later must have an end: And a serious mind can draw no true pleasure by looking forward, under the painful and positive conviction, that what he calls the present constitution is merely temporary. As parents, we can have no joy, knowing that this government is not sufficiently lasting to ensure any thing which we may bequeath to posterity: And by a plain method of argument, as we are running the next generation into debt, we ought to do the work of it, otherwise we use them meanly and pitifully. In order to discover the line of our duty rightly, we should take our children in our hand, and fix our station a few years farther into life; that eminence will present a prospect, which a few present fears and prejudices conceal from our sight.

Though I would carefully avoid giving unnecessary offence, yet I am inclined to believe, that all those who espouse the doctrine of reconciliation, may be included within the following descriptions. Interested men, who are not to be trusted; weak men who cannot see; prejudiced men who will not see; and a certain set of moderate men, who think better of the European world than it deserves; and this last class by an ill-judged deliberation, will be the cause of more calamities to this continent than all the other three.

It is the good fortune of many to live distant from the scene of sorrow; the evil is not sufficiently brought to their doors to make them feel the precariousness with which all American property is possessed. But let our imaginations transport us for a few moments to Boston, that seat of wretchedness will teach us wisdom, and instruct us for ever to renounce a power in whom we can have no trust. The inhabitants of that unfortunate city, who but a few months ago were in ease and affluence, have now no other alternative than to stay and starve, or turn out to beg. Endangered by the fire of their friends if they continue within the city, and plundered by the soldiery if they leave it. In their present condition they are prisoners without the hope of redemption, and in a general attack for their relief, they would be exposed to the fury of both armies.

Men of passive tempers look somewhat lightly over the offenses of Britain, and, still hoping for the best, are apt to call out, 'Come we shall be friends again for all this.' But examine the passions and feelings of mankind. Bring the doctrine of reconciliation to the touchstone of nature, and then tell me, whether you can hereafter love, honor, and faithfully serve the power that hath carried fire and sword into your land? If you cannot do all these, then are you only deceiving yourselves, and by your delay bringing ruin upon posterity. Your future connection with Britain, whom you can neither love nor honor, will be forced and unnatural, and being formed only on the plan of present convenience, will in a little time fall into a relapse more wretched than the first. But if you say, you can still pass the violations over, then I ask, Hath your house been burnt? Hath your property been destroyed before your face? Are your wife and children destitute of a bed to lie on, or bread to live on? Have you lost a parent or a child by their hands, and yourself the ruined and wretched survivor? If you have not, then are you not a judge of those who have. But if you have, and can still shake hands with the murderers, then are you unworthy the name of husband, father, friend, or lover, and whatever may be your rank or title in life, you have the heart of a coward, and the spirit of a sycophant.

This is not infaming or exaggerating matters, but trying them by those feelings and affections which nature justifies, and without which, we should be incapable of discharging the social duties of life, or enjoying the felicities of it. I mean not to exhibit horror for the purpose of provoking revenge, but to awaken us from fatal and unmanly slumbers, that we may pursue determinately some fixed object. It is not in the power of Britain or of Europe to conquer America, if she do not conquer herself by delay and timidity. The present winter is worth an age if rightly employed, but if lost or neglected, the whole continent will partake of the misfortune; and there is no punishment which that man will not deserve, be he who, or what, or where he will, that may be the means of sacrificing a season so precious and useful.

It is repugnant to reason, to the universal order of things, to all examples from the former ages, to suppose, that this continent can longer remain subject to any external power. The most sanguine in Britain does not think so. The utmost stretch of human wisdom cannot, at this time compass a plan short of separation, which can promise the continent even a year's security. Reconciliation is now a fallacious dream. Nature hath deserted the connection, and Art cannot supply her place. For, as Milton wisely expresses, 'never can true reconcilement grow where wounds of deadly hate have pierced so deep.'

Every quiet method for peace hath been ineffectual. Our prayers have been rejected with disdain; and only tended to convince us, that nothing flatters vanity, or confirms obstinacy in Kings more than repeated petitioning and nothing hath contributed more than that very measure to make the Kings of Europe absolute: Witness Denmark and Sweden. Wherefore since nothing but blows will do, for God's sake, let us come to a final separation, and not leave the next generation to be cutting throats, under the violated unmeaning names of parent and child. . . .

Small islands not capable of protecting themselves, are the proper objects for kingdoms to take under their care; but there is something very absurd, in supposing a continent to be perpetually governed by an island. In no instance hath nature made the satellite larger than its primary planet, and as England and America, with respect to each Other, reverses the common order of nature, it is evident they belong to different systems: England to Europe, America to itself. . . .

As Britain hath not manifested the least inclination towards a compromise, we may be assured that no terms can be obtained worthy the acceptance of the continent, or any ways equal to the expense of blood and treasure we have been already put to.

The object contended for, ought always to bear some just proportion to the expense. The removal of N–, or the whole detestable junto, is a matter unworthy the millions we have expended. A temporary stoppage of trade, was an inconvenience, which would have sufficiently balanced the repeal of all the acts complained of, had such repeals been obtained; but if the whole continent must take up arms, if every man must be a soldier, it is scarcely worth our while to fight against a contemptible ministry only. Dearly, dearly, do we pay for the repeal of the acts, if that is all we fight for; for in a just estimation, it is as great a folly to pay a Bunker Hill price for law, as for land. As I have always considered the independency of this continent, as an event, which sooner or later must arrive, so from the late rapid progress of the continent to maturity, the event could not be far off. Wherefore, on the breaking out of hostilities, it was not worth the while to have disputed a matter, which time would have finally redressed, unless we meant to be in earnest; otherwise, it is like wasting an estate of a suit at law, to regulate the trespasses of a tenant, whose lease is just expiring. No man was a warmer wisher for reconciliation than myself, before the fatal nineteenth of April 1775 [Lexington and Concord], but the moment the event of that day was made known, I rejected the hardened, sullen tempered Pharaoh of England [George III] for ever; and disdain the wretch, that with the pretended title of FATHER OF HIS PEOPLE can unfeelingly hear of their slaughter, and composedly sleep with their blood upon his soul.

But admitting that matters were now made up, what would be the event? I answer, the ruin of the continent. And that for several reasons.

First. The powers of governing still remaining in the hands of the king, he will have a negative over the whole legislation of this continent. And as he hath shown himself such an inveterate enemy to liberty, and discovered such a thirst for arbitrary power; is he, or is he not, a proper man to say to these colonies, 'You shall make no laws but what I please.' And is there any inhabitants in America so ignorant, as not to know, that according to what is called the present constitution, that this continent can make no laws but what the king gives leave to; and is there any man so unwise, as not to see, that (considering what has happened) he will suffer no Law to be made here, but such as suit his purpose. We may be as effectually enslaved by the want of laws in America, as by submitting to laws made for us in England. After matters are made up (as it is called) can there be any doubt but the whole power of the crown will be exerted, to keep this continent as low and humble as possible? Instead of going forward we shall go backward, or be perpetually quarrelling or ridiculously petitioning. We are already greater than the king wishes us to be, and will he not hereafter endeavor to make us less? To bring the matter to one point. Is the power who is jealous of our prosperity, a proper power to govern us? Whoever says No to this question is an independent, for independency means no more, than, whether we shall make our own laws, or whether the king, the greatest enemy this continent hath, or can have, shall tell us 'there shall be no laws but such as I like.'

But the king you will say has a negative in England; the people there can make no laws without his consent. in point of right and good order, there is something very ridiculous, that a youth of twenty-one (which hath often happened) shall say to several millions of people, older and wiser than himself, I forbid this or that act of yours to be law. But in this place I decline this sort of reply, tho' I will never cease to expose the absurdity of it, and only answer, that England being the king's residence, and America not so, make quite another case. The king's negative here is ten times more dangerous and fatal than it can be in England, for there he will scarcely refuse his consent to a bill for putting England into as strong a state of defence as possible, and in america he would never suffer such a bill to be passed.

America is only a secondary object in the system of British politics. England consults the good of this country, no farther than it answers her own purpose. Wherefore, her own interest leads her to suppress the growth of ours in every case which doth not promote her advantage, or in the least interfere with it. A pretty state we should soon be in under such a second-hand government, considering what has happened! Men do not change from enemies to friends by the alteration of a name: And in order to show that reconciliation now is a dangerous doctrine, I affirm, that it would be policy in the kingdom at this time, to repeal the acts for the sake of reinstating himself in the government of the provinces; in order, that HE MAY ACCOMPLISH BY CRAFT AND SUBTILTY, IN THE LONG RUN, WHAT HE CANNOT DO BY FORCE AND VIOLENCE IN THE SHORT ONE. Reconciliation and ruin are nearly related.

Secondly. That as even the best terms, which we can expect to obtain, can amount to no more than a temporary expedient, or a kind of government by guardianship, which can last no longer than till the colonies come of age, so the general face and state of things, in the interim, will be unsettled and unpromising.

Emigrants of property will not choose to come to a country whose form of government hangs but by a thread, and who is every day tottering on the brink of commotion and disturbance; and numbers of the present inhabitants would lay hold of the interval, to dispose of their effects, and quit the continent.

But the most powerful of all arguments, is, that nothing but independence, i. e. a continental form of government, can keep the peace of the continent and preserve it inviolate from civil wars. I dread the event of a reconciliation with Britain now, as it is more than probable, that it will be followed by a revolt somewhere or other, the consequences of which may be far more fatal than all the malice of Britain. . . .

A government of our own is our natural right: And when a man seriously reflects on the precariousness of human affairs, he will become convinced, that it is infinitely wiser and safer, to form a constitution of our own in a cool deliberate manner, while we have it in our power, than to trust such an interesting event to time and chance. . . .

Ye that tell us of harmony and reconciliation, can ye restore to us the time that is past? Can ye give to prostitution its former innocence? Neither can ye reconcile Britain and America. The last cord now is broken, the people of England are presenting addresses against us. There are injuries which nature cannot forgive; she would cease to be nature if she did. As well can the lover forgive the ravisher of his mistress, as the continent forgive the murders of Britain. The Almighty hath implanted in us these inextinguishable feelings for good and wise purposes. They are the guardians of his image in our hearts. They distinguish us from the herd of common animals. The social compact would dissolve, and justice be extirpated from the earth, or have only a casual existence were we callous to the touches of affection. The robber and the murderer, would often escape unpunished, did not the injuries which our tempers sustain, provoke us into justice.

O ye that love mankind! Ye that dare oppose, not only the tyranny, but the tyrant, stand forth! Every spot of the old world is overrun with oppression. Freedom hath been hunted round the globe. Asia, and Africa, have long expelled her. Europe regards her like a stranger, and England hath given her warning to depart. O! receive the fugitive, and prepare in time an asylum for mankind.

Abigail Adams (1744–1818) and John Adams (1735–1826)

Abigail Adams, wife of Founding Father John Adams, is often regarded as one of the earliest American feminists. She was extraordinarily intelligent, read widely, expressed her deeply held antislavery views openly, and supported equal education for girls and the rights of women. While her husband was in Philadelphia as a Massachusetts delegate to the Second Continental Congress in 1776, Abigail penned her famous, oft-quoted letter reminding him not to "forget the ladies" as he and the other delegates were debating the issues of independence and the creation of a new government.

John Adams, though he protested and revolted against the English Crown, did not extend his radical views to support women's rights, as his correspondence with Abigail suggests.

The four letters below are an intriguing glimpse into this issue. First, we have Abigail Adams's challenge to her husband; then we have his response and her reply. In the fourth letter, from John Adams to James Sullivan, Adams reveals what he thinks about his wife's opinions.

In what ways does Abigail Adams reveal that she is thoroughly conversant with the political ideology of the day, especially John Locke's natural rights philosophy? On what grounds does John Adams reject her argument? Does the letter to Sullivan show that John Adams has accepted his wife's convictions?

Letters, 1776

ABIGAIL ADAMS TO JOHN ADAMS, MARCH 31, 1776

I long to hear that you have declared an independency—and by the way, in the new Code of Laws which I suppose it will be necessary for you to make, I desire you would Remember the Ladies, and be more generous and favorable to them than your ancestors. Do not put such unlimited power into the hands of the Husbands. Remember, all Men would be tyrants if they could. If particular care and attention is not paid to the Ladies we are determined to foment a Rebellion, and will not hold ourselves bound by any Laws in which we have no voice, or Representation.

That your Sex are Naturally Tyrannical is a Truth so thoroughly established as to admit of no dispute, but such of you as wish to be happy willingly give up the harsh title of Master for the more tender and endearing one of Friend. Why then, not put it out of the power of the vicious and the Lawless to use us with cruelty and indignity with impunity? Men of Sense in all Ages abhor those customs which treat us only as the vassals of your Sex. Regard us then as Being placed by Providence under your protection, and in imitation of the Supreme Being make use of that power only for our happiness.

JOHN ADAMS TO ABIGAIL ADAMS, APRIL 14, 1776

As to Declarations of Independency, be patient. Read our Privateering Laws, and our Commercial Laws. What signifies a Word.

As to your extraordinary Code of Laws, I cannot but laugh. We have been told that our Struggle has loosened the bands of Government everywhere. That Children and Apprentices were disobedient—that schools and Colleges were grown turbulent—that Indians slighted their Guardians and Negroes grew insolent to their

---

SOURCE: L. H. Butterfield, ed., *Adams Family Correspondence* (Cambridge, MA: Harvard University Press, 1963).

Masters. But your Letter was the first Intimation that another Tribe more numerous and powerful than all the rest, were grown discontented.—This is rather too coarse a Compliment, but you are so saucy, I won't blot it out.

Depend upon it, We know better than to repeal our Masculine systems. Altho they are in full Force, you know they are little more than Theory. We dare not exert our Power in its full Latitude. We are obliged to go fair, and softly, and, in Practice, you know We are the subjects. We have only the Name of Masters, and rather than give up this, which would completely subject Us to the Despotism of the Petticoat, I hope General Washington, and all our brave Heroes would fight. I am sure every good Politician would plot, as long as he would against Despotism, Empire, Monarchy, Aristocracy, Oligarchy, or Ochlocracy.

ABIGAIL ADAMS TO JOHN ADAMS, MAY 7, 1776

I can not say that I think you are very generous to the Ladies, for whilst you are proclaiming peace and good will to Men, Emancipating all Nations, you insist upon retaining an absolute power over Wives. But you must remember that Arbitrary power is like most other things which are very hard, very liable to be broken—and notwithstanding all your wise Laws and Maxims we have it in our power not only to free ourselves but to subdue our Masters, and without violence, throw both your natural and legal authority at our feet.

JOHN ADAMS TO JAMES SULLIVAN, MAY 26, 1776

. . . It is certain in Theory, that the only moral Foundation of Government is the Consent of the People. But to what an Extent Shall We carry this Principle? Shall We Say, that every Individual of the Community, old and young, male and female, as well as rich and poor, must consent, expressly to every Act of Legislation? No, you will Say. This is impossible. How then does the Right arise in the Majority to govern the Minority, against their Will? Whence arises the Right of the Men to govern Women, without their Consent? Whence the Right of the old to bind the Young, without theirs.

But let us first Suppose, that the whole Community of every Age, Rank, Sex, and Condition, has a Right to vote. This Community, is assembled—a Motion is made and carried by a Majority of one Voice. The Minority will not agree to this. Whence arises the Right of the Majority to govern, and the Obligation of the Minority to obey? from Necessity, you will Say, because there can be no other Rule. But why exclude Women? You will Say, because their Delicacy renders them unfit for Practice and Experience, in the great Business of Life, and the hardy Enterprizes of War, as well as the arduous Cares of State. Besides, their attention is So much engaged with the necessary Nurture of their Children, that Nature has made them fittest for domestic Cares. And Children have not Judgment or Will of their own. True. But will not these Reasons apply to others? Is it not equally true, that Men in general in every Society, who are wholly destitute of Property, are also too little acquainted with

SOURCE: Robert J. Taylor, ed., *Papers of John Adams* (Cambridge, MA: Harvard University Press, 1979), Volume 4, 208–212.

public Affairs to form a Right Judgment, and too dependent upon other Men to have a Will of their own? If this is a Fact, if you give to every Man, who has no Property, a Vote, will you not make a fine encouraging provision for Corruption by your fundamental Law? Such is the Frailty of the human Heart, that very few Men, who have no Property, have any Judgment of their own. They talk and vote as they are directed by Some Man of Property, who has attached their Minds to his Interest. . . .

Harrington has Shewn that Power always follows Property. This I believe to be as infallible a Maxim, in Politicks, as, that Action and Re-action are equal, is in Mechanicks. Nay I believe We may advance one Step farther and affirm that the Ballance of Power in a Society, accompanies the Ballance of Property in Land. The only possible Way then of preserving the Ballance of Power on the side of equal Liberty and public Virtue, is to make the Acquisition of Land easy to every Member of Society: to make a Division of the Land into Small Quantities, So that the Multitude may be possessed of landed Estates. If the Multitude is possessed of the Ballance of real Estate, the Multitude will have the Ballance of Power, and in that Case the Multitude will take Care of the Liberty, Virtue, and Interest of the Multitude in all Acts of Government.

I believe these Principles have been felt, if not understood in the Massachusetts Bay, from the Beginning: And therefore I Should think that Wisdom and Policy would dictate in these Times, to be very cautious of making Alterations. Our people have never been very rigid in Scrutinizing into the Qualifications of Voters, and I presume they will not now begin to be so. But I would not advise them to make any alteration in the Laws, at present, respecting the Qualifications of Voters.

Your Idea, that those Laws, which affect the Lives and personal Liberty of all, or which inflict corporal Punishment, affect those, who are not qualified to vote, as well as those who are, is just. But, So they do Women, as well as Men, Children as well as Adults. What Reason Should there be, for excluding a Man of Twenty years, Eleven Months and twenty-seven days old, from a Vote when you admit one, who is twenty one? The Reason is, you must fix upon Some Period in Life, when the Understanding and Will of Men in general is fit to be trusted by the Public. Will not the Same Reason justify the State in fixing upon Some certain Quantity of Property, as a Qualification.

The Same Reasoning, which will induce you to admit all Men, who have no Property, to vote, with those who have, for those Laws, which affect the Person will prove that you ought to admit Women and Children: for generally Speaking, Women and Children, have as good Judgment, and as Independent Minds as those Men who are wholly destitute of Property: these last being to all Intents and Purposes as much dependent upon others, who will please to feed, cloath, and employ them, as Women are upon their Husbands, or Children on their Parents. . . .

Depend upon it, sir, it is dangerous to open So fruitfull a Source of Controversy and Altercation, as would be opened by attempting to alter the Qualifications of Voters. There will be no End of it. New Claims will arise. Women will demand a Vote. Lads from 12 to 21 will think their Rights not enough attended to, and every Man, who has not a Farthing, will demand an equal Voice with any other in all Acts of State. It tends to confound and destroy all Distinctions, and prostrate all Ranks, to one common Levell.

Thomas Hutchinson (1711–1780)

Perhaps the most famous Loyalist during the Revolutionary era was Thomas Hutchinson. He was active during the Stamp Act crisis, during which time his house was destroyed by a mob of anti–Stamp Tax protestors. When the Boston Massacre took place, he was acting governor of Massachusetts; later, at the time of the Boston Tea Party, he was governor. As an appointee of the Crown, Hutchinson had little sympathy for the agitators who insisted on breaking with the mother country. Like most colonists, he considered himself, above all, an Englishman who lived in the American colonies. His comment that "It is better to submit to some abridgement of our rights, than to break off our connection with our protector, England" earned him the hatred of the rebels. He fell quickly from his position as a member of the power structure to the status of persona non grata.

In 1776, Hutchinson published *Strictures upon the Declaration of the Congress at Philadelphia*, in which he vehemently protests and takes apart, point by point, each of the arguments set forth in the Declaration of Independence. As you read the following excerpts, examine Hutchinson's arguments. How valid are they? Does he distort or misrepresent the Declaration? Is there any validity to the Loyalist Perspective? How would Thomas Jefferson respond?

A Loyalist Critique of the Declaration of Independence, 1776

STRICTURES UPON THE DECLARATION OF THE CONGRESS AT PHILADELPHIA, 1776

MY LORD,

The last time I had the honour of being in your Lordships company, you observed that you was utterly at a loss to what facts many parts of the Declaration of Independence published by the Philadelphia Congress referred, and that you wished they had been more particularly mentioned, that you might better judge of the grievances, alleged as special causes of the separation of the Colonies from the other parts of the Empire. This hint from your Lordship induced me to attempt a few Strictures upon the Declaration. Upon my first reading it, I thought there would have been more policy in leaving the World altogether ignorant of the motives to this Rebellion, than in offering such false and frivolous reasons in support of it; and I flatter myself, that before I have finished this letter, your Lordship will be of the same mind. But I beg leave, first to make a few remarks upon its rise and progress.

SOURCE: Thomas Hutchinson, *Strictures upon the Declaration of the Congress of Philadelphia, in a Letter to a Noble Lord, &c.* (London, 1776), 3–32, passim.

I have often heard men, (who I believe were free from party influence) express their wishes, that the claims of the Colonies to an exemption from the authority of Parliament in imposing Taxes had been conceded; because they had no doubts that America would have submitted in all other cases; and so this unhappy Rebellion, which has already proved fatal to many hundreds of the Subjects of the Empire, and probably will to many thousands more, might have been prevented.

The Acts for imposing Duties and Taxes may have accelerated the Rebellion, and if this could have been foreseen, perhaps, it might have been good policy to have omitted or deferred them; but I am of opinion, that if no Taxes or Duties had been laid upon the Colonies, other pretences would have been found for exception to the authority of Parliament. The body of the people in the Colonies, I know, were easy and quiet. They felt no burdens. They were attached, indeed, in every Colony to their own particular Constitutions, but the Supremacy of Parliament over the whole gave them no concern. They had been happy under it for an hundred years past: They feared no imaginary evils for an hundred years to come. But there were men in each of the principal Colonies, who had Independence in view, before any of those Taxes were laid, or proposed, which have since been the ostensible cause of resisting the execution of Acts of Parliament. Those men have conducted the Rebellion in the several stages of it, until they have removed the constitutional powers of Government in each Colony, and have assumed to themselves, with others, a supreme authority over the whole. . . .

It does not, however, appear that there was any regular plan formed for attaining to Independence, any further than that every fresh incident which could be made to serve the purpose, by alienating the affections of the Colonie from the Kingdom, should be improved accordingly. One of these incidents happened in the year 1764. This was the Act of Parliament for granting certain duties on goods in the British Colonies, for the support of Government, &c. At the same time a proposal was made in Parliament, to lay a stamp duty upon certain writings in the Colonies; but this was deferred until the next Session, that the Agents of the Colonies might notify the several Assemblies in order to their proposing any way, to them more eligible, for raising a sum for the same purpose with that intended by a stamp duty. The Colony of Massachuset's Bay was more affected by the Act for granting duties, than any other Colony. More molasses, the principal article from which any duty could arise, was distilled into spirits in that Colony than in all the rest. The Assembly of Massachuset's Bay, therefore, was the first that took any publick notice of the Act, and the first which ever took exception to the right of Parliament to impose Duties or Taxes on the Colonies, whilst they had no representatives in the House of Commons. This they did in a letter to their Agent in the summer of 1764, which they took care to print and publish before it was possible for him to receive it. And in this letter they recommend to him a pamphlet, wrote by one of their members, in which there are proposals for admitting representatives from the Colonies to sit in the House of Commons.

I have this special reason, my Lord, for taking notice of this Act of the Massachuset's Assembly; that though an American representation is thrown out as an expedient which might obviate the objections to Taxes upon the Colonies, yet it was only intended to amuse the authority in England; and as soon as it was known to have its advocates here, it was renounced by the Colonies, and even by the Assembly of the

Colony which first proposed it, as utterly impracticable. In every stage of the Revolt, the same disposition has always appeared. No precise, unequivocal terms of submission to the authority of Parliament in any case, have ever been offered by any Assembly. A concession has only produced a further demand, and I verily believe if every thing had been granted short of absolute Independence, they would not have been contented; for this was the object from the beginning. One of the most noted among the American clergy, prophesied eight years ago, that within eight years from that time, the Colonies would be formed into three distinct independent Republics, Northern, Middle and Southern. I could give your Lordship many irrefragable proofs of this determined design, but I reserve them for a future letter, the subject of which shall be the rite and progress of the Rebellion in each of the Colonies. . . .

It will cause greater prolixity to analize the various parts of this Declaration, than to recite the whole. I will therefore present it to your Lordship's view in distinct paragraphs, with my remarks, in order as the paragraphs are published.

In Congress, July 4, 1776.

A Declaration by the Representatives of the United States of America in General Congress assembled.

When in the course of human events it becomes necessary for one People to dissolve the political bands which have connected them with another, and to assume among the Powers of the earth, the separate and equal station to which the laws of nature and of nature's God entitle them, a decent respect to the opinions of mankind requires that they should declare the causes which impel them to the separation.

We hold these truths to be self evident—That all men are created equal, that they are endowed by their Creator with certain unalienable rights, that among these are life, liberty and the pursuit of happiness, that to secure these rights, governments are instituted among men, deriving their just powers from the consent of the governed; and whenever any form of government becomes destructive of these ends, it is the right of the people to alter or abolish it, and to institute new government, laying its foundation on such principles, and organizing its powers in such form as to them shall seem most likely to effect their safety and happiness. Prudence indeed will dictate that governments long established, should not be changed for light and transient causes; and accordingly all experience hath shewn that mankind are more disposed to suffer while evils are sufferable, than to right themselves by abolishing the forms to which they are accustomed. But when a long train of abuses and usurpations pursuing invariably the same objects, evinces a design to reduce them under absolute despotism, it is their right, it is their duty to throw off such government, and to provide new guards for their future security. Such has been the patient sufferance of these Colonies, and such is now the necessity which constrains them to alter their former systems of Government. The history of the present King of Great Britain is a history of repeated injuries and usurpations, all having its direct object, the establishment of an absolute tyranny over these States. To prove this, let facts be submitted to a candid world.

They begin, my Lord, with a false hypothesis. That the Colonies are one *distinct people,* and the kingdom another, connected by *political* bands. The Colonies, *politically* considered, never were a *distinct* people from the kingdom. There never has been but one *political* band, and that was just the same before the first Colonists emigrated as it has been ever since, the Supreme Legislative Authority, which hath essential right, and is indispensably bound to keep all parts of the Empire entire, until there may be a separation consistent with the general good of the Empire, of which good, from the nature of government, this authority must be the sole judge. I should therefore be impertinent, if I attempted to shew in what case a *whole people* may be justified in rising up in oppugnation to the powers of government, altering or abolishing them, and substituting, in whole or in part, new powers in their stead; or in what sense all men are created equal; or how far life, liberty, and the *pursuit of happiness* may be said to be unalienable; only I could wish to ask the Delegates of Maryland, Virginia, and the Carolinas, how their Constituents justify the depriving more than an hundred thousand Africans of their rights to liberty, and *the pursuit of happiness,* and in some degree to their lives, if these rights are so absolutely unalienable; nor shall I attempt to confute the absurd notions of government, or to expose the equivocal or inconclusive expressions contained in this Declaration; but rather to shew the false representation made of the facts which are alledged to be the evidence of injuries and usurpations, and the special motives to Rebellion. There are many of them, with design, left obscure; for as soon as they are developed, instead of justifying, they rather aggravate the criminality of this Revolt.

The first in order, *He has refused his assent to laws the most wholesome and necessary for the public good;* is of so general a nature, that it is not possible to conjecture to what laws or to what Colonies it refers. I remember no laws which any Colony has been restrained from passing, so as to cause any complaint of grievance, except those for issuing a fraudulent paper currency, and making it a legal tender; but this is a restraint which for many years past has been laid on Assemblies by an act of Parliament, since which such laws cannot have been offered to the King for his allowance. I therefore believe this to be a general charge, without any particulars to support it; fit enough to be placed at the head of a list of imaginary grievances.

The laws of England are or ought to be the laws of its Colonies. To prevent a deviation further than the local circumstances of any Colony may make necessary, all Colony laws are to be laid before the King; and if disallowed, they then become of no force. Rhode-Island, and Connecticut, claim by Charters, an exemption from this rule, and as their laws are never presented to the King, they are out of the question. Now if the King is to approve of all laws, or which is the same thing, of all which the people judge for the public good, for we are to presume they pass no other, this reserve in all Charters and Commissions is futile. This charge is still more inexcusable, because I am well informed, the disallowance of Colony laws has been much more frequent in preceding reigns, than in the present. . . .

He has called together legislative bodies at places unusual, uncomfortable, and distant from the depository of their public records, for the sole purpose of fatiguing them into a compliance with his measures.

To the same Colony this article also has respect. Your Lordship must remember the riotous, violent opposition to Government in the Town of Boston, which alarmed the whole Kingdom, in the year 1768. Four Regiments of the King's forces were ordered to that Town, to be aiding to the Civil Magistrate in restoring and preserving peace and order. The House of Representatives, which was then sitting in the Town, remonstrated to the Governor against posting Troops there, as being an invasion of their rights. He thought proper to adjourn them to Cambridge, where the House had frequently sat at their own desire, when they had been alarmed with fear of the small pox in Boston; the place therefore was not unusual. The public rooms of the College, were convenient for the Assembly to sit in, and the private houses of the inhabitants for the Members to lodge in; it therefore was not *uncomfortable*. It was within four miles of the Town of Boston, and less *distant* than any other Town fit for the purpose.

When this step, taken by the Governor, was known in England, it was approved, and conditional instructions were given to continue the Assembly at Cambridge. The House of Representatives raised the most frivolous objections against the authority of the Governor to remove the Assembly from Boston, but proceeded, nevertheless, to the business of the Session as they used to do. In the next Session, without any new cause, the Assembly refused to do any business unless removed to Boston. This was making themselves judges of the place, and by the same reason, of the time of holding the Assembly, instead of the Governor, who thereupon was instructed not to remove them to Boston, so long as they continued to deny his authority to carry them to any other place.

They *fatigued* the Governor by adjourning from day to day, and refusing to do business one Session after another, while he gave his constant attendance to no purpose; and this they make the King's *fatiguing* them to compel them to comply with his measures.

A brief narrative of this unimportant dispute between an American Governor and his Assembly, needs an apology to your Lordship; how ridiculous then do those men make themselves, who offer it to the world as a ground to justify Rebellion?

He has dissolved Representatives Houses repeatedly for opposing with manly firmness his Invasions on the Rights of the People.

Contentions between Governors and their Assemblies have caused dissolutions of such Assemblies, I suppose, in all the Colonies, in former as well as later times. I recollect but one instance of the dissolution of an Assembly by special order from the King, and that was in Massachuset's Bay. In 1768, the House of Representatives passed a vote or resolve, in prosecution of the plan of Independence, imcompatible with the subordination of the Colonies to the supreme authority of the Empire; and directed their Speaker to send a copy of it in circular letters to the Assemblies of the other Colonies, inviting them to avow the principles of the resolve, and to join in supporting them. No Government can long subsist, which admits of combinations of the subordinate powers against the supreme. This proceeding was therefore, justly deemed highly unwarrantable; and indeed it was the beginning of that unlawful confederacy, which has gone on until it has caused at least a temporary Revolt of all the Colonies which joined in it.

The Governor was instructed to require the House of Representatives, in their next Session to rescind or disavow this resolve, and if they refused, to dissolve them, as the only way to prevent their prosecuting the plan of Rebellion. They delayed a definitive answer, and he indulged them, until they had finished all the business of the Province, and then appeared this *manly firmness* in a rude answer and a peremptory refusal to comply with the King's demand. Thus, my Lord, the regular use of the prerogative in suppressing a Revolt, is urged as a grievance to justify the Revolt.

He has refused for a long time after such dissolutions to cause others to be erected whereby the legislative powers, incapable of annihilation, have returned to the people at large for their exercise; the state remaining in the mean time exposed to all the dangers of invasions from without and convulsions within.

This is connected with the last preceding article, and must relate to the same Colony only; for no other ever presumed, until the year 1774, when the general dissolution of the established government in all the Colonies was taking place, to convene an Assembly, without the Governor, by the meer act of the People.

In less than three months after the Governor had dissolved the Assembly of Massachuset's Bay, the town of Boston, the first mover in all affairs of this nature, applied to him to call another Assembly. The Governor thought he was the judge of the proper time for calling an Assembly, and refused. The town, without delay, chose their former members, whom they called a *Committee,* instead of Representatives; and they sent circular letters to all the other towns in the Province inviting them to chuse *Committees* also; and all these *Committees* met in what they called a *Convention,* and chose the Speaker of the last house their *Chairman.* Here was a House of Representatives in every thing but name; and they were proceeding upon business in the town of Boston, but were interrupted by the arrival of two or three regiments and a spirited message from the Governor, and in two or three days returned to their homes.

This vacation of three months was the *long time* the people waited before they exercised their unalienable powers; the *Invasions from without* were the arrival or expectation of three or four regiments sent by the King to aid the Civil Magistrate in preserving the peace; and the *Convulsions within* were the tumults, riots and acts of violence which this Convention was called, not to suppress but to encourage. . . .

He has kept among us, in times of peace, standing armies, without the consent of our legislatures.

This is too nugatory to deserve any remark. He has kept no armies among them without the consent of the Supreme Legislature. It is begging the question, to suppose that this authority was not sufficient without the aid of their own Legislatures.

He has affected to render the Military independent of, and superior to, the Civil Power.

When the subordinate Civil Powers of the Empire became Aiders of the people in acts of Rebellion, the King, as well he might, has employed the Military Power to reduce those rebellious Civil Powers to their constitutional subjection to the Supreme Civil Power. In no other sense has he ever *affected* to render the Military independent of, and superior to, the Civil Power.

He has combined with others to subject us to a jurisdiction foreign to our Constitution and unacknowledged by our Laws; giving his assent to their pretended Acts of Legislation.

This is a strange way of defining the part which the Kings of England take in conjunction with the Lords and Commons in passing Acts of Parliament. But why is our present Sovereign to be distinguished from all his predecessors since Charles the Second? Even the Republic which they affect to copy after, and Oliver, their favourite, because an Usurper, *combined* against them also. And then, how can a jurisdiction submitted to for more than a century be *foreign* to their constitution? And is it not the grossest prevarication to say this jurisdiction is *unacknowledged* by their laws, when all Acts of Parliament which respect them, have at all times been their rule of law in all their judicial proceedings? If this is not enough; their own subordinate legislatures have repeatedly in addresses, and resolves, in the most express terms *acknowledged* the supremacy of Parliament; and so late as 1764, before the conductors of this Rebellion had settled their plan, the House of Representatives of the leading Colony made a public declaration in an address to their Governor, that, although they humbly apprehended they might propose their objections, to the late Act of Parliament for granting certain duties in the British Colonies and Plantations in America, yet they at the same time, *acknowledged* that it was their duty to yield obedience to it while it continued unrepealed.

If the jurisdiction of Parliament is foreign to their Constitution, what need of specifying instances, in which they have been subjected to it? Every Act must be an usurpation and injury. They must then be mentioned, my Lord, to shew, hypothetically, that even if Parliament had jurisdiction, such Acts would be a partial and injurious use of it. I will consider them, to know whether they are so or not.

For quartering large bodies of armed troops among us.

When troops were employed in America, in the last reign, to protect the Colonies against French invasion, it was necessary to provide against mutiny and desertion, and to secure proper quarters. Temporary Acts of Parliament were passed for that purpose, and submitted to in the Colonies. Upon the peace, raised ideas took place in the Colonies, of their own importance, and caused a reluctance against Parliamentary authority, and an opposition to the Acts for quartering troops, not because the provision made was in itself unjust or unequal, but because they were Acts of a Parliament whose authority was denied. The provision was as similar to that in England as the state of the Colonies would admit.

For protecting them by a mock trial from punishment, for any murder which they should commit on the Inhabitants of these States.

It is beyond human wisdom to form a system of laws so perfect as to be adapted to all cases. It is happy for a state, that there can be an interposition of legislative power in those cases, where an adherence to established rules would cause injustice. To try men before a biassed and pre-determined Jury would be *a mock trial.* To prevent this, the Act of Parliament, complained of, was passed. Surely, if in any case Parliament may interpose and alter the general rule of law, it may in this. America has not been distinguished from other parts of the Empire. Indeed, the removal of trials for the sake of unprejudiced disinterested Juries, is altogether consistent with the spirit of our laws, and the practice of courts in changing the venue from one county to another.

For cutting off our trade with all parts of the world.

Certainly, my Lord, this could not be a *cause* of Revolt. The Colonies had revolted from the Supreme Authority, to which, by their constitutions, they were subject, before the Act passed. A Congress had assumed an authority over the whole, and had rebelliously prohibited all commerce with the rest of the Empire. This act, therefore, will be considered by the *candid world,* as a proof of the reluctance in government against what is the dernier resort in every state, and as a milder measure to bring the Colonies to a re-union with the rest of the Empire.

For imposing taxes on us without our consent.

How often has your Lordship heard it said, that the Americans are willing to submit to the authority of Parliament in all cases except that of taxes? Here we have a declaration made to the world of the causes which have impelled to a separation. We are to presume that it contains all which they that publish it are able to say in support of a separation, and that if any one cause was distinguished from another, special notice would be taken of it. That of taxes seems to have been in danger of being forgot. It comes in late, and in as slight a manner as is possible. And, I know, my Lord, that these men, in the early days of their opposition to Parliament, have acknowledged that they pitched upon this subject of taxes, because it was most alarming to the people, every man perceiving immediately that he is personally affected by it; and it has, therefore, in all communities, always been a subject more dangerous to government than any other, to make innovation in; but as their friends in England had fell in with the idea that Parliament could have no right to tax them because not represented, they thought it best it should be believed they were willing to submit to other acts of legislation until this point of taxes could be gained; owning at the same time, that they could find no fundamentals in the English Constitution, which made representation more necessary in acts for taxes, than acts for any other purpose; and that the world must have a mean opinion of their understanding, if they should rebel rather than pay a duty of three-pence *per* pound on tea, and yet be content to submit to an act which restrained them from making a nail to shoe their own horses. Some of them, my Lord, imagine they are as well acquainted with the nature of government, and with the constitution and history of England, as many of their partisans in the kingdom; and they will sometimes laugh at the doctrine of fundamentals from which even Parliament itself can never deviate; and they say it has been often held and denied merely to serve the cause of party, and that it must be so until these unalterable fundamentals shall be ascertained; that the great Patriots in the reign of King Charles the Second, Lord Russell, Hampden, Maynard, &c. whose memories they reverence, declared their opinions, that there were no bounds to the power of Parliament by any fundamentals whatever, and that even the hereditary succession to the Crown might be, as it since has been, altered by Act of Parliament; whereas they who call themselves Patriots in the present day have held it to be a fundamental, that there can be no taxation without representation, and that Parliament cannot alter it.

But as this doctrine was held by their friends, and was of service to their cause until they were prepared for a total independence, they appeared to approve it: As they have now no further occasion for it, they take no more notice of an act for imposing taxes than of many other acts; for a distinction in the authority of Parliament in any particular case, cannot serve their claim to a general exemption, which they are now preparing to assert.

For depriving us, in many cases, of the benefit of a trial by jury.

Offences against the Excise Laws, and against one or more late Acts of Trade, are determined without a Jury in England. It appears by the law books of some of the Colonies, that offences against their Laws of Excise, and some other Laws, are also determined without a Jury; and civil actions, under a sum limited, are determined by a Justice of Peace, I recollect no cases in which trials by Juries are taken away in America, by Acts of Parliament, except such as are tried in the Courts of Admiralty, and these are either for breaches of the Acts of trade, or trespasses upon the King's woods. I take no notice of the Stamp Act, because it was repealed soon after it was designed to take place.

I am sorry, my Lord, that I am obliged to say, there could not be impartial trials by Juries in either of these cases. All regulation of commerce must cease, and the King must be deprived of all the trees reserved for the Royal Navy, if no trials can be had but by Jury. The necessity of the case justified the departure from the general rule; and in the reign of King William the Third, jurisdiction, in both these cases, was given to the Admiralty by Acts of Parliament; and it has ever since been part of the constitution of the Colonies; and it may be said, to the honour of those Courts, that there have been very few instances of complaint of injury from their decrees. Strange that in the reign of King George the Third, this jurisdiction should suddenly become an usurpation and ground of Revolt. . . .

For taking away our Charters, abolishing our most valuable laws, altering fundamentally the forms of our Governments.

For suspending our own legislatures and declaring themselves vested with power, to legislate for us in all cases whatsoever.

These two articles are so much of the same nature, that I consider them together. There has been no Colony Charter altered except that of Massachuset's Bay, and that in no respect, that I recollect, except that the appointment and power of the council are made to conform to that of the Council of the other Royal Governments, and the laws which relate to grand and petit juries are made to conform to the general laws of the Realm.

The only instance of the suspension of any legislative power is that of the Province of New York, for refusing to comply with an Act of Parliament for quartering the King's troops posted there for its protection and defence against the French and Indian enemies. . . .

He has abdicated Government here, by declaring us out of his protection and waging War against us.

He has plundered our Seas, ravaged our Coasts, burnt our Towns and destroyed the Lives of our People.

He is at this time, transporting large Armies of foreign mercenaries to compleat the works of death, desolation and tyranny, already begun with circumstances of cruelty and perfidy scarcely paralleled in the most barbarous ages, and totally unworthy the head of a civilized Nation.

He has constrained our fellow Citizens, taken captive on the high Seas, to bear arms against their Country, to become the executioners of their Friends and Brethren, or to fall themselves by their hands.

He has excited domestick insurrections amongst us and has endeavoured to bring on the Inhabitants of our frontiers the merciless Indian Savages, whose known rule of warfare, is an undistinguished destruction of all ages, sexes and conditions.

These, my Lord, would be weighty charges from a *loyal and dutiful* people against an *unprovoked* Sovereign: They are more than the people of England pretended to bring against King James the Second, in order to justify the Revolution. Never was there an instance of more consummate effrontery. The Acts of a *justly incensed* Sovereign for suppressing a most *unnatural, unprovoked* Rebellion, are here assigned as the *causes* of this Rebellion. It is immaterial whether they are true or false. They are all short of the penalty of the laws which had been violated. Before the date of any one of them, the Colonists had as effectually renounced their allegiance by their deeds as they have since done by their words. They had displaced the civil and military officers appointed by the King's authority and set up others in their stead. They had new modelled their civil governments, and appointed a general government, independent of the King, over the whole. They had taken up arms, and made a public declaration of their resolution to defend themselves, against the forces employed to support his legal authority over them. To subjects, who had forfeited their lives by acts of Rebellion, every act of the Sovereign against them, which falls short of the forfeiture, is an act of favour. A most ungrateful return has been made for this favour. It has been improved to strengthen and confirm the Rebellion against him. . . .

A Prince, whose character is thus marked, by every act which defines the tyrant, is unfit to be the ruler of a free people.

Indignant resentment must seize the breast of every loyal subject. A tyrant, in modern language, means, not merely an absolute and arbitrary, but a cruel, merciless Sovereign. Have these men given an instance of any one Act in which the King has exceeded the just Powers of the Crown as limited by the English Constitution? Has he ever departed from known established laws, and substituted his own will as the rule of his actions? Has there ever been a Prince by whom subjects in rebellion, have been treated with less severity, or with longer forbearance?

Nor have we been wanting in attention to our British Brethren. We have warned them from time to time of attempts by their legislature, to extend an unwarrantable jurisdiction over us. We have reminded them of the circumstances of our emigration and settlement here. We have appealed to their native justice and magnanimity, and we have conjured them by the ties of our common kindred to disavow those usurpations which would inevitably interrupt our connections and correspondence. They too have been deaf to the voice of justice and consanguinity. We must therefore acquiesce in the necessity which denounces our separation and hold them as we hold the rest of mankind, Enemies in War, in Peace, Friends.

We therefore, the Representatives of the United States of America, in General Congress assembled, appealing to the Supreme Judge of the World, for the rectitude of our intentions, do in the name and by the authority of the good People of these Colonies, solemnly publish and declare, That these United Colonies, are, and ought to be, Free and Independent States, and that they are absolved from all allegiance to the British Crown, and that all political connection between them and the State of Great Britain, is and ought to be totally dissolved, and that as free and Independent States they have full power to levy War, conclude Peace, contract Alliances, establish Commerce, and to do all other Acts and things which Independent States may of right do. And for the support of this Declaration, with a firm reliance on the protection of Divine Providence, we mutually pledge to each other, our Lives, our Fortunes and our sacred Honour. Signed by order and in behalf of the Congress.

JOHN HANCOCK, President.

They have, my Lord, in their late address to the people of Great Britain, fully avowed these principles of Independence, by declaring they will pay no obedience to the laws of the Supreme Legislature; they have also pretended, that these laws were the mandates or edicts of the Ministers, not the acts of a constitutional legislative power, and have endeavoured to persuade, such as they called their British Brethren, to justify the Rebellion begun in America; and from thence they expected a general convulsion in the Kingdom, and that measures to compel a submission would in this way be obstructed. These expectations failing, after they had gone too far in acts of Rebellion to hope for impunity, they were under the *necessity* of a separation, and of involving themselves, and all over whom they had usurped authority, in the distresses and horrors of war against that power from which they revolted, and against all who continued in their subjection and fidelity to it.

Gratitude, I am sensible, is seldom to be found in a community, but so sudden a revolt from the rest of the Empire, which had incurred so immense a debt, and with which it remains burdened, for the protection and defence of the Colonies, and at their most importunate request, is an instance of ingratitude no where to be paralleled.

Suffer me, my Lord, before I close this Letter, to observe, that though the professed reason for publishing the Declaration was a decent respect to the opinions of mankind, yet the real design was to reconcile the people of America to that Independence, which always before, they had been made to believe was not intended. This design has too well succeeded. The people have not observed the fallacy in reasoning from the *whole* to *part;* nor the absurdity of making the *governed* to be *governors.* From a disposition to receive willingly complaints against Rulers, facts misrepresented have passed without examining. Discerning men have concealed their sentiments, because under the present *free* government in America, no man may, by writing or speaking, contradict any part of this Declaration, without being deemed an enemy to his country, and exposed to the rage and fury of the populace.

> I have the honour to be,
> My Lord,
> Your Lordship's most humble,
> And most obedient servant.

To the Right Honourable
the E—— of ——

London, October, 15th. 1776.

Slave Petition

The notions of "freedom" and "liberty" that were echoing throughout the colonies in the 1770s sufficiently encouraged slaves that they began petitioning colonial legislatures for their own freedom. A few petitions were requests to be sent back to Africa, but most argued for either immediate or gradual emancipation. This 1777 petition to the Massachusetts Bay Colony legislature was an appeal for gradual emancipation.

What philosophical argument did the slaves use to support their request? Is it apparent that they were familiar with the Declaration of Independence?

Petition for Gradual Emancipation, 1777

TO THE HONORABLE LEGISLATURE OF THE STATE OF MASSACHUSETTS BAY, JANUARY 13, 1777

The petition of a great number of blacks detained in a state of slavery in the bowels of a free & Christian country humbly sheweth that your petitioners apprehend we have in common with all other men a natural and unalienable right to that freedom which the Great Parent of the Universe hath bestowed equally on all mankind, and which they have never forfeited by any compact or agreement whatever. But they were unjustly dragged by the hand of cruel power from their dearest friends and some of them even torn from the embraces of their tender parents—from a populous, pleasant, and plentiful country and in violation of laws of nature and nations—and, in defiance of all the tender feelings of humanity, brought here to be sold like beasts of burthen & like them condemned to slavery for life among a people professing the mild religion of Jesus—a people not insensible of the secrets of rational beings nor without spirit to resent the unjust endeavours of others to reduce them to a state of bondage and subjection. Your honours need not to be informed that a life of slavery like that of your petitioners, deprived of every social privilege, of every thing requisite to render life tolerable, is far worse than nonexistence.

In imitation of the laudable example of the good people of these states, your petitioners have long and patiently waited the event of petition after petition by them presented to the legislative body of this state and cannot but with grief reflect that their success hath been but too similar. They cannot but express their astonishment that it has never been considered that every principle from which Americans have acted in the course of their unhappy difficulties with Great Britain pleads stronger than a thousand arguments in favour of your petitioners. They therefore humbly beseech your honours to give this petition its due weight & consideration & cause an act of the legislature to be passed whereby they may be restored to the enjoyments of that which is the natural right of all men—and their children who were born in this land of liberty may not be held as slaves after they arrive at the age of twenty one years. So may the inhabitants of this state, no longer chargeable with the inconsistency of acting themselves the part which they condemn and oppose in others, be prospered in their present glorious struggle for liberty and have those blessings to them, &c.

Lancaster Hill
Peter Bess
Brister Slenser
Prince Hall
Jack Pierpont
Nero Funelo
Newport Sumner
Job Look

SOURCE: Massachusetts Historical Society, *Collections*, 5th ser., vol. 3 (Boston, 1877), 436–437.

Joseph Brant (1742–1807)

Joseph Brant was a Mohawk Indian who helped create an alliance between his people and the British during the Revolution. In 1776, he sailed to London, where he met George III and assured him that the Mohawks would be loyal subjects in the fight against the colonists. When the British, as part of the settlement of the Peace of Paris in 1783, ceded to the victorious Americans the territory between the Appalachians and the Mississippi River, their Indian allies were enraged. Joseph Brant vehemently protested to Frederick Haldimand, the governor of Quebec, and criticized the British for ignoring the rights of the native peoples.

In what ways had the Mohawk shown their loyalty to the Crown? Is Brant justified in his criticism of the treaty?

———————————

Speech to Governor Haldimand at Quebec, May 21, 1783

Brother Asharekowa and Representatives of the King, the sachems and War Chieftains of the Six United Nations of Indians and their Allies have heard that the King, their Father, has made peace with his children the Bostonians. The Indians distinguish by Bostonians, the Americans in Rebellion, as it first began in Boston, and when they heard of it, they found that they were forgot and no mention made of them in said Peace, wherefore they have now sent me to inform themselves before you of the real truth, whether it is so or not, that they are not partakers of that Peace with the King and the Bostonians.

Brother, listen with great attention to our words, we were greatly alarmed and cast down when we heard that news, and it occasions great discontent and surprise with our People; wherefore tell us the real truth from your heart, and we beg that the King will be put in mind by you and recollect what we have been when his people first saw us, and what we have since done for him and his subjects.

Brother, we, the Mohawks, were the first Indian Nation that took you by the hand like friends and brothers, and invited you to live amongst us, treating you with kindness upon your debarkation in small parties. The Oneidas, our neighbors, were equally well disposed towards you and as a mark of our sincerity and love towards you we fastened your ship to a great mountain at Onondaga, the Center of our Confederacy, the rest of the Five Nations approving of it. We were then a great people, conquering all Indian Nations round about us, and you in a manner but a handfull, after which you increased by degrees and we continued your friends and allies, joining you from time to time against your enemies, sacrificing numbers of our people and leaving their bones scattered in your enemies country. At last we assisted you in conquering all Canada, and then again, for joining you so firmly and faithfully, you

———————————

Source: Charles M. Johnston, ed., *The Valley of the Six Nations: A Collection of Documents on the Indian Lands of the Grand River* (Toronto: Champlain Society, 1964), 38–41.

renewed your assurances of protecting and defending ourselves, lands and posses-
sions against any encroachment whatsoever, procuring for us the enjoyment of fair
and plentiful trade of your people, and sat contented under the shade of the Tree of
Peace, tasting the favour and friendship of a great Nation bound to us by Treaty, and
able to protect us against all the world.

Brother, you have books and records of our mutual Treaties and Engagements,
which will confirm the truth of what I have been telling, and as we are unacquainted
with the art of writing, we keep it fresh in our memory by Belts of Wampum deposited
in our Council House at Onondaga. We have also received an ornament for the Head,
i.e. a crown, from her late Majesty, Queen Ann, as a token of her mutual and unalterable friendship and alliance with us and our Confederacy. Wherefore, we on our side
have maintained an uninterrupted attachment towards you, in confidence and expectation of a Reciprocity, and to establish a Perpetual Friendship and Alliance between
us, of which we can give you several instances, to wit, when a few years after the Conquest of Canada, your people in this country thought themselves confined on account
of their numbers with regard to a Scarcity of Land, we were applied to for giving up
some of ours, and fix a line or mark between them and Us. We considered upon it,
and relinquished a great Territory to the King for the use of his Subjects, for a Trifling
consideration, merely as a Confirmation of said Act, and as a proof of our sincere
Regard towards them. This happened so late as the year 1768 at Fort Stanwix, and was
gratefully Accepted and Ratified by the different Governors and Great men of the
respective Colonies on the Sea Side, in presence of our Late Worthy Friend and
Superintendent, Sir William Johnson, when we expected a Permanent, Brotherly
Love and Amity, would be the Consequence, but in vain. The insatiable thirst for
Power and the next Object of dissatisfaction to the King's Subjects on the Sea Coast,
and they to blind our Eyes, Sent Priests from New England amongst us, whom we took
for Messengers of Peace, but we were Surprisingly undeceived when we found soon
after, that they came to sow the Seeds of discord among our People, in order to alienate our ancient attachments and Alliance from the King our Father, and join them in
Rebellion against him, and when they stood up against him, they first endeavored to
ensnare us, the Mohawks, and the Indians of the Six Nations living on the Susque-
hanna River, and the Oneidas, by which division they imagined the remainder of the
Confederacy would soon follow, but to not the Least effect.

About this Sad Period we lost our Greatest Friend, Sir William Johnson, notwithstanding we were unalterably determined to stick to our Ancient Treaties with the
Crown of England and when the Rebels attempted to insult the Families and
Descendents of our late Superintendent, on whom the management of our affairs
devolved, we stuck to them and Protected them as much as in our Power, conduct-
ing them to Canada with a determined Resolution inviolably to adhere to our
Alliance at the Risque of our Lives Families and Property, the rest of the Six Nations
finding the Firmness and Steadiness of us, the Mohawks, and Aughuagos, followed
our Example and espoused the King's cause to this Present Instant.

It is as I tell you, Brother, and would be too tedious to repeat on this Pressing
Occasion the many Proofs of Fidelity we have given the King our Father.

Wherefore Brother, I am now Sent in behalf of all the King's Indian Allies to
receive a decisive answer from you, and to know whether they are included in the
Treaty with the Americans, as faithful Allies should be or not, and whether those

Lands which the Great Being above has pointed out for Our Ancestors, and their descendants, and Placed them there from the beginning and where the Bones of our forefathers are laid, is secure to them, or whether the Blood of their Grand Children is to be mingled with their Bones, thro' the means of Our Allies for whom we have often so freely Bled.

Alexander McGillivray (1759?–1793)

Alexander McGillivray, the son of a Creek-French mother and a Scots father, fought on the British side during the American Revolution. Unhappy with the result of the war, McGillivray became an influential Creek diplomat who helped to establish relations between the Creeks and the Spanish in Florida as a way to secure some protection against American aggression. In this 1785 speech to the governor of Florida, Arturo O'Neill, McGillivray denounces American claims to the lands of the Creek, Cherokee, and Chickasaw peoples.

What is the purpose of McGillivray's speech? In what way does he feel the Spanish can prevent the Americans from taking over Indian land?

Speech to the Governor of Florida, 1785

MCGILLIVRAY FOR THE CHIEFS OF THE CREEK, CHICKASAW, AND CHEROKEE NATIONS, JULY 10, 1785

WHEREAS We the Cheifs and Warriors of the Creek Chickesaw and Cherokee Nations having received information that an Envoy has been appointed by his Most Catholic Majesty the King of Spain for the purpose of settling the boundarys of his territorys and those of the States of America, and as we have reason to Apprehend that the American Congress in those important matters will endeavour to avail themselves of the Late treaty of peace between them & the British Nation and that they will aim at getting his Majesty the King of Spain to confirm to them that Extensive Territory the Lines of which are drawn by the Said treaty and which includes the whole of our hunting Grounds to our Great injury and ruin—It behoves us therefore to object to, and We Cheifs and Warriors of the Creek Chickesaw and Cherokee Nations, do hereby in the most solemn manner protest against any title claim or demand the American Congress may set up for or against our lands, Settlements, and hunting Grounds in Consequence of the Said treaty of peace between the King of Great Britain and the States of America declaring that as we were not partys, so we are

SOURCE: John Walton Caughey, *McGillivray of the Creeks* (Norman: University of Oklahoma Press, 1938), 90–93.

determined to pay no attention to the Manner in which the British Negotiators has drawn out the Lines of the Lands in question Ceded to the States of America—it being a Notorious fact known to the Americans, known to every person who is in any ways conversant in, or acquainted with American affairs, that his Brittannick Majesty was never possessed either by session purchase or by right of Conquest of our Territorys and which the Said treaty gives away. On the contrary it is well known that from the first Settlement of the English colonys of Carolina and Georgia up to the date of the Said treaty no title has ever been or pretended to be made by his Brittanic Majesty to our lands except what was obtained by free Gift or by purchase for good and valuable Considerations.

We can urge in Evidence upon this occasion the Cessions of Lands made to the Carolinians and Georgians by us at different periods and one so late as June 1773 of the Lands lying on the bank of the River OGeechee for which we were paid a Sum not less than one hundred and twenty thousand pounds Stg. nor has any treaty been held by us Since that period for the purpose of granting any land to any people whatever nor did we the Nations of Creeks, Chickesaws and Cherokees do any act to forfeit our Independance and natural Rights to the Said King of Great Britain that could invest him with the power of giving our property away unless fighting by the side of his soldiers in the day of battle and Spilling our best blood in the Service of his Nation can be deemed so.

The Americans altho' sensible of the Injustice done to us on this occasion in consequence of this pretended claim have divided our territorys into countys and Sate themselves down on our land, as if they were their own. Witness the Large Settlement called Cumberland and others on the Mississippi which with the Late attempts on the Occonnee Lands are all encroachments on our hunting Grounds.

We have repeatedly warned the States of Carolina and Georgia to desist from these Encroachments and to confine themselves within the Lands [granted] to Brittain in the Year 1773. To these remonstrances we have received friendly talks and replys it is true but while they are addressing us by the flattering appellations of Friends and Brothers they are Stripping us of our natural rights by depriving us of that inheritance which belonged to our ancestors and hath descended from them to us Since the beginning of time.

As His most Gracious Majesty was pleased to Express his favorable disposition toward all those Nations of Indians who implored his favor and protection and which we the Cheifs and Warriors of the Nations aforesaid did do in General Congress, held at Pensacola in June 1784 receiving at the same time his Gracious assurances of protection to us, our respective propertys and Hunting Grounds—Relying thereupon and having the greatest Confidence in the Good faith, humanity and Justice of His Most Gracious Majesty the King of Spain we trust that he will enter into no terms with the American States that may Strengthen their claims or that may tend to deprive us of our Just inheritance.

And we request that your Excellency will have the Goodness to forward this Memorial and representation so that it may reach the foot of his Majestys throne. Humbly entreating that he will be pleased to take the same into his Royal consideration and that he will give his Said Envoy at the Americans Congress such orders respecting the premises as he in his great wisdom and Goodness may think fitte.

We conclude with the Sincerest assurances of our firmest attachment to Him and Gratitude for any favor His Most Gracious Majesty may procure us on this occasion.

Done at Little Tallassie in the Upper Creek Nation
This 10th July 1785
by order and in behalf of the Said Indian Nations

United Indian Nations

As Americans continued to encroach upon Indian lands, the native people decided to take a page out of the newborn republic's history book. The only hope to resist American expansion was for the tribes to unite, just as the 13 states had united, and so, in 1786, representatives of the Shawnee, Delaware, Huron, Cherokee, Wabash, Chippewa, Ottawa, Pottawatomie, and Miami formed the United Indian Nations. They issued a message to the U.S. Congress in which they insisted that the Ohio River remain the boundary between the United States and Indian territory and that any further agreements, treaties, or sales of land had to have the unanimous consent of the tribes.

What measures did the Indians take to ensure harmony between them and the settlers? According to the United Indian Nations, what would be necessary to maintain peace? Do the Indians have a legitimate grievance against the United States?

Protest to the United States Congress, 1786

SPEECH AT THE CONFEDERATE COUNCIL, NOVEMBER 28 AND DECEMBER 18, 1786

Present:—The Five Nations, the Hurons, Delawares, Shawanese, Ottawas, Chippewas, Powtewattimies, Twichtwees, Cherokees, and the Wabash confederates

To the Congress of the United States of America:

Brethren of the United States of America: It is now more than three years since peace was made between the King of Great Britain and you, but we, the Indians, were disappointed, finding ourselves not included in that peace, according to our expectations: for we thought that its conclusion would have promoted a friendship between the United States and Indians, and that we might enjoy that happiness that formerly subsisted between us and our elder brethren. We have received two very agreeable messages from the thirteen United States. We also received a message from the King,

---

Source: *American State Papers, Class II: Indian Affairs* (Washington, 1832), 1:8–9.

whose war we were engaged in, desiring us to remain quiet, which we accordingly complied with. During the time of this tranquillity, we were deliberating the best method we could to form a lasting reconciliation with the thirteen United States. Pleased at the same time, we thought we were entering upon a reconciliation and friendship with a set of people born on the same continent with ourselves, certain that the quarrel between us was not of our own making. In the course of our councils, we imagined we hit upon an expedient that would promote a lasting peace between us.

Brothers: We still are of the same opinion as to the means which may tend to reconcile us to each other; and we are sorry to find, although we had the best thoughts in our minds, during the beforementioned period, mischief has, nevertheless, happened between you and us. We are still anxious of putting our plan of accommodation into execution, and we shall briefly inform you of the means that seem most probable to us of effecting a firm and lasting peace and reconciliation: the first step towards which should, in our opinion, be, that all treaties carried on with the United States, on our parts, should be with the general voice of the whole confederacy, and carried on in the most open manner, without any restraint on either side; and especially as landed matters are often the subject of our councils with you, a matter of the greatest importance and of general concern to us, in this case we hold it indispensably necessary that any cession of our lands should be made in the most public manner, and by the united voice of the confederacy; holding all partial treaties as void and of no effect.

Brothers: We think it is owing to you that the tranquillity which, since the peace between us, has not lasted, and that that essential good has been followed by mischief and confusion, having managed every thing respecting us your own way. You kindled your council fires where you thought proper, without consulting us, at which you held separate treaties, and have entirely neglected our plan of having a general conference with the different nations of the confederacy. Had this happened, we have reason to believe every thing would now have been settled between us in a most friendly manner. We did every thing in our power, at the treaty of fort Stanwix, to induce you to follow this plan, as our real intentions were, at that very time, to promote peace and concord between us, and that we might look upon each other as friends, having given you no cause or provocation to be otherwise.

Brothers: Notwithstanding the mischief that has happened, we are still sincere in our wishes to have peace and tranquillity established between us, earnestly hoping to find the same inclination in you. We wish, therefore, you would take it into serious consideration, and let us speak to you in the manner we proposed. Let us have a treaty with you early in the spring; let us pursue reasonable steps; let us meet half ways, for our mutual convenience; we shall then bring [bury] in oblivion the misfortunes that have happened, and meet each other on a footing of friendship.

Brothers: We say let us meet half way, and let us pursue such steps as become upright and honest men. We beg that you will prevent your surveyors and other people from coming upon our side the Ohio river. We have told you before, we wished to pursue just steps, and we are determined they shall appear just and reasonable in the eyes of the world. This is the determination of all the chiefs of our confederacy now assembled here, notwithstanding the accidents that have happened in our villages, even when in council, where several innocent chiefs were killed when absolutely engaged in promoting a peace with you, the thirteen United States.

Although then interrupted, the chiefs here present still wish to meet you in the spring, for the beforementioned good purpose, when we hope to speak to each other without either haughtiness or menaces.

Brothers: We again request of you, in the most earnest manner, to order your surveyors and others, that mark out lands, to cease from crossing the Ohio, until we shall have spoken to you, because the mischief that has recently happened has originated in that quarter; we shall likewise prevent our people from going over until that time.

Brothers: It shall not be our faults if the plans which we have suggested to you should not be carried into execution; in that case the event will be very precarious, and if fresh ruptures ensue, we hope to be able to exculpate ourselves, and shall most assuredly, with our united force, be obliged to defend those rights and privileges which have been transmitted to us by our ancestors; and if we should be thereby reduced to misfortunes, the world will pity us when they think of the amicable proposals we now make to prevent the unnecessary effusion of blood. These are our thoughts and firm resolves, and we earnestly desire that you will transmit to us, as soon as possible, your answer, be it what it may.

Done at our Confederated Council Fire, at the Huron village, near the mouth of the Detroit river, December 18th, 1786.

The Five Nations,
Hurons, Ottawas, Twichtwees, Shawanese,
Chippewas, Cherokees, Delawares,
Powtewatimies, The Wabash Confederates.

Shays's Rebellion

In 1786, western Massachusetts farmers had fallen on hard times, which they blamed on the bankers and merchants of Boston. They petitioned the state legislature to ease their financial distress by lowering taxes, issuing paper money, and putting a moratorium on farm foreclosures. When their pleas were disregarded, Daniel Shays led a group of farmers into Springfield, where they occupied the court house in August 1786. Shays spearheaded a subsequent attack on the Springfield Arsenal in January, but state militiamen repelled this attack and, after several days of pursuing the rebels, finally arrested Shays and the other leaders of the rebellion. Though Shays and 14 others were convicted and sentenced to death, they were later pardoned by Governor John Hancock.

Shays's Rebellion is considered one of the major factors that convinced American political leaders to call for a Constitutional Convention later that year in order to form a more efficient government to replace the Articles of Confederation. It was this rebellion that prompted Thomas Jefferson to write: "I hold it that a little rebellion now and then is a good thing, and as necessary in the political world as storms in the physical. Unsuccessful rebellions, indeed, generally establish the encroachments on the rights of the people which have produced them. An observation of this truth should render honest republican governors so mild in their punishment of rebellions as not to discourage them too much. It is a medicine necessary for the sound health of the government."

One of the Shaysites, Daniel Gray, wrote a statement of their grievances. What is the writ of habeas corpus? Is the suspension of this writ justification for armed rebellion? Are any of their grievances eventually resolved by the U. S. Constitution?

Statement of Grievances, 1786

AN ADDRESS TO THE PEOPLE OF THE SEVERAL TOWNS IN THE COUNTY OF HAMPSHIRE, NOW AT ARMS

GENTLEMEN,

We have thought proper to inform you of some of the principal causes of the late risings of the people, and also of their present movement, viz.

1st. The present expensive mode of collecting debts, which, by reason of the great scarcity of cash, will of necessity fill our gaols with unhappy debtors, and thereby a reputable body of people rendered incapable of being serviceable either to themselves or the community.

2d. The monies raised by impost and excise being appropriated to discharge the interest of governmental securities, and not the foreign debt, when these securities are not subject to taxation.

3d. A suspension of the writ of *Habeas corpus,* by which those persons who have stepped forth to assert and maintain the rights of the people, are liable to be taken and conveyed even to the most distant part of the Commonwealth, and thereby subjected to an unjust punishment.

4th. The unlimited power granted to Justices of the Peace and Sheriffs, Deputy Sheriffs, and Constables, by the Riot Act, indemnifying them to the prosecution thereof; when perhaps, wholly actuated from a principle of revenge, hatred and envy.

Furthermore, Be assured, that this body, now at arms, despise the idea of being instigated by British emissaries, which is so strenuously propagated by the enemies of our liberties: And also wish the most proper and speedy measures may be taken, to discharge both our foreign and domestic debt.

Per Order,
Daniel Gray, *Chairman of the Committee, for the above purpose.*

SOURCE: George Richards Minot, ed., *History of the Insurrection in Massachusetts in 1786 and of the Rebellion Consequent Thereon,* (New York: Da Capo Press, 1971) 83.

George Mason (1725–1792)

George Mason was one of the most vocal participants at the Constitutional Convention in 1787. Because of his strong stand on states' rights, he refused to sign the Constitution when it was completed; in his eyes, it gave too much power to the federal government. Returning to Virginia, he campaigned against ratification of the Constitution and published one of the most influential Anti-Federalist pamphlets, "Objections to this Constitution of Government." Mason echoed one of the chief Anti-Federalist criticisms, that the Constitution contained no declaration (or bill) of rights, and he specifically deplored the absence of guarantees for freedom of the press and trial by jury. Such objections to the Constitution had the meritorious effect of convincing the Federalists to consent to the addition of the Bill of Rights.

Which is more important to Mason: the lack of a bill of rights or the fear that southern states would lose power? How valid are his views that law is "tedious, intricate and expensive," and that justice is "unattainable"? What are his chief objections to the executive branch?

Objections to This Constitution of Government, 1787

There is no Declaration of Rights, and the laws of the general government being paramount to the laws and constitution of the several States, the Declarations of Rights in the separate States are no security. Nor are the people secured even in the enjoyment of the benefit of the common law. . . .

The Judiciary of the United States is so constructed and extended, as to absorb and destroy the judiciaries of the several States; thereby rendering law as tedious, intricate and expensive, and justice as unattainable, by a great part of the community, as in England, and enabling the rich to oppress and ruin the poor.

The President of the United States has no Constitutional Council, a thing unknown in any safe and regular government. He will therefore be unsupported by proper information and advice, and will generally be directed by minions and favorites; or he will become a tool to the Senate—or a Council of State will grow out of the principal officers of the great departments; the worst and most dangerous of all ingredients for such a Council in a free country. . . . From this fatal defect has arisen the improper power of the Senate in the appointment of public officers, and the alarming dependence and connection between that branch of the legislature and the supreme Executive.

Hence also sprung that unnecessary officer the Vice-President, who for want of other employment is made president of the Senate, thereby dangerously blending

SOURCE: Kate Mason Rowland, *The Life of George Mason, 1725–1792* (New York: Russell & Russell, 1964), vol. II, 387–390.

the executive and legislative powers, besides always giving to some one of the States an unnecessary and unjust pre-eminence over the others.

The President of the United States has the unrestrained power of granting pardons for treason, which may be sometimes exercise to screen from punishment those whom he had secretly instigated to commit the crime, and thereby prevent a discovery of his own guilt.

By declaring all treaties supreme laws of the land, the Executive and the Senate have, in many cases, an exclusive power of legislation; which might have been avoided by proper distinctions with respect to treaties, and requiring the assent of the House of Representatives, where it could be done with safety.

By requiring only a majority to make all commercial and navigation laws, the five Southern States, whose produce and circumstances are totally different from that of the eight Northern and Eastern States, may be ruined, for such rigid and premature regulations may be made as will enable the merchants of the Northern and Eastern States not only to demand an exhorbitant freight, but to monopolize the purchase of the commodities at their own price, for many years, to the great injury of the landed interest, and impoverishment of the people; and the danger is the greater as the gain on one side will be in proportion to the loss on the other. Whereas requiring two-thirds of the members present in both Houses would have produced mutual moderation, promoted the general interest, and removed an insuperable objection to the adoption of this government.

Under their own construction of the general clause, at the end of the enumerated powers, the Congress may grant monopolies in trade and commerce, constitute new crimes, inflict unusual and severe punishments, and extend their powers as far as they shall think proper; so that the State legislatures have no security for the powers now presumed to remain to them, or the people for their rights.

There is no declaration of any kind, for preserving the liberty of the press, or the trial by jury in civil causes; nor against the danger of standing armies in time of peace. . . .

This government will set out a moderate aristocracy: it is at present impossible to foresee whether it will, in its operation, produce a monarchy, or a corrupt, tyrannical aristocracy; it will most probably vibrate some years between the two, and then terminate in the one or the other.

Judith Sargent Murray (1751–1820)

Although her name is not widely known today, Judith Sargent Murray was one of the first Enlightenment thinkers to write an eloquent argument in favor of the equality of women. Her "On the Equality of the Sexes" (appearing two years before Mary Wollstonecraft published A *Vindication of the Rights of Woman*) establishes her as one of the first feminists. Although she was disparaged by her contemporaries, she influenced many of those who followed her. Denied a formal education because of her sex, she was tutored by her brother in Latin,

Greek, and literature. This experience led her to believe that an important means for women to secure equal rights was universal female education.

How does she prove that women are equal? How do men create gender inequality? In what ways do her arguments anticipate those of Angelina Grimké, Elizabeth Cady Stanton, Susan B. Anthony, and Betty Friedan?

"On the Equality of the Sexes," 1790

That minds are not alike, full well I know,
This truth each day's experience will show;
To heights surprising some great spirits soar,
With inborn strength mysterious depths explore;
Their eager gaze surveys the path of light,
Confest it stood to Newton's piercing sight.
Deep science, like a bashful maid retires,
And but the ardent *breast her worth inspires;*
By perseverance the coy fair is won.
And Genius, led by Study, wears the crown.
But some there are who wish not to improve,
Who never can the path of knowledge love,
Whose souls almost with the dull body one,
With anxious care each mental pleasure shun;
Weak is the level'd, enervated mind,
And but while here to vegetate design'd.
The torpid spirit mingling with its clod,
Can scarcely boast its origin from God;
Stupidly dull—they move progressing on—
They eat, and drink, and all their work is done.
While others, emulous of sweet applause,
Industrious seek for each event a cause,
Tracing the hidden springs whence knowledge flows,
Which nature all in beauteous order shows.
Yet cannot I their sentiments imbibe,
Who this distinction to the sex ascribe,
As if a woman's form must needs enrol,
A weak, a servile, an inferior soul;
And that the guise of man must still proclaim,
Greatness of mind, and him, to be the same:

SOURCE: Sharon M. Harris, ed., *Selected Writings of Judith Sargent Murray* (New York: Oxford University Press, 1995), 3–14.

Yet as the hours revolve fair proofs arise,
Which the bright wreath of growing fame supplies;
And in past times some men have sunk *so* low,
That female records nothing less *can show.*
But imbecility is still confin'd,
And by the lordly sex to us consign'd;
They rob us of the power t'improve,
And then declare we only trifles love;
Yet haste the era, when the world shall know,
That such distinctions only dwell below;
The soul unfetter'd, to no sex confin'd,
Was for the abodes of cloudless day design'd.
Mean time we emulate their manly fires,
Though erudition all their thoughts inspires,
Yet nature with equality *imparts,*
And noble passions, *swell e'en* female hearts.

Is it upon mature consideration we adopt the idea, that nature is thus partial in her distributions? Is it indeed a fact, that she hath yielded to one half of the human species so unquestionable a mental superiority? I know that to both sexes elevated understandings, and the reverse, are common. But, suffer me to ask, in what the minds of females are so notoriously deficient, or unequal. May not the intellectual powers be ranged under these four heads—imagination, reason, memory and judgment. The province of imagination hath long since been surrendered up to us, and we have been crowned undoubted sovereigns of the regions of fancy. Invention is perhaps the most arduous effort of the mind; this branch of imagination hath been particularly ceded to us, and we have been time out of mind invested with that creative faculty. Observe the variety of fashions (here I bar the contemptuous smile) which distinguish and adorn the female world; how continually are they changing, insomuch that they almost render the whole man's assertion problematical, and we are ready to say, *there is something new under the sun.* Now, what a playfulness, what an exuberance of fancy, what strength of inventive imagination, doth this continual variation discover? Again, it hath been observed, that if the turpitude of the conduct of our sex, hath been ever so enormous, so extremely ready are we, that the very first thought presents us with an apology, so plausible, as to produce our actions even in an amiable light. Another instance of our creative powers, is our talent for slander; how ingenious are we at inventive scandal? what a formidable story can we in a moment fabricate merely from the force of a prolifick imagination? how many reputations, in the fertile brain of a female, have been utterly despoiled? how industrious are we at improving a hint? suspicion how easily do we convert into conviction, and conviction, embellished by the power of eloquence, stalks abroad to the surprise and confusion of unsuspecting innocence. Perhaps it will be asked if I furnish these facts as instances of excellency in our sex. Certainly not; but as proofs of a creative faculty, of a lively imagination. Assuredly great activity of mind is thereby discovered, and was this activity properly directed, what beneficial effects would follow. Is the needle and kitchen sufficient to employ the operations of a soul thus organized? I should conceive not. Nay, it is a truth that those very departments leave the intelligent principle vacant, and at liberty for speculation. Are we deficient in reason? we can only reason from what we know, and if opportunity of acquiring knowledge hath been denied us, the inferiority of our sex cannot fairly be deduced from thence. Memory, I believe, will be allowed us in common, since every one's experience must testify, that a loquacious old woman is as frequently met with, as a communicative old man; their subjects are alike drawn from the fund of other times and the transactions of their youth, or of maturer life, entertain, or perhaps fatigue you, in the evening of their lives. "But our judgement is not so strong—we do not distinguish so well."—Yet it may be questioned, from what doth this superiority, in this determining faculty of the soul, proceed. May we not trace its source in the difference of education, and continued advantages? Will it be said that the judgment of a male of two years old, is more sage than that of a female's of the same age? I believe the reverse is generally observed to be true. But from that period what partiality! how is the one exalted and the other depressed, by the contrary modes of education which are adopted! the one is taught to aspire, and the other is early confined and limited. As their years increase, the sister must be wholly domesticated, while the brother is led by the hand through all the flowery paths of science. Grant that their minds are by nature equal, yet who shall wonder at the *apparent* superiority, if indeed custom becomes *second nature;* nay if it taketh place of nature, and that it doth the experience of each day will evince. At length arrived at womanhood, the uncultivated fair one feels a void, which the employments allotted her are by no means capable of filling. What can she do? to books she may not apply; or if she doth, *to those only of the novel kind,* lest she merit the appellation of a *learned lady;* and what ideas have been affixed to this term, the observation of many can testify. Fashion, scandal, and sometimes what is still more reprehensible, are then called in to her relief; and who can say to what lengths the liberties she takes may proceed. Meantime she herself is most unhappy; she feels the want of a cultivated mind. Is she single, she in vain seeks to fill up time from sexual employments or amusements. Is she united to a person whose soul nature made equal to her own, education hath set him so far above her, that in those entertainments which are productive of such rational felicity, she is not qualified to accompany him. She experiences a mortifying consciousness of inferiority, which embitters every enjoyment. Doth the person to whom her adverse fate hath consigned her, possess a mind incapable of improvement, she is equally wretched, in being so closely connected with an individual whom she cannot but despise. Now, was she permitted the same instructors as her brother, (with an eye however to their particular departments) for the employment of a rational mind an ample field would be opened. In astronomy she might catch a glimpse of the immensity of the Deity, and thence she would form amazing conceptions of the august and supreme Intelligence. In geography she would admire Jehova in the midst of his benevolence; thus adapting this globe to the various wants and amusements of its inhabitants. In natural philosophy she would adore the infinite majesty of heaven, clothed in condescension; and as she traversed the reptile world, she would hail the goodness of a creating God. A mind, thus filled, would have little room for the trifles with which our sex are, with too much justice, accused of amusing themselves, and they would thus be rendered fit companions for those, who should one day wear them as their crown. Fashions, in their variety, would then give place to conjectures, which might perhaps conduce to the improvement of the literary world; and there would be no leisure for slander or detraction. Reputation would not then be blasted, but serious speculations would occupy the lively imaginations of the sex. Unnecessary visits would be precluded, and that custom would only be indulged by way of relaxation, or to answer the demands of consanguinity and friendship. Females would become discreet, their judgements would be invigorated, and their partners for life being circumspectly chosen, an unhappy Hymen would then be as rare, as is now the reverse.

Will it be urged that those acquirements would supersede our domestick duties. I answer that every requisite in female economy is easily attained; and, with truth I can add, that when once attained, they require no further *mental attention.* Nay, while we are pursuing the needle, or the superintendency of the family, I repeat, that our minds are at full liberty for reflection; that imagination may exert itself in full vigour; and that if a just foundation is early laid, our ideas will then be worthy of rational beings. If we were industrious we might easily find time to arrange them upon paper, or should avocations press too hard for such an indulgence, the hours allotted for conversation would at least become more refined and rational. Should it still be vociferated, "Your domestick employments are sufficient"—I would calmly ask, is it reasonable, that a candidate for immortality, for the joys of heaven, an intelligent being, who is to spend an eternity in contemplating the works of Deity, should at present be so degraded, as to be allowed no other ideas, than those which are suggested by the mechanism of a pudding, or the sewing [of] the seams of a garment? Pity that all such censurers of female improvement do not go one step further, and deny their future existence; to be consistent they surely ought.

Yes, ye lordly, ye haughty sex, our souls are by nature *equal* to yours; the same breath of God animates, enlivens, and invigorates us; and that we are not fallen lower than yourselves, let those witness who have greatly towered above the various discouragements by which they have been so heavily oppressed; and though I am unacquainted with the list of celebrated characters on either side, yet from the observations I have made in the contracted circle in which I have moved, I dare confidently believe, that from the commencement of time to the present day, there hath been as many females, as males, who, by the *mere force of natural powers,* have merited the crown of applause; who, *thus assisted,* have seized the wreath of fame. I know there are [those] who assert, that as the animal powers of the one sex are superiour, of course their mental faculties also must be stronger; thus attributing strength of mind to the transient organization of this earth born tenement. But if this reasoning is just, man must be content to yield the palm to many of the brute creation, since by not a few of his brethren of the field, he is far surpassed in bodily strength. Moreover, was this argument admitted, it would prove too much, for occular demonstration evinceth, that there are many robust masculine ladies, and effeminate gentlemen. Yet I fancy that Mr. Pope, though clogged with an enervated body, and distinguished by a diminutive stature, could nevertheless lay claim to greatness of soul; and perhaps there are many other instances which might be adduced to combat so unphilosophical an opinion. Do we not often see, that when the clay built tabernacle is well nigh dissolved, when it is just ready to mingle with the parent soil, the immortal inhabitant aspires to, and even attaineth heights the most sublime, and which were before wholly unexplored. Besides, were we to grant that animal strength proved any thing, taking into consideration the accustomed impartiality of nature, we should be induced to imagine, that she had invested the female mind with superiour strength as an equivalent for the bodily powers of man. But waving this however palpable advantage, for *equality only,* we wish to contend.

. . .

I AM aware that there are many passages in the sacred oracles which seem to give the advantage to the other sex; but I consider all these as wholly metaphorical. Thus David was a man after God's own heart, yet see him enervated by his licentious passions! behold him following Uriah to the death, and shew me wherein could consist the immaculate Being's complacency. Listen to the curses which Job bestoweth upon the day of his nativity, and tell me where is his perfection, where his patience—*literally* it existed not. David and Job were types of him who was to come; and the superiority of man, as exhibited in scripture, being also emblematical, all arguments deduced from thence, of course fall to the ground. The exquisite delicacy of the female mind proclaimeth the exactness of its texture, while its nice sense of honour announceth its innate, its native grandeur. And indeed, in one respect, the preeminence seems to be tacitly allowed us; for after an education which limits and confines, and employments and recreations which naturally tend to enervate the body, and debilitate the mind; after we have from our early youth been adorned with ribbons, and other gewgaws, dressed out like the ancient victims previous to a sacrifice, being taught by the care of our parents in collecting the most showy materials that the ornamenting our exteriour ought to be the principal object of our attention; after, I say, fifteen years thus spent, we are introduced into the world, amid the united adulation of every beholder. Praise is sweet to the soul; we are immediately intoxicated by large draughts of flattery, which being plentifully administered, is to the pride of our hearts the most acceptable incense. It is expected that with the other sex we should commence immediate war, and that we should triumph over the machinations of the most artful. We must be constantly upon our guard; prudence and discretion must be our characteristicks; and we must rise superiour to, and obtain a complete victory over those who have been long adding to the native strength of their minds, by an unremitted study of men and books, and who have, moreover, conceived from the loose characters which they have seen portrayed in the extensive variety of their reading, a most contemptible opinion of the sex. Thus unequal, we are, notwithstanding, forced to the combat, and the infamy which is consequent upon the smallest deviation in our conduct, proclaims the high idea which was formed of our native strength; and thus, indirectly at least, is the preference acknowledged to be our due. And if we are allowed an equality of acquirement, let serious studies equally employ our minds, and we will bid our souls arise to equal strength. We will meet upon every ground, the despot man; we will rush with alacrity to the combat, and, crowned by success, we shall then answer the exalted expectations which are formed. Though sensibility, soft compassion, and gentle commiseration, are inmates in the female bosom, yet against every deep laid art, altogether fearless of the event, we will set them in array; for assuredly the wreath of victory will encircle the spotless brow. If we meet an equal, a sensible friend, we will reward him with the hand of amity, and through life we will be assiduous to promote his happiness; but from every deep laid scheme for our ruin, retiring into ourselves, amid the flowery paths of science, we will indulge in all the refined and sentimental pleasures of contemplation. And should it still be urged, that the studies thus insisted upon would interfere with our more peculiar department, I must further reply, that *early hours,* and close application, will do wonders; and to her who is from the first dawn of reason taught to fill up time rationally, both the requisites will be easy. I grant that niggard fortune is too generally unfriendly to the mind; and that much of that valuable treasure, time, is necessarily expended upon the wants of the body; but it should be remembered, that in embarrassed circumstances our companions have as little leisure for literary improvement, as is afforded to us; for most certainly their provident care is at least as requisite as our exertions. Nay, we have even more leisure for sedentary pleasures, as our avocations are more retired, much less laborious, and, as hath been observed, by no means require that avidity of attention which is proper to the employments of the other sex. In high life, or, in other words, where the parties are in possession of affluence, the objection respecting time is wholly obviated, and of course falls to the ground; and it may also be repeated, that many of those hours which are at present swallowed up in fashion and scandal, might be redeemed, were we habituated to useful reflections. But in one respect, O ye arbiters of our fate! we confess that the superiority is indubitably yours; you are by nature formed for our protectors; we pretend not to vie with you in bodily strength; upon this point we will never contend for victory. Shield us then, we beseech you, from external evils, and in return *we* will transact *your* domestick affairs. Yes, *your,* for are you not equally interested in those matters with ourselves? Is not the elegancy of neatness as agreeable to your sight as to ours; is not the well savoured viand equally delightful to your taste; and doth not your sense of hearing suffer as much, from the discordant sounds prevalent in an ill regulated family, produced by the voices of children and many *et ceteras?*

CONSTANTIA

By way of supplement to the foregoing pages, I subjoin the following extract from a letter, wrote to a friend in the December of 1780.

And now assist me, O thou genius of my sex, while I undertake the ardous task of endeavouring to combat that vulgar, that almost universal errour, which hath, it seems, enlisted even Mr. P— under its banners. The superiority of your sex hath, I grant, been time out of mind esteemed a truth incontrovertible; in consequence of which persuasion, every plan of education hath been calculated to establish this favourite tenet. Not long since, weak and presuming as I was, I amused myself with selecting some arguments from nature, reason, and experience, against this so generally received idea. I confess that to sacred testimonies I had not recourse. I held them to be merely metaphorical, and thus regarding them, I could not persuade myself that there was any propriety in bringing them to decide in this *very important debate.* However, as you, sir, confine yourself entirely to the sacred oracles, I mean to bend the whole of my artillery against those supposed proofs, which you have from thence provided, and from which you have formed an intrenchment *apparently* so invulnerable. And first, to begin with our great progenitors; but here, suffer me to premise, that it is for mental strength I mean to contend, for with respect to animal powers, I yield them undisputed to that sex, which enjoys them in common with the lion, the tyger, and many other beasts of prey; therefore your observations respecting the *rib under the arm, at a distance from the head,* &c.&c. in no sort mitigate against my view. Well, but the woman was first in the transgression. Strange how blind *self love* renders you men; were you not wholly absorbed in a partial admiration of your own abilities, you would long since have acknowledged the force of what I am now going to urge. It is true some ignoramuses have absurdly enough informed us, that the beauteous fair of paradise, was seduced from her obedience, by a malignant demon, *in the guise of a baleful serpent;* but we, who are better informed, know that the fallen spirit presented himself to her view, *a shining angel still;* for thus, saith the criticks in the Hebrew tongue, ought the word to be rendered. Let us examine her motive— Hark! the seraph declares that she shall attain a perfection of knowledge; for is there aught which is not comprehended under one or other of the terms *good* and *evil.* It doth not appear that she was governed by any one sensual appetite; but merely by a desire of adorning her mind; a laudable ambition fired her soul, and a thirst for knowledge impelled the predilection so fatal in its consequences. Adam could not plead the same deception; assuredly he was not deceived; nor ought we to admire his superiour strength, or wonder at his sagacity, when we so often confess that example is much more influential than precept. His gentle partner stood before him, a melancholy instance of the direful effects of disobedience; he saw her not possessed of that wisdom which she had fondly hoped to obtain, but he beheld the once blooming female, disrobed of that innocence, which had heretofore rendered her so lovely. To him then deception became impossible, as he had proof positive of the fallacy of the argument, which the deceiver had suggested. What then could be his inducement to burst the barriers, and to fly directly in the face of that command, which *immediately* from the mouth of deity *he* had received, since, I say, he could not plead that fascinating stimulus, the accumulation of knowledge, as indisputable conviction was so visibly portrayed before him. What mighty cause impelled him to sacrifice myriads of beings yet unborn, and by one impious act, which *he saw* would be productive of such fatal effects, entail undistinguished ruin upon a race of beings, which he was yet to produce. Blush, ye vaunters of fortitude; ye boasters of resolution; ye haughty lords of the creation; blush when ye remember, that he was influenced by no other motive than a bare pusillanimous attachment to a woman! by sentiments so exquisitely soft, that all his sons have, from that period, when they have designed to degrade them, described as highly feminine. Thus it should seem, that all the arts of the grand deceiver (since means adequate to the purpose are, I conceive, invariably pursued) were requisite to mislead our general mother, while the father of mankind forfeited his own, and relinquished the happiness of posterity, merely in compliance with the blandishments of a female. The subsequent subjection the apostle Paul explains as a figure; after enlarging upon the subject, he adds, *"This is a great mystery; but I speak concerning Christ and the church."* Now we know with what consummate wisdom the unerring father of eternity hath formed his plans; all the types which he hath displayed, he hath permitted *materially* to fail, in the very virtue for which *they* were famed. The reason for this is obvious, we might otherwise mistake his economy, and render that honour to the creature, which is due only to the creator. I know that Adam was a figure of him who was to come. The grace contained in this figure, is the reason of my rejoicing, and while I am very far from prostrating before the shadow, I yield joyfully in all things the preeminence to the second federal head. Confiding faith is prefigured by Abraham, yet he exhibits a contrast to affiance, when he says of his fair companion, she is my sister. Gentleness was the characteristick of Moses, yet he hesitated not to reply to Jehovah himself, which unsaintlike tongue he murmured at the waters of strife, and with rash hands he break the tables, which were inscribed by the finger of divinity. David, dignified with the title of the man after God's own heart, and yet how stained was his life. Solomon was celebrated for wisdom, but folly is wrote in legible characters upon his almost every action. Lastly, let us turn our eyes to man in the aggregate. He is manifested as the figure of strength, but that we may not regard him as anything more than a figure, his soul is formed in no sort superiour, but every way equal to the mind of her, who is the emblem of weakness, and whom he hails the gentle companion of his better days.

Shawnee, Miami, Ottawa, and Seneca Proposal

During the presidency of George Washington, a number of tribes in the old northwest banded together in a confederacy to resist further American encroachment into the lands north of the Ohio River. After the Indians, under Little Turtle and Blue Jacket, had defeated an army led by the governor of the Northwest Territory, Arthur St. Clair, American envoys met with tribal representatives to work out some sort of settlement. During the meeting, the Indians criticized the American government for failing to enforce previous treaties. What solution did the tribal emissaries offer? Was it viable?

Proposal to Maintain Indian Lands, 1793

Brothers;—

Money, to us, is of no value, & to most of us unknown, and as no consideration whatever can induce us to sell the lands on which we get sustenance for our women and children; we hope we may be allowed to point out a mode by which your settlers may be easily removed, and peace thereby obtained.

Brothers;—

We know that these settlers are poor, or they would never have ventured to live in a country which have been in continual trouble ever since they crossed the Ohio; divide therefore this large sum of money which you have offered to us, among these people, give to each also a portion of what you say you would give us annually over

---

SOURCE: E. A. Cruikshank, ed., *The Correspondence of Lieut. Governor John Graves Simcoe,* 5 vols. (Toronto: Ontario Historical Society, 1923–1931), vol. 2, 17–19.

and above this very large sum of money, and we are persuaded they would most readily accept of it in lieu of the lands you sold to them, if you add also the great sums you must expend in raising and paying Armies, with a view to force us to yield you our Country, you will certainly have more than sufficient for the purposes of repaying these settlers for all their labor and improvements.

Brothers;—

You have talked to us about concessions. It appears strange that you should expect any from us, who have only been defending our just Rights against your invasion; We want Peace; Restore to us our Country and we shall be Enemies no longer.

Brothers;—

You make one concession to us, by offering us your money, and another by having agreed to do us justice, after having long and injuriously withheld it. We mean in the acknowledgement you have now made, that the King of England never did, nor ever had a right, to give you our Country, by the Treaty of peace, and you want to make this act of Common Justice, a great part of your concessions, and seem to expect that because you have at last acknowledged our independence, we should for such a favor surrender to you our Country.

Brothers;—

You have talked also a great deal about pre-emption and your exclusive right to purchase Indian lands, as ceded to you by the King at the Treaty of peace.

Brothers;—

We never made any agreement with the King, nor with any other Nation that we would give to either the exclusive right of purchasing our lands. And we declare to you that we consider ourselves free to make any bargain or cession of lands, whenever & to whomsoever we please, if the white people as you say, made a treaty that none of them but the King should purchase of us, and that he has given that right to the U. States, it is an affair which concerns you & him & not us. We have never parted with such a power.

Brothers;—

At our General Council held at the Glaize last Fall, we agreed to meet Commissioners from the U. States, for the purpose of restoring Peace, provided they consented to acknowledge and confirm our boundary line to be the Ohio; and we determined not to meet you until you gave us satisfaction on that point; that is the reason we have never met.

We desire you to consider Brothers, that our only demand, is the peaceable possession of a small part of our once great Country. Look back and view the lands from whence we have been driven to this spot, we can retreat no further, because the country behind hardly affords food for its present inhabitants. And we have therefore resolved, to leave our bones in this small space, to which we are now confined.

Brothers;—

We shall be persuaded that you mean to do us justice if you agree, that the Ohio, shall remain the boundary line between us, if you will not consent thereto, our meeting will be altogether unnecessary.

Protest Against the Alien and Sedition Acts

Passed by the Federalist majority in Congress, the Alien Act was designed to limit immigration, and the Sedition Act to make illegal written and spoken criticism of the government. Both of these acts were aimed at the Jeffersonian Republican opposition, and the Sedition Act in particular, which equated political criticism with sedition, especially infuriated the Jeffersonians. Claiming that the Sedition Act nullified the First Amendment, Thomas Jefferson and James Madison wrote eloquent attacks on the Federalist attempt to limit free speech and, simultaneously, made a strong case for states' rights and for limiting the federal government. The Virginia State Legislature adopted Madison's text as the Virginia Resolutions, and Jefferson's was adopted by the Kentucky State Legislature as the Kentucky Resolutions. The other states refused to approve the resolutions, and therefore they had no effect at the time. Decades later, they surfaced again to be used to support the southern position on secession and nullification.

What type of a compact was the Constitution, according to Jefferson and Madison? Why did they argue that the states were superior to the federal government? What is their view of the First Amendment?

The Virginia Resolutions, 1798

RESOLVED, That the General Assembly of Virginia, doth unequivocally express a firm resolution to maintain and defend the Constitution of the United States, and the Constitution of this State, against every aggression either foreign or domestic, and that they will support the government of the United States in all measures warranted by the former.

That this assembly most solemnly declares a warm attachment to the Union of the States, to maintain which it pledges all its powers; and that for this end, it is their duty to watch over and oppose every infraction of those principles which constitute the only basis of that Union, because a faithful observance of them, can alone secure it's existence and the public happiness.

That this Assembly doth explicitly and peremptorily declare, that it views the powers of the federal government, as resulting from the compact, to which the states are parties; as limited by the plain sense and intention of the instrument constituting the compact; as no further valid that they are authorized by the grants enumerated in that compact; and that in case of a deliberate, palpable, and dangerous exercise of other powers, not granted by the said compact, the states who are parties thereto, have the right, and are in duty bound, to interpose for arresting the progress of the

SOURCE: Jonathan Elliot, ed., *The Debates in the Several State Conventions on the Adoption of the Federal Constitution*, vol. 4 (1836; New York: Burt Franklin Reprints, 1974).

evil, and for maintaining within their respective limits, the authorities, rights and liberties appertaining to them. . . .

That the General Assembly doth also express its deep regret, that a spirit has in sundry instances, been manifested by the federal government, to enlarge its powers by forced constructions of the constitutional charter which defines them; and that implications have appeared of a design to expound certain general phrases (which having been copied from the very limited grant of power, in the former articles of confederation were the less liable to be misconstrued) so as to destroy the meaning and effect, of the particular enumeration which necessarily explains and limits the general phrases; and so as to consolidate the states by degrees, into one sovereignty, the obvious tendency and inevitable consequence of which would be, to transform the present republican system of the United States, into an absolute, or at best a mixed monarchy.

That the General Assembly doth particularly protest against the palpable and alarming infractions of the Constitution, in the two late cases of the "Alien and Sedition Acts" passed at the last session of Congress; the first of which exercises a power no where delegated to the federal government, and which by uniting legislative and judicial powers to those of executive, subverts the general principles of free government; as well as the particular organization, and positive provisions of the federal constitution; and the other of which acts, exercises in like manner, a power not delegated by the constitution, but on the contrary, expressly and positively forbidden by one of the amendments thereto; a power, which more than any other, ought to produce universal alarm, because it is levelled against that right of freely examining public characters and measures, and of free communication among the people thereon, which has ever been justly deemed, the only effectual guardian of every other right.

That this state having by its Convention, which ratified the federal Constitution, expressly declared, that among other essential rights, "the Liberty of Conscience and of the Press cannot be cancelled, abridged, restrained, or modified by any authority of the United States," and from its extreme anxiety to guard these rights from every possible attack of sophistry or ambition, having with other states, recommended an amendment for that purpose, which amendment was, in due time, annexed to the Constitution; it would mark a reproachable inconsistency, and criminal degeneracy, if an indifference were now shewn, to the most palpable violation of one of the Rights, thus declared and secured; and to the establishment of a precedent which may be fatal to the other.

That the good people of this commonwealth, having ever felt, and continuing to feel, the most sincere affection for their brethren of the other states; the truest anxiety for establishing and perpetuating the union of all; and the most scrupulous fidelity to that constitution, which is the pledge of mutual friendship, and the instrument of mutual happiness; the General Assembly doth solemnly appeal to the like dispositions of the other states, in confidence that they will concur with this commonwealth in declaring, as it does hereby declare, that the acts aforesaid, are unconstitutional; and that the necessary and proper measures will be taken by each, for co-operating with this state, in maintaining the Authorities, Rights, and Liberties, referred to the States respectively, or to the people. . . .

Agreed to by the Senate, December 24, 1798.

The Kentucky Resolutions, 1799

THE representatives of the good people of this commonwealth in general assembly convened, having maturely considered the answers of sundry states in the Union, to their resolutions passed at the last session, respecting certain unconstitutional laws of Congress, commonly called the alien and sedition laws, would be faithless indeed to themselves, and to those they represent, were they silently to acquiesce in principles and doctrines attempted to be maintained in all those answers, that of Virginia only excepted. To again enter the field of argument, and attempt more fully or forcibly to expose the unconstitutionality of those obnoxious laws, would, it is apprehended be as unnecessary as unavailing.

We cannot however but lament, that in the discussion of those interesting subjects, by sundry of the legislatures of our sister states, unfounded suggestions, and uncandid insinuations, derogatory of the true character and principles of the good people of this commonwealth, have been substituted in place of fair reasoning and sound argument. Our opinions of those alarming measures of the general government, together with our reasons for those opinions, were detailed with decency and with temper, and submitted to the discussion and judgment of our fellow citizens throughout the Union. Whether the decency and temper have been observed in the answers of most of those states who have denied or attempted to obviate the great truths contained in those resolutions, we have now only to submit to a candid world. Faithful to the true principles of the federal union, unconscious of any designs to disturb the harmony of that Union, and anxious only to escape the fangs of despotism, the good people of this commonwealth are regardless of censure or calumniation.

Least however the silence of this commonwealth should be construed into an acquiescence in the doctrines and principles advanced and attempted to be maintained by the said answers, or least those of our fellow citizens throughout the Union, who so widely differ from us on those important subjects, should be deluded by the expectation, that we shall be deterred from what we conceive our duty; or shrink from the principles contained in those resolutions: therefore.

RESOLVED, That this commonwealth considers the federal union, upon the terms and for the purposes specified in the late compact, as conducive to the liberty and happiness of the several states: That it does now unequivocally declare its attachment to the Union, and to that compact, agreeable to its obvious and real intention, and will be among the last to seek its dissolution: That if those who administer the general government be permitted to transgress the limits fixed by that compact, by a total disregard to the special delegations of power therein contained, annihilation of the state governments, and the erection upon their ruins, of a general consolidated government, will be the inevitable consequence: That the principle and construction contended for by sundry of the state legislatures, that the general government is the exclusive judge of the extent of the powers delegated to it, stop nothing short of despotism; since the discretion of those who administer the government, and not the constitution, would be the measure of their powers: That the several states who formed that instrument, being sovereign and independent, have the unquestionable right to judge of its infraction; and that a nullification, by those sovereignties, of all unauthorized acts done under colour of that instrument, is the rightful remedy: That this commonwealth does upon the most deliberate reconsideration declare, that the said alien and sedition laws, are in their opinion, palpable violations of the said constitution; and however cheerfully it may be disposed to surrender its opinion to a majority of its sister states in matters of ordinary or doubtful policy; yet, in momentous regulations like the present, which so vitally wound the best rights of the citizen, it would consider a silent acquiescence as highly criminal: That although this commonwealth as a party to the federal compact; will bow to the laws of the Union, yet it does at the same time declare, that it will not now, nor ever hereafter, cease to oppose in a constitutional manner, every attempt from what quarter soever offered, to violate that compact:

AND FINALLY, in order that no pretexts or arguments may be drawn from a supposed acquiescence on the part of this commonwealth in the constitutionality of those laws, and be thereby used as precedents for similar future violations of federal compact; this commonwealth does now enter against them, its SOLEMN PROTEST.

Approved December 3rd, 1799.

Tecumseh (1768–1813)

The Indian alliance led by Little Turtle in the aftermath of the American Revolution had disintegrated by the 1790s during George Washington's administration. In the early nineteenth century, a Shawnee chief, Tecumseh, set about resurrecting the alliance. Tecumseh believed that an alliance of the tribes north of the Ohio River would not be sufficient to resist American encroachment, and so, for several years, he traveled in an attempt to convince the southern tribes (the Cherokee, Chickasaw, Choctaw, and Creek) to unite with the northern tribes (the Miami, Shawnee, Potawatomi, and others) in order to present a united front. In 1809, while Tecumseh was undertaking his diplomatic mission, William Henry Harrison, the governor of Indiana Territory, negotiated a treaty with several of the Ohio tribes to purchase 3 million acres of land in southern Indiana. Outraged, Tecumseh wrote a letter to Harrison in which he vehemently protested this purchase, which had not been unanimously endorsed by the tribes. In November 1811, while Tecumseh was again in the South and trying to negotiate an Indian alliance, American forces under William Henry Harrison attacked the northern tribes at their encampment on Tippecanoe Creek. Although the battle was a stalemate, the Indians withdrew the following day, and Harrison declared a victory. By the following year, the United States was at war with England, and Tecumseh went to Canada, where he became a brigadier general in the British Army. In 1813, at the Battle of the Thames, Tecumseh was killed.

The first text is from Tecumseh's letter to Governor Harrison, in which he expresses his view that all the tribes of North America are linked together by blood and that the land belongs to them by birthright. The second document is a speech Tecumseh delivered to the southern tribes in an attempt to persuade them to make common cause with the northern tribes in resisting white encroachment.

What does Tecumseh's letter reveal about the Indian stance on private property? Does an individual have the right to sell property? According to Tecumseh, why should the southern tribes join his confederacy? What would happen if they continue to remain complacent? What is the character of Americans?

Letter to Governor William Henry Harrison, 1810

It is true I am a Shawnee. My forefathers were warriors. Their son is a warrior. From them I take only my existence; from my tribe I take nothing. I am the maker of my own fortune; and oh! that I could make of my own fortune; and oh! that I could make that of my red people, and of my country, as great as the conceptions of my mind, when I think of the Spirit that rules the universe. I would not then come to Governor Harrison to ask him to tear the treaty and to obliterate the landmark; but I would say to him: "Sir, you have liberty to return to your own country."

The being within, communing with past ages, tells me that once, nor until lately, there was no white man on this continent; that it then all belonged to red men, children of the same parents, placed on it by the Great Spirit that made them, to keep it, to traverse it, to enjoy its productions, and to fill it with the same race, once a happy race, since made miserable by the white people, who are never contented but always encroaching. The way, and the only way, to check and to stop this evil, is for all the red men to unite in claiming a common and equal right in the land, as it was at first, and should be yet; for it never was divided, but belongs to all for the use of each. For no part has a right to sell, even to each other, much less to strangers—those who want all, and will not do with less.

The white people have no right to take the land from the Indians, because they had it first; it is theirs. They may sell, but all must join. Any sale not made by all is not valid. The late sale is bad. It was made by a part only. Part do not know how to sell. All red men have equal rights to the unoccupied land. The right of occupancy is as good in one place as in another. There can not be two occupations in the same place. The first excludes all others. It is not so in hunting or traveling; for there the same ground will serve many, as they may follow each other all day; but the camp is stationary, and that is occupancy. It belongs to the first who sits down on his blanket or skins which he has thrown upon the ground; and till he leaves it no other has a right.

SOURCE: C. M. Depew, ed., *The Library of Oratory* (New York, 1902) vol. 4, 363–364.

Speech to the Southern Tribes, 1811

SLEEP NOT LONGER, O CHOCTAWS AND CHICKASAWS

. . . [H]ave we not courage enough remaining to defend our country and maintain our ancient independence? Will we calmly suffer the white intruders and tyrants to enslave us? Shall it be said of our race that we knew not how to extricate ourselves from the three most dreadful calamities—folly, inactivity and cowardice? But what need is there to speak of the past? It speaks for itself and asks, Where today is the Pequod? Where the Narragansetts, the Mohawks, Pocanokets, and many other once powerful tribes of our race? They have vanished before the avarice and oppression of the white men, as snow before a summer sun. In the vain hope of alone defending their ancient possessions, they have fallen in the wars with the white men. Look abroad over their once beautiful country, and what see you now? Naught but the ravages of the paleface destroyers meet our eyes. So it will be with you Choctaws and Chickasaws! Soon your mighty forest trees, under the shade of whose wide spreading branches you have played in infancy, sported in boyhood, and now rest your wearied limbs after the fatigue of the chase, will be cut down to fence in the land which the white intruders dare to call their own. Soon their broad roads will pass over the grave of your fathers, and the place of their rest will be blotted out forever. The annihilation of our race is at hand unless we unite in one common cause against the common foe. Think not, brave Choctaws and Chickasaws, that you can remain passive and indifferent to the common danger, and thus escape the common fate. Your people, too, will soon be as falling leaves and scattering clouds before their blighting breath. You, too, will be driven away from your native land and ancient domains as leaves are driven before the wintry storms.

Sleep not longer, O Choctaws and Chickasaws, in false security and delusive hopes. Our broad domains are fast escaping from our grasp. Every year our white intruders become more greedy, exacting, oppressive and overbearing. Every year contentions spring up between them and our people and when blood is shed we have to make atonement whether right or wrong, at the cost of the lives of our greatest chiefs, and the yielding up of large tracts of our lands. Before the palefaces came among us, we enjoyed the happiness of unbounded freedom, and were acquainted with neither riches, wants nor oppression. How is it now? Wants and oppression are our lot; for are we not controlled in everything, and dare we move without asking, by your leave? Are we not being stripped day by day of the little that remains of our ancient liberty? Do they not even kick and strike us as they do their blackfaces? How long will it be before they will tie us to a post and whip us, and make us work for them in their cornfields as they do them? Shall we wait for that moment or shall we die fighting before submitting to such ignominy?

Have we not for years had before our eyes a sample of their designs, and are they not sufficient harbingers of their future determinations? Will we not soon be driven from our respective countries and the graves of our ancestors? Will not the bones of

---

SOURCE: W. C. Vanderwerth, *Indian Oratory: Famous Speeches by Noted Indian Chieftains* (Norman: University of Oklahoma Press, 1971), 62–65.

our dead be plowed up, and their graves be turned into fields? Shall we calmly wait until they become so numerous that we will no longer be able to resist oppression? Will we wait to be destroyed in our turn, without making an effort worthy of our race? Shall we give up our homes, our country, bequeathed to us by the Great Spirit, the graves of our dead, and everything that is dear and sacred to us, without a struggle? I know you will cry with me: Never! Never! Then let us by unity of action destroy them all, which we now can do, or drive them back whence they came. War or extermination is now our only choice. Which do you choose? I know your answer. Therefore, I now call on you, brave Choctaws and Chickasaws, to assist in the just cause of liberating our race from the grasp of our faithless invaders and heartless oppressors. The white usurpation in our common country must be stopped, or we, its rightful owners, be forever destroyed and wiped out as a race of people. I am now at the head of many warriors backed by the strong arm of English soldiers. Choctaws and Chickasaws, you have too long borne with grievous usurpation inflicted by the arrogant Americans. Be no longer their dupes. If there be one here tonight who believes that his rights will not sooner or later be taken from him by the avaricious American palefaces, his ignorance ought to excite pity, for he knows little of the character of our common foe.

And if there be one among you mad enough to undervalue the growing power of the white race among us, let him tremble in considering the fearful woes he will bring down upon our entire race, if by his criminal indifference he assists the designs of our common enemy against our common country. Then listen to the voice of duty, of honor, of nature and of your endangered country. Let us form one body, one heart, and defend to the last warrior our country, our homes, our liberty, and the graves of our fathers.

Choctaws and Chickasaws, you are among the few of our race who sit indolently at ease. You have indeed enjoyed the reputation of being brave, but will you be indebted for it more from report than fact? Will you let the whites encroach upon your domains even to your very door before you will assert your rights in resistance? Let no one in this council imagine that I speak more from malice against the paleface Americans than just grounds of complaint. Complaint is just toward friends who have failed in their duty; accusation is against enemies guilty of injustice. And surely, if any people ever had, we have good and just reasons to believe we have ample grounds to accuse the Americans of injustice; especially when such great acts of injustice have been committed by them upon our race, of which they seem to have no manner of regard, or even to reflect. They are a people fond of innovations, quick to contrive and quick to put their schemes into effectual execution no matter how great the wrong and injury to us; while we are content to preserve what we already have. Their designs are to enlarge their possessions by taking yours in turn; and will you, can you longer dally, O Choctaws and Chickasaws?

Do you imagine that that people will not continue longest in the enjoyment of peace who timely prepare to vindicate themselves, and manifest a determined resolution to do themselves right whenever they are wronged? Far otherwise. Then haste to the relief of our common cause, as by consanguinity of blood you are bound; lest the day be not far distant when you will be left single-handed and alone to the cruel mercy of our most inveterate foe.

Congressmen Protest the War of 1812

During the animated debate in Congress over the issue of going to war against Great Britain, a group of fervent antiwar Federalist congressmen, led by Josiah Quincy, released a statement denouncing the "war hawks" (led by Henry Clay and John C. Calhoun) and President James Madison's resolve to ally the United States with France. These pro-British Federalists also opposed the war because they perceived it as an imperial venture that would add more territory, from which additional states would be carved and into which southern planters could expand the cotton kingdom. Do they use a moral argument against the war? How important are economic issues to these men? Why would they oppose the expansion of the cotton kingdom?

Federalist Protest, 1812

If our ills were of a nature that war would remedy, if war would compensate any of our losses or remove any of our complaints, there might be some alleviation of the suffering in the charm of the prospect. But how will war upon the land protect commerce upon the ocean? What balm has Canada for wounded honor? How are our mariners benefited by a war which exposes those who are free, without promising release to those who are impressed?

But it is said that war is demanded by honor. Is national honor a principle which thirsts after vengeance, and is appeased only by blood? . . . If honor demands a war with England, what opiate lulls that honor to sleep over the wrongs done us by France? On land, robberies, seizures, imprisonments, by French authority; at sea, pillage, sinkings, burnings, under French orders. These are notorious. Are they unfelt because they are French? . . .

It would be some relief to our anxiety if amends were likely to be made for the weakness and wildness of the project by the prudence of the preparation. But in no aspect of this anomalous affair can we trace the great and distinctive properties of wisdom. There is seen a headlong rushing into difficulties, with little calculation about the means, and little concern about the consequences. With a navy comparatively nominal, we are about to enter into the lists against the greatest marine [power] on the globe. With a commerce unprotected and spread over every ocean, we propose to make a profit by privateering, and for this endanger the wealth of which we are honest proprietors. An invasion is threatened of the colonies of a power which, without putting a new ship into commission, or taking another soldier into pay, can spread alarm or desolation along the extensive range of our seaboard. . . .

The undersigned can not refrain from asking, what are the United States to gain by this war? Will the gratification of some privateersmen compensate the nation for that sweep of our legitimate commerce by the extended marine of our

---

SOURCE: *Annals of Congress*, 12th Congress, 1st session, volume 2, columns 2219–2221.

enemy which this desperate act invites? Will Canada compensate the Middle states for New York; or the Western states for New Orleans?

Let us not be deceived. A war of invasion may invite a retort of invasion. When we visit the peaceable, and as to us innocent, colonies of Great Britain with the horrors of war, can we be assured that our own coast will not be visited with like horrors? At a crisis of the world such as the present, and under impressions such as these, the undersigned could not consider the war, in which the United States have in secret been precipitated, as necessary, or required by any moral duty, or any political expediency.

Hartford Convention

One of the remarkable episodes in the ongoing controversy over states' rights took place not in the South, but in New England, during the War of 1812. New England Federalists were very much opposed to "Mr. Madison's War" (as they called it), primarily because the British embargo was devastating to the New England economy and their tax dollars were being used to fight battles elsewhere. New Englanders also were fearful that one of the outcomes of the war would be the addition of new states that would effectively dilute New England's power in Congress. Federalists held a convention at Hartford, Connecticut, during which they openly discussed the issue of secession. Moderate delegates, however, prevailed, and the resolutions that were passed did not openly call for secession but instead proposed several new constitutional amendments that would offset the Three-fifths Clause, which they felt had given the South inequitable political power. Unfortunately for the Federalists, news of Andrew Jackson's unexpected victory at New Orleans and the signing of the Treaty of Ghent ended the war, made the resolutions irrelevant, and tainted the party as treasonous. The Hartford Convention was the death knell of the Federalist Party and had the long-term effect of boosting the states' rights issue during the antebellum period.

Do any of these proposals reflect legitimate grievances? Which ones, if any, had a chance of being adopted?

Proposals, 1814–1815

Therefore resolved, That it be and hereby is recommended to the Legislatures of the several states represented in this Convention to adopt all such measures as may be necessary effectually to protect the citizens of said states from the operation and effects of all acts which have been or may be passed by the Congress of the United

SOURCE: Timothy Dwight, *History of the Hartford Convention* (1833), 377–378.

States, which shall contain provisions, subjecting the militia or other citizens to forcible drafts, conscriptions, or impressments, not authorized by the Constitution of the United States.

Resolved, That it be and hereby is recommended to the said Legislatures, to authorize an immediate and earnest application to be made to the Government of the United States, requesting their consent to some arrangement, whereby the said states may, separately or in concert, be empowered to assume upon themselves the defense of their territory against the enemy, and a reasonable portion of the taxes, collected within said states, may be paid into the respective treasuries thereof, and appropriated to the payment of the balance due said states, and to the future defense of the same. The amount so paid into the said treasuries to be credited, and the disbursements made as aforesaid to be charged to the United States.

Resolved, That it be, and it hereby is, recommended to the Legislatures of the aforesaid states, to pass laws (where it has not already been done) authorizing the Governors or Commanders-in-Chief of their militia to make detachments from the same, or to form voluntary corps, as shall be most convenient and conformable to their Constitutions, and to cause the same to be well armed equipped and disciplined, and held in readiness for service; and upon the request of the Governor of either of the other states, to employ the whole of such detachment or corps, as well as the regular forces of the state, or such part thereof as may be required and can be spared consistently with the safety of the state, in assisting the state, making such request to repel any invasion thereof which shall be made or attempted by the public enemy.

Resolved, That the following amendments of the Constitution of the United States, be recommended to the states. . . .

First. Representatives and direct taxes shall be apportioned among the several states which may be included within this union, according to their respective numbers of free persons, including those bound to serve for a term of years, and excluding Indians not taxed, and all other persons. [This is an attack on the Three-fifths Clause which allowed slave states to count slaves as three-fifths of a person in determining representation in Congress.]

Second. No new state shall be admitted into the union by Congress in virtue of the power granted by the Constitution, without the concurrence of two-thirds of both Houses.

Third. Congress shall not have power to lay any embargo on the ships or vessels of the citizens of the United States, in the ports or harbors thereof, for more than sixty days.

Fourth. Congress shall not have power, without the concurrence of two-thirds of both Houses, to interdict the commercial intercourse between the United States and any foreign nation or the dependencies thereof.

Fifth. Congress shall not make or declare war, or authorize acts of hostility against any foreign nation, without the concurrence of two-thirds of both Houses, except such acts of hostility be in defense of the territories of the United States when actually invaded.

Sixth. No person who shall hereafter be naturalized, shall be eligible as a member of the Senate or House of Representatives of the United States, nor capable of holding any civil office under the authority of the United States.

Seventh. The same person shall not be elected President of the United States a second time; nor shall the President be elected from the same state two terms in succession.

Resolved, That if the application of these states to the government of the United States, recommended in a foregoing Resolution, should be unsuccessful, and peace should not be concluded and the defense of these states should be neglected, as it has been since the commencement of the war, it will in the opinion of this Convention be expedient for the Legislatures of the several states to appoint Delegates to another Convention, to meet at Boston . . . with such powers and instructions as the exigency of a crisis so momentous may require. [A not-so-veiled hint at secession.]

Free Blacks of Philadelphia

The American Colonization Society was founded in 1817 by northern and southern abolitionists who wanted to eliminate slavery gradually. Although the society loathed slavery, its members considered blacks to be an inferior race. Emancipation therefore posed another difficult question: What should be done with the freed slaves? The answer was colonization. Send them back to Africa. Indeed, during James Monroe's presidency, the colony of Liberia was founded (its capital named Monrovia in honor of the American president) with the express purpose of providing a home to emancipated slaves. Free blacks throughout the United States were painfully aware of the racism of American society, and they wanted to see slavery ended. However, they had no desire whatsoever to "return" to Africa. They were, after all, Americans.

Shortly after the founding of the American Colonization Society, free blacks in Philadelphia sent their congressman a protest against the colonization policy. What does this petition reveal about the daily life of free blacks? What is the basis for their anticolonization argument?

Protest Against Colonization Policy, 1817

WHEREAS OUR ANCESTORS

Whereas our ancestors (not of choice) were the first successful cultivators of the wilds of America, we their descendants feel ourselves entitled to participate in the blessings of her luxuriant soil, which their blood and sweat manured; and that any measure or system of measures, having a tendency to banish us from her bosom, would not only be cruel, but in direct violation of those principles, which have been the boast of this republic.

Source: Herbert Aptheker, ed., *A Documentary History of the Negro People in the United States: From Colonial Times Through the Civil War* (Secaucus, NJ: Citadel Press, 1973), 71–72.

Resolved, That we view with deep abhorrence the unmerited stigma attempted to be cast upon the reputation of the free people of color, by the promoters of this measure, "that they are a dangerous and useless part of the community," when in the state of disfranchisement in which they live, in the hour of danger they ceased to remember their wrongs, and rallied around the standard of their country.

Resolved, That we never will separate ourselves voluntarily from the slave population in this country; they are our brethren by the ties of consanguinity, of suffering, and of wrong; and we feel that there is more virtue in suffering privations with them, than fancied advantages for a season.

Resolved, That without arts, without science, without a proper knowledge of government, to cast into the savage wilds of Africa the free people of color, seems to us the circuitous route through which they must return to perpetual bondage.

Resolved, That having the strongest confidence in the justice of God, and philanthropy of the free states, we cheerfully submit our destinies to the guidance of Him who suffers not a sparrow to fall, without his special providence.

Resolved, That a committee of eleven persons be appointed to open a correspondence with the honorable Joseph Hopkinson, member of Congress from this city, and likewise to inform him of the sentiments of this meeting, when they in their judgment may deem it proper.

WEB RESOURCES FOR PART TWO

SITES FEATURING A NUMBER OF THE DISSENTERS IN PART TWO

John Woolman
www.quakerinfo.com/woolman.shtml
http://etext.lib.virginia.edu/toc/modeng/public/WooJour.html
www.uoregon.edu/~rbear/woolman.html
www.strecorsoc.org/jwoolman/title.html

Slavery and Antislavery Sentiment During the Revolutionary Period
www.americanrevolution.com/AmINotaManandaBrother.htm
www.usconstitution.com/AnActfortheGradualAbolitionofSlavery.htm
www.royalprovincial.com/military/rhist/blkpion/blklist.htm

Samuel Adams
www.colonialhall.com/adamss/adamss.php
http://history.hanover.edu/texts/adamss.html
www.americanrevwar.homestead.com/files/ADAMS2.HTM

Thomas Paine
www.infidels.org/library/historical/thomas_paine/index.shtml
www.ushistory.org/paine/

Thomas Hutchinson
www.pbs.org/ktca/liberty/chronicle-boston1774.html
www.americanrevwar.homestead.com/files/HUTCH.HTM

Abigail Adams
http://abigailadams.org/

Joseph Brant
www.indians.org/welker/brant.htm

Shays's Rebellion
www.sjchs-history.org/Shays.html

George Mason
http://gunstonhall.org/georgemason/

Judith Sargent Murray
www.hurdsmith.com/judith/

Tecumseh
www.jmu.edu/madison/center/main_pages/madison_archives/era/native/tecumseh/bio.htm

OTHER DISSENTING VOICES OF THE TIME

Anthony Benezet
Like fellow Quaker John Woolman, Anthony Benezet was an early outspoken critic of slavery. For information about this important figure, see:

http://wesley.nnu.edu/WesleyanTheology/theojrnl/31-35/32-1-7.htm
www.learningtogive.org/papers/people/anthony_benezet.html

Sons of Liberty
For information on this semi-secret revolutionary organization, see:

http://earlyamerica.com/review/fall96/sons.html.

Mercy Otis Warren
For information on writer and patriot Mercy Otis Warren, see::

www.csustan.edu/english/reuben/pal/chap2/warren.html

The Whiskey Rebellion
For information on the 1794 rebellion against the excise tax, see:

www.whiskeyrebellion.org/rebell.htm

The Paxton Boys Protesting Pennsylvania's Neglect of Frontier Defense
This site has information about the Paxton Boys, a group of western Pennsylvania settlers who protested against the colonial government's policy of protecting the Indians against settlers' raiding parties and the laws fashioned to criminalize those who attacked the Indians.

http://conspiracy.pasleybrothers.com/readings/paxton_boys.htm

Pontiac's Rebellion

For information on Chief Pontiac and his rebellion against the British after the French and Indian War, see:

www.u-s-history.com/pages/h598.html
www.ohiohistorycentral.org/ohc/history/h_indian/events/pontwar.shtml

The Regulator Movement in North Carolina

For information on the Regulators who protested against the tax policies in North Carolina prior to the American Revolution, see:

www.u-s-history.com/pages/h630.html

PART THREE

Questioning the Nation, 1820–1860

Four young Lowell Mill girls, c. 1850, taking time off work to pose for the photographer.

Henry David Thoreau. "If a man does not keep pace with his companions, perhaps it is because he hears a different drummer. Let him step to the music which he hears, however measured or far away." *A daguerreotype taken around the time of Thoreau's experiment at Walden Pond.*

Introduction: The Reforming Impulse

During the administrations of the first five presidents, a rapidly growing number of Americans were extraordinarily proud of their young republic. An emergent sense of nationalism was at work as the United States strove to set itself apart from Europe by glorifying its brief history and by creating and reinforcing its myths, unconcerned with facts or evidence. Parson Weems's popular biography of George Washington was the source of the charming fiction of the chopped-down cherry tree and little George's inability to tell a lie, which elevated the first president into a messianic stratosphere. Noah Webster actively promoted American spelling standards to separate the American language from the King's English. Washington Irving's Sleepy Hollow tales were widely read and helped create a distinctively American literature.

Nevertheless, pervasive regionalism and divisive forces of sectionalism threatened this evolving yet fragile national identity. In 1819, there were 22 states in the Union—11 slave states, 11 free. This meant that each section had 22 senators. When Missouri applied that year to enter the Union as a slave state, Northerners were alarmed that slaveholding interests would control the Senate. A crisis was averted when the county of York, Massachusetts, was admitted as the free state of Maine simultaneously with the admission of Missouri as a slave state. It was also agreed that any future states carved out of the Louisiana Purchase north of the 36° 30′ parallel would be free and that those south of that line would be slave. The Missouri Compromise ensured that, for the time being at least, the balance of power in the Senate would be preserved. However, far from being a solution, the compromise served only to sweep under the rug the "serpent that was coiled under the table" at the Constitutional Convention—the unresolved issue of slavery.

The antebellum period—roughly from 1820 to 1860—was therefore a time when sectionalism threatened to tear apart the new nation. As more settlers moved west, the issue of slavery continued to fester. Settlers from the North carved new free states out of the western territories. Those from the South, seeking new lands for the cultivation of the country's most lucrative crop, cotton, took their slaves with them into northern Mexico. By 1836, enough slaveholding Americans had moved into the Mexican province of Tejas to instigate a rebellion that secured independence for the Lone Star Republic. Though the urge for expansion was becoming more and more intoxicating, many Northerners were filled with moral indignation over the fact that most settlers in Texas were from the South and appeared to be conspiring to acquire new land for slaveholding. From such new territories, new states would be carved, and this would increase Southern dominance in Congress. To Northerners who already felt that Southerners controlled the Union—all but three of the first ten presidents were from the South, and the three Northern presidents served only one term each—this apparent "conspiracy" to extend slavery was a Southern plot to take over the nation. Still, in 1845, as a fervor swept over the land that it was the United States's "manifest destiny" to conquer the entire North American continent, Texas was admitted to the Union as a slave state. The following year, as Southerners thirsting to spread the cotton kingdom fixed their eyes on the lands of the Southwest and California, the United States went to war with Mexico. By the end of 1848, with Mexico defeated, the United States took the territory that later would be carved into the states of California, Nevada, Utah, Arizona, and New Mexico. It is ironic that the expansion of the nation, which appealed to strong nationalist sentiments, widened the gulf between North and South and thrust the explosive issue of slavery, already being stirred up by a burgeoning abolitionist movement, into the foremost place in the nation's consciousness. Manifest destiny led, seemingly inevitably, to disunion.

For Native Americans, of course, manifest destiny meant disaster. No tribe had adapted to and accepted the white man's ways more fully than the Cherokee of

Georgia, and yet their ancestral lands were unceremoniously appropriated by President Andrew Jackson against the ruling of the Supreme Court. In spite of their determined resistance, they were forced along the Trail of Tears to a bleak reservation west of the Mississippi. Other tribes, like the Winnebago, and the Sauk and Fox, also attempted to defend themselves from white encroachment, to no avail.

The antebellum period also witnessed a flood of reform movements. Many people, believing in the principles of American democracy, protested against injustice by promoting change. In a sense, this was actually influenced by the intensity of nationalistic sentiment that was particularly highlighted during the events of 1826. As Americans celebrated the fiftieth anniversary of the Declaration of Independence, congratulating themselves on the wonders of democracy, a number of people became acutely aware that their own circumstances, as well as those of others, were preventing them from achieving the equal opportunity that the new American nation had promised. Workers agitated for better wages, a 10-hour day, and universal manhood suffrage, by which all adult white men would be granted the vote without having to meet a property qualification. After William Lloyd Garrison began publishing *The Liberator* in 1831, and Nat Turner's Rebellion later that year, sentiments for and against slavery intensified rapidly. Within another two years, the American Anti-Slavery Society was founded, with tens of thousands of members. By the time of the Mexican War, abolitionists were in a position to exert an enormous influence on the debate over the extension of slavery.

Female abolitionists and their male supporters, recognizing that slaves were not the only people held in subjugation, and infuriated that since the American Revolution women had actually lost ground, began agitating for women's suffrage and equal rights. Many within the abolitionist crusade and the feminist movement also raised their dissenting voices against other social problems. They worked for prison and asylum reform, universal education to enable workers and immigrants to assimilate more easily into middle-class society (ironically strengthening class differences), and the temperance crusade to limit alcohol consumption and the concomitant vices of spousal abuse, unemployment, poverty, and crime.

Romanticism and its offspring transcendentalism also had a powerful impact on the strivings for reform, especially in the North, where there were serious attempts to erect utopian communities, like Brooke Farm in Massachusetts, New Harmony in Indiana, and the Oneida Community in New York. Each of these utopian experiments sought to rectify the ills of society and to expand notions of democracy by making America more inclusive.

Shortly after the Mexican War had come to an end, gold was discovered at Sutter's Mill, California. The resulting rush of forty-niners into California swelled the population so rapidly that the territory was ready for admission to the Union before the year was out. Its application to join the Union as a free state would tip the balance in the Senate, and so in 1850 the crisis over the slavery issue again reared its head. By the summer, Congress had worked out the Compromise of 1850: California would be admitted as a free state; other states to be carved out of the Mexican territories would decide for themselves whether they would be slave or free; the slave trade in the District of Columbia would be abolished (but not slavery in the district); and the Fugitive Slave Law would be vigorously enforced, thereby ensuring that Northern states would return escaped slaves to their masters. Again, the basic issue of slavery remained unresolved.

Events began to move rapidly. Senator Stephen A. Douglas, passionate to secure a Northern route for the proposed Transcontinental Railroad through the territory of Kansas, thereby guaranteeing the development of Chicago as a major railroad hub, proposed the Kansas-Nebraska Act to organize those territories under the principle of "popular sovereignty." Recognizing that nothing sounded more agreeable to the American ear than championing the people's right to choose for themselves, Douglas pushed the notion that settlers in the territories should make their own decisions on the issue of slavery when forming a state constitution. Because both Kansas and Nebraska were north of the Missouri Compromise line prohibiting slavery, however, abolitionists immediately and vehemently denounced the proposed act as a devious scheme to extend slavery. Opposition to the act led directly to the founding of the Republican Party, while proslavery and antislavery forces sent settlers to Kansas to gain a majority to elect delegates to a convention to write a state constitution. In 1856, after abolitionist John Brown murdered several proslavery settlers, brutal guerrilla warfare that would last a decade broke out. "Bleeding Kansas" thus became the harbinger of the Civil War.

Other events in the 1850s hastened the country toward civil war. The 1852 publication of Harriet Beecher Stowe's heartrending *Uncle Tom's Cabin* opened the eyes of many Americans to the evils of slavery as it angered Southerners. Senator Charles Sumner's blistering speech on "The Crime Against Kansas" in 1856 led to his being beaten nearly to death in the Senate chamber by an enraged congressman from South Carolina. The Supreme Court's ruling in the Dred Scott case in 1857 declared the Missouri Compromise unconstitutional and ruled that African Americans had "no rights which the white man was bound to respect." And in 1859 John Brown's raid on Harper's Ferry, an abortive attempt to lead a slave insurrection, was the final factor convincing both North and South that compromise was no longer possible.

Disunion seemed inescapable.

Theodore Frelinghuysen (1787–1862)

Theodore Frelinghuysen, U.S. senator from New Jersey, vice-presidential running mate of Henry Clay in the 1844 election, and later president of Rutgers University, is remembered mostly for his passionate speech to the Senate arguing against the removal of the Cherokee in 1830. Despite Frelinghuysen's efforts, Congress passed the Indian Removal Bill that forced the Cherokee, at bayonet point, from their lands in Georgia and relocated them to a reservation in present-day Oklahoma. It has been estimated that as many as 15,000 of the 60,000 Indians died on the Trail of Tears.

According to Frelinghuysen, do the Indians have a valid claim to their land? Why does the senator refer to natural law? Is he correct in maintaining that the Cherokee grievance against the U.S. government is comparable to the colonists' grievances against George III and Parliament in the 1770s?

Speech Protesting the Indian Removal Bill, April 9, 1830

. . . I now proceed to the discussion of those principles which, in my humble judgment, fully and clearly sustain the claims of the Indians to all their political and civil rights, as by them asserted. And here, I insist that, by immemorial possession, as the original tenants of the soil, they hold a title beyond and superior to the British Crown and her colonies, and to all adverse pretensions of our confederation and subsequent Union. God, in his providence, planted these tribes on this Western continent, so far as we know, before Great Britain herself had a political existence. I believe, sir, it is not now seriously denied that the Indians are men, endowed with kindred faculties and powers with ourselves: that they have a place in human sympathy, and are justly entitled to a share in the common bounties of a benignant Providence. And, with this conceded, I ask in what code of the law of nations, or by what process of abstract deduction, their rights have been extinguished? . . .

In the light of natural law, can a reason for a distinction exist in the mode of enjoying that which is my own? If I use it for hunting, may another take it because he needs it for agriculture? I am aware that some writers have, by a system of artificial reasoning, endeavored to justify, or rather excuse the encroachments made upon Indian territory; and they denominate these abstractions the law of nations, and, in this ready way, the question is despatched. Sir, as we trace the sources of this law, we find its authority to depend either upon the conventions or common consent of

SOURCE: *Register of Debates in Congress*, 21st Congress, 1st session, vol. 6, part 1, April 9, 1830, 311, 312, 318.

nations. And when, permit me to inquire, were the Indian tribes ever consulted on the establishment of such a law? Whoever represented them or their interests in any Congress of nations, to confer upon the public rules of intercourse, and the proper foundations of dominion and property? The plain matter of fact is, that all these partial doctrines have resulted from the selfish plans and pursuits of more enlightened nations; and it is not matter for any great wonder, that they should so largely partake of a mercenary and exclusive spirit toward the claims of the Indians. . . .

Our ancestors found these people, far removed from the commotions of Europe, exercising all the rights, and enjoying the privileges, of free and independent sovereigns of this new world. They were not a wild and lawless horde of banditti, but lived under the restraints of government, patriarchal in its character, and energetic in its influence. They had chiefs, head men, and councils. The white men, the authors of all their wrongs, approached them as friends—they extended the olive branch; and, being then a feeble colony and at the mercy of the native tenants of the soil, by presents and professions, propitiated their good will. The Indian yielded a slow, but substantial confidence; granted to the colonists an abiding place; and suffered them to grow up to man's estate beside him. He never raised the claim of elder title: as the white man's wants increased, he opened the hand of his bounty wider and wider. By and by, conditions are changed. His people melt away; his lands are constantly coveted; millions after millions are ceded. The Indian bears it all meekly; he complains, indeed, as well he may; but suffers on: and now he finds that this neighbor, whom his kindness had nourished, has spread an adverse title over the last remains of his patrimony, barely adequate to his wants, and turns upon him, and says, "away we cannot endure you so near us! These forests and rivers, these groves of your fathers, these firesides and hunting grounds, are ours by the right of power, and the force of numbers." Sir, let every treaty be blotted from our records, and in the judgment of natural and unchangeable truth and justice, I ask, who is the injured, and who is the aggressor? Let conscience answer, and I fear not the result. . . . Do the obligations of justice change with the color of the skin? Is it one of the prerogatives of the white man, that he may disregard the dictates of moral principles, when an Indian shall be concerned? No, sir. . . , if the contending parties were to exchange positions, place the white man where the Indian stands, load him with all these wrongs, and what path would his outraged feelings strike out for his career? . . . A few pence of duty on tea, that invaded no fireside, excited no fears, disturbed no substantial interest whatever, awakened in the American colonies a spirit of firm resistance; and how was the tea tax met, sir? Just as it should be. There was lurking beneath this trifling imposition of duty, a covert assumption of authority, that led directly to oppressive exactions. "No taxation without representation," became our motto. We would neither pay the tax nor drink the tea. Our fathers buckled on their armor, and, from the water's edge, repelled the encroachments of a misguided cabinet. We successfully and triumphantly contended for the very rights and privileges that our Indian neighbors now implore us to protect and preserve to them. Sir, this thought invests the subject under debate with most singular and momentous interest. We, whom God has exalted to the very summit of prosperity—whose brief career forms the brightest page in history; the wonder and praise of the world; freedom's hope, and her consolation; we, about to turn traitors to our principles and our fame—about to become the oppressors of the feeble, and to cast away our birthright! Sir, I hope for better things. . . .

The end, however, is to justify the means. "The removal of the Indian tribes to the west of the Mississippi is demanded by the dictates of humanity." This is a word of conciliating import. But it often makes its way to the heart under very doubtful titles, and its present claims deserve to be rigidly questioned. Who urges this plea? They who covet the Indian lands—who wish to rid themselves of a neighbor that they despise, and whose State pride is enlisted in rounding off their territories.

Cherokee Chief John Ross (1790–1866)

Although Senator Theodore Frelinghuysen strongly opposed Andrew Jackson's Indian Removal Bill that stipulated sending the Cherokee from their native Georgia to Indian Territory (present-day Oklahoma), the bill passed both houses of Congress in 1830. The Cherokee themselves were not silent in standing up for their rights and made a strong effort first to challenge the law and then to forestall enforcement of it. Their case made it all the way to the Supreme Court. In *Cherokee Nation v. Georgia* and in *Worcester v. Georgia*, Chief Justice John Marshall ruled in the Cherokee's favor. Unfortunately, a contingent of Cherokee, without the authorization of the Cherokee nation, met with representatives of the U.S. Government at New Echota, Georgia, and signed a removal treaty. Once the Senate ratified the Treaty of New Echota, President Jackson had the authority he needed to force the removal.

In 1836, in protest, Cherokee Chief John Ross wrote a letter to Congress denouncing the Treaty of New Echota. His protest was to no avail, and in 1838 the Cherokee began the thousand-mile march along the infamous Trail of Tears. Why, according to Chief Ross, was the Treaty of New Echota invalid?

Letter Protesting the Treaty of New Echota, 1836

TO THE SENATE AND HOUSE OF REPRESENTATIVES, RED CLAY COUNCIL GROUND, CHEROKEE NATION, SEPTEMBER 28, 1836

It is well known that for a number of years past we have been harassed by a series of vexations, which it is deemed unnecessary to recite in detail, but the evidence of which our delegation will be prepared to furnish. With a view to bringing our troubles to a close, a delegation was appointed on the 23rd of October, 1835, by the General Council of the nation, clothed with full powers to enter into arrangements

SOURCE: Gary E. Moulton, ed., *The Papers of Chief John Ross*, vol. 1, 1807–1839 (Norman: University of Oklahoma Press, 1985).

with the Government of the United States, for the final adjustment of all our exist-ing difficulties. The delegation failing to effect an arrangement with the United States commissioner, then in the nation, proceeded, agreeably to their instructions in that case, to Washington City, for the purpose of negotiating a treaty with the authori-ties of the United States.

After the departure of the Delegation, a contract was made by the Rev. John F. Schermerhorn, and certain individual Cherokees, purporting to be a "treaty, con-cluded at New Echota, in the State of Georgia, on the 29th day of December, 1835, by General William Carroll and John F. Schermerhorn, commissioners on the part of the United States, and the chiefs, headmen, and people of the Cherokee tribes of Indians." A spurious Delegation, in violation of a special injunction of the general council of the nation, proceeded to Washington City with this pretended treaty, and by false and fraudulent representations supplanted in the favor of the Government the legal and accredited Delegation of the Cherokee people, and obtained for this instrument, after making important alterations in its provisions, the recognition of the United States Government. And now it is presented to us as a treaty, ratified by the Senate, and approved by the President [Andrew Jackson], and our acquiescence in its requirements demanded, under the sanction of the displeasure of the United States, and the threat of summary compulsion, in case of refusal. It comes to us, not through our legitimate authorities, the known and usual medium of communica-tion between the Government of the United States and our nation, but through the agency of a complication of powers, civil and military.

By the stipulations of this instrument, we are despoiled of our private posses-sions, the indefeasible property of individuals. We are stripped of every attribute of freedom and eligibility for legal self-defence. Our property may be plundered before our eyes; violence may be committed on our persons; even our lives may be taken away, and there is none to regard our complaints. We are denationalized; we are disfranchised. We are deprived of membership in the human family! We have neither land nor home, nor resting place that can be called our own. And this is effected by the provisions of a compact which assumes the venerated, the sacred appellation of treaty.

We are overwhelmed! Our hearts are sickened, our utterance is paralized, when we reflect on the condition in which we are placed, by the audacious practices of unprincipled men, who have managed their stratagems with so much dexterity as to impose on the Government of the United States, in the face of our earnest, solemn, and reiterated protestations.

The instrument in question is not the act of our Nation; we are not parties to its covenants; it has not received the sanction of our people. The makers of it sustain no office nor appointment in our Nation, under the designation of Chiefs, Head men, or any other title, by which they hold, or could acquire, authority to assume the reins of Government, and to make bargain and sale of our rights, our posses-sions, and our common country. And we are constrained solemnly to declare, that we cannot but contemplate the enforcement of the stipulations of this instrument on us, against our consent, as an act of injustice and oppression, which, we are well persuaded, can never knowingly be countenanced by the Government and people of the United States; nor can we believe it to be the design of these honorable and highminded individuals, who stand at the head of the Govt., to bind a whole Nation, by the acts of a few unauthorized individuals. And, therefore, we, the parties to be affected by the result, appeal with confidence to the justice, the magnanimity, the compassion, of your honorable bodies, against the enforcement, on us, of the provisions of a compact, in the formation of which we have had no agency.

Sylvia Dubois (1788?–1889)

Sylvia Dubois spent most of her life as a slave. In 1883, when she was in her 90s, she related her life story to C. W. Larison, who published it under the title *Silvia Dubois, a Biografy of the Slav Who Whipt Her Mistress and Gand Her Fredom*. The following excerpt, although it was recounted decades after the event took place and should therefore be regarded as a blend of folklore and fact, does suggest that slaves did not completely acquiesce to the South's "peculiar institution" and that many were not afraid to resist their masters. Why did Sylvia's master free her?

Reminiscences from *Sylvia Dubois, a Biografy of the Slav Who Whipt Her Mistress and Gand Her Fredom*, 1883

"Well, your mistress was always kind to you, wasn't she?"

"Kind to me? Why, she was the very devil himself. Why, she'd level me with anything she could get hold of—club, stick of wood, tongs, fire-shovel, knife, axe, hatchet, anything that was handiest—and then she was so damned quick about it too. I tell you, if I intended to sauce her, I made sure to be off always."

"Well, did she ever hit you?"

"Yes, often. Once she knocked me till I was so stiff that she thought I was dead. Once after that, because I was a little saucy, she leveled me with the fire-shovel and broke my pate. She thought I was dead then, but I wasn't."

"Broke your pate?"

"Yes, broke my skull. You can put your fingers here, in the place where the break was, in the side of my head, yet. She smashed it right in—she didn't do things to the halves."

(Hereupon I examined Sylvia's head and found that at some time long ago the skull had been broken and depressed for a space not less than three inches, that the deepest fragment had not been elevated as surgeons now do, and that in consequence there is to this day a depression in which I can bury a large part of the index finger.)

SOURCE: C. W. Larison, *Silvia Dubois, a Biografy of the Slav Who Whipt Her Mistress and Gand Her Fredom*, edited by Jared C. Lobdell (New York: Oxford University Press, 1988), 63–70.

"Well, Sylvia, what did your master say about such as was done by your mistress?"

"Say? Why, he knew how passionate she was. He saw her kick me in the stomach one day so badly that he interfered. I was not grown up then; I was too young to stand such. He didn't tell her so when I was by, but I have heard him tell her when they thought I was not listening that she was too severe—that such work would not do—she'd kill me next."

"Well, did his remonstrating with her make her any better?"

"Not a bit—made her worse. Just put the devil in her. And then, just as soon as he was out of the way, if I was a little saucy, or a little neglectful, I'd catch hell again. But I fixed her. I paid her up for all her spunk. I made up my mind that when I grew up I would do it, and when I had a good chance, when some of her grand company was around, I fixed her."

"Well, what did you do?"

"I knocked her down and blamed near killed her."

"Well, where and how did that happen?"

"It happened in the barroom. There was some grand folks stopping there, and she wanted things to look pretty stylish, and so she set me to scrubbing up the barroom. I felt a little glum and didn't do it to suit her. She scolded me about it and I sauced her. She struck me with her hand. Thinks I, it's a good time now to dress you out, and damned if I won't do it. I set down my tools and squared for a fight. The first whack, I struck her a hell of a blow with my fist. I didn't knock her entirely through the panels of the door, but her landing against the door made a terrible smash, and I hurt her so badly that all were frightened out of their wits, and I didn't know myself but that I'd killed the old devil."

"Were there anyone in the barroom then?"

"It was full of folks. Some of them were Jersey folks who were going from the Lake Countries home to visit their friends. Some were drovers on their way to the west. And some were hunters and boatmen staying a while to rest."

"What did they do when they saw you knock your mistress down?"

"Do? Why they were going to take her part, of course. But I just sat down the slop bucket and straightened up, and smacked my fists at 'em, and told 'em to wade in if they dared and I'd thrash every devil of 'em, and there wasn't a damned a one that dared to come."

"Well, what next?"

"Then I got out and pretty quick too. I knew it wouldn't do to stay there, so I went down to Chenang Point and there went to work."

"Where was your master during this fracas?"

"He? He was gone to tend court at Wilkes-Barre. He was a grand jury man and had to be gone a good many days. He often served as grand jury man, and then he was always gone a week or two. Things would have gone better if he had been home."

"When he came home what did he do?"

"He sent for me to come back."

"Did you go?"

"Of course I did; I had to go. I was a slave, and if I didn't go, he would have brought me, and in a hurry too. In those days the masters made the niggers mind, and when he spoke I knew I must obey.

"Them old masters, when they got mad, had no mercy on a nigger—they'd cut a nigger all up in a hurry—cut 'em all up into strings, just leave the life, that's all. I've seen 'em do it, many a time."

"Well, what did your master say when you came back?"

"He didn't scold me much. He told me that as my mistress and I got along so badly, if I would take my child and go to New Jersey and stay there, he would give me free. I told him I would go. It was late at night; he wrote me a pass, gave it to me, and early the next morning I set out for Flagtown, New Jersey."

"It seems that you got along with your master much better than you did with your mistress?"

"Yes, I got along with him first rate. He was a good man and a great man too; all the grand folks liked Minical Dubois. When the great men had their meetings, Minical Dubois was always invited to be with 'em, and he always went, too. He was away from home a great deal; he had a great deal of business and he was known all over the country. I liked my master and everybody liked him."

"He never whipped me unless he was sure that I deserved it. He used to let me go to frolics and balls and to have good times away from home, with other black folks, whenever I wanted to. He was a good man and a good master. But when he told me I must come home from a ball at a certain time, when the time came, the jib was out. I knew I must go; it wouldn't do to disappoint Minical Dubois. . . ."

"How did you go to Flagtown?"

"On foot, to be sure. I came right down through the Beech Woods, all alone, excepting my young one in my arms. Sometimes I didn't see a person for half a day; sometimes I didn't get half enough to eat, and never had any bed to sleep in; I just slept anywhere. My baby was about a year and a half old, and I had to carry it all the way. The wood was full of panthers, bears, wildcats, and wolves; I often saw 'em in the daytime, and always heard 'em howling in the night. O! that old panther—when he howled it made the hair stand up all over my head.

"At Easton, I went on board of a raft to go down the Delaware. A man by the name of Brink had his wife and family on board of a raft, bound for Philadelphia. I went on board to help the wife, for my passage. They were nice folks and I had a good time; I left the raft not far from Trenton, but I do not know exactly where—there was no town at the place at which I got off the raft.

"Then I proceeded directly to Flagtown, to see my mother. I did not find her there—she had moved to New Brunswick. On my way, a man called to me, asking me 'Whose nigger are you?' I replied 'I'm no man's nigger—I belong to God—I belong to no man.'

"He then said 'Where are you going?' I replied 'That's none of your business. I'm free. I go where I please.'

"He came toward me. I sat down my young one, showed him my fist, and looked at him; and I guess he saw 't was no use. He moseyed off, telling me that he would have me arrested as soon as he could find a magistrate.

"You see that in those days the negroes were all slaves, and they were sent nowhere, nor allowed to go anywhere without a pass; and when anyone met a negro who was not with his master, he had a right to demand of him whose negro he was; and if the negro did not show his pass, or did not give good evidence whose he was, he was arrested at once and kept until his master came for him, paid whatever charges were made, and took him away. You see, in those days anybody had authority to arrest vagrant negroes. They got paid for arresting them and charges for their keeping till their master redeemed them. But he didn't arrest me—not a bit.

"When I got to New Brunswick, I found my mother. Soon after I went to work, and remained in New Brunswick several years. From New Brunswick I went to Princeton to work for Victor Tulane. I remained in his family a long while; I worked for him when Paul Tulane was a child; I worked there when he was born. Victor Tulane was a great man and a good man, and he used his servants well. And Paul was a nice boy and Madam Tulane was a good woman; and I liked 'em all, and all the servants liked 'em.

"After a long while, I visited my grandfather, Harry Compton, who lived at the forks of the road, near this place. He was then an old man; they say he was more than a hundred years old, and I guess he was. But he was yet quite active; he wanted me to stay with him and take of him and I stayed; and at his death I inherited his property. I lived on the old homestead until a few years ago, when them damned Democrats set fire to my house, and burned up my home and all that I had. Since that time I have lived at this place, with my youngest daughter."

David Walker (1785–1830)

David Walker was a free North Carolina black who became an ardent and outspoken abolitionist. By the 1820s he had moved to Boston, opened a clothing store, and enjoyed a reputation as a leader of the city's black community of about 1500 people. He helped form the Massachusetts General Colored Association and became a distributor of the first national black newspaper in the United States, *Freedom's Journal*. Then, in 1829, he published his *Appeal to the Coloured Citizens of the World*, which uncompromisingly condemned both the institution of slavery and racism. If whites would not emancipate the slaves, he argued, then the slaves should rise up in revolt: Kill or be killed. Abolitionists worked hard to disseminate thousands of copies of this incendiary pamphlet to slaves throughout the South, and Southerners worked equally hard to prevent its distribution. So outraged were slaveholders that rumors began circulating that the South had put a price on Walker's head, and in June 1830 David Walker was found dead. Historians have established that he probably died of a respiratory disease, but, at the time, it was widely supposed that he had been poisoned.

Walker's *Appeal* is very significant because it marks the transition from the rather mild-mannered antislavery protests of Quakers and moderates to the more zealous and inflammatory antislavery protests of William Lloyd Garrison (who began publication of *The Liberator* in 1831), Theodore Weld, Elijah

Lovejoy, Frederick Douglass, and eventually John Brown. When Nat Turner's Rebellion occurred in 1831, Southerners had no doubt that Walker's *Appeal* had instigated it. And so, as the abolitionist crusade became more radical, so, too, did the Southern defense of its peculiar institution.

This excerpt from the *Appeal* is taken from the 1830 edition. Why does Walker refer to Jefferson in his critique of slavery? How effective is this? What is Walker's view of Christianity? What response might slaveholders have made to the *Appeal*?

Appeal to the Coloured Citizens of the World, 1830

PREAMBLE.

My dearly beloved Brethren and Fellow Citizens.

Having traveled over a considerable portion of these United States, and having, in the course of my travels, taken the most accurate observations of things as they exist—the result of my observations has warranted the full and unshaken conviction, that we, (coloured people of these United States,) are the most degraded, wretched, and abject set of beings that ever lived since the world began; and I pray God that none like us ever may live again until time shall be no more. They tell us of the Israelites in Egypt, the Helots in Sparta, and of the Roman Slaves, which last were made up from almost every nation under heaven, whose sufferings under those ancient and heathen nations, were, in comparison with ours, under this enlightened and Christian nation, no more than a cypher—or, in other words, those heathen nations of antiquity, had but little more among them than the name and form of slavery; while wretchedness and endless miseries were reserved, apparently in a phial, to be poured out upon our fathers, ourselves and our children, by Christian Americans!

These positions I shall endeavour, by the help of the Lord, to demonstrate in the course of this Appeal, to the satisfaction of the most incredulous mind—and may God Almighty, who is the Father of our Lord Jesus Christ, open your hearts to understand and believe the truth.

The causes, my brethren, which produce our wretchedness and miseries, are so very numerous and aggravating, that I believe the pen only of a Josephus or a Plutarch, can well enumerate and explain them. Upon subjects, then, of such incomprehensible magnitude, so impenetrable, and so notorious, I shall be obliged to omit a large class of, and content myself with giving you an exposition of a few of those, which do indeed rage to such an alarming pitch, that they cannot but be a perpetual source of terror and dismay to every reflecting mind.

SOURCE: Charles M. Wiltse, ed., *David Walker's Appeal in Four Articles; Together with a Preamble, to the Coloured Citizens of the World* (New York: Hill and Wang, 1965), 1–18.

I am fully aware, in making this appeal to my much afflicted and suffering brethren, that I shall not only be assailed by those whose greatest earthly desires are, to keep us in abject ignorance and wretchedness, and who are of the firm conviction that Heaven has designed us and our children to be slaves and beasts of burden to them and their children. I say, I do not only expect to be held up to the public as an ignorant, impudent and restless disturber of the public peace, by such avaricious creatures, as well as a mover of insubordination—and perhaps put in prison or to death, for giving a superficial exposition of our miseries, and exposing tyrants. But I am persuaded, that many of my brethren, particularly those who are ignorantly in league with slaveholders or tyrants, who acquire their daily bread by the blood and sweat of their more ignorant brethren—and not a few of those too, who are too ignorant to see an inch beyond their noses, will rise up and call me cursed—Yea, the jealous ones among us will perhaps use more abject subtlety, by affirming that this work is not worth perusing, that we are well situated, and there is no use in trying to better our condition, for we cannot. I will ask one question here.—Can our condition be any worse?—Can it be more mean and abject? If there are any changes, will they not be for the better though they may appear for the worst at first? Can they get us any lower? Where can they get us? They are afraid to treat us worse, for they know well, the day they do it they are gone. But against all accusations which may or can be preferred against me, I appeal to Heaven for my motive in writing—who knows what my object is, if possible, to awaken in the breasts of my afflicted, degraded and slumbering brethren, a spirit of inquiry and investigation respecting our miseries and wretchedness in this Republican Land of Liberty!!!!!!

The sources from which our miseries are derived, and on which I shall comment, I shall not combine in one, but shall put them under distinct heads and expose them in their turn; in doing which, keeping truth on my side, and not departing from the strictest rules of morality, I shall endeavour to penetrate, search out, and lay them open for your inspection. If you cannot or will not profit by them, I shall have done my duty to you, my country and my God.

And as the inhuman system of slavery, is the source from which most of our miseries proceed, I shall begin with that curse to nations, which has spread terror and devastation through so many nations of antiquity, and which is raging to such a pitch at the present day in Spain and in Portugal. It had one tug in England, in France, and in the United States of America; yet the inhabitants thereof, do not learn wisdom, and erase it entirely from their dwellings and from all with whom they have to do. The fact is, the labour of slaves comes so cheap to the avaricious usurpers, and is (as they think) of such great utility to the country where it exists, that those who are actuated by sordid avarice only, overlook the evils, which will as sure as the Lord lives, follow after the good. In fact, they are so happy to keep in ignorance and degradation, and to receive the homage and the labour of the slaves, they forget that God rules in the armies of heaven and among the inhabitants of the earth, having his ears continually open to the cries, tears and groans of his oppressed people; and being a just and holy Being will at one day appear fully in behalf of the oppressed, and arrest the progress of the avaricious oppressors; for although the destruction of the oppressors God may not effect by the oppressed, yet the Lord our God will bring other destructions upon them—for not unfrequently will he cause them to rise up one against another, to be split and divided, and to oppress each other, and sometimes to open hostilities with sword in hand. Some may ask, what is the matter with this united and happy people?—Some say it is the cause of political usurpers, tyrants, oppressors, But has not the Lord an oppressed and suffering people among them? Does the Lord condescend to hear their cries and see their tears in consequence of oppression? Will he let the oppressors rest comfortably and happy always? Will he not cause the very children of the oppressors to rise up against them, and oftimes put them to death? "God works in many ways his wonders to perform." . . .

All persons who are acquainted with history, and particularly the Bible, who are not blinded by the God of this world, and are not actuated solely by avarice—who are able to lay aside prejudice long enough to view candidly and impartially, things as they were, are, and probably will be—who are willing to admit that God made man to serve Him alone, and that man should have no other Lord or Lords but Himself—that God Almighty is the sole proprietor or master of the WHOLE human family, and will not on any consideration admit of a colleague, being unwilling to divide his glory with another—and who can dispense with prejudice long enough to admit that we are men, notwithstanding our improminent noses and woolly heads, and believe that we feel for our fathers, mothers, wives and children, as well as the whites do for theirs.—I say, all who are permitted to see and believe these things, can easily recognize the judgments of God among the Spaniards. Though others may lay the cause of the fierceness with which they cut each other's throats, to some other circumstance, yet they who believe that God is a God of justice, will believe that SLAVERY is the principal cause.

While the Spaniards are running about upon the field of battle cutting each other's throats, has not the Lord an afflicted and suffering people in the midst of them, whose cries and groans in consequence of oppression are continually pouring into the ears of the God of justice? Would they not cease to cut each other's throats, if they could? But how can they? The very support which they draw from government to aid them in perpetrating such enormities, does it not arise in a great degree from the wretched victims of oppression among them? And yet they are calling for Peace!—Peace!! Will any peace be given unto them? Their destruction may indeed be procrastinated awhile, but can it continue long, while they are oppressing the Lord's people? Has He not the hearts of all men in His hand? Will he suffer one part of his creatures to go on oppressing another like brutes always, with impunity? And yet, those avaricious wretches are calling for Peace!!!! I declare, it does appear to me, as though some nations think God is asleep, or that he made the Africans for nothing else but to dig their mines and work their farms, or they cannot believe history, sacred or profane. I ask every man who has a heart, and is blessed with the privilege of believing—Is not God a God of justice to all his creatures? Do you say he is? Then if he gives peace and tranquillity to tyrants, and permits them to keep our fathers, our mothers, ourselves and our children in eternal ignorance and wretchedness, to support them and their families, would he be to us a God of justice? I ask, O ye Christians!!! who hold us and our children in the most abject ignorance and degradation, that ever a people were afflicted with since the world began—I say, if God gives you peace and tranquillity, and suffers you thus to go on afflicting us, and our children, who have never given you the least provocation—would he be to us a God of justice? If you will allow that we are MEN, who feel for each other, does not the blood of our fathers and of us their children, cry aloud to the Lord of Sabaoth against you, for the cruelties and murders with which you have, and do continue to afflict us. But it is time for me to close my remarks on the suburbs, just to enter more fully into the interior of this system of cruelty and oppression.

ARTICLE I. OUR WRETCHEDNESS IN CONSEQUENCE OF SLAVERY.

My beloved brethren:—The Indians of North and of South America—the Greeks—the Irish, subjected under the king of Great Britain—the Jews, that ancient people of the Lord—the inhabitants of the islands of the sea—in fine, all the inhabitants of the earth, (except however, the sons of Africa) are called men, and of course are, and ought to be free. But we, (coloured people) and our children are brutes!! and of course are, and ought to be SLAVES to the American people and their children forever!! to dig their mines and work their farms; and thus go on enriching them, from one generation to another with our blood and our tears!!!!

I promised in a preceding page to demonstrate to the satisfaction of the most incredulous, that we, (coloured people of these United States of America) are the most wretched, degraded and abject set of beings that ever lived since the world began, and that the white Americans having reduced us to the wretched state of slavery, treat us in that condition more cruel (they being an enlightened and Christian people,) than any heathen nation did any people whom it had reduced to our condition. These affirmations are so well confirmed in the minds of all unprejudiced men, who have taken the trouble to read histories, that they need no elucidation from me. But to put them beyond all doubt, I refer you in the first place to the children of Jacob, or of Israel in Egypt, under Pharaoh and his people. Some of my brethren do not know who Pharaoh and the Egyptians were—I know it to be a fact, that some of them take the Egyptians to have been a gang of devils, not knowing any better, and that they (Egyptians) having got possession of the Lord's people, treated them nearly as cruel as Christian Americans do us, at the present day. For the information of such, I would only mention that the Egyptians, were Africans or coloured people, such as we are—some of them yellow and others dark—a mixture of Ethiopians and the natives of Egypt—about the same as you see the coloured people of the United States at the present day.—I say, I call your attention then, to the children of Jacob, while I point out particularly to you his son, among the rest, in Egypt.

"And Pharaoh, said unto Joseph, . . . thou shalt be over my house, and according unto thy word shall all my people be ruled: only in the throne will I be greater than thou."

"And Pharaoh said unto Joseph, see, I have set thee over all the land of Egypt."

"And Pharaoh said unto Joseph, I am Pharaoh, and without thee shall no man lift up his hand or foot in all the land of Egypt."

Now I appeal to heaven and to earth, and particularly to the American people themselves, who cease not to declare that our condition is not hard, and that we are comparatively satisfied to rest in wretchedness and misery, under them and their chil-

dren. Not, indeed, to show me a coloured President, a Governor, a Legislator, a Senator, a Mayor, or an Attorney at the Bar.—But to show me a man of colour, who holds
the low office of Constable, or one who sits in a Juror Box, even on a case of one of his
wretched brethren, throughout this great Republic!!—But let us pass Joseph the son
of Israel a little farther in review, as he existed with that heathen nation.

"And Pharaoh called Joseph's name Zaphnathpaaneah; and he gave him to wife
Asenath the daughter of Potipherah priest of On. And Joseph went out over all the
land of Egypt."

Compare the above, with the American institutions. Do they not institute laws to
prohibit us from marrying among the whites? I would wish, candidly, however,
before the Lord, to be understood, that I would not give a pinch of snuff to be married to any white person I ever saw in all the days of my life. And I do say it, that the
black man, or man of colour, who will leave his own colour (provided he can get
one, who is good for any thing) and marry a white woman, to be a double slave to
her, just because she is white, ought to be treated by her as he surely will be, viz: as a
NIGGER!!!! It is not, indeed, what I care about inter-marriages with the whites,
which induced me to pass this subject in review; for the Lord knows, that there is a
day coming when they will be glad enough to get into the company of the blacks,
notwithstanding, we are, in this generation, levelled by them, almost on a level with
the brute creation: and some of us they treat even worse than they do the brutes that
perish. I only made this extract to show how much lower we are held, and how much
more cruel we are treated by the Americans, than were the children of Jacob, by the
Egyptians.—We will notice the sufferings of Israel some further, under heathen
Pharaoh, compared with ours under the enlightened Christians of America.

"And Pharaoh spoke unto Joseph, saying, thy father and thy brethren are come
unto thee:

"The land of Egypt is before thee: in the best of the land make thy father and
brethren to dwell; in the land of Goshen let them dwell: and if thou knowest any
men of activity among them, then make them rulers over my cattle."

I ask those people who treat us so well, Oh! I ask them, where is the most barren
spot of land which they have given unto us? Israel had the most fertile land in all
Egypt. Need I mention the very notorious fact, that I have known a poor man of
colour, who laboured night and day, to acquire a little money, and having acquired it,
he vested it in a small piece of land, and got him a house erected thereon, and having
paid for the whole, he moved his family into it, where he was suffered to remain but
nine months, when he was cheated out of his property by a white man, and driven
out of door! And is not this the case generally? Can a man of colour buy a piece of
land and keep it peaceably? Will not some white man try to get it from him, even if it
is in a mud hole? I need not comment any farther on a subject, which all both black
and white, will readily admit. But I must, really, observe that in this very city, when a
man of colour dies, if he owned any real estate it most generally falls into the hands
of some white person. The wife and children of the deceased may weep and lament if
they please, but the estate will be kept snug enough by its white possessor.

But to prove farther that the condition of the Israelites was better under the
Egyptians than ours is under the whites. I call upon the professing Christians, I call
upon the philanthropist, I call upon the very tyrant himself, to show me a page of

history, either sacred or profane, on which a verse can be found, which maintains, that the Egyptians heaped the insupportable insult upon the children of Israel, by telling them that they were not of the human family. Can the whites deny this charge? Have they not, after having reduced us to the deplorable condition of slaves under their feet, held us up as descending originally from the tribes of Monkeys or Orang-Outangs? O! my God! I appeal to every man of feeling—is not this insupportable? Is it not heaping the most gross insult upon our miseries, because they have got us under their feet and we cannot help ourselves? Oh! pity us we pray thee, Lord Jesus, Master.—Has Mr. Jefferson declared to the world, that we are inferior to the whites, both in the endowments of our bodies and our minds? It is indeed surprising, that a man of such great learning, combined with such excellent natural parts, should speak so of a set of men in chains. I do not know what to compare it to, unless, like putting one wild deer in an iron cage, where it will be secured, and hold another by the side of the same, then let it go, and expect the one in the cage to run as fast as the one at liberty. So far, my brethren, were the Egyptians from heaping these insults upon their slaves, that Pharaoh's daughter took Moses, a son of Israel for her own, as will appear by the following.

"And Pharaoh's daughter said unto her, [Moses' mother] take this child away, and nurse it for me, and I will pay thee thy wages. And the woman took the child and nursed it.

"And the child grew, and she brought him unto Pharaoh's daughter and he became her son. And she called his name Moses: and she said because I drew him out of the water."

In all probability, Moses would have become Prince Regent to the throne, and no doubt, in process of time but he would have been seated on the throne of Egypt. But he had rather suffer shame, with the people of God, than to enjoy pleasures with that wicked people for a season. O! that the coloured people were long since of Moses' excellent disposition, instead of courting favour with, and telling news and lies to our natural enemies, against each other—aiding them to keep their hellish chains of slavery upon us. Would we not long before this time, have been respectable men, instead of such wretched victims of oppression as we are? Would they be able to drag our mothers, our fathers, our wives, our children and ourselves, around the world in chains and handcuffs as they do, to dig up gold and silver for them and theirs? This question, my brethren, I leave for you to digest: and may God Almighty force it home to your hearts. Remember that unless you are united, keeping your tongues within your teeth, you will be afraid to trust your secrets to each other, and thus perpetuate our miseries under the Christians!!!!

ADDITION.—Remember, also to lay humble at the feet of our Lord and Master Jesus Christ, with prayers and fastings. Let our enemies go on with their butcheries, and at once fill up their cup. Never make an attempt to gain our freedom or natural right, from under our cruel oppressor, and murderers, until you see your way clear—when that hour arrives and you move, be not afraid or dismayed; for be you assured that Jesus Christ the King of heaven and of earth who is the God of justice and of armies, will surely go before you. And those enemies who have for hundreds of years stolen our rights, and kept us ignorant of Him and His divine worship, he will remove. Millions of whom, are this day, so ignorant and avaricious, that they cannot conceive how God can have an attribute of justice, and show mercy to us because it pleased Him to make us black—which colour, Mr. Jefferson calls unfortunate!!!!!! As though we are not as thankful to our God, for having made us as it pleased himself, as they, (the whites,) are for having made them white. They think because they hold us in their infernal chains of slavery, that we wish to be white, or of their color—but they are dreadfully deceived—we wish to be just as it pleased our Creator to have made us, and no avaricious and unmerciful wretches, have any business to make slaves of, or hold us in slavery. How would they like for us to make slaves of, and hold them in cruel slavery, and murder them as they do us?—But is Mr. Jefferson's assertions true? viz. "that it is unfortunate for us that our Creator has been pleased to make us black." We will not take his say so, for the fact. The world will have an opportunity to see whether it is unfortunate for us, that our Creator has made us darker than the whites. . . .

I have been for years troubling the pages of historians, to find out what our fathers have done to the white Christians of America, to merit such condign punishment as they have inflicted on them, and do continue to inflict on us their children. But I must aver, that my researches have hitherto been to no effect. I have therefore, come to the immoveable conclusion, that they (Americans) have, and do continue to punish us for nothing else, but for enriching them and their country. For I cannot conceive of anything else. Nor will I ever believe otherwise, until the Lord shall convince me.

The world knows, that slavery as it existed among the Romans, (which was the primary cause of their destruction) was, comparatively speaking, no more than a cypher, when compared with ours under the Americans. Indeed I should not have noticed the Roman slaves, had not the very learned and penetrating Mr. Jefferson said, "when a master was murdered, all his slaves in the same house, or within hearing, were condemned to death."—Here let me ask Mr. Jefferson, (but he is gone to answer at the bar of God, for the deeds done in his body while living,) I therefore ask the whole American people, had I not rather die, or be put to death, than to be a slave to any tyrant, who takes not only my own, but my wife and children's lives by the inches? Yea, would I meet death with avidity far! far!! in preference to such servile submission to the murderous hands of tyrants. Mr. Jefferson's very severe remarks on us have been so extensively argued upon by men whose attainments in literature, I shall never be able to reach, that I would not have meddled with it, were it not to solicit each of my brethren, who has the spirit of a man, to buy a copy of Mr. Jefferson's "Notes on Virginia," and put it in the hand of his son. For let no one of us suppose that the refutations which have been written by our white friends are enough—they are whites—we are blacks. We, and the world wish to see the charges of Mr. Jefferson refuted by the blacks themselves, according to their chance; for we must remember that what the whites have written respecting this subject, is other men's labours, and did not emanate from the blacks. I know well, that there are some talents and learning among the coloured people of this country, which we have not a chance to develope, in consequence of oppression; but our oppression ought not to hinder us from acquiring all we can. For we will have a chance to develope them by and by. God will not suffer us, always to be oppressed. Our sufferings will come to an end, in spite of all the Americans this side of eternity. Then we will want all the learning and talents among ourselves, and perhaps more, to govern ourselves.—"Every dog must have its day," the American's is coming to an end.

But let us review Mr. Jefferson's remarks respecting us some further. Comparing our miserable fathers, with the learned philosophers of Greece, he says: "Yet notwithstanding these and other discouraging circumstances among the Romans, their slaves were often their rarest artists. They excelled too, in science, insomuch as to be usually employed as tutors to their master's children; Epictetus, Terence and Phaedrus, were slaves,—but they were of the race of whites. It is not their condition then, but nature, which has produced the distinction." See this, my brethren!! Do you believe that this assertion is swallowed by millions of the whites? Do you know that Mr. Jefferson was one of as great characters as ever lived among the whites? See his writings for the world, and public labours for the United States of America. Do you believe that the assertions of such a man, will pass away into oblivion unobserved by this people and the world? If you do you are much mistaken—See how the American people treat us—have we souls in our bodies? Are we men who have any spirits at all? I know that there are many swell-bellied fellows among us, whose greatest object is to fill their stomachs. Such I do not mean—I am after those who know and feel, that we are MEN, as well as other people; to them, I say, that unless we try to refute Mr. Jefferson's arguments respecting us, we will only establish them.

But the slaves among the Romans. Every body who has read history, knows, that as soon as a slave among the Romans obtained his freedom, he could rise to the greatest eminence in the State, and there was no law instituted to hinder a slave from buying his freedom. Have not the Americans instituted laws to hinder us from obtaining our freedom? Do any deny this charge? Read the laws of Virginia, North Carolina, etc. Further: have not the Americans instituted laws to prohibit a man of colour from obtaining and holding any office whatever, under the government of the United States of America? Now, Mr. Jefferson tells us, that our condition is not so hard, as the slaves were under the Romans!!!!!!

It is time for me to bring this article to a close. But before I close it, I must observe to my brethren that at the close of the first Revolution in this country, with Great Britain, there were but thirteen States in the Union, now there are twenty four, most of which are slave-holding States, and the whites are dragging us around in chains and in handcuffs, to their new States and Territories to work their mines and farms, to enrich them and their children—and millions of them believing firmly that we being a little darker than they, were made by our Creator to be an inheritance to them and their children for ever—the same as a parcel of brutes.

Are we MEN!!—I ask you, O my brethren! are we MEN? Did our Creator make us to be slaves to dust and ashes like ourselves? Are they not dying worms as well as we? Have they not to make their appearance before the tribunal of Heaven, to answer for the deeds done in the body, as well as we? Have we any other Master but Jesus Christ alone? Is he not their Master as well as ours?—What right then, have we to obey and call any other Master, but Himself? How we could be so submissive to a gang of men, whom we cannot tell whether they are as good as ourselves or not, I never could conceive. However, this is shut up with the Lord, and we cannot precisely tell—but I declare, we judge men by their works.

The whites have always been an unjust, jealous, unmerciful, avaricious and bloodthirsty set of beings, always seeking after power and authority.—We view them all over the confederacy of Greece, where they were first known to be any thing, (in consequence of education) we see them there, cutting each other's throats—trying to subject each other to wretchedness and misery—to effect which, they used all kinds of deceitful, unfair, and unmerciful means. We view them next in Rome, where the spirit of tyranny and deceit raged still higher. We view them in Gaul, Spain, and in Britain.—In fine, we view them all over Europe, together with what were scattered about in Asia and Africa, as heathens, and we see them acting more like devils than accountable men. But some may ask, did not the blacks of Africa, and the mulattoes of Asia, go on in the same way as did the whites of Europe. I answer, no—they never were half so avaricious, deceitful and unmerciful as the whites, according to their knowledge.

But we will leave the whites or Europeans as heathens, and take a view of them as Christians, in which capacity we see them as cruel, if not more so than ever. In fact, take them as a body, they are ten times more cruel, avaricious and unmerciful than ever they were; for while they were heathens, they were bad enough it is true, but it is positively a fact that they were not quite so audacious as to go and take vessel loads of men, women and children, and in cold blood, and through devilishness, throw them into the sea, and murder them in all kind of ways. While they were heathens, they were too ignorant for such barbarity. But being Christians, enlightened and sensible, they are completely prepared for such hellish cruelties. Now suppose God were to give them more sense, what would they do? If it were possible, would they not dethrone Jehovah and seat themselves upon his throne? I therefore, in the name and fear of the Lord God of Heaven and of earth, divested of prejudice either on the side of my colour or that of the whites, advance my suspicion of them, whether they are as good by nature as we are or not. Their actions, since they were known as a people, have been the reverse, I do indeed suspect them, but this, as I before observed, is shut up with the Lord, we cannot exactly tell, it will be proved in succeeding generations.—The whites have had the essence of the gospel as it was preached by my master and his apostles—the Ethiopians have not, who are to have it in its meridian splendor—the Lord will give it to them to their satisfaction. I hope and pray my God, that they will make good use of it, that it may be well with them.

William Lloyd Garrison (1805–1879)

In the years after the American Revolution, Northern states gradually eliminated slavery. By the 1820s, antislavery people were arguing for the emancipation of all slaves through a process whereby the federal government would compensate slaveholders for their property and the freedmen would be relocated to Africa. Indeed, during James Monroe's presidency, several thousand freed slaves had been sent to the newly established nation of Liberia in West Africa. At this time William Lloyd Garrison was in Baltimore writing for the *Genius of Universal Emancipation*, a gradualist antislavery newspaper published by Quaker William Lundy. By 1830, however, Garrison no longer viewed gradualism as a viable strategy to eliminate slavery. He moved to Boston and in January 1831 began publishing his own newspaper,

The Liberator. In the first issue, he condemned the gradualist approach in no uncertain terms and advocated the *immediate* abolition of slavery. The intensity of his views and the uncompromising nature of his language alarmed and distressed Southern slaveholders so thoroughly that they began more earnestly defending slavery. By 1832, Garrison had founded the New England Anti-Slavery Society and in 1833 the American Anti-Slavery Society. The state of Georgia offered a $5000 reward for Garrison's capture, trial, and conviction. In 1835, he was rescued from a proslavery mob that had dragged him through the streets of Boston with a rope around his neck when the mayor intervened and put him in jail. While incarcerated, Garrison wrote on the wall of his cell, "Wm. Lloyd Garrison was put into this cell Wednesday afternoon, October 21, 1835, to save him from the violence of a 'respectable and influential' mob, who sought to destroy him for preaching the abominable and dangerous doctrine that 'all men are created equal. . . .'"

Never afraid to challenge the powers that be, Garrison became increasingly radical in the 1840s and 1850s. One of his most controversial acts was the public burning of a copy of the U.S. Constitution on July 4, 1854. To Garrison, the Constitution, because it acquiesced in the institution of slavery, was "an agreement with death and a covenant with hell." By this time the debate over slavery had become so intense that many Americans began to believe that the only resolution would be through civil war.

On what grounds does Garrison call for the immediate abolition of slavery? Why does he oppose gradualism?

The Liberator, Vol. I, No. I, January 1, 1831

To the Public

In the month of August, I issued proposals for publishing *"The Liberator"* in Washington City; but the enterprise, though hailed in different sections of the country, was palsied by public indifference. Since that time, the removal of the *Genius of Universal Emancipation* to the Seat of Government has rendered less imperious the establishment of a similar periodical in that quarter.

During my recent tour for the purpose of exciting the minds of the people by a series of discourses on the subject of slavery, every place that I visited gave fresh evidence of the fact, that a greater revolution in public sentiment was to be effected in the free states—*and particularly in New England*—than at the south. I found contempt more bitter, opposition more active, detraction more relentless, prejudice more stubborn, and apathy more frozen, than among slave owners themselves. Of course, there were individual exceptions to the contrary. This state of things afflicted, but did not

---

SOURCE: *The Liberator* (Boston), January 1, 1831.

dishearten me. I determined, at every hazard, to lift up the standard of emancipation in the eyes of the nation, *within sight of Bunker Hill and in the birth place of liberty.* That standard is now unfurled; and long may it float, unhurt by the spoliations of time or the missiles of a desperate foe—yea, till every chain be broken, and every bondman set free! Let Southern oppressors tremble—let their secret abettors tremble—let their Northern apologists tremble—let all the enemies of the persecuted blacks tremble.

I deem the publication of my original Prospectus unnecessary, as it has obtained a wide circulation. The principles therein inculcated will be steadily pursued in this paper, excepting that I shall not array myself as the political partisan of any man. In defending the great cause of human rights, I wish to derive the assistance of all religions and of all parties.

Assenting to the "self evident truth" maintained in the American Declaration of Independence, "that all men are created equal, and endowed by their Creator with certain inalienable rights—among which are life, liberty and the pursuit of happiness," I shall strenuously contend for the immediate enfranchisement of our slave population. In Park-Street Church, on the Fourth of July, 1829, in an address on slavery, I unreflectingly assented to the popular but pernicious doctrine of *gradual* abolition. I seize this opportunity to make a full and unequivocal recantation, and thus publicly to ask pardon of my God, of my country, and of my brethren the poor slaves, for having uttered a sentiment so full of timidity, injustice and absurdity. A similar recantation, from my pen, was published in the *Genius of Universal Emancipation* at Baltimore, in September, 1829. My conscience is now satisfied.

I am aware, that many object to the severity of my language; but is there not cause for severity? I *will be* as harsh as truth, and as uncompromising as justice. On this subject, I do not wish to think, or speak, or write, with moderation. No! No! Tell a man whose house is on fire, to give a moderate alarm; tell him to moderately rescue his wife from the hands of the ravisher; tell the mother to gradually extricate her babe from the fire into which it has fallen;—but urge me not to use moderation in a cause like the present. I am in earnest—I will not equivocate—I will not excuse—I will not retreat a single inch—**AND I *WILL BE HEARD.*** The apathy of the people is enough to make every statue leap from its pedestal, and to hasten the resurrection of the dead.

It is pretended, that I am retarding the cause of emancipation by the coarseness of my invective, and the precipitancy of my measures. *The charge is not true.* On this question my influence,—humble as it is,—is felt at this moment to a considerable extent, and shall be felt in coming years—not perniciously, but beneficially—not as a curse, but as a blessing; and posterity will bear testimony that I was right. I desire to thank God, that he enables me to disregard "the fear of man which bringeth a snare," and to speak his truth in its simplicity and power. . . .

William Lloyd Garrison.

William Apess (1798–1839?)

William Apess, a Pequot Indian, was "bound out" (like many other homeless children in the early nineteenth century) to a white family in Massachusetts. By the time he was 15, he had lived with several different white families and had adapted reasonably well to white society. After a stint in the army during the War of 1812, he returned to Connecticut in 1817 and became a lay preacher for several years until his official ordination as a Methodist minister in 1829. In that same year he published *A Son of the Forest* (the first autobiography ever written by an Indian) and then, four years later, a second personal memoir, *The Experiences of Five Christian Indians of the Pequod Tribe.* In this book, his essay "An Indian's Looking-Glass for the White Man" is a strong indictment, from a Christian perspective, of the whites' treatment of the Indians. Effectively using the Bible to condemn racism, Apess became one of the most articulate nineteenth-century Indian protest voices. While continuing to work for Indian rights in the 1830s, he published two more important protest works: *Indian Nullification of the Unconstitutional Laws of Massachusetts, Relative to the Marshpee* [sic] *Tribe* (1835) and *Eulogy on King Philip* (1836). But after this last book was published, he seems to have dropped out of sight, and very little is known about the rest of his life.

Why does he use scripture to condemn white attitudes about race? Is this an effective technique? How does his view on race compare with David Walker's view?

———————————

"An Indian's Looking-Glass for the White Man," 1833

Having a desire to place a few things before my fellow creatures who are traveling with me to the grave, and to that God who is the maker and preserver both of the white man and the Indian, whose abilities are the same and who are to be judged by one God, who will show no favor to outward appearances but will judge righteousness. Now I ask if degradation has not been heaped long enough upon the Indians? And if so, can there not be a compromise? Is it right to hold and promote prejudices? If not, why not put them all away? I mean here, among those who are civilized. It may be that many are ignorant of the situation of many of my brethren with the limits of New England. Let me for a few moments turn your attention to the reservations in the different states of New England, and, with but few exceptions, who shall find them as follows: the most mean, abject, miserable race of beings in the world—a complete place of prodigality and prostitution.

Let a gentleman and lady of integrity and respectability visit these places, and they would be surprised; as they wandered from one hut to the other they would view,

Source: Barry O'Connell, ed., *On Our Own Ground: The Complete Writings of William Apess, A Pequot* (Amherst: University of Massachusetts Press, 1992), 155–161.

with the females who are left alone, children half-starved and some almost as naked as they came into the world. And it is a fact that I have seen them as much so—while the females are left without protection, and are seduced by white men, and are finally left to be common prostitutes for them and to be destroyed by that burning, fiery curse, that has swept millions, both of red and white men, into the grave with sorrow and disgrace—rum. One reason why they are left so is because their most sensible and active men are absent at sea. Another reason is because they are made to believe they are minors and have not the abilities given them from God to take care of themselves, without it is to see to a few little articles, such as baskets and brooms. Their land is in common stock, and they have nothing to make them enterprising.

Another reason is because those men who are Agents, many of them are unfaithful and care not whether the Indians live or die; they are much imposed upon by their neighbors, who have no principle. They would think it no crime to go upon Indian lands and cut and carry off their most valuable timber, or anything else they chose; and I doubt not but they think it clear gain. Another reason is because they have no education to take care of themselves; if they had, I would risk them to take care of their own property.

Now I will ask if the Indians are not called the most ingenious people among us. And are they not said to be men of talents? And I would ask: Could there be a more efficient way to distress and murder them by inches than the way they have taken? And there is no people in the world but who may be destroyed in the same way. Now, if these people are what they are held up in our view to be, I would take the liberty to ask why they are not brought forward and pains taken to educate them, to give them all a common education, and those of the brightest and first-rate talents put forward and held up to office. Perhaps some unholy, unprincipled men would cry out, "The skin was not good enough"; but stop, friends—I am not talking about the skin but about principles. I would ask if there cannot be as good feelings and principles under a red skin as there can be under a white. And let me ask: Is it not on the account of a bad principle that we who are red children have had to suffer so much as we have? And let me ask: Did not this bad principle proceed from the whites or their forefathers? And I would ask: Is it worthwhile to nourish it any longer? If not then let us have a change, although some men no doubt will spout their corrupt principles against it, that are in the halls of legislation and elsewhere. But I presume this kind of talk will seem surprising and horrible. I do not see why it should so long as they (the whites) say that they think as much of us as they do of themselves.

This I have heard repeatedly, from the most respectable gentlemen and ladies—and having heard so much precept, I should now wish to see the example. And I would ask who has a better right to look for these things than the naturalist himself—the candid man would say none.

I know that many say they are willing, perhaps the majority of the people, that we should enjoy our rights and privileges as they do. If so, I would ask, Why are not we protected in our persons and property throughout the Union? Is it not because there reigns in the breast of many who are leaders a most unrighteous, unbecoming, and impure black principle, and as corrupt and unholy as it can be—while these very same unfeeling, self-esteemed characters pretend to take the skin as a pretext to keep us from our unalienable and lawful rights? I would ask you if you would like to be disfranchised from all your rights, merely because your skin is white, and for no other crime. I'll venture to say, these very characters who hold the skin to be such a barrier in the way would be the first to cry out, "Injustice! awful injustice!"

But, reader, I acknowledge that this is a confused world, and I am not seeking for office, but merely placing before you the black inconsistency that you place before me—which is ten times blacker than any skin that you will find in the universe. And now let me exhort you to do away with that principle, as it appears ten times worse in the sight of God and candid men than skins of color—more disgraceful than all the skins that Jehovah ever made. If black or red skins or any other skin of color is disgraceful to God, it appears that he has disgraced himself a great deal—for he has made fifteen colored people to one white and placed them here upon this earth.

Now let me ask you, white man, if it is a disgrace for to eat, drink, and sleep with the image of God, or sit, or walk and talk with them. Or have you the folly to think that the white man, being one in fifteen or sixteen, are the only beloved images of God? Assemble all nations together in your imagination, and then let the whites be seated among them, and then let us look for the whites, and I doubt not it would be hard finding them; for to the rest of the nations, they are still but a handful. Now suppose these skins were put together, and each skin has its national crimes written upon it—which skin do you think would have the greatest? I will ask one question more. Can you charge the Indians with robbing a nation almost of their whole continent, and murdering their women and children, and then depriving the remainder of their lawful rights, that nature and God require them to have? And to cap the climax, rob another nation to till their grounds and welter out their days under the lash with hunger and fatigue under the scorching rays of a burning sun? I should look at all the skins, and I know that when I cast my eye upon that white skin, and if I saw those crimes written upon it, I should enter my protest against it immediately and cleave to that which is more honorable. And I can tell you that I am satisfied with the manner of my creation, fully—whether others are or not.

But we will strive to penetrate more fully into the conduct of those who profess to have pure principles and who tell us to follow Jesus Christ and imitate him and have his Spirit. Let us see if they come anywhere near him and his ancient disciples. The first thing we are to look at are his precepts, of which we will mention a few. "Thou shalt love the Lord thy God with all thy heart, with all thy soul, with all thy mind, and with all thy strength. The second is like unto it. Thou shalt love thy neighbor as thyself. On these two precepts hang all the law and the prophets" (Matt. 22:37, 38, 39, 40). "By this shall all men know that they are my disciples, if ye have love one to another" (John 13:35). Our Lord left this special command with his followers, that they should love one another.

Again, John in his Epistles says, "He who loveth God loveth his brother also" (1 John 4:21). "Let us not love in word but in deed" (1 John 3: 18). "Let your love be without dissimulation. See that ye love one another with a pure heart fervently" (1 Peter 1:22). "If any man say, I love God, and hateth his brother, he is a liar" (1 John 4:20). "Whosoever hateth his brother is a murderer, and no murderer hath eternal life abiding in him" (1 John 3:15). The first thing that takes our attention is the saying of Jesus, "Thou shalt love," etc. The first question I would ask my brethren in the ministry, as well as that of the membership: What is love, or its effects? Now, if they who teach are not essentially affected with pure love, the love of God, how can they teach as they ought? Again, the holy teachers of old said, "Now if any man have not the spirit of Christ, he is none of his" (Rom. 8:9). Now, my brethren in the ministry, let me ask you a few sincere questions. Did you ever hear or read of Christ teaching his disciples that they ought to despise one because his skin was different from theirs? Jesus Christ being a Jew, and those of his Apostles certainly were not whites—and did not he who completed the plan of salvation complete it for the whites as well as for the Jews, and others? And were not the whites the most degraded people on the earth at that time? And none were more so, for they sacrificed their children to dumb idols! And did not St. Paul labor more abundantly for building up a Christian nation among you than any of the Apostles? And you know as well as I that you are not indebted to a principle beneath a white skin for your religious services but to a colored one.

What then is the matter now? Is not religion the same now under a colored skin as it ever was? If so, I would ask, why is not a man of color respected? You may say, as many say, we have white men enough. But was this the spirit of Christ and his Apostles? If it had been, there would not have been one white preacher in the world—for Jesus Christ never would have imparted his grace or word to them, for he could forever have withheld it from them. But we find that Jesus Christ and his Apostles never looked at the outward appearances. Jesus in particular looked at the hearts, and his Apostles through him, being discerners of the spirit, looked at their fruit without any regard to the skin, color, or nations; as St. Paul himself speaks, "Where there is neither Greek nor Jew, circumcision nor uncircumcision, Barbarian nor Scythian, bond nor free—but Christ is all, and in all" (Col. 3: 11). If you can find a sprit like Jesus Christ and his Apostles prevailing now in any of the white congregations, I should like to know it. I ask: Is it not the case that everybody that is not white is treated with contempt and counted as barbarians? And I ask if the word of God justifies the white man in so doing. When the prophets prophesied, of whom did they speak? When they spoke of heathens, was it not the whites and others who were counted Gentiles? And I ask if all nations with the exception of the Jews were not counted heathens. And according to the writings of some, it could not mean the Indians, for they are counted Jews. And now I would ask: Why is all this distinction made among these Christian societies? I would ask: What is all this ado about missionary societies, if it be not to Christianize those who are not Christians? And what is it for? To degrade them worse, to bring them into society where they must welter out their days in disgrace merely because their skin is of a different complexion. What folly it is to try to make the state of human society worse than it is. How astonished some may be at this—but let me ask: Is it not so? Let me refer you to the churches only. And, my brethren, is there any agreement? Do brethren and sisters love one another? Do they not rather hate one another? Outward forms and ceremonies, the lusts of the flesh, the lusts of the eye, and pride of life is of more value to many professors than the love of God shed abroad in their hearts, or an attachment to his altar, to his ordinances, or to his children. But you may ask: Who are the children of God? Perhaps you may say, none but white. If so, the word of the Lord is not true.

I will refer you to St. Peter's precepts (Acts 10): "God is no respecter of persons," etc. Now if this is the case, my white brother, what better are you than God? And if no better, why do you, who profess his Gospel and to have his spirit, act so contrary to it? Let me ask why the men of a different skin are so despised. Why are not they educated and placed in your pulpits? I ask if his services well performed are not as good as if a white man performed them. I ask if a marriage or a funeral ceremony or the ordinance of the Lord's house would not be as acceptable in the sight of God as though he was white. And if so, why is it not to you? I ask again: Why is it not as acceptable to have men to exercise their office in one place as well as in another? Perhaps you will say that if we admit you to all of these privileges you will want more. I expect that I can guess what that is—Why, say you, there would be intermarriages. How that would be I am not able to say—and if it should be, it would be nothing strange or new to me; for I can assure you that I know a great many that have intermarried, both of the whites and the Indians—and many are their sons and daughters and people, too, of the first respectability. And I could point to some in the famous city of Boston and elsewhere. You may look now at the disgraceful act in the state law passed by the legislature of Massachusetts, and behold the fifty-pound fine levied upon any clergyman or justice of the peace that dare to encourage the laws of God and nature by a legitimate union in holy wedlock between the Indians and whites. I would ask how this looks to your lawmakers. I would ask if this corresponds with your sayings—that you think as much of the Indians as you do of the whites. I do not wonder that you blush, many of you, while you read; for many have broken the ill-fated laws made by man to hedge up the laws of God and nature. I would ask if they who have made the law have not broken it—but there is no other state in New England that has this law but Massachusetts; and I think, as many of you do not, that you have done yourselves no credit.

But as I am not looking for a wife, having one of the finest cast, as you no doubt would understand while you read her experience and travail of soul in the way to heaven, you will see that it is not my object. And if I had none, I should not want anyone to take my right from me and choose a wife for me; for I think that I or any of my brethren have a right to choose a wife for themselves as well as the whites—and as the whites have taken the liberty to choose my brethren, the Indians, hundreds and thousands of them, as partners in life, I believe the Indians have as much right to choose their partners among the whites if they wish. I would ask you if you can see anything inconsistent in your conduct and talk about the Indians. And if you do, I hope you will try to become more consistent. Now, if the Lord Jesus Christ, who is counted by all to be a Jew—and it is well known that the Jews are a colored people, especially those living in the East, where Christ was born—and if he should appear among us, would he not be shut out of doors by many, very quickly? And by those too who profess religion?

By what you read, you may learn how deep your principles are. I should say they were skin-deep. I should not wonder if some of the most selfish and ignorant would spout a charge of their principles now and then at me. But I would ask: How are you to love your neighbors as yourself? Is it to cheat them? Is it to wrong them in anything? Now, to cheat them out of any of their rights is robbery. And I ask: Can you deny that you are not robbing the Indians daily, and many others? But at last you may think I am what is called a hard and uncharitable man. But not so. I believe there are many who would not hesitate to advocate our cause; and those too who are men of fame and respectability—as well as ladies of honor and virtue. There is a

Webster, and Everett, and a Wirt, and many others who are distinguished characters—besides a host of my fellow citizens, who advocate our cause daily. And how I congratulate such noble spirits—how they are to be prized and valued; for they are well calculated to promote the happiness of mankind. They well know that man was made for society, and not for hissing-stocks and outcasts. And when such a principle as this lies within the hearts of men, how much it is like its God—and how it honors its Maker—and how it imitates the feelings of the Good Samaritan, that had his wounds bound up, who had been among thieves and robbers.

Do not get tired, ye noble-hearted—only think how many poor Indians want their wounds done up daily; the Lord will reward you, and pray you stop not till this tree of distinction shall be leveled to the earth, and the mantle of prejudice torn from every American heart—then shall peace pervade the Union.

Laborers of Boston

Although many contemporaries, as well as later historians, have called the Jacksonian era the Age of the Common Man because of the elimination of property qualifications for white men's right to vote and because of President Jackson's assault on the moneyed interests of the Northeast, it was a time of considerable inequality and exploitation of the lower classes. Many workers, including the Lowell Mill girls (in 1834), began agitating against exploitive employers and sought to improve their working conditions, wages, and hours. In 1835, in Boston, after three strikes had vainly sought to reduce the work day from 13 hours to 10, a group of carpenters, masons, and stonecutters issued a circular in which they once again articulated their position.

What was the employers' reasoning against the 10-hour day? What was the workers' counterargument? What does the circular reveal about class structure in the United States?

Ten-Hour Circular, 1835

. . . In the name of the Carpenters, Masons, and Stone Cutters, [we] do respectfully represent—

That we are now engaged in a cause, which is not only of vital importance to ourselves, our families, and our children, but is equally interesting and equally important to every Mechanic in the United States and the whole world. We are contending

Source: Irving Mark and E. I. Schwaab, *The Faith of Our Fathers* (New York: Alfred A. Knopf, Inc., 1952), 342–343.

for the recognition of the Natural Right to dispose of our own time in such quantities as we deem and believe to be most conducive to our own happiness, and the welfare of all those engaged in Manual Labor.

The work in which we are now engaged is neither more nor less than a contest between Money and Labor: Capital, which can only be made productive by labor, is endeavoring to crush labor the only source of all wealth.

We have been too long subjected to the odious, cruel, unjust, and tyrannical system which compels the operative Mechanic to exhaust his physical and mental powers by excessive toil, until he has no desire but to eat and sleep, and in many cases he has no power to do either from extreme debility.

We contend that no man or body of men, have a right to require of us that we should toil as we have hitherto done under the old system of labor.

We go further. No man or body of men who require such excessive labor can be friends to the country or the Rights of Man. We also say, that we have rights, and we have duties to perform as American Citizens and members of society, which forbid us to dispose of more than Ten Hours for a day's work.

We cannot, we will not, longer be mere slaves to inhuman, insatiable and unpitying avarice. We have taken a firm and decided stand, to obtain the acknowledgment of those rights to enable us to perform those duties to God, our Country and ourselves.

Our opponents have no arguments to adduce against our determination. We have invited them to the contest in a fair and honorable manner, but they have declined. They have used trickery, obloquy and abuse instead of reasoning. We warn all brother Mechanics, especially Carpenters, Masons and Stone Cutters, to beware of advertisements for hands. Be assured in all cases from this time, now, henceforth and forever, that whenever a Carpenter, Mason or Stone Cutter, advertises for a large number of hands as wanted in Boston or any other city or town, that it is a mere trick, to deceive and oppress you. They never guarantee to you one single day's work, and you will, as in all similar cases, get only your labor for your pains. There are men enough now in this city who are skillful, able, and willing to work on an equitable and just method, and the advertisements for hands are only traps to "Catch Gulls." In no instance, in no part of the United States have such calls for hands been designed for any other purpose, than the most unjustifiable and wicked deception.

Beware also of the offers of high wages. We have not asked for an increase of wages, but are willing that demand and supply should govern the price as it does that of all other disposable property. To induce you to assist them to form shackles and fetters for your own limbs and your own minds, they offer you an increase of wages. Will you be deceived by this old and shallow artifice? We believe you will not—we know you will not.

When you understand that we are contending for your rights, for the rights of your families and your children as well as our own, we feel full confidence that you will make no movement to retard the accomplishment of the glorious and holy enterprise, both yours and ours. It is for the rights of humanity we contend. Our cause is the cause of philanthropy. Our opposers resort to the most degrading obloquy to injure us. Not degrading to us, but to the authors of such unmerited opprobrium which they attempt to cast upon us. They tell us "We shall spend all our hours of leisure in Drunkenness and Debauchery if the hours of labor are reduced."

We hurl from us the base, ungenerous, ungrateful, detestable, cruel, malicious slander, with scorn and indignation.

We assert and challenge the world to controvert the position that excessive labor has been the immediate cause of more intemperance than all other causes combined. Physical exhaustion craves and will have excitement of some kind, and the cause of Temperance never will prevail until slavery among Mechanics shall cease from the land.

We are friends to temperance "in all things," but any man who requires of us excessive labor is intemperate; if he is not actuated by ardent spirits, he is controlled by a spirit of inhumanity equally fatal to human happiness.

It is not a long period since some of our opposers made it a rule to furnish a half pint of ardent spirits to each man, every day, for no other purpose than to urge the physical powers to excessive exertion; thank God, those days have passed away, but they will ever remain a foul blot on the pages of History. Now we are told that excessive labor is the only security against intemperance.

To show the utter fallacy of their idiotic reasoning, if reasoning it may be called, we have only to say, they employ us about eight months in the year during the longest and the hottest days, and in short days, hundreds of us remain idle for want of work, for three or four months, when our expenses must of course be the heaviest during winter. When the long days again appear, our guardians set us to work as they say, "to keep us from getting drunk." No fear has ever been expressed by these benevolent employers respecting our morals while we are idle in short days, through their avarice. We would not be too severe on our employers, they are slaves to the Capitalists, as we are to them. "The power behind" their "throne is greater than the throne itself." But we cannot bear to be the servant of servants and slaves to oppression, let the source be where it may. We will be so no longer, for it is rank injustice. Further, they threaten to starve us into submission to their will. Starve us to prevent us from getting drunk! Wonderful Wisdom! Refined Benevolence! Exalted Philanthropy!

The property holders in this city are dependent night and day upon the Mechanics, to man their Fire Engines; good policy might seem to dictate to them the expediency of providing a new set of firemen, before they starve the present ones or drive them to the extremity of leaving their Engine Houses desolate unto them. We are willing to bear our portion of the burthens, and perform our part of the services of social life, if we can be treated as men and not as beasts of burthen. We claim by the blood of our fathers, shed on our battle-fields in the War of the Revolution, the rights of American Freemen, and no earthly power shall resist our righteous claims with impunity. When we hear men, not only Employers, but "highminded" and honorable Merchants and Capitalists, as they are called, who are not only dependent on us for the protection of their property, but for a safe night's rest. When we hear such men say that we shall all become drunkards, and they intend to starve us into submission to their high will, we pity their infatuation and have painful apprehensions for the safety of the social Fabric. But the public mind is with us. The glorious work goes nobly on. Many employers have acceded to our reasonable demands, and in a few days we sincerely hope and believe that the victory over old prejudices and antiquated customs will be triumphantly complete.

Mechanics of Boston—stand firm—Be true to your selves. Now is the time to enroll your names on the scroll of history as the undaunted enemies of oppression, as the enemies of mental, moral and physical degradation, as the friends of the human race.

The God of the Universe has given us time, health and strength. We utterly deny the right of any man to dictate to us how much of it we shall sell. Brethren in the City, Towns and Country, our cause is yours, the cause of Liberty, the cause of God. . . .

Angelina Grimké (1805–1879)
and Sarah Grimké (1792–1873)

Angelina and Sarah Grimké, daughters of a South Carolina slaveholder, disapproved of slavery all their lives. In the 1820s, the sisters moved to Philadelphia, where they became Quakers and eventually prominent abolitionists and feminists. In the 1830s, William Lloyd Garrison published one of Angelina's letters in his newspaper *The Liberator*, and shortly thereafter both sisters began traveling to speak at antislavery meetings. In 1836, Angelina published her first pamphlet, an appeal to Southern women to join the abolition crusade, not only because the institution was evil but also because slave owners were fathering children with their slaves. Slavery, thus, was destroying the sanctity of marriage and driving white women deeper into subjection. This pamphlet caused quite a furor among a population that was horrified that a woman should be so outspoken—especially about such a volatile issue. As both sisters continued to speak publicly and publish impassioned indictments of slavery, they were increasingly attacked, even by other abolitionists, because of their gender. The attacks convinced the sisters that they had to become feminists as well as abolitionists.

In the following excerpts from Angelina Grimké's *Appeal to the Christian Women of the South* and Sarah Grimké's "The Original Equality of Woman," the sisters tackle the popular arguments that made use of the Bible to validate the institution of slavery and the subjugation of women. How effective is their use of the Bible to condemn both the proslavery cause and the gender assumptions of the 1830s? Is slavery primarily a Southern problem? Why should women be at the forefront of abolition? What other arguments does Angelina use to censure slavery?

Appeal to the Christian Women of the South, 1836

RESPECTED FRIENDS,

. . . All that sophistry of argument which has been employed to prove, that although it is sinful to send to Africa to procure men and women as slaves, who have never been in slavery, that still, it is not sinful to keep those in bondage who have come down by inheritance, will be utterly overthrown. We must come back to the good old doctrine of our forefathers who declared to the world, "this self evident truth that *all* men are created equal, and that they have certain *inalienable* rights among which are life, *liberty*, and the pursuit of happiness." It is even a greater absurdity to suppose a man can be legally born a slave under *our free Republican* Government, than under the petty despotisms of barbarian Africa. If then, we have no right to enslave an African, surely we can have none to enslave an American; if it is a self evident truth that *all* men, every where and of every color are born equal, and have an *inalienable right to liberty*, then it is equally true that *no* man can be born a slave, and no man can ever *rightfully* be reduced to *involuntary* bondage and held as a slave, however fair may be the claim of his master or mistress through wills and title-deeds.

But after all, it may be said, our fathers were certainly mistaken, for the Bible sanctions Slavery, and that is the highest authority. Now the Bible is my ultimate appeal on all matters of faith and practice, and it is to *this test* I am anxious to bring the subject at issue between us. Let us then begin with Adam and examine the charter of privileges which was given to him. "Have dominion over the fish of the sea, and over the fowl of the air, and over every living thing that moveth upon the earth." In the eighth Psalm we have a still fuller description of this charter which through Adam was given to all mankind. "Thou madest him to have dominion over the works of thy hands; thou hast put all things under his feet. All sheep and oxen, yea, and the beasts of the field, the fowl of the air, the fish of the sea, and whatsoever passeth through the paths of the seas." And after the flood when this charter of human rights was renewed, we find *no additional* power vested in man. "And the fear of you and the dread of you shall be upon every beast of the earth, and upon all the fishes of the sea, into your hand are they delivered." In this charter, although the different kinds of *irrational* beings are so particularly enumerated, and supreme dominion over *all of them* is granted, yet *man* is *never* vested with this dominion *over his fellow man;* he was never told that any of the human species were put *under his feet;* it was only all *things,* and man, who was created in the image of his Maker, *never* can properly be termed a *thing,* though the laws of Slave States do call him "a chattel personal;" *Man,* then I assert *never* was put *under the feet of man,* by that first charter of human rights which was given by God, to the Fathers of the Antediluvian and Postdiluvian worlds, therefore this doctrine of equality is based on the Bible.

But it may be argued, that in the very chapter of Genesis from which I have last quoted, will be found the curse pronounced upon Canaan, by which his posterity

SOURCE: Angelina E. Grimké, *Appeal to the Christian Women of the South* (New York: New York Anti-Slavery Society, 1836), 4–67 *passim*.

was consigned to servitude under his brothers Shem and Japheth. I know this prophecy was uttered, was most fearfully and wonderfully fulfilled, through the immediate descendants of Canaan, i.e. the Canaanites, and I do not know but that it has been through all the children of Ham, but I do know that prophecy does *not* tell us what *ought to be,* but what actually does take place, ages after it has been delivered, and that if we justify America for enslaving the children of Africa, we must also justify Egypt for reducing the children of Israel to bondage, for the latter was foretold as explicitly as the former. I am well aware that prophecy has often been urged as an excuse for Slavery, but be not deceived, the fulfilment of prophecy will *not cover one sin* in the awful day of account. Hear what our Saviour says on this subject; "it must needs be that offences come, but *woe unto that man through whom they come*"—Witness some fulfilment of this declaration in the tremendous destruction of Jerusalem, occasioned by that most nefarious of all crimes the crucifixion of the Son of God. Did the fact of that event having been foretold, exculpate the Jews from sin in perpetuating it; No—for hear what the Apostle Peter says to them on this subject, "Him being delivered by the determinate counsel and foreknowledge of God, ye have taken, and by *wicked* hands have crucified and slain." Other striking instances might be adduced, but these will suffice. . . .

But I shall be told, God sanctioned Slavery, yea commanded Slavery under the Jewish Dispensation. Let us examine this subject calmly and prayerfully. I admit that a species of *servitude* was permitted to the Jews, but in studying the subject I have been struck with wonder and admiration at perceiving how carefully the servant was guarded from violence, injustice and wrong. I will first inform you how these servants became servants, for I think this a very important part of our subject. From consulting Horne, Calmet, and the Bible, I find there were six different ways by which the Hebrews became servants legally.

1. If reduced to extreme poverty, a Hebrew might sell himself, i.e. his services, for six years, in which case *he* received the purchase money *himself.* Lev. xxv, 39.
2. A father might sell his children as servants, i.e. his *daughters,* in which circumstance it was understood the daughter was to be the wife or daughter-in-law of the man who bought her, and the *father* received the price. In other words, Jewish women were sold as *white women* were in the first settlement of Virginia—as *wives, not* as slaves. Ex. xxi, 7.
3. Insolvent debtors might be delivered to their creditors as servants. 2 Kings iv, 1.
4. Thieves not able to make restitution for their thefts, were sold for the benefit of the injured person. Ex. xxii, 3.
5. They might be born in servitude. Ex. xxi, 4.
6. If a Hebrew had sold himself to a rich Gentile, he might be redeemed by one of his brethren at any time the money was offered; and he who redeemed him, was *not* to take advantage of the favor thus conferred, and rule over him with rigor. Lev. xxv, 47-55.

Before going into an examination of the laws by which these servants were protected, I would just ask whether American slaves have become slaves in any of the ways in which the Hebrews became servants. Did they sell themselves into slavery and receive the purchase money into their own hands? No! Did they become insolvent, and by their own imprudence subject themselves to be sold as slaves? No! Did they steal the property of another, and were they sold to make restitution for their crimes? No! Did their present masters, as an act of kindness, redeem them from some heathen tyrant to whom *they had sold themselves* in the dark hour of adversity? No! Were they born in slavery? No! No! not according to *Jewish Law,* for the servants who were born in servitude among them, were born of parents who had *sold themselves* for six years: Ex. xxi, 4. Were the female slaves of the South sold by their fathers? How shall I answer this question? Thousands and tens of thousands never were, *their* fathers *never* have received the poor compensation of silver or gold for the tears and toils, the suffering, the anguish, and hopeless bondage of *their* daughters. They labor day by day, and year by year, side by side, in the same field, if haply their daughters are permitted to remain on the same plantation with them, instead of being as they often are, separated from their parents and sold into distant states, never again to meet on earth. But do the *fathers of the South ever sell their daughters?* My heart beats, and my hand trembles, as I write the awful affirmative, Yes! The fathers of this Christian land often sell their daughters, *not* as Jewish parents did, to be the wives and daughters-in-law of the man who buys them, but to be the abject slaves of petty tyrants and irresponsible masters. Is it not so, my friends? I leave it to your own candor to corroborate my assertion. Southern slaves then have *not* become slaves in any of the six different ways in which Hebrews became servants, and I hesitate not to say that American masters *cannot* according to *Jewish law* substantiate their claim to the men, women, or children they now hold in bondage. . . .

Where, then, I would ask, is the warrant, the justification, or the palliation of American slavery from Hebrew servitude? How many of the southern slaves would now be in bondage according to the laws of Moses; Not one. You may observe that I have carefully avoided using the term *slavery* when speaking of Jewish servitude; and simply for this reason, that *no such thing* existed among that people; the word translated servant does *not* mean *slave,* it is the same that is applied to Abraham, to Moses, to Elisha and the prophets generally. *Slavery* then *never* existed under the Jewish Dispensation at all, and I cannot but regard it as an aspersion on the character of Him who is "glorious in Holiness" for any one to assert that "*God sanctioned, yea commanded slavery* under the old dispensation." I would fain lift my feeble voice to vindicate Jehovah's character from so foul a slander. If slaveholders are determined to hold slaves as long as they can, let them not dare to say that the God of mercy and of truth *ever* sanctioned such a system of cruelty and wrong. It is blasphemy against Him. . . .

The Ladies Anti-Slavery Society of Boston was called last fall, to a severe trial of their faith and constancy. They were mobbed by "the gentlemen of property and standing," in that city at their anniversary meeting, and their lives were jeoparded by an infuriated crowd; but their conduct on that occasion did credit to our sex, and affords a full assurance that they will *never* abandon the cause of the slave. The pamphlet, Right or Wrong in Boston, issued by them in which a particular account is given of that "mob of broad cloth in broad day," does equal credit to the head and the heart of her who wrote it. I wish my Southern sisters could read it; they would then understand that the women of the North have engaged in this work from a sense of *religious duty,* and that nothing will ever induce them to take their hands from it until it is fully accomplished. They feel no hostility to you, no bitterness or wrath; they rather sympathize in your trials and difficulties; but they well know that the first thing to be done to help you, is to pour in the light of truth on your minds, to urge you to reflect on, and pray over the subject. This is all *they* can do for you, *you* must work out your own deliverance with fear and trembling, and with the direction and blessing of God, *you can do it.* Northern women may labor to produce a correct public opinion at the North, but if Southern women sit down in listless indifference and criminal idleness, public opinion cannot be rectified and purified at the South. It is manifest to every reflecting mind, that slavery must be abolished; the era in which we live, and the light which is overspreading the whole world on this subject, clearly show that the time cannot be distant when it will be done. Now there are only two ways in which it can be effected, by moral power or physical force, and it is for *you* to choose which you prefer. Slavery always has, and always will produce insurrections, wherever it exists, because it is a violation of the natural order of things, and no human power can much longer perpetuate it. The opposers of abolitionists fully believe this; one of them remarked to me not long since, there is no doubt there will be a most terrible overturning at the South in a few years, such cruelty and wrong, must be visited with divine vengeance soon. Abolitionists believe, too, that this must inevitably be the case if you do not repent, and they are not willing to leave you to perish without entreating you, to save yourselves from destruction; well may they say with the apostle, "am I then your enemy because I tell you the truth," and warn you to flee from impending judgments.

But why, my dear friends, have I thus been endeavoring to lead you through the history of more than three thousand years, and to point you to that great cloud of witnesses who have gone before, "from works to rewards?" Have I been seeking to magnify the sufferings, and exalt the character of woman, that she "might have praise of men?" No! no! my object has been to arouse *you*, as the wives and mothers, the daughters and sisters, of the South, to a sense of your duty as *women*, and as Christian women, on that great subject, which has already shaken our country, from the St. Lawrence and the lakes, to the Gulf of Mexico, and from the Mississippi to the shores of the Atlantic; *and will continue mightily to shake it*, until the polluted temple of slavery fall and crumble into ruin. I would say unto each one of you, "what meanest thou, O sleeper! arise and call upon thy God, if so be that God will think upon us that we perish not." Perceive you not that dark cloud of vengeance which hangs over our boasting Republic? Saw you not the lightnings of Heaven's wrath, in the flame which leaped from the Indian's torch to the roof of yonder dwelling, and lighted with its horrid glare the darkness of midnight? Heard you not the thunders of Divine anger, as the distant roar of the cannon came rolling onward, from the Texian country, where Protestant American Rebels are fighting with Mexican Republicans—for what? For the reestablishment of *slavery*; yes! of American slavery in the bosom of a Catholic Republic, where that system of robbery, violence, and wrong, had been legally abolished for twelve years. Yes! citizens of the United States, after plundering Mexico of her land, are now engaged in deadly conflict, for the privilege of fastening chains, and collars, and manacles—upon whom? upon the subjects of some foreign prince? No! upon native born American Republican citizens, although the fathers of these very men declared to the whole world, while struggling to free themselves from the three penny taxes of an English king, that they believed it to be a *self-evident* truth that *all men* were created equal, and had an *unalienable right to liberty*. . . .

The *women of the South can overthrow* this horrible system of oppression and cruelty, licentiousness and wrong. Such appeals to your legislatures would be irresistible, for there is something in the heart of man which *will bend under moral suasion.* There is a swift witness for truth in his bosom, which *will respond to truth* when it is uttered with calmness and dignity. If you could obtain but six signatures to such a petition in only one state, I would say, send up that petition, and be not in the least discouraged by the scoffs and jeers of the heartless, or the resolution of the house to lay it on the table. It will be a great thing if the subject can be introduced into your legislatures in any way, even by *women,* and *they* will be the most likely to introduce it there in the best possible manner, as a matter of *morals* and *religion,* not of expediency or politics. You may petition, too, the different ecclesiastical bodies of the slave states. Slavery must be attacked with the whole power of truth and the sword of the spirit. You must take it up on *Christian* ground, and fight against it with Christian weapons, whilst your feet are shod with the preparation of the gospel of peace. And *you are now* loudly called upon by the cries of the widow and the orphan, to arise and gird yourselves for this great moral conflict, with the whole armour of righteousness upon the right hand and on the left. . . .

But I will now say a few words on the subject of Abolitionism. Doubtless you have all heard Anti-Slavery societies denounced as insurrectionary and mischievious, fanatical and dangerous. It has been said they publish the most abominable untruths, and that they are endeavoring to excite rebellions at the South. Have you believed these reports, my friends? Have *you* also been deceived by these false assertions? Listen to me, then, whilst I endeavor to wipe from the fair character of Abolitionism such unfounded accusations. You know that *I* am a Southerner; you know that my dearest relatives are now in a slave State. Can you for a moment believe I would prove so recreant to the feelings of a daughter and a sister, as to join a society which was seeking to overthrow slavery by falsehood, bloodshed, and murder? I appeal to you who have known and loved me in days that are passed, can *you* believe it? No! my friends. As a Carolinian, I was peculiarly jealous of any movements on this subject; and before I would join an Anti-Slavery Society, I took the precaution of becoming acquainted with some of the leading Abolitionists, of reading their publications and attending their meetings, at which I heard addresses both from colored and white men; and it was not until I was fully convinced that their principles were *entirely pacific,* and their efforts *only moral,* that I gave my name as a member to the Female Anti-Slavery Society of Philadelphia. Since that time, I have regularly taken the Liberator, and read many Anti-Slavery pamphlets and papers and books, and can assure you I *never* have seen a single insurrectionary paragraph, and never read any account of cruelty which I could not believe. Southerners may deny the truth of these accounts, but why do they not *prove* them to be false. Their violent expressions of horror at such accounts being believed, *may* deceive some, but they cannot deceive *me,* for I lived too long in the midst of slavery, not to know what slavery is. When *I* speak of this system "I speak that I do know," and I am not at all afraid to assert, that Anti-Slavery publications have *not* overdrawn the monstrous features of slavery at all. And many a Southerner *knows* this as well as I do. A lady in North

Carolina remarked to a friend of mine, about eighteen months since, "Northerners know nothing at all about slavery; they think it is perpetual bondage only; but of the *depth of degradation* that word involves, they have no conception; if they had, *they would never cease* their efforts until so *horrible* a system was overthrown." She did not know how faithfully some Northern men and Northern women had studied this subject; how diligently they had searched out the cause of "him who had none to help him," and how fearlessly they had told the story of the negro's wrongs. Yes, Northerners know *every* thing about slavery now. This monster of iniquity has been unveiled to the world, her frightful features unmasked, and soon, very soon will she be regarded with no more complacency by the American republic than is the idol of Juggernaut, rolling its bloody wheels over the crushed bodies of its prostrate victims.

But you will probably ask, if Anti-Slavery societies are not insurrectionary, who do Northerners tell us they are? Why, I would ask you in return, did Northern senators and Northern representatives give their votes, at the last sitting of congress, to the admission of Arkansas Territory as a state? Take those men, one by one, and ask them in their parlours, do you *approve of slavery*? Ask them on *Northern* ground, where they will speak the truth, and I doubt not *every man* of them will tell you, *no!* Why then, I ask, did *they* give their votes to enlarge the mouth of that grave which has already destroyed its tens of thousands? All our enemies tell *us* they are as much anti-slavery as we are. Yes, my friends, thousands who are helping you to bind the fetters of slavery on the negro, despise you in their hearts for doing it; they rejoice that such an institution has not been entailed upon them. Why then, I would ask, do *they* lend you their help? I will tell you, "they love *the praise of men more* than the praise of God." The Abolition cause has not yet become so popular as to induce them to believe, that by advocating it in congress, they shall sit still more securely in their seats there, and like the *chief rulers* of the days of our Saviour, though *many* believed on him, yet they did *not* confess him, lest they should be *put out of the synagogue;* John xii, 42, 43. Or perhaps like Pilate, thinking they could prevail nothing, and fearing a tumult, they determined to release Barabbas and surrender the just man, the poor innocent slave to be stripped of his rights and scourged. In vain will such men try to wash their hands, and say, with the Roman governor, "I am innocent of the blood of this just person." Northern American statesmen are no more innocent of the crime of slavery, than Pilate was of the murder of Jesus, or Saul of that of Stephen. These are high charges, but I appeal to *their hearts;* I appeal to public opinion ten years from now. Slavery then is a national sin.

But you will say, a great many other Northerners tell us so, who can have no political motives. The interests of the North, you must know, my friends, are very closely combined with those of the South. The Northern merchants and manufacturers are making *their* fortunes out of the *produce of slave labor;* the grocer is selling your rice and sugar; how then can these men bear a testimony against slavery without condemning themselves? But there is another reason, the North is most dreadfully afraid of Amalgamation. She is alarmed at the very idea of a thing so monstrous, as she thinks. And lest this consequence *might* flow from emancipation, she is determined to resist all efforts at emancipation without expatriation. It is not because *she approves of slavery,* or believes it to be "corner stone of our republic," for she is as much *anti-slavery* as we are; but amalgamation is too horrible to think of. Now I would ask *you,* is it right, is it generous, to refuse the colored people in this country the advantages of education and the privilege, or rather the *right,* to follow honest trades and callings merely because they are colored? The same prejudice exists here against our colored brethren that existed against the Gentiles in Judea. Great numbers cannot bear the idea of equality, and fearing lest, if they had the same advantages we enjoy, they would become as intelligent, as moral, as religious, and as respectable and wealthy, they are determined to keep them as low as they possibly can. Is this doing as they would be done by? Is this loving their neighbor as *themselves*? Oh! that *such* opposers of Abolitionism would put their souls in the stead of the free colored man's and obey the apostolic injunction, to "remember them that are in bonds *as bound with them*." I will leave you to judge whether the fear of amalgamation ought to induce men to oppose anti-slavery efforts, when *they* believe *slavery* to be *sinful.* Prejudice against color, is the most powerful enemy we have to fight with at the North.

You need not be surprised, then, at all, at what is said *against* Abolitionists by the North, for they are wielding a two-edged sword, which even here, cuts through the *cords of caste,* on the one side and the *bonds of interest* on the other. They are only sharing the fate of other reformers, abused and reviled whilst they are in the minority; but they are neither angry nor discouraged by the invective which has been heaped upon them by slaveholders at the South and their apologists at the North. . . .

There is nothing to fear from immediate Emancipation, but *every thing* from the consequences of slavery. . . .

"The Original Equality of Woman," 1837

LETTER TO MARY S. PARKER, PRESIDENT OF THE BOSTON FEMALE ANTI-SLAVERY SOCIETY

Amesbury, 7th Mo., 11th, 1837

My Dear Friend,

In attempting to comply with thy request to give my views on the Province of Woman, I feel that I am venturing on nearly untrodden ground, and that I shall advance arguments in opposition to a corrupt public opinion, and to the perverted interpretation of Holy Writ, which has so universally obtained. But I am in search of truth; and no obstacle shall prevent my prosecuting that search, because I believe the welfare of the world will be materially advanced by every new discovery we make of the designs of Jehovah in the creation of woman. It is impossible that we can answer the purpose of our being, unless we understand that purpose. It is impossible that we should fulfill our duties, unless we comprehend them or live up to our privileges, unless we know what they are.

SOURCE: Sarah Grimké, *Letters on the Equality of the Sexes and the Condition of Woman, Addressed to Mary S. Parker, President of the Boston Female Anti-Slavery Society,* 1838; Larry Ceplair, ed., *The Public Years of Sarah and Angelina Grimké: Selected Writings 1835–1839* (New York: Columbia University Press, 1989), 205–207.

In examining this important subject, I shall depend solely on the bible to desig-nate the sphere of woman, because I believe almost every thing that has been writ-ten on this subject, has been the result of a misconception of the simple truths revealed in the Scriptures, in consequence of the false translation of many passages of Holy Writ. My mind is entirely delivered from the superstitious reverence which is attached to the English version of the Bible. King James's translators certainly were not inspired. I therefore claim the original as my standard, *believing that to have been inspired,* and I also claim to judge for myself what is the meaning of the inspired writ-ers, because I believe it to be the solemn duty of every individual to search the Scrip-tures for themselves, with the aid of the Holy Spirit, and not be governed by the views of any man, or set of men.

We must first view woman at the period of her creation. "And God said, Let us make man in our own image, after our likeness; and let them have dominion over the fish of the sea, and over the fowl of the air, and over the cattle, and over all the earth. So God created man in his own image, in the image of God created he him, male and female, created he them." [Gen. 1:26-27]. In all this sublime description of the creation of man, (which is a generic term including man and woman), there is not one particle of difference intimated as existing between them. They were both made in the image of God; dominion was given to both over every other creature, but not over each other. Created in perfect equality, they were expected to exercise the vicegerence intrusted to them by their Maker, in harmony and love.

Let us pass on now to the recapitulation of the creation of man—"The Lord God formed man of the dust of the ground, and breathed into his nostrils the breath of life; and man became a living soul. And the Lord God said, it is not good that man should be alone, I will make him an help meet for him" [Gen. 2:7-18]. All creation swarmed with animated beings capable of natural affection, as we know they still are; it was not, therefore, merely to give man a creature susceptible of lov-ing, obeying, and looking up to him, for all that the animals could do and did do. It was to give him a companion, *in all respects his equal;* one who was like himself a *free agent,* gifted with intellect and endowed with immortality; not a partaker merely of his animal gratifications, but able to enter into all his feelings as a moral and respon-sible being. If this had not been the case, how could she have been an help meet for him? I understand this as applying not only to the parties entering into the marriage contract, but to all men and women, because I believe God designed woman to be an help meet for man in every good and perfect work. She was a part of himself, as if Jehovah designed to make the oneness and identity of man and woman perfect and complete; and when the glorious work of their creation was finished, "the morning stars stand together, and all the sons of God shouted for joy" [Job 38:7].

This blissful condition was not long enjoyed by our first parents. Eve, it would seem from the history, was wandering alone amid the bowers of Paradise, when the serpent met with her. From her reply to Satan, it is evident that the command not to eat "of the tree that is in the midst of the garden," was given to both, although the term man was used when the prohibition was issued by God. "And the woman said unto the serpent, WE may eat of the fruit of the trees of the garden, but of the fruit of the tree which is in the midst of the garden, God hath said, YE shall not eat of it, neither shall YE touch it, lest YE die" [Gen. 3:3]. Here the woman was exposed to temptation from a being with whom she was unacquainted. She had been accustomed to associate with her believed partner, and to hold communion with God and with angels; but of satanic intelligence, she was in all probability entirely ignorant. Through the subtlety of the serpent, she was beguiled. And "when she saw that the tree was good for food, and that it was pleasant to the eyes, and a tree to be desired to make one wise, she took the fruit thereof and did eat" [Gen. 3:6].

We next find Adam involved in the same sin, not through the instrumentality of a supernatural agent, but through that of his equal, a being whom he must have known was liable to transgress the divine command, because he must have felt that he was himself a free agent, and that he was restrained from disobedience only by the exercise of faith and love towards his Creator. Had Adam tenderly reproved his wife, and endeavored to lead her to repentance instead of sharing in her guilt, I should be much more ready to accord to man that superiority which he claims; but as the facts stand disclosed by the sacred historian, it appears to me that to say the least, there was as much weakness exhibited by Adam as by Eve. They both fell from innocence, and consequently from happiness, *but not from equality.*

Let us next examine the conduct of this fallen pair, when Jehovah interrogated them respecting their fault. they both frankly confessed their guilt. "The man said, the woman whom thou gavest to be with me, she gave me of the tree and I did eat. And the woman said, the serpent beguiled me and I did eat." [Gen. 3:12]. And the Lord God said unto the woman, "Thou wilt be subject unto thy husband, he will rule over thee" [Gen 3:16]. That this did not allude to the subjection of woman to man is manifest, because the same mode of expression is used in speaking to Cain of Abel [Gen. 4:10-12]. The truth is that the curse, as it is termed, which was pronounced by Jehovah upon woman, is a simple prophecy. The Hebrew, like the French language, uses the same word to express shall and will. Our translators having been accustomed to exercise lordship over their wives, and seeing only through the medium of a perverted judgment, very naturally, though I think not very learnedly or very kindly, translated it *shall* instead of *will*, and thus converted a prediction to Eve into a command to Adam; for observe, it is addressed to the woman and not to the man. The consequence of the fall was an immediate struggle for dominion, and Jehovah foretold which would gain the ascendancy; but as he created them in his image, as that image manifestly was not lost by the fall, because it is urged in Gen. 9:6, as an argument why the life of man should not be taken by his fellow man, there is no reason to suppose that sin produced any distinction between them as moral, intellectual and responsible beings. Man might just as well have endeavored by hard labor to fulfil the prophecy, thorns and thistles will the earth bring forth to thee, as to pretend to accomplish the other, "he will rule over thee," by asserting dominion over his wife.

Authority usurped from God, not given.
He gave him only over beast, flesh, and fowl,
Dominion absolute: that right he holds
By God's donation: but man o'er woman
He made not Lord, such title to himself
Reserving, human left from human free.

Here then I plant myself. God created us equal;—he created us free agents;—he is our Lawgiver, our King, and our Judge, and to him alone is woman bound to be in subjection, and to him alone is she accountable for the use of those talents with which her Heavenly Father has entrusted her. One is her Master even Christ.

Thine for the oppressed in the bonds of womanhood,

Sarah M. Grimké

Wendell Phillips (1811–1884)

Many people in the United States were stunned when, in 1837, abolitionist newspaper editor Elijah P. Lovejoy was murdered by a proslavery mob in Alton, Illinois. That a white man had been killed because of his opposition to slavery caused a lively debate in many Northern states. At a meeting in Faneuil Hall, Boston, several people gave speeches about Lovejoy's murder. Massachusetts Attorney General James Austin declared that Lovejoy deserved exactly what he got. When Austin finished, an unknown young man, Wendell Phillips, rose to his feet and passionately condemned Austin's view. The speech launched Phillips's career as one of the leading abolitionists in the nation.

Why does Phillips take exception to Austin's comparison of the mob that killed Lovejoy with the patriots of Boston who resisted the British in the 1770s? Why is Lovejoy's cause superior to that of the patriots?

On the Murder of Lovejoy, December 8, 1837

. . . A comparison has been drawn between the events of the Revolution and the tragedy at Alton. We have heard it asserted here, in Faneuil Hall, that Great Britain had a right to tax the Colonies, and we have heard the mob at Alton, the drunken murderers of Lovejoy, compared to those patriot fathers who threw the tea overboard! [*Great applause.*] Fellow-citizens, is this Faneuil Hall doctrine? [*"No, no."*] The mob at Alton were met to wrest from a citizen his just rights,—met to resist the laws. We have been told that our fathers did the same; and the glorious mantle of Revolutionary precedent has been thrown over the mobs of our day.

To make out their title to such defence, the gentleman says that the British Parliament had a *right* to tax these Colonies. It is manifest that, without this, his parallel falls

---

SOURCE: Wendell Phillips, *Speeches, Lectures, and Letters* (Boston: James Redpath, 1863), 1–10.

to the ground; for Lovejoy had stationed himself within constitutional bulwarks. He was not only defending the freedom of the press, but he was under his own roof, in arms with the sanction of the civil authority. The men who assailed him went against and over the laws. The *mob,* as the gentleman terms it,—mob, forsooth! certainly we sons of the tea-spillers are a marvellously patient generation!—the "orderly mob" which assembled in the Old South [Church] to destroy the tea were met to resist, not the laws, but illegal exactions.

Shame on the American who calls the tea-tax and stamp-act *laws!* Our fathers resisted, not the King's prerogative, but the King's usurpation. To find any other account, you must read our Revolutionary history upside down. Our State archives are loaded with arguments of John Adams to prove the taxes laid by the British Parliament unconstitutional,—beyond its power. It was not till this was made out that the men of New England rushed to arms. The arguments of the Council Chamber and the House of Representatives preceded and sanctioned the contest. To draw the conduct of our ancestors into a precedent for mobs, for a right to resist laws we ourselves have enacted, is an insult to their memory. The difference between the excitements of those days and our own which the gentleman in kindness to the latter has overlooked, is simply this: the men of that day went for the right, as secured by the laws. They were the people rising to sustain the laws and constitution of the Province. The rioters of our day go for their own wills, right or wrong. . . .

I must find some fault with the statement which has been made of the events at Alton. It has been asked why Lovejoy and his friends did not appeal to the executive,— trust their defence to the police of the city. It has been hinted that, from hasty and ill-judged excitement, the men within the building provoked a quarrel, and that he fell in the course of it, one mob resisting another.

Recollect, Sir, that they did act with the approbation and sanction of the Mayor. In strict truth, there was no executive to appeal to for protection. The Mayor acknowledged that he could not protect them. They asked him if it was lawful for them to defend themselves. He told them it was, and sanctioned their assembling in arms to do so. They were not, then, a mob; they were not merely citizens defending their own property; they were in some sense the *posse comitatus,* adopted for the occasion into the police of the city, acting under the order of a magistrate. It was civil authority resisting lawless violence.

Where, then, was the imprudence? Is the doctrine to be sustained here that it is *imprudent* for men to aid magistrates in executing the laws?

Men are continually asking each other, Had Lovejoy a right to resist? Sir, I protest against the question, instead of answering it. Lovejoy did not resist, in the sense they mean. He did not throw himself back on the natural right of self-defence. He did not cry anarchy, and let slip the dogs of civil war, careless of the horrors which would follow.

Sir, as I understand this affair, it was not an individual protecting his property; it was not one body of armed men resisting another, and making the streets of a peaceful city run blood with their contentions. It did not bring back the scenes in some old Italian cities, where family met family, and faction met faction, and mutually trampled the laws under foot.

No; the men in that house were regularly *enrolled,* under the sanction of the Mayor. There being no militia in Alton, about seventy men were enrolled with the approbation of the Mayor. These relieved each other every other night. About thirty men were in arms on the night of the sixth, when the press was landed. The next evening, it was not thought necessary to summon more than half that number; among these was Lovejoy. It was, therefore, you perceive, Sir, the police of the city resisting rioters,—civil government breasting itself to the shock of lawless men.

Here is no question about the right of self-defence. It is in fact simply this: Has the civil magistrate a *right* to put down a riot?

Some persons seem to imagine that anarchy existed at Alton from the commencement of these disputes. Not at all. "No one of us," says an eyewitness and a comrade of Lovejoy, "has taken up arms during these disturbances but at the command of the Mayor."

Anarchy did not settle down on that devoted city till Lovejoy breathed his last. Till then the law, represented in his person, sustained itself against its foes. When he fell, civil authority was trampled under foot. He had "planted himself on his constitutional rights,"—appealed to the laws,—claimed the protection of the civil authority,—taken refuge under "the broad shield of the Constitution. When through that he was pierced and fell, he fell but one sufferer in a common catastrophe." He took refuge under the banner of liberty,—amid its folds; and when he fell, its glorious stars and stripes, the emblem of free institutions, around which cluster so many heart-stirring memories, were blotted out in the martyr's blood.

It has been stated, perhaps inadvertently, that Lovejoy or his comrades fired first. This is denied by those who have the best means of knowing. Guns were first fired by the mob. After being twice fired on, those within the building consulted together and deliberately returned the fire.

But suppose they did fire first. They had a right so to do; not only the right which every citizen has to defend himself, but the further right which every civil officer has to resist violence. Even if Lovejoy fired the first gun, it would not lessen his claim to our sympathy, or destroy his title to be considered a martyr in defence of a free press.

The question now is, Did he act within the Constitution and the laws? The men who fell in State Street on the 5th of March 1770, did more than Lovejoy is charged with. They were the *first* assailants. Upon some slight quarrel they pelted the troops with every missile within reach. Did this bate one jot of the eulogy with which Hancock and Warren hallowed their memory, hailing them as the first martyrs in the cause of American liberty?

If, Sir, I had adopted what are called Peace principles, I might lament the circumstances of this case. But all you who believe, as I do, in the right and duty of magistrates to execute the laws, join with me and brand as base hypocrisy the conduct of those who assemble year after year on the 4th of July, to fight over the battles of the Revolution and yet "damn with faint praise," or load with obloquy, the memory of this man, who shed his blood in defence of life, liberty, property, and the freedom of the press!

Throughout that terrible night I find nothing to regret but this, that within the limits of our country, civil authority should have been so prostrated as to oblige a citizen to arm in his own defence, and to arm in vain.

The gentleman says Lovejoy was presumptuous and imprudent,—he "died as a fool dieth." And a reverend clergyman of the city tells us that no citizen has a right to publish opinions disagreeable to the community! If any mob follows such publication, on *him* rests its guilt! He must wait, forsooth, till the people come up to it and agree with him!

This libel on liberty goes on to say that the want of right to speak as we think is an evil inseparable from republican institutions! If this be, what are they worth? Welcome the despotism of the Sultan, where one knows what he may publish and what he may not, rather than the tyranny of this many-headed monster, the mob, where we know not what we may do or say, till some fellow-citizen has tried it, and paid for the lesson with his life.

This clerical absurdity chooses as a check for the abuses of the press, not the *law,* but the dread of a mob. By so doing, it deprives not only the individual and the minority of their rights, but the majority also, since the expression of *their* opinion may sometimes provoke disturbance from the minority. A few men may make a mob as well as many. The majority, then, have no right, as Christian men, to utter their sentiments, if by any possibility it may lead to a mob! Shades of Hugh Peters and John Cotton, save us from such pulpits!

Imprudent to defend the liberty of the press! Why? Because the defence was unsuccessful? Does success gild crime into patriotism, and the want of it change heroic self-devotion to imprudence? . . .

Presumptuous to assert the freedom of the press on American ground! Is the assertion of such freedom before the age? So much before the age as to leave one no right to make it because it displeases the community? Who invents this libel on his country? It is this very thing which entitles Lovejoy to greater praise. The disputed right which provoked the Revolution— taxation without representation—is far beneath that for which he died. [Here there was a strong and general expression of disapprobation.]

One word, gentlemen. As much as *thought* is better than money, so much is the cause in which Lovejoy died nobler than a mere question of taxes. James Otis thundered in this Hall when the King did but touch his *pocket.* Imagine, if you can, his indignant eloquence, had England offered to put a gag upon his lips. [Great applause.]

The question that stirred the Revolution touched our civil interests. *This* concerns us not only as citizens, but as immortal beings. Wrapped up in its fate, saved or lost with it, are not only the voice of the statesman, but the instructions of the pulpit, and the progress of our faith. . . .

Mr. Chairman, from the bottom of my heart I thank that brave little band at Alton for resisting. We must remember that Lovejoy had fled from city to city,—suffered the destruction of three presses patiently. At length he took counsel with friends, men of character, of tried integrity, of wide views, of Christian principle. They thought the crisis had come: it was full time to assert the laws. They saw around them, not a community like our own, of fixed habits, of character moulded and settled, but one "in the gristle, not yet hardened into the bone of manhood." The people there, children of our older States, seem to have forgotten the blood-tried principles of their fathers the moment they lost sight of our New England hills. Something was to be done to show them the priceless value of the freedom of the press, to bring back and set right their wandering and confused ideas.

He and his advisers looked out on a community, staggering like a drunken man, indifferent to their rights and confused in their feelings. Deaf to argument, haply they might be stunned into sobriety. They saw that of which we cannot judge, the *necessity* of resistance. Insulted law called for it. Public opinion, fast hastening on the downward course, must be arrested.

Does not the event show they judged rightly? Absorbed in a thousand trifles, how has the nation all at once come to a stand? Men begin, as in 1776 and 1640, to discuss principles, to weigh characters, to find out where they are. Haply we may awake before we are borne over the precipice. . . .

Ralph Waldo Emerson (1803–1882)

Transcendentalists Ralph Waldo Emerson, Henry David Thoreau, and Margaret Fuller had an enormous impact on thinking in the first half of the nineteenth century. Transcendental philosophy grew out of the romantic movement, which, in rejecting the Enlightenment's veneration of reason, had emphasized the ineffable beauty of nature and spirit. Going a step further, transcendentalists urged individuals to transcend the confines of book learning and formal knowledge and cultivate instead the innate ability of each person to know beauty and truth. Each of us must become aware of our original connection to the universe, to nature, to life. We must learn who we are and become conscious that there is a spark of divinity within each individual. Ours souls are part of the "Oversoul." And in this sense, each individual is interconnected with all of nature. But this does not mean that we are to be concerned only with ourselves. We must also be engaged in the world, for we are a part of the world. Since we are all part of the godhead, there is no fundamental difference between humans. Masculine and feminine principles exist in each individual, and it is through the union of the masculine and the feminine that humankind can discover the path to a truly new utopian humanity. The soul, the spirit, and the mind, therefore, favor no gender, no class, and no race. It is not surprising that transcendentalists were among the most outspoken advocates of abolitionism and feminism.

The title of Emerson's "Essay on Self-Reliance" is self-explanatory. Each person, according to Emerson, in order to live a full, meaningful life, must not conform to society but instead cultivate self-reliance. How does self-reliance lead to a deeper engagement with the world at large? What does Emerson mean when he writes, "A foolish consistency is the hobgoblin of little minds"? The speech Emerson gave at Concord, Massachusetts (the beginning of which is excerpted here), in May 1851 to oppose the Fugitive Slave Law makes it quite clear that his emphasis on self-reliance does not preclude commitment to political action. In what way does Emerson echo Thoreau's argument in "Resistance to Civil Government"?

"Self-Reliance," 1841

. . . To believe your own thought, to believe that what is true for you in your private heart is true for all men,—that is genius. . . . A man should learn to detect and watch that gleam of light which flashes across his mind from within, more than the lustre of the firmament of bards and sages. Yet he dismisses without notice his thought, because it is his. In every work of genius we recognize our own rejected thoughts: they come back to us with a certain alienated majesty. Great works of art have no more affecting lesson for us than this. They teach us to abide by our spontaneous impression with good-humored inflexibility then most when the whole cry of voices is on the other side. Else, to-morrow a stranger will say with masterly good sense precisely what we have thought and felt all the time, and we shall be forced to take with shame our own opinion from another.

There is a time in every man's education when he arrives at the conviction that envy is ignorance; that imitation is suicide; that he must take himself for better, for worse, as his portion; that though the wide universe is full of good, no kernel of nourishing corn can come to him but through his toil bestowed on that plot of ground which is given to him to till. The power which resides in him is new in nature, and none but he knows what that is which he can do, nor does he know until he has tried. . . .

Trust thyself: every heart vibrates to that iron string. Accept the place the divine providence has found for you, the society of your contemporaries, the connection of events. Great men have always done so, and confided themselves childlike to the genius of their age, betraying their perception that the absolutely trustworthy was seated at their heart, working through their hands, predominating in all their being. And we are now men, and must accept in the highest mind the same transcendent destiny; and not minors and invalids in a protected corner, not cowards fleeing before a revolution, but guides, redeemers, and benefactors, obeying the Almighty effort, and advancing on Chaos and the Dark.

. . . Society everywhere is in conspiracy against the manhood of every one of its members. Society is a joint-stock company, in which the members agree, for the better securing of his bread to each shareholder, to surrender the liberty and culture of the eater. The virtue in most request is conformity. Self-reliance is its aversion. It loves not realities and creators, but names and customs.

SOURCE: Ralph Waldo Emerson, *The Essay on Self-Reliance* (East Aurora, NY: Roycroft Press, 1908), 1–59, passim.

Whoso would be a man must be a nonconformist. He who would gather immortal palms must not be hindered by the name of goodness, but must explore if it be goodness.

Nothing is at last sacred but the integrity of your own mind. Absolve you to yourself, and you shall have the suffrage of the world. I remember an answer which when quite young I was prompted to make to a valued adviser, who was wont to importune me with the dear old doctrines of the church. On my saying, What have I to do with the sacredness of traditions, if I live wholly from within? my friend suggested,—"But these impulses may be from below, not from above." I replied, "They do not seem to me to be such; but if I am the Devil's child, I will live then from the Devil." No law can be sacred to me but that of my nature. Good and bad are but names very readily transferable to that or this; the only right is what is after my constitution, the only wrong what is against it. A man is to carry himself in the presence of all opposition, as if every thing were titular and ephemeral but he. I am ashamed to think how easily we capitulate to badges and names, to large societies and dead institutions. Every decent and well-spoken individual affects and sways me more than is right. I ought to go upright and vital, and speak the rude truth in all ways. . . .

Virtues are, in the popular estimate, rather the exception than the rule. There is the man and his virtues. Men do what is called a good action, as some piece of courage or charity, much as they would pay a fine in expiation of daily non-appearance on parade. Their works are done as an apology or extenuation of their living in the world,—as invalids and the insane pay a high board. Their virtues are penances. I do not wish to expiate, but to live. My life is for itself and not for a spectacle. I much prefer that it should be of a lower strain, so it be genuine and equal, than that it should be glittering and unsteady. I wish it to be sound and sweet, and not to need diet and bleeding. I ask primary evidence that you are a man, and refuse this appeal from the man to his actions. I know that for myself it makes no difference whether I do or forbear those actions which are reckoned excellent. I cannot consent to pay for a privilege where I have intrinsic right. Few and mean as my gifts may be, I actually am, and do not need for my own assurance or the assurance of my fellows any secondary testimony.

What I must do is all that concerns me, not what the people think. This rule, equally arduous in actual and in intellectual life, may serve for the whole distinction between greatness and meanness. It is the harder, because you will always find those who think they know what is your duty better than you know it. It is easy in the world to live after the world's opinion; it is easy in solitude to live after our own; but the great man is he who in the midst of the crowd keeps with perfect sweetness the independence of solitude.

The objection to conforming to usages that have become dead to you is, that it scatters your force. It loses your time and blurs the impression of your character. If you maintain a dead church, contribute to a dead Bible-society, vote with a great party either for the government or against it, spread your table like base housekeepers,—under all these screens I have difficulty to detect the precise man you are. And, of course, so much force is withdrawn from your proper life. But do your work, and I shall know you. Do your work, and you shall reinforce yourself. A man must consider what a blindman's-buff is this game of conformity. If I know your sect, I anticipate your argument. I hear a preacher announce for his text and topic the expediency of one of the institutions of his church. Do I not know beforehand that not possibly can he say a new and spontaneous word? Do I not know that, with all this ostentation of examining the grounds of the institution, he will do no such thing? Do I not know that he is pledged to himself not to look but at one side,—the permitted side, not as a man, but as a parish minister? He is a retained attorney, and these airs of the bench are the emptiest affectation. Well, most men have bound their eyes with one or another handkerchief, and attached themselves to some one of these communities of opinion. This conformity makes them not false in a few particulars, authors of a few lies, but false in all particulars. Their every truth is not quite true. Their two is not the real two, their four not the real four; so that every word they say chagrins us, and we know not where to begin to set them right. Meantime nature is not slow to equip us in the prison-uniform of the party to which we adhere. We come to wear one cut of face and figure, and acquire by degrees the gentlest asinine expression. There is a mortifying experience in particular, which does not fail to wreak itself also in the general history; I mean "the foolish face of praise," the forced smile which we put on in company where we do not feel at ease in answer to conversation which does not interest us. The muscles, not spontaneously moved, but moved by a low usurping wilfulness, grow tight about the outline of the face with the most disagreeable sensation.

For nonconformity the world whips you with its displeasure. And therefore a man must know how to estimate a sour face. The by-standers look askance on him in the public street or in the friend's parlour. If this aversation had its origin in contempt and resistance like his own, he might well go home with a sad countenance; but the sour faces of the multitude, like their sweet faces, have no deep cause, but are put on and off as the wind blows and a newspaper directs. Yet is the discontent of the multitude more formidable than that of the senate and the college. It is easy enough for a firm man who knows the world to brook the rage of the cultivated classes. Their rage is decorous and prudent, for they are timid as being very vulnerable themselves. But when to their feminine rage the indignation of the people is added, when the ignorant and the poor are aroused, when the unintelligent brute force that lies at the bottom of society is made to growl and mow, it needs the habit of magnanimity and religion to treat it godlike as a trifle of no concernment.

The other terror that scares us from self-trust is our consistency; a reverence for our past act or word, because the eyes of others have no other data for computing our orbit than our past acts, and we are loath to disappoint them.

But why should you keep your head over your shoulder? Why drag about this corpse of your memory, lest you contradict somewhat you have stated in this or that public place? Suppose you should contradict yourself; what then? It seems to be a rule of wisdom never to rely on your memory alone, scarcely even in acts of pure memory, but to bring the past for judgment into the thousand-eyed present, and live ever in a new day. In your metaphysics you have denied personality to the Deity: yet when the devout motions of the soul come, yield to them heart and life, though they should clothe God with shape and color. Leave your theory, as Joseph his coat in the hand of the harlot, and flee.

A foolish consistency is the hobgoblin of little minds, adored by little statesmen and philosophers and divines. With consistency a great soul has simply nothing to do. He may as well concern himself with his shadow on the wall. Speak what you think now in hard words, and to-morrow speak what to-morrow thinks in hard words again, though it contradict every thing you said to-day.—'Ah, so you shall be sure to be misunderstood.'—Is it so bad, then, to be misunderstood? Pythagoras was misunderstood, and Socrates, and Jesus, and Luther, and Copernicus, and Galileo, and Newton, and every pure and wise spirit that ever took flesh. To be great is to be misunderstood.

I suppose no man can violate his nature. All the sallies of his will are rounded in by the law of his being, as the inequalities of Andes and Himmaleh are insignificant in the curve of the sphere. Nor does it matter how you gauge and try him. A character is like an acrostic or Alexandrian stanza;—read it forward, backward, or across, it still spells the same thing. In this pleasing, contrite wood-life which God allows me, let me record day by day my honest thought without prospect or retrospect, and, I cannot doubt, it will be found symmetrical, though I mean it not, and see it not. My book should smell of pines and resound with the hum of insects. The swallow over my window should interweave that thread or straw he carries in his bill into my web also. We pass for what we are. Character teaches above our wills. Men imagine that they communicate their virtue or vice only by overt actions, and do not see that virtue or vice emit a breath every moment. . . .

I hope in these days we have heard the last of conformity and consistency. Let the words be gazetted and ridiculous henceforward. Instead of the gong for dinner, let us hear a whistle from the Spartan fife. Let us never bow and apologize more. A great man is coming to eat at my house. I do not wish to please him; I wish that he should wish to please me. I will stand here for humanity, and though I would make it kind, I would make it true. Let us affront and reprimand the smooth mediocrity and squalid contentment of the times, and hurl in the face of custom, and trade, and office, the fact which is the upshot of all history, that there is a great responsible Thinker and Actor working wherever a man works; that a true man belongs to no other time or place, but is the centre of things. Where he is, there is nature. He measures you, and all men, and all events. Ordinarily, every body in society reminds us of somewhat else, or of some other person. Character, reality, reminds you of nothing else; it takes place of the whole creation. The man must be so much, that he must make all circumstances indifferent. Every true man is a cause, a country, and an age; requires infinite spaces and numbers and time fully to accomplish his design;—and posterity seem to follow his steps as a train of clients. A man Caesar is born, and for ages after we have a Roman Empire. Christ is born, and millions of minds so grow and cleave to his genius, that he is confounded with virtue and the possible of man. An institution is the lengthened shadow of one man. . . .

Let a man then know his worth, and keep things under his feet. Let him not peep or steal, or skulk up and down with the air of a charity-boy, a bastard, or an interloper, in the world which exists for him. But the man in the street, finding no worth in himself which corresponds to the force which built a tower or sculptured a marble god, feels poor when he looks on these. To him a palace, a statue, or a costly book have an alien and forbidding air, much like a gay equipage, and seem to say like that, 'Who are you, Sir?' Yet they all are his, suitors for his notice, petitioners to his faculties that they will come out and take possession. The picture waits for my verdict: it is not to command me, but I am to settle its claims to praise. That popular fable of the sot who was picked up dead drunk in the street, carried to the duke's house, washed and dressed and laid in the duke's bed, and, on his waking, treated with all obsequious ceremony like the duke, and assured that he had been insane, owes its popularity to the fact, that it symbolizes so well the state of man, who is in the world a sort of sot, but now and then wakes up, exercises his reason, and finds himself a true prince. . . .

The relations of the soul to the divine spirit are so pure, that it is profane to seek to interpose helps. It must be that when God speaketh he should communicate, not one thing, but all things; should fill the world with his voice; should scatter forth light, nature, time, souls, from the centre of the present thought; and new date and new create the whole. Whenever a mind is simple, and receives a divine wisdom, old things pass away,—means, teachers, texts, temples fall; it lives now, and absorbs past and future into the present hour. All things are made sacred by relation to it,—one as much as another. All things are dissolved to their centre by their cause, and, in the universal miracle, petty and particular miracles disappear. If, therefore, a man claims to know and speak of God, and carries you backward to the phraseology of some old mouldered nation in another country, in another world, believe him not. Is the acorn better than the oak which is its fulness and completion? Is the parent better than the child into whom he has cast his ripened being? Whence, then, this worship of the past? The centuries are conspirators against the sanity and authority of the soul. Time and space are but physiological colors which the eye makes, but the soul is light; where it is, is day; where it was, is night; and history is an impertinence and an injury, if it be any thing more than a cheerful apologue or parable of my being and becoming.

Man is timid and apologetic; he is no longer upright; he dares not say 'I think,' 'I am,' but quotes some saint or sage. He is ashamed before the blade of grass or the blowing rose. These roses under my window make no reference to former roses or to better ones; they are for what they are; they exist with God to-day. There is no time to them. There is simply the rose; it is perfect in every moment of its existence. Before a leaf-bud has burst, its whole life acts; in the full-blown flower there is no more; in the leafless root there is no less. Its nature is satisfied, and it satisfies nature, in all moments alike. But man postpones or remembers; he does not live in the present, but with reverted eye laments the past, or, heedless of the riches that surround him, stands on tiptoe to foresee the future. He cannot be happy and strong until he too lives with nature in the present, above time.

. . . If we live truly, we shall see truly. It is as easy for the strong man to be strong, as it is for the weak to be weak. When we have new perception, we shall gladly disburden the memory of its hoarded treasures as old rubbish. When a man lives with God, his voice shall be as sweet as the murmur of the brook and the rustle of the corn.

And now at last the highest truth on this subject remains unsaid; probably cannot be said; for all that we say is the far-off remembering of the intuition. That thought, by what I can now nearest approach to say it, is this. When good is near you, when you have life in yourself, it is not by any known or accustomed way; you shall not discern the foot-prints of any other; you shall not see the face of man; you shall not hear any name;—the way, the thought, the good, shall be wholly strange and new. It shall exclude example and experience. You take the way from man, not to man. All persons that ever existed are its forgotten ministers. Fear and hope are alike beneath it. There is somewhat low even in hope. In the hour of vision, there is nothing that can be called gratitude, nor properly joy. The soul raised over passion beholds identity and eternal causation, perceives the self-existence of Truth and Right, and calms itself with knowing that all things go well. Vast spaces of nature, the Atlantic Ocean, the South Sea,—long intervals of time, years, centuries,—are of no account. This which I think and feel underlay every former state of life and circumstances, as it does underlie my present, and what is called life, and what is called death.

Life only avails, not the having lived. Power ceases in the instant of repose; it resides in the moment of transition from a past to a new state, in the shooting of the gulf, in the darting to an aim. This one fact the world hates, that the soul becomes; for that for ever degrades the past, turns all riches to poverty, all reputation to a shame, confounds the saint with the rogue, shoves Jesus and Judas equally aside. Why, then, do we prate of self-reliance? Inasmuch as the soul is present, there will be power not confident but agent. To talk of reliance is a poor external way of speaking. Speak rather of that which relies, because it works and is. Who has more obedience than I masters me, though he should not raise his finger. Round him I must revolve by the gravitation of spirits. We fancy it rhetoric, when we speak of eminent virtue. We do not yet see that virtue is Height, and that a man or a company of men, plastic and permeable to principles, by the law of nature must overpower and ride all cities, nations, kings, rich men, poets, who are not.

This is the ultimate fact which we so quickly reach on this, as on every topic, the resolution of all into the ever-blessed ONE. Self-existence is the attribute of the Supreme Cause, and it constitutes the measure of good by the degree in which it enters into all lower forms. All things real are so by so much virtue as they contain. Commerce, husbandry, hunting, whaling, war, eloquence, personal weight, are somewhat, and engage my respect as examples of its presence and impure action. I see the same law working in nature for conservation and growth. Power is in nature the essential measure of right. Nature suffers nothing to remain in her kingdoms which cannot help itself. The genesis and maturation of a planet, its poise and orbit, the bended tree recovering itself from the strong wind, the vital resources of every animal and vegetable, are demonstrations of the self-sufficing, and therefore self-relying soul. . . .

But now we are a mob. Man does not stand in awe of man, nor is his genius admonished to stay at home, to put itself in communication with the internal ocean, but it goes abroad to beg a cup of water of the urns of other men. We must go alone. I like the silent church before the service begins, better than any preaching. How far off, how cool, how chaste the persons look, begirt each one with a precinct or sanctuary! So let us always sit. Why should we assume the faults of our friend, or wife, or father, or child, because they sit around our hearth, or are said to have the same blood? All men have my blood, and I have all men's. Not for that will I adopt their petulance or folly, even to the extent of being ashamed of it. But your isolation must not be mechanical, but spiritual, that is, must be elevation. At times the whole world seems to be in conspiracy to importune you with emphatic trifles. Friend, client, child, sickness, fear, want, charity, all knock at once at thy closet door, and say,—"Come out unto us." But keep thy state; come not into their confusion. The power men possess to annoy me, I give them by a weak curiosity. No man can come near me but through my act. "What we love that we have, but by desire we bereave ourselves of the love." . . .

If any man consider the present aspects of what is called by distinction society, he will see the need of these ethics. The sinew and heart of man seem to be drawn out, and we are become timorous, desponding whimperers. We are afraid of truth, afraid of fortune, afraid of death, and afraid of each other. Our age yields no great and perfect persons. We want men and women who shall renovate life and our social state, but we see that most natures are insolvent, cannot satisfy their own wants, have an ambition out of all proportion to their practical force, and do lean and beg day and night continually. Our housekeeping is mendicant, our arts, our occupations, our marriages, our religion, we have not chosen, but society has chosen for us. We are parlour soldiers. We shun the rugged battle of fate, where strength is born. . . .

Insist on yourself; never imitate. Your own gift you can present every moment with the cumulative force of a whole life's cultivation; but of the adopted talent of another, you have only an extemporaneous, half possession. That which each can do best, none but his Maker can teach him. No man yet knows what it is, nor can, till that person has exhibited it. Where is the master who could have taught Shakspeare? Where is the master who could have instructed Franklin, or Washington, or Bacon, or Newton? Every great man is a unique. The Scipionism of Scipio is precisely that part he could not borrow. Shakspeare will never be made by the study of Shakspeare. Do that which is assigned you, and you cannot hope too much or dare too much. . . .

The civilized man has built a coach, but has lost the use of his feet. He is supported on crutches, but lacks so much support of muscle. He has a fine Geneva watch, but he fails of the skill to tell the hour by the sun. A Greenwich nautical almanac he has, and so being sure of the information when he wants it, the man in the street does not know a star in the sky. The solstice he does not observe; the equinox he knows as little; and the whole bright calendar of the year is without a dial in his mind. His note-books impair his memory; his libraries overload his wit; the insurance-office increases the number of accidents; and it may be a question whether machinery does not encumber; whether we have not lost by refinement some energy, by a Christianity entrenched in establishments and forms, some vigor of wild virtue. For every Stoic was a Stoic; but in Christendom where is the Christian? . . .

Society is a wave. The wave moves onward, but the water of which it is composed does not. The same particle does not rise from the valley to the ridge. Its unity is only phenomenal. The persons who make up a nation to-day, next year die, and their experience with them.

And so the reliance on Property, including the reliance on governments which protect it, is the want of self-reliance. Men have looked away from themselves and at things so long, that they have come to esteem the religious, learned, and civil institutions as guards of property, and they deprecate assaults on these, because they feel them to be assaults on property. They measure their esteem of each other by what each has, and not by what each is. But a cultivated man becomes ashamed of his property, out of new respect for his nature. Especially he hates what he has, if he see that it is accidental,—came to him by inheritance, or gift, or crime; then he feels that it is not having; it does not belong to him, has no root in him, and merely lies there, because no revolution or no robber takes it away. But that which a man is does always by necessity acquire, and what the man acquires is living property, which does not wait the beck of rulers, or mobs, or revolutions, or fire, or storm, or bankruptcies, but perpetually renews itself wherever the man breathes. "Thy lot or portion of life," said the Caliph Ali, "is seeking after thee; therefore be at rest from seeking after it." Our dependence on these foreign goods leads us to our slavish respect for numbers. The political parties meet in numerous conventions; the greater the concourse, and with each new uproar of announcement, The delegation from Essex! The Democrats from New Hampshire! The Whigs of Maine! the young patriot feels himself stronger than before by a new thousand of eyes and arms. In like manner the reformers summon conventions, and vote and resolve in multitude. Not so, O friends! will the God deign to enter and inhabit you, but by a method precisely the reverse. It is only as a man puts off all foreign support, and stands alone, that I see him to be strong and to prevail. He is weaker by every recruit to his banner. Is not a man better than a town? Ask nothing of men, and in the endless mutation, thou only firm column must presently appear the upholder of all that surrounds thee. He who knows that power is inborn, that he is weak because he has looked for good out of him and elsewhere, and so perceiving, throws himself unhesitatingly on his thought, instantly rights himself, stands in the erect position, commands his limbs, works miracles; just as a man who stands on his feet is stronger than a man who stands on his head.

So use all that is called Fortune. Most men gamble with her, and gain all, and lose all, as her wheel rolls. But do thou leave as unlawful these winnings, and deal with Cause and Effect, the chancellors of God. In the Will work and acquire, and thou hast chained the wheel of Chance, and shalt sit hereafter out of fear from her rotations. A political victory, a rise of rents, the recovery of your sick, or the return of your absent friend, or some other favorable event, raises your spirits, and you think good days are preparing for you. Do not believe it. Nothing can bring you peace but yourself. Nothing can bring you peace but the triumph of principles.

Address to the Citizens of Concord, 1851

ON THE FUGITIVE SLAVE LAW, MAY 3, 1851

. . . I accepted your invitation to speak to you on the great question of these days in the very moment it came to me, with very little consideration of what I might have to offer; for there seems to be no option. The last year has forced us all into politics, and made it a paramount duty to seek what it is often a duty to shun.

We do not breathe well. There is infamy in the air. I have a new experience. I wake in the morning with a painful sensation, which I carry about all day, & which, when traced home, is the odious remembrance of that ignominy that has fallen on Massachusetts, that robs the landscape of beauty, & takes the sunshine out of every hour. I have lived all my life in this state, and never had any experience of personal inconvenience from the laws. They never came near me to my discomfort before. I find the same sensibility in my neighbours. And in that class who take no interest in

SOURCE: Ralph Waldo Emerson, *Emerson's Antislavery Writings,* ed. by Len Gougeon and Joel Myerson (New Haven: Yale University Press, 1995), 53–58.

the ordinary questions of party politics. There are men who are as sure indexes of the equity of legislation & of the sane state of public feeling, as the barometer is of the weight of the air, and it is a bad sign if they are discontented. For though they snuff oppression & dishonour at a distance in the air, it is because they are more impressionable; the whole population will in a short time be as painfully affected.

Every hour brings us from distant quarters of the Union the natural expression of mortification at the late events in Massachusetts and the behaviour of Boston. The tameness was indeed shocking. Boston, of whose fame for spirit & character, we have all been so proud. . . .

The levity of the public mind has been shown, in the past year, by the most extravagant actions. Who could have believed it, if foretold, that a hundred guns would be fired in Boston, on the passage of the Fugitive-slave-bill? Nothing proves the want of all thought, the absence of standard in men's minds, more than the dominion of party. Here are humane people who have tears for misery, an open purse for want, who should have been the defenders of the poor man, are found his embittered enemies, rejoicing in his rendition,—merely from party ties. I thought none that was not ready to go on all fours would back this law. And yet here are upright men, *compotes mentis,* husbands, fathers, trustees, friends, open, generous, brave, who can see nothing in this claim for bare humanity, & the health & honor of their native state, but canting, fanaticism, sedition, & "one idea." Because of this preoccupied mind, the whole wealth & power of Boston 200,000 souls & 180 millions of money, are thrown into the scale of crime; and the poor black boy, whom the fame of Boston had reached, in the recesses of a rice swamp, or in the alleys of Savannah, on arriving here, finds all this force employed to catch him. The famous town of Boston is his master's hound. The learning of the universities, the culture of elegant society, the acumen of lawyers, majesty of the Bench, the eloquence of the Christian pulpit, the stoutness of Democracy, the respectability of the Whig Party are all combined to kidnap him.

The crisis is interesting, as it shows the selfprotecting nature of the world, & of the divine laws. It is the law of the world, as much immorality as there is, so much misery. The greatest prosperity will in vain escape the greatest calamity. You borrow the succour of the devil, & he must have his fee. He was never known to abate a penny of his rents. In every nation all the immorality that exists breeds plagues. Out of the corrupt society that exists, we have never been able to combine any pure prosperity. There is always something in the very advantages of a condition which hurts it. Africa has its malformation, England has its Ireland, Germany its hatred of classes, France, its love of gunpowder, Italy, its pope; and America, the most prosperous country in the universe, has the greatest calamity in the universe, negro slavery. . . .

By the sentiment of Duty. An immoral law makes it a man's duty to break it, at every hazard. For Virtue is the very self of every man. It is, therefore, a principle of law, that an immoral contract is void, and that an immoral statute is void, for, as laws do not make right, but are simply declaratory of a right which already existed, it is not to be presumed that they can so stultify themselves, as to command injustice.

It is remarkable how rare, even in the history of the worst tyrants, is an immoral law. Some colour, some indirection, was always used. If you take up the volumes of the Universal History, you will find it difficult searching. The precedents are few. It is not easy to parallel the wickedness of this American law. And that is the head & body of this discontent, that the law is immoral; that you have ordained a crime. Here is a statute which enacts the crime of kidnapping,—a crime on one footing with arson and murder. A man's right to liberty, is as inalienable as his right to life.

Pains seem to have been taken to give us in this statute a wrong pure from any mixture of right. If our resistance to this law, is not right, there is no right. This is not meddling with other people's affairs: This is hindering other people from meddling with us. This is not going crusading into Virginia & Georgia after slaves, who, it is alleged, are very comfortable where they are:—that amiable argument falls to the ground: But this is befriending in our own state, on our own farms, a man who has taken the risk of being shot, or burned alive, or cast into the sea, or starved to death, or suffocated in a wooden box, to get away from his driver; and this man, who has run this gauntlet of a thousand miles for his freedom, the statute says, you men of Massachusetts shall hunt, & catch, & send back again to the dog-hutch he fled from. . . .

Margaret Fuller (1810–1850)

During the 1830s, Margaret Fuller lived in Cambridge, Massachusetts, where she was part of Ralph Waldo Emerson and Henry David Thoreau's transcendentalist circle. In 1840, Fuller and Emerson founded a literary journal, *The Dial*, which Fuller edited until 1844, when she accepted Horace Greeley's offer to become the book review editor of the New York *Tribune*. In 1846, she moved to Europe as the *Tribune*'s foreign correspondent, and in 1848 she became involved in the Italian revolution. Returning to the United States in 1850, she drowned when her ship sank during a hurricane within sight of land at Fire Island, New York.

Despite her short life, Margaret Fuller was an influential transcendentalist and feminist. Her ardent plea for women's rights, "The Great Lawsuit: Man versus Men, Woman versus Women," was published in *The Dial* in 1843, and then in 1845 it was incorporated in her book *Woman in the Nineteenth Century*. Like Emerson and Thoreau, Margaret Fuller argued that the United States was a land of hypocrisy that did not live up to its self-proclaimed ideals and that the path to equality and liberty was through self-reliance and personal enlightenment.

She argued also that women must gain economic independence in order to achieve equality. Why is this so? What does Fuller mean when she argues that "there is no wholly masculine man, no purely feminine woman"? Are men and women androgynous?

Woman in the Nineteenth Century, Part 3, 1844

. . . In our own country, women are, in many respects, better situated than men. Good books are allowed, with more time to read them. They are not so early forced into the bustle of life, nor so weighed down by demands for outward success. The perpetual changes, incident to our society, make the blood circulate freely through the body politic, and, if not favorable at present to the grace and bloom of life, they are so to activity, resource, and would be to reflection, but for a low materialist tendency, from which the women are generally exempt in themselves, though its existence, among the men, has a tendency to repress their impulses and make them doubt their instincts, thus often paralyzing their action during the best years.

But they have time to think, and no traditions chain them, and few conventionalities, compared with what must be met in other nations. There is no reason why they should not discover that the secrets of nature are open, the revelations of the spirit waiting, for whoever will seek them. When the mind is once awakened to this consciousness, it will not be restrained by the habits of the past, but fly to seek the deeds of a heavenly future.

Their employments are more favorable to meditation than those of men.

Woman is not addressed religiously here more than elsewhere. She is told that she should be worthy to be the mother of a Washington, or the companion of some good man. But in many, many instances, she has already learned that all bribes have the same flaw; that truth and good are to be sought solely for their own sakes. And, already, an ideal sweetness floats over many forms, shines in many eyes.

Already deep questions are put by young girls on the great theme: What shall I do to enter upon the eternal life?

Men are very courteous to them. They praise them often, check them seldom. There is chivalry in the feeling toward "the ladies," which gives them the best seats in the stage-coach, frequent admission, not only to lectures of all sorts, but to courts of justice, balls of legislature, reform conventions. The newspaper editor "would be better pleased that the Lady's Book should be filled up exclusively by ladies. It would then, indeed, be a true gem, worthy to be presented by young men to the mistress of their affections." Can gallantry go further?

In this country is venerated, wherever seen, the character which Goethe spoke of as an Ideal, which he saw actualized in his friend and patroness, the Grand Duchess Amelia: "The excellent woman is she, who, if the husband dies, can be a father to the children." And this, if read aright, tells a great deal.

Women who speak in public, if they have a moral power, such as has been felt from Angelina Grimké and Abby Kelly,—that is, if they speak for conscience' sake, to serve a cause which they hold sacred,—invariably subdue the prejudices of their hearers, and excite an interest proportionate to the aversion with which it had been the purpose to regard them.

Source: Margaret Fuller, *Woman in the Nineteenth Century,* (New York: Greeley and McElrath, 1845), 96–107.

A passage in a private letter so happily illustrates this, that it must be inserted here. Abby Kelly in the Town-House of——.

"The scene was not unheroic—to see that woman, true to humanity and her own nature, a centre of rude eyes and tongues, even gentlemen feeling licensed to make part of a species of mob around a female out of her sphere. As she took her seat in the desk amid the great noise, and in the throng, full, like a wave, of something to ensue, I saw her humanity in a gentleness and unpretension, tenderly open to the sphere around her, and, had she not been supported by the power of the will of genuineness and principle, she would have failed. It led her to prayer, which, in Woman especially, is childlike; sensibility and will going to the side of God and looking up to him; and humanity was poured out in aspiration.

"She acted like a gentle hero, with her mild decision and womanly calmness. All heroism is mild, and quiet, and gentle, for it is life and possession; and combativeness and firmness show a want of actualness. She is as earnest, fresh and simple, as when she first entered the crusade. I think she did much good, more than the men in her place could do, for Woman feels more as being and reproducing—this brings the subject more into home relations. Men speak through, and mostly from intellect, and this addresses itself to that in others which is combative."

Not easily shall we find elsewhere, or before this time, any written observations on the same subject, so delicate and profound.

The late Dr. Channing, whose enlarged and tender and religious nature shared every onward impulse of his time, though his thoughts followed his wishes with a deliberative caution which belonged to his habits and temperament, was greatly interested in these expectations for women. His own treatment of them was absolutely and thoroughly religious. He regarded them as souls, each of which had a destiny of its own, incalculable to other minds, and whose leading it must follow, guided by the light of a private conscience. He had sentiment, delicacy, kindness, taste; but they were all pervaded and ruled by this one thought, that all beings had souls, and must vindicate their own inheritance. Thus all beings were treated by him with an equal, and sweet, though solemn, courtesy. The young and unknown, the woman and the child, all felt themselves regarded with an infinite expectation, from which there was no reaction to vulgar prejudice. He demanded of all he met, to use his favorite phrase, "great truths."

His memory, every way dear and reverend, is, by many, especially cherished for this intercourse of unbroken respect.

At one time, when the progress of Harriet Martineau through this country, Angelina Grimké's appearance in public, and the visit of Mrs. Jameson, had turned his thoughts to this subject, he expressed high hopes as to what the coming era would bring to Woman. He had been much pleased with the dignified courage of Mrs. Jameson in taking up the defence of her sex in a way from which women usually shrink, because, if they express themselves on such subjects with sufficient force and clearness to do any good, they are exposed to assaults whose vulgarity makes them painful. In intercourse with such a woman, he had shared her indignation at the base injustice, in many respects, and in many regions, done to the sex; and been led to think of it far more than ever before. He seemed to think that he might some time write upon the subject. That his aid is withdrawn from the cause is a subject of great regret; for, on this question as on others, he would have known how to sum up the evidence, and take, in the noblest spirit, middle ground. He always furnished a platform on which opposing parties could stand and look at one another under the influence of his mildness and enlightened candor.

Two younger thinkers, men both, have uttered noble prophecies, auspicious for Woman. Kinmont, all whose thoughts tended towards the establishment of the reign of love and peace, thought that the inevitable means of this would be an increased predominance given to the idea of Woman. Had he lived longer, to see the growth of the Peace Party, the reforms in life and medical practice which seek to substitute water for wine and drugs, pulse for animal food, he would have been confirmed in his view of the way in which the desired changes are to be effected.

In this connection I must mention Shelley, who, like all men of genius, shared the feminine development, and, unlike many, knew it. His life was one of the first pulse-beats in the present reform-growth. He, too, abhorred blood and heat, and, by his system and his song, tended to reinstate a plant-like gentleness in the development of energy. In harmony with this, his ideas of marriage were lofty, and, of course, no less so of Woman, her nature, and destiny.

For Woman, if, by a sympathy as to outward condition, she is led to aid the enfranchisement of the slave, must be no less so, by inward tendency, to favor measures which promise to bring the world more thoroughly and deeply into harmony with her nature. When the lamb takes place of the lion as the emblem of nations, both women and men will be as children of one spirit, perpetual learners of the word and doers thereof, not hearers only.

A writer in the New York Pathfinder, in two articles headed "Femality," has uttered a still more pregnant word than any we have named. He views Woman truly from the soul, and not from society, and the depth and leading of his thoughts are proportionably remarkable. He views the feminine nature as a harmonizer of the vehement elements, and this has often been hinted elsewhere; but what he expresses most forcibly is the lyrical, the inspiring and inspired apprehensiveness of her being.

This view being identical with what I have before attempted to indicate, as to her superior susceptibility to magnetic or electric influence, I will now try to express myself more fully.

There are two aspects of Woman's nature, represented by the ancients as Muse and Minerva. It is the former to which the writer in the Pathfinder looks. It is the latter which Wordsworth has in mind, when he says,

> *"With a placid brow,*
> *Which woman ne'er should forfeit, keep thy vow."*

The especial genius of Woman I believe to be electrical in movement, intuitive in function, spiritual in tendency. She excels not so easily in classification, or recreation, as in an instinctive seizure of causes, and a simple breathing out of what she receives, that has the singleness of life, rather than the selecting and energizing of art.

More native is it to her to be the living model of the artist than to set apart from herself any one form in objective reality; more native to inspire and receive the poem, than to create it. In so far as soul is in her completely developed, all soul is the same; but in so far as it is modified in her as Woman, it flows, it breathes, it sings, rather than deposits soil, or finishes work; and that which is especially feminine flushes, in blossom, the face of earth, and pervades, like air and water, all this seeming solid globe, daily renewing and purifying its life. Such may be the especially feminine element spoken of as Femality. But it is no more the order of nature that it should be incarnated pure in any form, than that the masculine energy should exist unmingled with it in any form.

Male and female represent the two sides of the great radical dualism. But, in fact, they are perpetually passing into one another. Fluid hardens to solid, solid rushes to fluid. There is no wholly masculine man, no purely feminine woman.

. . . Yet sight comes first, and of this sight of the world of causes, this approximation to the region of primitive motions, women I hold to be especially capable. Even without equal freedom with the other sex, they have already shown themselves so; and should these faculties have free play, I believe they will open new, deeper and purer sources of joyous inspiration than have as yet refreshed the earth.

Let us be wise, and not impede the soul. Let her work as she will. Let us have one creative energy, one incessant revelation. Let it take what form it will, and let us not bind it by the past to man or woman, black or white. . . .

Every relation, every gradation of nature is incalculably precious, but only to the soul which is poised upon itself, and to whom no loss, no change, can bring dull discord, for it is in harmony with the central soul.

If any individual live too much in relations, so that he becomes a stranger to the resources of his own nature, he falls, after a while, into a distraction, or imbecility, from which he can only be cured by a time of isolation, which gives the renovating fountains time to rise up. With a society it is the same. Many minds, deprived of the traditionary or instinctive means of passing a cheerful existence, must find help in self-impulse, or perish. It is therefore that, while any elevation, in the view of union, is to be hailed with joy, we shall not decline celibacy as the great fact of the time. It is one from which no vow, no arrangement, can at present save a thinking mind. For now the rowers are pausing on their oars; they wait a change before they can pull together. All tends to illustrate the thought of a wise contemporary. Union is only possible to those who are units. To be fit for relations in time, souls, whether of Man or Woman, must be able to do without them in the spirit.

It is therefore that I would have Woman lay aside all thought, such as she habitually cherishes, of being taught and led by men. I would have her, like the Indian girl, dedicate herself to the Sun, the Sun of Truth, and go nowhere if his beams did not make clear the path. I would have her free from compromise, from complaisance, from helplessness, because I would have her good enough and strong enough to love one and all beings, from the fulness, not the poverty of being.

Men, as at present instructed, will not help this work, because they also are under the slavery of habit. . . .

Lowell Mill Girls

In the early 1830s, in an effort to increase production, textile mills in Lowell, Massachusetts, began an experiment in which young farm women were hired in large numbers. At a time when the idea of young, unmarried women working and living away from home was scandalous, the mill provided a safe and secure environment. The girls resided in supervised housing, were given boarding house–style meals, followed a strict dress and behavior code, and were expected to attend educational lectures and expand their minds by using the library. This uncommon opportunity for women to leave home and earn money in a secure setting created a great deal of camaraderie among them, and the Lowell Mills thrived. However, in 1834, when increasing competition forced the mills to cut wages, the tight-knit Lowell Mill girls decided to strike. The strike was unsuccessful, as was a second strike in 1836, but the workers showed that they had a strong sense of their own interests and were not timid about attempting to organize. In 1846, they struck again, and this time they were partially successful. One of the Lowell employees, Sarah Bagley, founded the Lowell Female Labor Association in 1844 and became a staunch labor reformer who helped to guide the Lowell Mill girls as they called for a 10-hour workday and increased wages. Thus, although women were a minority in the workforce of the nineteenth century, some of the earliest attempts at labor organization were spearheaded by working women.

In 1846, Sarah Bagley and others wrote a constitution for their union, and in 1847, after they changed their name to Lowell Female Industrial Reform and Mutual Aid Society, they wrote a second constitution. What do these documents say about labor conditions in the mills? What are the workers' major grievances? What do they reveal about the political consciousness and organizational capabilities of nineteenth-century working-class women?

Lowell Female Labor Reform Association, 1846

Whereas we, the Operatives of Lowell, believing that in the present age of improvement, nothing can escape the searching glances of reform; and when men begin to inquire why the Laborer does not hold that place in the social, moral and intellectual world, which a bountiful Creator designed him to occupy, the *reason* is obvious. He is a slave to a false and debasing state of society. Our merciful Father in his infinite wisdom surely, has not bestowed all his blessings, both mental and moral on a

SOURCE: Retrieved on 10/26/2003 from http://irw.rutgers.edu/research/ugresearch/birthplaces/preamble.html and http://irw.rutgers.edu/research/ugresearch/birthplaces/lowellconstitution.html.

few, on whom also he has showered all of pecuniary gifts. No! to us *all* has he given minds capable of eternal progression and improvement!

It now only remains for us to throw off the shackles which are binding us in ignorance and servitude and which prevent us from rising to that scale of being for which God designed us.

But how shall this be done? How shall the mass become educated? With the present system of labor it is impossible. There must be reasonable hours for manual labor, and a just portion of time allowed for the cultivation of the mental and moral faculties and no other way *can* the great work be accomplished.

We know no employment is respectable only as long as these employed are such, and no farther than they are intelligent and moral, can they merit the companionship and esteem of their fellow-beings. It is evident, that with the present system of labor, the minds of the mass *must* remain uncultivated, their morals unimproved and our country be flooded with vice and misery!

Shall we, Operatives of America, the land where Democracy claims to be the principle by which we live and by which we are governed, see the evil daily increasing which separates more widely and more effectually the favored few and the unfortunate many, without one exertion to stay the progress?—God forbid! Let the daughters of New England kindle the spark of philanthropy on every heart till its brightness shall *fill* the whole earth!

In consideration of which we adopt the following Constitution:

ART. 1st. This Association shall be called the Lowell Female Labor Reform Association.

ART. 2d. This Association shall be governed by the following officers: President, two Vice Presidents, a Secretary, Treasurer and board of Directors, consisting of eight in number.

ART. 3d. It shall be the duty of the President to preside at the meetings of the Association and board of Directors, and call especial meetings whenever any three members of the same shall request it.

ART. 4th. It shall be the duty of the Vice Presidents to preside in case of the absence of the President.

ART. 5th. It shall be the duty of the Secretary to be present at all meetings of the Association, and be prepared to read the proceedings of the last meeting, if requested. Also, to keep a correct account of the business of the Association.

ART. 6th. It shall be the duty of the Treasurer to receive all money paid into the treasury, and keep a correct account of the same also, to pay all bills presented by the Association, and signed by the President and Secretary.

ART. 7th. It shall be the duty of the Directors to present all plans of operation to the Association, and to assist in all labors of the same.

ART. 8th. Any person signing this Constitution, shall literally pledge herself to labor *actively* for Reform in the present system of labor.

ART. 9th. The members of this Association disapprove of all hostile measures, strikes and turn outs until all pacific measures prove abortive, and then that is the imperious duty of every one to assert and maintain that independence which our brave ancestors bequeathed to us, and sealed with their blood.

ART. 10th. This Constitution may be altered and amended by a vote of two thirds of the members present, provided the amendment be proposed at a previous meeting. It shall be the duty of the Board of Directors to revise the Constitution at the time of the Annual meeting for choosing Officers, which shall be holden on the first Tuesday of January.

The following Officers were chosen Jan. 1846.

SARAH G. BAGLEY, *President*
HANNAH C. TARLTON, *Vice Pres.*

MARY EMERSON,
HULDAH J. STONE, *Rec'g. Sec'y.*
SARAH A. YOUNG, *Cor. Sec'y.*
MARY A. K. TARLTON, *Treasurer.*
CLIMENA BUTLER
MISS GILMAN
ABBEY KEMP
CATHERINE MAXEY

Directors

MARY J. ROBINSON
ELIZA SIMPSON
ELIZABETH L. TRUE
ELMIRA B. STONE

Voice of Industry, February 27, 1846.

Lowell Female Industrial Reform and Mutual Aid Society, 1847

The following Preamble and Constitution having been adopted, we would most strongly urge upon every female operative, as well as others who are compelled by necessity to support themselves of this opportunity to help us in this humane enterprise: Let us unite together and protect each other. In health and prosperity we can enjoy each other's society from week to week—in sickness and despondency share in and kindly relieve each other's distresses. The young and defenceless female, far away from home and loving hearts, can here find true sympathy and aid. We do hope and confidently believe that many of our toiling sisters will come in next Tuesday, sign the Constitution, and engage heart and hand in this benevolent cause.

Our meetings will be holden every Tuesday evening, at eight o'clock, at the Reading Room, 76 Central street. The officers for the coming year will be chosen Jan. 12. Let there be full attendance. Now is the time for ACTION.

H. J. Stone, Sec'y.

PREAMBLE

The time having come when the claims of Industry and the Rights of all, are engrossing the deep attention, the profoundest thought and energetic action of the wisest and best in this and other lands—when the worthy toiling millions of earth are waking from the deathlike stupor which has so long held them in ignorance and degredation, to a sense of their true dignity and worth as God's free men and women, destined to eternal progression and ultimate perfection, we, females of Lowell, feel that *we* also have a *work* to accomplish—a high and holy destiny to achieve. We deem it a privelage and also a *duty* we owe to ourselves and our race, to lend a helping hand, feeble though it may be, to assist in carrying forward the great "Industrial Reform" already commenced, and which is progressing with such unlooked for success, in the Old and New World. To assist in scattering light and knowledge among the people—to encourage in every good word and work, those who are devoting themselves, and all that they have, to the cause of human elevation and human happiness.

We feel that by our mutual, *united* action, and with the blessing of high heaven, we can accomplish much, which shall tell for the progress of Industrial Reform— the elevation and cultivation of mind and morals, in our midst—the comfort and relief of destitute and friendless females in this busy city.

With this high aim and these noble objects in view, we most solemnly pledge ourselves to labor actively, energetically and unitedly, to bring about a better state of society. In order the more successfully to accomplish these objects, we adopt the following

CONSTITUTION

ART. I. This Association shall be called the LOWELL FEMALE INDUSTRIAL REFORM AND MUTUAL AID SOCIETY.

ART. II. The objects of this Society shall be the diffusion of correct principles and useful practical knowledge among its members—the rendering of Industry honorable and attractive—the relieving and aiding of all who may be sick, or in want of the comforts and necessaries of life, or standing in need of the counsels and sympathies of true and benevolent hearts. Also to encourage and assist each other in self-culture, intellectual and moral, that we may be fitted for and occupy that station in society, which the truly good and useful ever should. That we may know and respect our own individual rights and privileges as females, and be prepared, understandingly, to maintain and enjoy them, irrespective of concentrated wealth or aristocratic usages of an anti-republican state of society.

ART. III. Any female can become a member by signing the Constitution and paying an initiation fee of fifty cents.

ART. IV. The officers of this society shall consist of a President, two Vice Presidents, Secretary, Treasurer and Board of Directors, four in number, all of which officers shall be members, ex-officio, of the Board.

ART. V. It shall be the duty of the President to preside at all meetings of the Society, and in case of absence, the Vice President shall fill the chair.

ART. VI. It shall be the duty of the Secretary to be present at all meetings, and prepared to read the minutes of the previous meeting, if requested.

ART. VII. It shall be the duty of the Treasurer to receive all money paid into the Treasury, and to pay all bills presented by the Society and signed by the President and Secretary; also to keep a correct amount of the same.

ART. VIII. It shall be the duty of the Board to appoint a Charitable Committee the first Tuesday of each month, or oftener if necessary.

ART. IX. That Committee shall be styled the Sisters of Charity. It shall be their duty to ascertain who is needy or sick in the Society, and report the same at each meeting, that their wants may be attended to faithfully, their hearts cheered by the voice of sympathy and love. It shall also be their duty to furnish watchers for the sick so long as deemed necessary.

ART. X. Every member shall deposit not less than six cents weekly in the hands of the Treasurer, which sum, with the initiation fee and fines, shall go to make up a sick fund, which shall be appropriated no other way, except by vote of two thirds of the Board.

ART. XI. No member shall draw from this fund until she has contributed to the same three months the amount specified in article tenth; and then not less than two nor over five dollars a week, or longer than four weeks, unless the Board see fit to order otherwise.

ART. XII. Any member who shall absent herself from the meetings three weeks in succession, without a reasonable excuse, shall be subjected to a fine of thirty-seven and a half cents per week. If at the end of three months said member does not come in and pay up her fines, she shall not be entitled to any of the benefits of the sick fund.

ART. XIII. The officers of this Society shall be chosen on the first Tuesdays of January and July, two weeks notice being previously given.

ART. XIV. This Constitution may be altered or amended by a vote of two thirds of the members present, provided it be proposed at a previous meeting.

Voice of Industry, January 8, 1847

Elizabeth Cady Stanton (1815–1902)

Elizabeth Cady Stanton, an abolitionist and an advocate of women's rights, sailed with her husband to London in 1840 to attend the World Anti-Slavery Convention. After making the arduous voyage, she was dismayed and angered to discover that women were not allowed to speak at the convention. In a sense, this was an epiphany for her, a revelation that the fight for women's rights was at least as important as the fight against slavery. At the convention, she met Lucretia Mott, and the two women resolved that they would arrange a women's rights convention in the United States. In July 1848, 300 women and 40 men gathered in Seneca Falls, New York, to "discuss the social, civil, and religious condition and rights of women." The principal outcome of this convention was the "Declaration of Sentiments." Modeling the manifesto on the Declaration of Independence and the Bill of Rights, Stanton called not only for women's suffrage but also for complete social and economic equality and a restructuring of societal stereotypes about the roles of the two sexes. Though the Seneca Falls declaration kicked off the modern women's movement, the struggle for women's rights remained in the background during the 1850s, as the crusade against slavery took center stage. At the end of the Civil War, Stanton and Mott, along with Susan B. Anthony, Lucy Stone, and many others, focused their considerable energies on women's rights.

Why does Stanton claim, in her speech, that there has never been a truly virtuous nation in the history of the world? How were women treated unequally? How effective is the device of modeling the Seneca Falls declaration on the Declaration of Independence? What do you suppose was public reaction to the declaration? What counterarguments would men use to oppose Stanton's position?

Speech at Seneca Falls, July 19, 1848

We have met here today to discuss our rights and wrongs, civil and political, and not, as some have supposed, to go into the detail of social life alone. We do not propose to petition the legislature to make our husbands just, generous, and courteous, to seat every man at the head of a cradle, and to clothe every woman in male attire. None of these points, however important they may be considered by leading men, will be touched in this convention. As to their costume, the gentlemen need feel no fear of our imitating that, for we think it in violation of every principle of taste, beauty, and dignity; notwithstanding all the contempt cast upon our loose, flowing garments, we still admire the graceful folds, and consider our costume far more

SOURCE: Ellen Carol Dubois, ed. *The Elizabeth Cady Stanton-Susan B. Anthony Reader: Correspondence, Writings, Speeches* (Boston: Northeastern University Press, 1992) 27–35.

artistic than theirs. Many of the nobler sex seem to agree with us in this opinion, for the bishops, priests, judges, barristers, and lord mayors of the first nation on the globe, and the Pope of Rome, with his cardinals, too, all wear the loose flowing robes, thus tacity acknowledging that the male attire is neither dignified nor imposing. No, we shall not molest you in your philosophical experiments with stocks, pants, high-heeled boots, and Russian belts. Yours be the glory to discover, by personal experience, how long the kneepan can resist the terrible strapping down which you impose, in how short time the well-developed muscles of the throat can be reduced to mere threads by the constant pressure of the stock, how high the heel of a boot must be to make a short man tall, and how tight the Russian belt may be drawn and yet have wind enough left to sustain life.

But we are assembled to protest against a form of government existing without the consent of the governed—to declare our right to be free as man is free, to be represented in the government which we are taxed to support, to have such disgraceful laws as give man the power to chastise and imprison his wife, to take the wages which she earns, the property which she inherits, and, in case of separation, the children of her love; laws which make her the mere dependent on his bounty. It is to protest against such unjust laws as these that we are assembled today, and to have them, if possible, forever erased from our statute books, deeming them a shame and a disgrace to a Christian republic in the nineteenth century. We have met to uplift woman's fallen divinity upon an even pedestal with man's.

And, strange as it may seem to many, we now demand our right to vote according to the declaration of the government under which we live. This right no one pretends to deny. We need not prove ourselves equal to Daniel Webster to enjoy this privilege, for the ignorant Irishman in the ditch has all the civil rights he has. We need not prove our muscular power equal to this same Irishman to enjoy this privilege, for the most tiny, weak, ill-shaped stripling of twenty-one has all the civil rights of the Irishman. We have no objection to discuss the question of equality, for we feel that the weight of argument lies wholly with us, but we wish the question of equality kept distinct from the question of rights, for the proof of the one does not determine the truth of the other. All white men in this country have the same rights, however they may differ in mind, body, or estate.

The right is ours. The question now is: how shall we get possession of what rightfully belongs to us? We should not feel so sorely grieved if no man who had not attained the full stature of a Webster, Clay, Van Buren, or Gerrit Smith could claim the right of the elective franchise. But to have drunkards, idiots, horse-racing, rum-selling rowdies, ignorant foreigners, and silly boys fully recognized, while we ourselves are thrust out from all the rights that belong to citizens, it is too grossly insulting to the dignity of woman to be longer quietly submitted to. The right is ours. Have it, we must. Use it, we will. The pens, the tongues, the fortunes, the indomitable wills of many women are already pledged to secure this right. The great truth that no just government can be formed without the consent of the governed we shall echo and re-echo in the ears of the unjust judge, until by continual coming we shall weary him.

There seems now to be a kind of moral stagnation in our midst. Philanthropists have done their utmost to rouse the nation to a sense of its sins. War, slavery, drunkenness, licentiousness, gluttony, have been dragged naked before the people, and all their abominations and deformities fully brought to light, yet with idiotic laugh we hug those monsters to our breasts and rush on to destruction. Our churches are multiplying on all sides, our missionary societies, Sunday schools, and prayer meetings and innumerable charitable and reform organizations are all in operation, but still the tide of vice is swelling, and threatens the destruction of everything, and the battlements of righteousness are weak against the raging elements of sin and death. Verily, the world waits the coming of some new element, some purifying power, some spirit of mercy and love. The voice of woman has been silenced in the state, the church, and the home, but man cannot fulfill his destiny alone, he cannot redeem his race unaided. There are deep and tender chords of sympathy and love in the hearts of the downfallen and oppressed that woman can touch more skillfully than man.

The world has never yet seen a truly great and virtuous nation, because in the degradation of woman the very fountains of life are poisoned at their source. It is vain to look for silver and gold from mines of copper and lead. It is the wise mother that has the wise son. So long as your women are slaves you may throw your colleges and churches to the winds. You can't have scholars and saints so long as your mothers are ground to powder between the upper and nether millstone of tyranny and lust. How seldom, now, is a father's pride gratified, his fond hopes realized, in the budding genius of his son! The wife is degraded, made the mere creature of caprice, and the foolish son is heaviness to his heart. Truly are the sins of the fathers visited upon the children to the third and fourth generation. God, in His wisdom, has so linked the whole human family together that any violence done at one end of the chain is felt throughout its length, and here, too, is the law of restoration, as in woman all have fallen, so in her elevation shall the race be recreated.

"Voices" were the visitors and advisers of Joan of Arc. Do not "voices" come to us daily from the haunts of poverty, sorrow, degradation, and despair, already too long unheeded. Now is the time for the women of this country, if they would save our free institutions, to defend the right, to buckle on the armor that can best resist the keenest weapons of the enemy—contempt and ridicule. The same religious enthusiasm that nerved Joan of Arc to her work nerves us to ours. In every generation God calls some men and women for the utterance of truth, a heroic action, and our work today is the fulfilling of what has long since been foretold by the Prophet—Joel 2:28: "And it shall come to pass afterward, that I will pour out my spirit upon all flesh; and your sons and your daughters shall prophesy." We do not expect our path will be strewn with the flowers of popular applause, but over the thorns of bigotry and prejudice will be our way, and on our banners will beat the dark storm clouds of opposition from those who have entrenched themselves behind the stormy bulwarks of custom and authority, and who have fortified their position by every means, holy and unholy. But we will steadfastly abide the result. Unmoved we will bear it aloft. Undauntedly we will unfurl it to the gale, for we know that the storm cannot rend from it a shred, that the electric flash will but more clearly show to us the glorious words inscribed upon it, "Equality of Rights."

Declaration of Sentiments, 1848

When, in the course of human events, it becomes necessary for one portion of the family of man to assume among the people of the earth a position different from that which they have hitherto occupied, but one to which the laws of nature and of nature's God entitle them, a decent respect to the opinions of mankind requires that they should declare the causes that impel them to such a course.

We hold these truths to be self-evident: that all men and women are created equal; that they are endowed by their Creator with certain inalienable rights; that among these are life, liberty, and the pursuit of happiness; that to secure these rights governments are instituted, deriving their just powers from the consent of the governed. Whenever any form of government becomes destructive of these ends, it is the right of those who suffer from it to refuse allegiance to it, and to insist upon the institution of a new government, laying its foundation on such principles, and organizing its powers in such form, as to them shall seem most likely to effect their safety and happiness. Prudence, indeed, will dictate that governments long established should not be changed for light and transient causes; and accordingly all experience hath shown that mankind are more disposed to suffer, while evils are sufferable, than to right themselves by abolishing the forms to which they are accustomed. But when a long train of abuses and usurpations, pursuing invariably the same object, evinces a design to reduce them under absolute despotism, it is their duty to throw off such government, and to provide new guards for their future security. Such has been the patient sufferance of the women under this government, and such is now the necessity which constrains them to demand the equal station to which they are entitled. The history of mankind is a history of repeated injuries and usurpations on the part of man toward woman, having in direct object the establishment of an absolute tyranny over her. To prove this, let facts be submitted to a candid world.

He has never permitted her to exercise her inalienable right to the elective franchise.

He has compelled her to submit to laws, in the formation of which she had no voice.

He has withheld from her rights which are given to the most ignorant and degraded men—both natives and foreigners.

Having deprived her of this first right of a citizen, the elective franchise, thereby leaving her with but representation in the halls of legislation, he has oppressed her on all sides.

He has made her, if married, in the eye of the law, civilly dead. He has taken from her all right in property. even to the wages she earns.

He has made her, morally, an irresponsible being, as she can commit many crimes with impunity, provided they be done in the presence of her husband.

In the covenant of marriage, she is compelled to promise obedience to her husband, he becoming, to all intents and purposes, her master—the law giving him power to deprive her of her liberty. and to administer chastisement.

SOURCE: Elizabeth Cady Stanton, Susan B. Anthony, and Matilda Joslyn Gage, eds., *History of Woman Suffrage*, vol. I (1881; New York: Arno Press and the New York Times, 1969), 70–72.

He has so framed the laws of divorce, as to what shall be the proper causes, and in case of separation, to whom the guardianship of the children shall be given, as to be wholly regardless of the happiness of women—the law, in all cases, going upon a false supposition of the supremacy of man, and giving all power into his hands.

After depriving her of all rights as a married woman, if single, and the owner of property, he has taxed her to support a government which recognizes her only when her property can be made profitable to it.

He has monopolized nearly all the profitable employments, and from those she is permitted to follow, she receives but a scanty remuneration. He closes against her all the avenues to wealth and distinction which he considers most honorable to himself. As a teacher of theology, medicine, or law, she is not known.

He has denied her the facilities for obtaining a thorough education, all colleges being closed against her.

He allows her in Church, as well as State, but a subordinate position, claiming Apostolic authority for her exclusion from the ministry, and, with some exceptions, from any public participation in the affairs of the Church.

He has created a false public sentiment by giving to the world a different code of morals for men and women, by which moral delinquencies which exclude women from society, are not only tolerated, but deemed of little account in man.

He has usurped the prerogative of Jehovah himself, claiming it as his right to assign for her a sphere of action, when that belongs to her conscience and to her God.

He has endeavored, in every way that he could, to destroy her confidence in her own powers, to lessen her self-respect and to make her willing to lead a dependent and abject life.

Now, in view of this entire disfranchisement of one-half the people of this country, their social and religious degradation—in view of the unjust laws above mentioned, and because women do feel themselves aggrieved, oppressed, and fraudulently deprived of their most sacred rights, we insist that they have immediate admission to all the rights and privileges which belong to them as citizens of the United States.

In entering upon the great work before us, we anticipate no small amount of misconception, misrepresentation, and ridicule; but we shall use every instrumentality within our power to effect our object. We shall employ agents, circulate tracts, petition the State and National legislatures, and endeavor to enlist the pulpit and the press in our behalf. We hope this Convention will be followed by a series of Conventions embracing every part of the country.

RESOLUTIONS

WHEREAS, The great precept of nature is conceded to be, that "man shall pursue his own true and substantial happiness." Blackstone in his Commentaries remarks, that this law of Nature being coeval with mankind, and dictated by God himself, is of course superior in obligation to any other. It is binding over all the globe, in all countries and at all times; no human laws are of any validity if contrary to this. and such of them as are valid, derive all their force, and all their validity, and all their authority, mediately and immediately, from this original; therefore,

Resolved, That such laws as conflict, in any way with the true and substantial happiness of woman, are contrary to the great precept of nature and of no validity, for this is "superior in obligation to any other."

Resolved, That all laws which prevent woman from occupying such a station in society as her conscience shall dictate, or which place her in a position inferior to that of man, are contrary to the great precept of nature, and therefore of no force or authority.

Resolved, That woman is man's equal—was intended to be so by the Creator, and the highest good of the race demands that she should be recognized as such.

Resolved, That the women of this country ought to be enlightened in regard to the laws under which they live, that they may no longer publish their degradation by declaring themselves satisfied with their present position, nor their ignorance, by asserting that they have all the rights they want.

Resolved, That inasmuch as man, while claiming for himself intellectual superiority, does accord to woman moral superiority, it is pre-eminently his duty to encourage her to speak and teach, as she has an opportunity, in all religious assemblies.

Resolved, That the same amount of virtue, delicacy, and refinement of behavior that is required of woman in the social state, should also be required of man, and the same transgressions should be visited with equal severity on both man and woman.

Resolved, That the objection of indelicacy and impropriety, which is so often brought against woman when she addresses a public audience, comes with a very ill-grace from those who encourage, by their attendance, her appearance on the stage, in the concert. Or in feats of the circus.

Resolved, That woman has too long rested satisfied in the circumscribed limits which corrupt customs and a perverted application of the Scriptures have marked out for her, and that it is time she should move in the enlarged sphere which her great Creator has assigned her.

Resolved, That it is the duty of the women of this country to secure to themselves their sacred right to the elective franchise.

Resolved, That the equality of human rights results necessarily from the fact of the identity of the race in capabilities and responsibilities.

Resolved, therefore. That, being invested by the creator with the same capabilities, and the same consciousness of responsibility for their exercise, it is demonstrably the right and duty of woman, equally with man, to promote every righteous cause by every righteous means; and especially in regard to the great subjects of morals and religion, it is self-evidently her right to participate with her brother in teaching them, both in private and in public, by writing and by speaking, by any instrumentalities proper to be used, and in any assemblies proper to be held; and this being a self evident truth growing out of the divinely implanted principles of human nature, any custom or authority adverse to it, whether modern or wearing the hoary sanction of antiquity, is to be regarded as a self- evident falsehood, and at war with mankind.

Resolved, That the speedy success of our cause depends upon the zealous and untiring efforts of both men and women, for the overthrow of the monopoly of the pulpit, and for the securing to women an equal participation with men in the various trades, professions. and commerce.

Sojourner Truth (c. 1797–1883)

Isabella Baumfree is a legendary figure in American history. After escaping from slavery, she dedicated herself equally to the causes of abolition and feminism. Proclaiming that she would travel the nation speaking nothing but the truth, she changed her name to Sojourner Truth. Uneducated and untrained in grammatical niceties, she was nevertheless an extraordinary speaker who invariably mesmerized audiences wherever she went. Her most famous speech was given at the 1851 Women's Rights Convention in Akron, Ohio. There is some dispute about her exact words because the written version (transcribed some 12 years after the event by Frances Gage, the president of the convention) differs from a contemporary newspaper account of the speech. In any case, the speech enthralled her audience and still resonates today as a compelling example of nineteenth-century feminism.

According to Sojourner Truth, why should women be treated no differently from men?

Ain't I A Woman?, 1851

Well, children, where there is so much racket there must be something out of kilter. I think that 'twixt the negroes of the South and the women at the North, all talking about rights, the white men will be in a fix pretty soon. But what's all this here talking about? That man over there says that women need to be helped into carriages, and lifted over ditches, and to have the best place everywhere. Nobody ever helps me into carriages, or over mud-puddles, or gives me any best place! And ain't I a woman? Look at me! Look at my arm! I have ploughed and planted, and gathered into barns, and no man could head me! And ain't I a woman? I could work as much and eat as much as a man—when I could get it—and bear the lash as well! And ain't I a woman? I have borne thirteen children, and seen most all sold off to slavery, and when I cried out with my mother's grief, none but Jesus heard me! And ain't I a woman?

Then they talk about this thing in the head; what's this they call it? [a member of the audience calls out, "intellect"] That's it, honey. What's that got to do with women's rights or negroes' rights? If my cup won't hold but a pint, and yours holds a quart, wouldn't you be mean not to let me have my little half measure full?

Then that little man in black there, he says women can't have as much rights as men, 'cause Christ wasn't a woman! Where did your Christ come from? Where did your Christ come from? From God and a woman! Man had nothing to do with Him. If the first woman God ever made was strong enough to turn the world upside down

---

Source: Elizabeth Cady Stanton, Susan B. Anthony, and Matilda J. Gage, eds., *History of Woman Suffrage* (Rochester: Charles Mann, 1881), vol. I, 403–404.

all alone, these women together ought to be able to turn it back, and get it right side up again! And now they is asking to do it, the men better let them.

Obliged to you for hearing me, and now old Sojourner ain't got nothing more to say.

Frederick Douglass (1818–1895)

Frederick Douglass was perhaps the most articulate and influential black abolitionist during the antebellum period. After his escape from slavery in 1838, he surfaced in Massachusetts, where he met William Lloyd Garrison. Soon thereafter he became an ardent and tireless campaigner for abolition. The story is often repeated of Garrison introducing Douglass as a speaker at a Nantucket antislavery meeting in 1841. When Douglass spoke, he eloquently confessed that he was a "thief," for he had stolen his limbs, his head, and his body from his master by running away. He gave speeches around the country and in England, he wrote an autobiography, and he published an abolitionist newspaper, *The North Star*. Not only was Frederick Douglass committed to the campaign against slavery but also he fought for complete civil and political rights for African Americans and allied himself to the women's rights movement.

Shortly after the Seneca Falls convention, he reported on the event in *The North Star*. What is the basis for Douglass's argument that women should have equal rights with men?

Perhaps Frederick Douglass's most powerful (and acerbic) speech is the one he delivered at the 1852 Fourth of July celebration in Rochester, New York. How effective is Douglass's denunciation of American hypocrisy? If he could confront Thomas Jefferson, would he agree with him or would he challenge him to rewrite the Declaration of Independence?

The North Star, July 28, 1848

One of the most interesting events of the past week, was the holding of what is technically styled a Woman's Rights Convention at Seneca Falls. The speaking, addresses, and resolutions of this extraordinary meeting was wholly conducted by women; and although they evidently felt themselves in a novel position, it is but simple justice to

SOURCE: Philip S. Foner, ed., *Frederick Douglass on Women's Rights* (New York: Da Capo Press, 1992), 49–51.

say that their whole proceedings were characterized by marked ability and dignity. No one present, we think, however much he might be disposed to differ from the views advanced by the leading speakers on that occasion, will fail to give them credit for brilliant talents and excellent dispositions. In this meeting, as in other deliberative assemblies, there were frequent differences of opinion and animated discussion; but in no case was there the slightest absence of good feeling and decorum. Several interesting documents setting forth the rights as well as the grievances of women were read. Among these was a Declaration of Sentiments, to be regarded as the basis of a grand movement for attaining the civil, social, political, and religious rights of women. We should not do justice to our own convictions, or to the excellent persons connected with this infant movement, if we did not in this connection offer a few remarks on the general subject which the Convention met to consider and the objects they seek to attain. In doing so, we are not insensible that the bare mention of this truly important subject in any other than terms of contemptuous ridicule and scornful disfavor, is likely to excite against us the fury of bigotry and the folly of prejudice. A discussion of the rights of animals would be regarded with far more complacency by many of what are called the "wise" and the "good" of our land, than would a discussion of the rights of women. It is, in their estimation to be guilty of evil thoughts, to think that woman is entitled to equal rights with man. Many who have at last made the discovery that the negroes have some rights as well as other members of the human family, have yet to be convinced that women are entitled to any. Eight years ago a number of persons of this description actually abandoned the anti-slavery cause, lest by giving their influence in that direction they might possibly be giving countenance to the dangerous heresy that woman, in respect to rights, stands on an equal footing with man. In the judgment of such persons the American slave system, with all its concomitant horrors, is less to be deplored than this "wicked" idea. It is perhaps needless to say, that we cherish little sympathy for such sentiments or respect for such prejudices. Standing as we do up on the watch-tower of human freedom, we cannot be deterred from an expression of our approbation of any movement, however humble, to improve and elevate the character of any members of the human family. While it is impossible for us to go into this subject at length, and dispose of the various objections which are often urged against such a doctrine as that of female equality, we are free to say that in respect to political rights, we hold woman to be justly entitled to all we claim for man. We go farther, and express our conviction that all political rights which it is expedient for man to exercise, it is equally for woman. All that distinguishes man as an intelligent and accountable being, is equally true of woman, and if that government only is just which governs by the free consent of the governed, there can be no reason in the world for denying to woman the exercise of the elective franchise, or a hand in making and administering the laws of the land. Our doctrine is that "right is of no sex." We therefore bid the women engaged in this movement our humble Godspeed.

What to the Slave Is the Fourth of July?, July 5, 1852

Mr. President, Friends and Fellow Citizens: He who could address this audience without a quailing sensation, has stronger nerves than I have. I do not remember ever to have appeared as a speaker before any assembly more shrinkingly, nor with greater distrust of my ability, than I do this day. A feeling has crept over me, quite unfavorable to the exercise of my limited powers of speech. The task before me is one which requires much previous thought and study for its proper performance. I know that apologies of this sort are generally considered flat and unmeaning. I trust, however, that mine will not be so considered. Should I seem at ease, my appearance would much misrepresent me. The little experience I have had in addressing public meetings, in country school houses, avails me nothing on the present occasion.

The papers and placards say, that I am to deliver a 4th [of] July oration. This certainly sounds large, and out of the common way, for it is true that I have often had the privilege to speak in this beautiful Hall, and to address many who now honor me with their presence. But neither their familiar faces, nor the perfect gage I think I have of Corinthian Hall, seems to free me from embarrassment.

The fact is, ladies and gentlemen, the distance between this platform and the slave plantation, from which I escaped, is considerable—and the difficulties to be overcome in getting from the latter to the former, are by no means slight. That I am here to-day is, to me, a matter of astonishment as well as of gratitude. You will not, therefore, be surprised, if in what I have to say I evince no elaborate preparation, nor grace my speech with any high sounding exordium. With little experience and with less learning, I have been able to throw my thoughts hastily and imperfectly together; and trusting to your patient and generous indulgence, I will proceed to lay them before you. . . .

This, for the purpose of this celebration, is the 4th of July. It is the birthday of your National Independence, and of your political freedom. This, to you, is what the Passover was to the emancipated people of God. It carries your minds back to the day, and to the act of your great deliverance; and to the signs, and to the wonders, associated with that act, and that day. This celebration also marks the beginning of another year of your national life; and reminds you that the Republic of America is now 76 years old. . . .

Fellow Citizens, I am not wanting in respect for the fathers of this republic. The signers of the Declaration of Independence were brave men. They were great men, too, great enough to give frame to a great age. It does not often happen to a nation to raise, at one time, such a number of truly great men. The point from which I am compelled to view them is not, certainly, the most favorable; and yet I cannot contemplate their great deeds with less than admiration. They were statesmen, patriots and heroes, and for the good they did, and the principles they contended for, I will unite with you to honor their memory. . . .

Fellow-citizens, pardon me, allow me to ask, why am I called upon to speak here to-day? What have I, or those I represent, to do with your national independence?

Source: John W. Blassingame, ed., *The Frederick Douglass Papers: Series One: Speeches, Debates, and Interviews,* 1847–1854 (New Haven: Yale University Press, 1982), vol. 2, 359–371, 386–387.

Are the great principles of political freedom and of natural justice, embodied in that Declaration of Independence, extended to us? and am I, therefore, called upon to bring our humble offering to the national altar, and to confess the benefits and express devout gratitude for the blessings resulting from your independence to us?

Would to God, both for your sakes and ours, that an affirmative answer could be truthfully returned to these questions! Then would my task be light, and my burden easy and delightful. For who is there so cold, that a nation's sympathy could not warm him? Who so obdurate and dead to the claims of gratitude, that would not thankfully acknowledge such priceless benefits? Who so stolid and selfish, that would not give his voice to swell the hallelujahs of a nation's jubilee, when the chains of servitude had been torn from his limbs? I am not that man. In a case like that, the dumb might eloquently speak, and the "lame man leap as an hart."

But such is not the state of the case. I say it with a sad sense of the disparity between us. I am not included within the pale of glorious anniversary! Your high independence only reveals the immeasurable distance between us. The blessings in which you, this day, rejoice, are not enjoyed in common. The rich inheritance of justice, liberty, prosperity and independence, bequeathed by your fathers, is shared by you, not by me. The sunlight that brought light and healing to you, has brought stripes and death to me. This Fourth July is yours, not mine. You may rejoice, I must mourn. To drag a man in fetters into the grand illuminated temple of liberty, and call upon him to join you in joyous anthems, were inhuman mockery and sacrilegious irony. Do you mean, citizens, to mock me, by asking me to speak to-day? If so, there is a parallel to your conduct. And let me warn you that it is dangerous to copy the example of a nation whose crimes, towering up to heaven, were thrown down by the breath of the Almighty, burying that nation in irrevocable ruin! I can to-day take up the plaintive lament of a peeled and woe-smitten people!

"By the rivers of Babylon, there we sat down. Yea! we wept when we remembered Zion. We hanged our harps upon the willows in the midst thereof. For there, they that carried us away captive, required of us a song; and they who wasted us required of us mirth, saying, Sing us one of the songs of Zion. How can we sing the Lord's song in a strange land? If I forget thee, O Jerusalem, let my right hand forget her cunning. If I do not remember thee, let my tongue cleave to the roof of my mouth."

Fellow-citizens, above your national, tumultuous joy, I hear the mournful wail of millions! whose chains, heavy and grievous yesterday, are, to-day, rendered more intolerable by the jubilee shouts that reach them. If I do forget, if I do not faithfully remember those bleeding children of sorrow this day, "may my right hand forget her cunning, and may my tongue cleave to the roof of my mouth!" To forget them, to pass lightly over their wrongs, and to chime in with the popular theme, would be treason most scandalous and shocking, and would make me a reproach before God and the world.

My subject, then, fellow-citizens, is American slavery. I shall see this day and its popular characteristics from the slave's point of view. Standing there identified with the American bondman, making his wrongs mine, I do not hesitate to declare, with all my soul, that the character and conduct of this nation never looked blacker to me than on this 4th of July!

Whether we turn to the declarations of the past, or to the professions of the present, the conduct of the nation seems equally hideous and revolting. America is false to the past, false to the present, and solemnly binds herself to be false to the future. Standing with God and the crushed and bleeding slave on this occasion, I will, in the name of humanity which is outraged, in the name of liberty which is fettered, in the name of the constitution and the Bible which are disregarded and trampled upon, dare to call in question and to denounce, with all the emphasis I can command, everything that serves to perpetuate slavery—the great sin and shame of America! "I will not equivocate; I will not excuse"; I will use the severest language I can command; and yet not one word shall escape me that any man, whose judgment is not blinded by prejudice, or who is not at heart a slaveholder, shall not confess to be right and just.

But I fancy I hear some one of my audience say, "It is just in this circumstance that you and your brother abolitionists fail to make a favorable impression on the public mind. Would you argue more, and denounce less; would you persuade more, and rebuke less; your cause would be much more likely to succeed."

But, I submit, where all is plain there is nothing to be argued. What point in the anti-slavery creed would you have me argue? On what branch of the subject do the people of this country need light? Must I undertake to prove that the slave is a man? That point is conceded already. Nobody doubts it. The slaveholders themselves acknowledge it in the enactment of laws for their government. They acknowledge it when they punish disobedience on the part of the slave. There are seventy-two crimes in the State of Virginia which, if committed by a black man (no matter how ignorant he be), subject him to the punishment of death; while only two of the same crimes will subject a white man to the like punishment. What is this but the acknowledgment that the slave is a moral, intellectual, and responsible being? The manhood of the slave is conceded. It is admitted in the fact that Southern statute books are covered with enactments forbidding, under severe fines and penalties, the teaching of the slave to read or to write. When you can point to any such laws in reference to the beasts of the field, then I may consent to argue the manhood of the slave. When the dogs in your streets, when the fowls of the air, when the cattle on your hills, when the fish of the sea, and the reptiles that crawl, shall be unable to distinguish the slave from a brute, then will I argue with you that the slave is a man!

For the present, it is enough to affirm the equal manhood of the Negro race. Is it not astonishing that, while we are ploughing, planting, and reaping, using all kinds of mechanical tools, erecting houses, constructing bridges, building ships, working in metals of brass, iron, copper, silver and gold; that, while we are reading, writing and ciphering, acting as clerks, merchants and secretaries, having among us lawyers, doctors, ministers, poets, authors, editors, orators and teachers; that, while we are engaged in all manner of enterprises common to other men, digging gold in California, capturing the whale in the Pacific, feeding sheep and cattle on the hill-side, living, moving, acting, thinking, planning, living in families as husbands, wives and children, and, above all, confessing and worshipping the Christian's God, and looking hopefully for life and immortality beyond the grave, we are called upon to prove that we are men!

Would you have me argue that man is entitled to liberty? that he is the rightful owner of his own body? You have already declared it. Must I argue the wrongfulness of slavery? Is that a question for Republicans? Is it to be settled by the rules of logic and argumentation, as a matter beset with great difficulty, involving a doubtful application of the principle of justice, hard to be understood? How should I look today, in the presence of Americans, dividing, and subdividing a discourse, to show that men have a natural right to freedom? speaking of it relatively and positively, negatively and affirmatively. To do so, would be to make myself ridiculous, and to offer an insult to your understanding. There is not a man beneath the canopy of heaven that does not know that slavery is wrong for him.

What, am I to argue that it is wrong to make men brutes, to rob them of their liberty, to work them without wages, to keep them ignorant of their relations to their fellow men, to beat them with sticks, to flay their flesh with the lash, to load their limbs with irons, to hunt them with dogs, to sell them at auction, to sunder their families, to knock out their teeth, to burn their flesh, to starve them into obedience and submission to their masters? Must I argue that a system thus marked with blood, and stained with pollution, is wrong? No! I will not. I have better employment for my time and strength than such arguments would imply.

What, then, remains to be argued? Is it that slavery is not divine; that God did not establish it; that our doctors of divinity are mistaken? There is blasphemy in the thought. That which is inhuman, cannot be divine! Who can reason on such a proposition? They that can, may; I cannot. The time for such argument is passed.

At a time like this, scorching irony, not convincing argument, is needed. O! had I the ability, and could reach the nation's ear, I would, to-day, pour out a fiery stream of biting ridicule, blasting reproach, withering sarcasm, and stern rebuke. For it is not light that is needed, but fire; it is not the gentle shower, but thunder. We need the storm, the whirlwind, and the earthquake. The feeling of the nation must be quickened; the conscience of the nation must be roused; the propriety of the nation must be startled; the hypocrisy of the nation must be exposed; and its crimes against God and man must be proclaimed and denounced.

What, to the American slave, is your 4th of July? I answer; a day that reveals to him, more than all other days in the year, the gross injustice and cruelty to which he is the constant victim. To him, your celebration is a sham; your boasted liberty, an unholy license; your national greatness, swelling vanity; your sounds of rejoicing are empty and heartless; your denunciation of tyrants, brass fronted impudence; your shouts of liberty and equality, hollow mockery; your prayers and hymns, your sermons and thanksgivings, with all your religious parade and solemnity, are, to Him, mere bombast, fraud, deception, impiety, and hypocrisy—a thin veil to cover up crimes which would disgrace a nation of savages. There is not a nation on the earth guilty of practices more shocking and bloody than are the people of the United States, at this very hour.

Go where you may, search where you will, roam through all the monarchies and despotisms of the Old World, travel through South America, search out every abuse, and when you have found the last, lay your facts by the side of the everyday practices of this nation, and you will say with me, that, for revolting barbarity and shameless hypocrisy, America reigns without a rival. . . .

Allow me to say, in conclusion, notwithstanding the dark picture I have this day presented, of the state of the nation, I do not despair of this country. There are forces in operation which must inevitably work the downfall of slavery. "The arm of the Lord is not shortened," and the doom of slavery is certain. I, therefore, leave off where I began, with hope. While drawing encouragement from "the Declaration of Independence," the great principles it contains, and the genius of American Institutions, my spirit is also cheered by the obvious tendencies of the age. . . .

Henry David Thoreau (1817–1862)

When hostilities with Mexico broke out in 1846, there was little doubt in anyone's mind that the war was going to be a war for expansion. Many Northerners were aware that the South had set its sights on the northern provinces of Mexico as suitable territory into which slavery could be expanded and out of which new slave states could be carved. But, on the whole, there was widespread enthusiasm and patriotic fervor in favor of war. Two hundred thousand men volunteered for the army, while politicians and newspapers claimed that the war would be a blessing for Mexico by bestowing the American benefits of liberty and equality. Abolitionists and some clergymen and politicians, however, raised their voices in opposition to a war that would expand slavery. William Lloyd Garrison staunchly condemned the war. So, too, did Theodore Parker, Henry Clay, and David Wilmot. A little-known one-term congressman from Illinois, responding to President Polk's statement that "American blood had been spilled on American soil," introduced the "Spot Resolution" to Congress, which demanded that the president reveal the exact spot on which American blood had been spilled. Abraham Lincoln's resolution, however, was defeated, and war was declared. Eventually, enthusiasm for the war began to wane, especially after reports out of Mexico revealed that tens of thousands of American soldiers were dying of dysentery and other diseases, hundreds were deserting, and atrocities were being perpetrated against the civilian population.

The most famous dissenter against the Mexican War was Henry David Thoreau. Thoreau, like his close friend Ralph Waldo Emerson, was a transcendentalist. In the summer of 1846, Thoreau was in the midst of his experiment in living life simply and deliberately at Walden Pond. He believed that most men were living lives of "quiet desperation" because they were unable to connect with their own spirits. "However mean your life is," Thoreau wrote, "meet it and live it; do not shun it and call it hard names." In July 1846, after refusing to pay his poll tax because he refused to support a government that was undertaking a war to expand slavery, Thoreau was arrested and put in jail. Though he spent only one night in the cell (against his wishes, his aunt paid the tax for him), the experience led him to write one of the most influential essays in American literature. In "On Resistance to Civil Government" (also referred to as "On the Duty of Civil Disobedience"), Thoreau argued that when there is injustice, it is the duty of every just man to oppose that injustice. If a law is unjust—as any law supporting the institution of slavery was—then it is the duty of every just person to break that law and pay the consequences. In this way, enough pressure would be put on the government so that the authorities would have no recourse but to change the law. The story (perhaps apocryphal) has been told that Emerson, scandalized that his friend had been locked up, visited Thoreau that night and asked, "Henry, what are you doing in there?" Thoreau, looking back through the bars, without hesitation replied, "Ralph, what are you doing *out* there!"

"Civil Disobedience" would go on to have a far wider impact than perhaps Thoreau himself could have foreseen. Later in the century a young law student in London read it and spent the rest of his life using Thoreau's principles to fight apartheid in South Africa and British imperialism in his native India. This, of course, was Mohandas K. Gandhi. In the 1940s, a young theology student at Morehouse College who had been following Gandhi's career also fell under the spell of "Civil Disobedience" and put its ideas to the test after he became a minister in Montgomery, Alabama, in 1955. Eight years later, in 1963, the Rev. Martin Luther King Jr. wrote "Letter from Birmingham Jail," in which he, too, echoing Thoreau, made a distinction between just laws and unjust laws.

Though Thoreau pointed out repeatedly that individuals must strive for self-realization, he did not lose sight of the fact that individuals must operate within society and that they have an obligation to do what is right. According to Thoreau, what is the best form of government? Is the state separate from its citizens? When is the majority right?

"I learned this, at least, by my experiment," Thoreau wrote at the end of *Walden*, "that if one advances confidently in the direction of his dreams, and endeavors to live the life which he has imagined, he will meet with a success unexpected in common hours."

"On Resistance to Civil Government," 1849

I heartily accept the motto, "That government is best which governs least"; and I should like to see it acted up to more rapidly and systematically. Carried out, it finally amounts to this, which also I believe—"That government is best which governs not at all"; and when men are prepared for it, that will be the kind of government which they will have. Government is at best but an expedient; but most governments are usually, and all governments are sometimes, inexpedient. The objections which have been brought against a standing army, and they are many and weighty, and deserve to prevail, may also at last be brought against a standing government. The standing army is only an arm of the standing government. The government itself, which is only the mode which the people have chosen to execute their will, is equally liable to be abused and perverted before the people can act through it. Witness the present Mexican war, the work of comparatively a few individuals using the standing government as their tool; for in the outset, the people would not have consented to this measure.

This American government—what is it but a tradition, though a recent one, endeavoring to transmit itself unimpaired to posterity, but each instant losing some of its integrity? It has not the vitality and force of a single living man; for a single man can bend it to his will. It is a sort of wooden gun to the people themselves. But

SOURCE: Henry David Thoreau, *Walden and Resistance to Civil Government*, ed. by William Rossi (New York: W. W. Norton, 1992), 226–245.

it is not the less necessary for this; for the people must have some complicated machinery or other, and hear its din, to satisfy that idea of government which they have. Governments show thus how successfully men can be imposed upon, even impose on themselves, for their own advantage. It is excellent, we must all allow. Yet this government never of itself furthered any enterprise, but by the alacrity with which it got out of its way. It does not keep the country free. It does not settle the West. It does not educate. The character inherent in the American people has done all that has been accomplished; and it would have done somewhat more, if the government had not sometimes got in its way. For government is an expedient, by which men would fain succeed in letting one another alone; and, as has been said, when it is most expedient, the governed are most let alone by it. Trade and commerce, if they were not made of india-rubber, would never manage to bounce over obstacles which legislators are continually putting in their way; and if one were to judge these men wholly by the effects of their actions and not partly by their intentions, they would deserve to be classed and punished with those mischievious persons who put obstructions on the railroads.

But, to speak practically and as a citizen, unlike those who call themselves no-government men, I ask for, not at once no government, but at once a better government. Let every man make known what kind of government would command his respect, and that will be one step toward obtaining it.

After all, the practical reason why, when the power is once in the hands of the people, a majority are permitted, and for a long period continue, to rule is not because they are most likely to be in the right, nor because this seems fairest to the minority, but because they are physically the strongest. But a government in which the majority rule in all cases can not be based on justice, even as far as men understand it. Can there not be a government in which the majorities do not virtually decide right and wrong, but conscience?—in which majorities decide only those questions to which the rule of expediency is applicable? Must the citizen ever for a moment, or in the least degree, resign his conscience to the legislator? Why has every man a conscience then? I think that we should be men first, and subjects afterward. It is not desirable to cultivate a respect for the law, so much as for the right. The only obligation which I have a right to assume is to do at any time what I think right. It is truly enough said that a corporation has no conscience; but a corporation of conscientious men is a corporation with a conscience. Law never made men a whit more just; and, by means of their respect for it, even the well-disposed are daily made the agents of injustice. A common and natural result of an undue respect for the law is, that you may see a file of soldiers, colonel, captain, corporal, privates, powder-monkeys, and all, marching in admirable order over hill and dale to the wars, against their wills, ay, against their common sense and consciences, which makes it very steep marching indeed, and produces a palpitation of the heart. They have no doubt that it is a damnable business in which they are concerned; they are all peaceably inclined. Now, what are they? Men at all? or small movable forts and magazines, at the service of some unscrupulous man in power? Visit the Navy Yard, and behold a marine, such a man as an American government can make, or such as it can make a man with its black arts—a mere shadow and reminiscence of humanity, a man laid out alive and standing, and already, as one may say, buried under arms with funeral accompaniment, though it may be,

"Not a drum was heard, not a funeral note,
      As his corse to the rampart we hurried;
Not a soldier discharged his farewell shot
      O'er the grave where our hero was buried."

The mass of men serve the state thus, not as men mainly, but as machines, with their bodies. They are the standing army, and the militia, jailers, constables, posse comitatus, etc. In most cases there is no free exercise whatever of the judgement or of the moral sense; but they put themselves on a level with wood and earth and stones; and wooden men can perhaps be manufactured that will serve the purpose as well. Such command no more respect than men of straw or a lump of dirt. They have the same sort of worth only as horses and dogs. Yet such as these even are commonly esteemed good citizens. Others—as most legislators, politicians, lawyers, ministers, and office-holders—serve the state chiefly with their heads; and, as they rarely make any moral distinctions, they are as likely to serve the devil, without intending it, as God. A very few—as heroes, patriots, martyrs, reformers in the great sense, and men—serve the state with their consciences also, and so necessarily resist it for the most part; and they are commonly treated as enemies by it. A wise man will only be useful as a man, and will not submit to be "clay," and "stop a hole to keep the wind away," but leave that office to his dust at least:

"I am too high born to be propertied,
To be a second at control,
Or useful serving-man and instrument
To any sovereign state throughout the world."

He who gives himself entirely to his fellow men appears to them useless and selfish; but he who gives himself partially to them is pronounced a benefactor and philanthropist.

How does it become a man to behave toward the American government today? I answer, that he cannot without disgrace be associated with it. I cannot for an instant recognize that political organization as my government which is the slave's government also.

All men recognize the right of revolution; that is, the right to refuse allegiance to, and to resist, the government, when its tyranny or its inefficiency are great and unendurable. But almost all say that such is not the case now. But such was the case, they think, in the Revolution of '75. If one were to tell me that this was a bad government because it taxed certain foreign commodities brought to its ports, it is most probable that I should not make an ado about it, for I can do without them. All machines have their friction; and possibly this does enough good to counter-balance the evil. At any rate, it is a great evil to make a stir about it. But when the friction comes to have its machine, and oppression and robbery are organized, I say, let us not have such a machine any longer. In other words, when a sixth of the population of a nation which has undertaken to be the refuge of liberty are slaves, and a whole country is unjustly overrun and conquered by a foreign army, and subjected to military law, I think that it is not too soon for honest men to rebel and revolutionize. What makes this duty the more urgent is the fact that the country so overrun is not our own, but ours is the invading army.

Paley, a common authority with many on moral questions, in his chapter on the "Duty of Submission to Civil Government," resolves all civil obligation into expediency; and he proceeds to say that "so long as the interest of the whole society requires it, that it, so long as the established government cannot be resisted or changed without public inconveniencey, it is the will of God . . . that the established government be obeyed—and no longer. This principle being admitted, the justice of every particular case of resistance is reduced to a computation of the quantity of the danger and grievance on the one side, and of the probability and expense of redressing it on the other." Of this, he says, every man shall judge for himself. But Paley appears never to have contemplated those cases to which the rule of expediency does not apply, in which a people, as well as an individual, must do justice, cost what it may. If I have unjustly wrested a plank from a drowning man, I must restore it to him though I drown myself. This, according to Paley, would be inconvenient. But he that would save his life, in such a case, shall lose it. This people must cease to hold slaves, and to make war on Mexico, though it cost them their existence as a people.

In their practice, nations agree with Paley; but does anyone think that Massachusetts does exactly what is right at the present crisis?

> *"A drab of state, a cloth-o'-silver slut,*
> *To have her train borne up, and her soul trail in the dirt."*

Practically speaking, the opponents to a reform in Massachusetts are not a hundred thousand politicians at the South, but a hundred thousand merchants and farmers here, who are more interested in commerce and agriculture than they are in humanity, and are not prepared to do justice to the slave and to Mexico, cost what it may. I quarrel not with far-off foes, but with those who, near at home, co-operate with, and do the bidding of, those far away, and without whom the latter would be harmless. We are accustomed to say, that the mass of men are unprepared; but improvement is slow, because the few are not as materially wiser or better than the many. It is not so important that many should be good as you, as that there be some absolute goodness somewhere; for that will leaven the whole lump. There are thousands who are in opinion opposed to slavery and to the war, who yet in effect do nothing to put an end to them; who, esteeming themselves children of Washington and Franklin, sit down with their hands in their pockets, and say that they know not what to do, and do nothing; who even postpone the question of freedom to the question of free trade, and quietly read the prices-current along with the latest advices from Mexico, after dinner, and, it may be, fall asleep over them both. What is the price-current of an honest man and patriot today? They hesitate, and they regret, and sometimes they petition; but they do nothing in earnest and with effect. They will wait, well disposed, for others to remedy the evil, that they may no longer have it to regret. At most, they give up only a cheap vote, and a feeble countenance and Godspeed, to the right, as it goes by them. There are nine hundred and ninety-nine patrons of virtue to one virtuous man. But it is easier to deal with the real possessor of a thing than with the temporary guardian of it.

All voting is a sort of gaming, like checkers or backgammon, with a slight moral tinge to it, a playing with right and wrong, with moral questions; and betting naturally accompanies it. The character of the voters is not staked. I cast my vote, perchance, as I think right; but I am not vitally concerned that that right should prevail. I am willing to leave it to the majority. Its obligation, therefore, never exceeds that of expediency. Even voting for the right is doing nothing for it. It is only expressing to men feebly your desire that it should prevail. A wise man will not leave the right to the mercy of chance, nor wish it to prevail through the power of the majority. There is but little virtue in the action of masses of men. When the majority shall at length vote for the abolition of slavery, it will be because they are indifferent to slavery, or because there is but little slavery left to be abolished by their vote. They will then be the only slaves. Only his vote can hasten the abolition of slavery who asserts his own freedom by his vote.

I hear of a convention to be held at Baltimore, or elsewhere, for the selection of a candidate for the Presidency, made up chiefly of editors, and men who are politicians by profession; but I think, what is it to any independent, intelligent, and respectable man what decision they may come to? Shall we not have the advantage of this wisdom and honesty, nevertheless? Can we not count upon some independent votes? Are there not many individuals in the country who do not attend conventions? But no: I find that the respectable man, so called, has immediately drifted from his position, and despairs of his country, when his country has more reasons to despair of him. He forthwith adopts one of the candidates thus selected as the only available one, thus proving that he is himself available for any purposes of the demagogue. His vote is of no more worth than that of any unprincipled foreigner or hireling native, who may have been bought. O for a man who is a man, and, as my neighbor says, has a bone is his back which you cannot pass your hand through! Our statistics are at fault: the population has been returned too large. How many men are there to a square thousand miles in the country? Hardly one. Does not America offer any inducement for men to settle here? The American has dwindled into an Odd Fellow—one who may be known by the development of his organ of gregariousness, and a manifest lack of intellect and cheerful self-reliance; whose first and chief concern, on coming into the world, is to see that the almshouses are in good repair; and, before yet he has lawfully donned the virile garb, to collect a fund to the support of the widows and orphans that may be; who, in short, ventures to live only by the aid of the Mutual Insurance company, which has promised to bury him decently.

It is not a man's duty, as a matter of course, to devote himself to the eradication of any, even to most enormous, wrong; he may still properly have other concerns to engage him; but it is his duty, at least, to wash his hands of it, and, if he gives it no thought longer, not to give it practically his support. If I devote myself to other pursuits and contemplations, I must first see, at least, that I do not pursue them sitting upon another man's shoulders. I must get off him first, that he may pursue his contemplations too. See what gross inconsistency is tolerated. I have heard some of my townsmen say, "I should like to have them order me out to help put down an insurrection of the slaves, or to march to Mexico—see if I would go"; and yet these very men have each, directly by their allegiance, and so indirectly, at least, by their money, furnished a substitute. The soldier is applauded who refuses to serve in an unjust war by those who do not refuse to sustain the unjust government which makes the war; is applauded by those whose own act and authority he disregards and sets at naught; as if the state were penitent to that degree that it hired one to scourge it while it sinned, but not to that degree that it left off sinning for a moment. Thus, under the name of Order and Civil Government, we are all made at last to pay homage to and support our own meanness. After the first blush of sin comes its indifference; and from immoral it becomes, as it were, unmoral, and not quite unnecessary to that life which we have made.

The broadest and most prevalent error requires the most disinterested virtue to sustain it. The slight reproach to which the virtue of patriotism is commonly liable, the noble are most likely to incur. Those who, while they disapprove of the character and measures of a government, yield to it their allegiance and support are undoubtedly its most conscientious supporters, and so frequently the most serious obstacles to reform. Some are petitioning the State to dissolve the Union, to disregard the requisitions of the President. Why do they not dissolve it themselves—the union between themselves and the State—and refuse to pay their quota into its treasury? Do not they stand in the same relation to the State that the State does to the Union? And have not the same reasons prevented the State from resisting the Union which have prevented them from resisting the State?

How can a man be satisfied to entertain an opinion merely, and enjoy it? Is there any enjoyment in it, if his opinion is that he is aggrieved? If you are cheated out of a single dollar by your neighbor, you do not rest satisfied with knowing you are cheated, or with saying that you are cheated, or even with petitioning him to pay you your due; but you take effectual steps at once to obtain the full amount, and see to it that you are never cheated again. Action from principle, the perception and the performance of right, changes things and relations; it is essentially revolutionary, and does not consist wholly with anything which was. It not only divided States and churches, it divides families; ay, it divides the individual, separating the diabolical in him from the divine.

Unjust laws exist: shall we be content to obey them, or shall we endeavor to amend them, and obey them until we have succeeded, or shall we transgress them at once? Men, generally, under such a government as this, think that they ought to wait until they have persuaded the majority to alter them. They think that, if they should resist, the remedy would be worse than the evil. But it is the fault of the government itself that the remedy is worse than the evil. It makes it worse. Why is it not more apt to anticipate and provide for reform? Why does it not cherish its wise minority? Why does it cry and resist before it is hurt? Why does it not encourage its citizens to put out its faults, and do better than it would have them? Why does it always crucify Christ and excommunicate Copernicus and Luther, and pronounce Washington and Franklin rebels?

One would think, that a deliberate and practical denial of its authority was the only offense never contemplated by its government; else, why has it not assigned its definite, its suitable and proportionate, penalty? If a man who has no property refuses but once to earn nine shillings for the State, he is put in prison for a period unlimited by any law that I know, and determined only by the discretion of those who put him there; but if he should steal ninety times nine shillings from the State, he is soon permitted to go at large again.

If the injustice is part of the necessary friction of the machine of government, let it go, let it go: perchance it will wear smooth—certainly the machine will wear out. If the injustice has a spring, or a pulley, or a rope, or a crank, exclusively for itself, then perhaps you may consider whether the remedy will not be worse than the evil; but if it is of such a nature that it requires you to be the agent of injustice to another, then I say, break the law. Let your life be a counter-friction to stop the machine. What I have to do is to see, at any rate, that I do not lend myself to the wrong which I condemn.

As for adopting the ways which the State has provided for remedying the evil, I know not of such ways. They take too much time, and a man's life will be gone. I have other affairs to attend to. I came into this world, not chiefly to make this a good place to live in, but to live in it, be it good or bad. A man has not everything to do, but something; and because he cannot do everything, it is not necessary that he should be petitioning the Governor or the Legislature any more than it is theirs to petition me; and if they should not hear my petition, what should I do then? But in this case the State has provided no way: its very Constitution is the evil. This may seem to be harsh and stubborn and unconciliatory; but it is to treat with the utmost kindness and consideration the only spirit that can appreciate or deserves it. So is all change for the better, like birth and death, which convulse the body.

I do not hesitate to say, that those who call themselves Abolitionists should at once effectually withdraw their support, both in person and property, from the government of Massachusetts, and not wait till they constitute a majority of one, before they suffer the right to prevail through them. I think that it is enough if they have God on their side, without waiting for that other one. Moreover, any man more right than his neighbors constitutes a majority of one already.

I meet this American government, or its representative, the State government, directly, and face to face, once a year—no more—in the person of its tax-gatherer; this is the only mode in which a man situated as I am necessarily meets it; and it then says distinctly, Recognize me; and the simplest, the most effectual, and, in the present posture of affairs, the indispensablest mode of treating with it on this head, of expressing your little satisfaction with and love for it, is to deny it then. My civil neighbor, the tax-gatherer, is the very man I have to deal with—for it is, after all, with men and not with parchment that I quarrel—and he has voluntarily chosen to be an agent of the government. How shall he ever know well that he is and does as an officer of the government, or as a man, until he is obliged to consider whether he will treat me, his neighbor, for whom he has respect, as a neighbor and well-disposed man, or as a maniac and disturber of the peace, and see if he can get over this obstruction to his neighborliness without a ruder and more impetuous thought or speech corresponding with his action. I know this well, that if one thousand, if one hundred, if ten men whom I could name—if ten honest men only—ay, if one HONEST man, in this State of Massachusetts, ceasing to hold slaves, were actually to withdraw from this co-partnership, and be locked up in the county jail therefor, it would be the abolition of slavery in America. For it matters not how small the beginning may seem to be: what is once well done is done forever. But we love better to talk about it: that we say is our mission. Reform keeps many scores of newspapers in its service, but not one man. If my esteemed neighbor, the State's ambassador, who will devote his days to the settlement of the question of human rights in the Council Chamber, instead of being threatened with the prisons of Carolina, were to sit down the prisoner of Massachusetts, that State which is so anxious to foist the sin of slavery upon her sister—though at present she can discover only an act of inhospitality to be the ground of a quarrel with her—the Legislature would not wholly waive the subject of the following winter.

Under a government which imprisons unjustly, the true place for a just man is also a prison. The proper place today, the only place which Massachusetts has provided for her freer and less despondent spirits, is in her prisons, to be put out and locked out of the State by her own act, as they have already put themselves out by their principles. It is there that the fugitive slave, and the Mexican prisoner on parole, and the Indian come to plead the wrongs of his race should find them; on that separate but more free and honorable ground, where the State places those who are not with her, but against her—the only house in a slave State in which a free man can abide with honor. If any think that their influence would be lost there, and their voices no longer afflict the ear of the State, that they would not be as an enemy within its walls, they do not know by how much truth is stronger than error, nor how much more eloquently and effectively he can combat injustice who has experienced a little in his own person. Cast your whole vote, not a strip of paper merely, but your whole influence. A minority is powerless while it conforms to the majority; it is not even a minority then; but it is irresistible when it clogs by its whole weight. If the alternative is to keep all just men in prison, or give up war and slavery, the State will not hesitate which to choose. If a thousand men were not to pay their tax bills this year, that would not be a violent and bloody measure, as it would be to pay them, and enable the State to commit violence and shed innocent blood. This is, in fact, the definition of a peaceable revolution, if any such is possible. If the tax-gatherer, or any other public officer, asks me, as one has done, "But what shall I do?" my answer is, "If you really wish to do anything, resign your office." When the subject has refused allegiance, and the officer has resigned from office, then the revolution is accomplished. But even suppose blood shed when the conscience is wounded? Through this wound a man's real manhood and immortality flow out, and he bleeds to an everlasting death. I see this blood flowing now.

I have contemplated the imprisonment of the offender, rather than the seizure of his goods—though both will serve the same purpose—because they who assert the purest right, and consequently are most dangerous to a corrupt State, commonly have not spent much time in accumulating property. To such the State renders comparatively small service, and a slight tax is wont to appear exorbitant, particularly if they are obliged to earn it by special labor with their hands. If there were one who lived wholly without the use of money, the State itself would hesitate to demand it of him. But the rich man—not to make any invidious comparison—is always sold to the institution which makes him rich. Absolutely speaking, the more money, the less virtue; for money comes between a man and his objects, and obtains them for him; it was certainly no great virtue to obtain it. It puts to rest many questions which he would otherwise be taxed to answer; while the only new question which it puts is the hard but superfluous one, how to spend it. Thus his moral ground is taken from under his feet. The opportunities of living are diminished in proportion as that are called the "means" are increased. The best thing a man can do for his culture when he is rich is to endeavor to carry out those schemes which he entertained when he was poor. Christ answered the Herodians according to their condition. "Show me the tribute-money," said he—and one took a penny out of his pocket—if you use money which has the image of Caesar on it, and which he has made current and valuable, that is, if you are men of the State, and gladly enjoy the advantages of Caesar's government, then pay him back some of his own when he demands it. "Render therefore to Caesar that which is Caesar's and to God those things which are God's"—leaving them no wiser than before as to which was which; for they did not wish to know.

When I converse with the freest of my neighbors, I perceive that, whatever they may say about the magnitude and seriousness of the question, and their regard for the public tranquillity, the long and the short of the matter is, that they cannot spare the protection of the existing government, and they dread the consequences to their property and families of disobedience to it. For my own part, I should not like to think that I ever rely on the protection of the State. But, if I deny the authority of the State when it presents its tax bill, it will soon take and waste all my property, and so harass me and my children without end. This is hard. This makes it impossible for a man to live honestly, and at the same time comfortably, in outward respects. It will not be worth the while to accumulate property; that would be sure to go again. You must hire or squat somewhere, and raise but a small crop, and eat that soon. You must live within yourself, and depend upon yourself always tucked up and ready for a start, and not have many affairs. A man may grow rich in Turkey even, if he will be in all respects a good subject of the Turkish government. Confucius said: "If a state is governed by the principles of reason, poverty and misery are subjects of shame; if a state is not governed by the principles of reason, riches and honors are subjects of shame." No: until I want the protection of Massachusetts to be extended to me in some distant Southern port, where my liberty is endangered, or until I am bent solely on building up an estate at home by peaceful enterprise, I can afford to refuse allegiance to Massachusetts, and her right to my property and life. It costs me less in every sense to incur the penalty of disobedience to the State than it would to obey. I should feel as if I were worth less in that case.

Some years ago, the State met me in behalf of the Church, and commanded me to pay a certain sum toward the support of a clergyman whose preaching my father attended, but never I myself. "Pay," it said, "or be locked up in the jail." I declined to pay. But, unfortunately, another man saw fit to pay it. I did not see why the schoolmaster should be taxed to support the priest, and not the priest the schoolmaster; for I was not the State's schoolmaster, but I supported myself by voluntary subscription. I did not see why the lyceum should not present its tax bill, and have the State to back its demand, as well as the Church. However, as the request of the selectmen, I condescended to make some such statement as this in writing: "Know all men by these presents, that I, Henry Thoreau, do not wish to be regarded as a member of any society which I have not joined." This I gave to the town clerk; and he has it. The State, having thus learned that I did not wish to be regarded as a member of that church, has never made a like demand on me since; though it said that it must adhere to its original presumption that time. If I had known how to name them, I should then have signed off in detail from all the societies which I never signed on to; but I did not know where to find such a complete list.

I have paid no poll tax for six years. I was put into a jail once on this account, for one night; and, as I stood considering the walls of solid stone, two or three feet thick, the door of wood and iron, a foot thick, and the iron grating which strained the light, I could not help being struck with the foolishness of that institution which treated me as if I were mere flesh and blood and bones, to be locked up. I wondered that it should have concluded at length that this was the best use it could put me to, and had never thought to avail itself of my services in some way. I saw that, if there was a wall of stone between me and my townsmen, there was a still more difficult one to climb or break through before they could get to be as free as I was. I did not for a moment feel confined, and the walls seemed a great waste of stone and mortar. I felt as if I alone of all my townsmen had paid my tax. They plainly did not know how to treat me, but behaved like persons who are underbred. In every threat and in every compliment there was a blunder; for they thought that my chief desire was to stand the other side of that stone wall. I could not but smile to see how industriously they locked the door on my meditations, which followed them out again without let or hindrance, and they were really all that was dangerous. As they could not reach me, they had resolved to punish my body; just as boys, if they cannot come at some person against whom they have a spite, will abuse his dog. I saw that the State was half-witted, that it was timid as a lone woman with her silver spoons, and that it did not know its friends from its foes, and I lost all my remaining respect for it, and pitied it.

Thus the state never intentionally confronts a man's sense, intellectual or moral, but only his body, his senses. It is not armed with superior wit or honesty, but with superior physical strength. I was not born to be forced. I will breathe after my own fashion. Let us see who is the strongest. What force has a multitude? They only can force me who obey a higher law than I. They force me to become like themselves. I do not hear of men being forced to live this way or that by masses of men. What sort of life were that to live? When I meet a government which says to me, "Your money or your life," why should I be in haste to give it my money? It may be in a great strait, and not know what to do: I cannot help that. It must help itself; do as I do. It is not worth the while to snivel about it. I am not responsible for the successful working of the machinery of society. I am not the son of the engineer. I perceive that, when an acorn and a chestnut fall side by side, the one does not remain inert to make way for the other, but both obey their own laws, and spring and grow and flourish as best they can, till one, perchance, overshadows and destroys the other. If a plant cannot live according to nature, it dies; and so a man.

The night in prison was novel and interesting enough. The prisoners in their shirtsleeves were enjoying a chat and the evening air in the doorway, when I entered. But the jailer said, "Come, boys, it is time to lock up"; and so they dispersed, and I heard the sound of their steps returning into the hollow apartments. My room-mate was introduced to me by the jailer as "a first-rate fellow and clever man." When the door was locked, he showed me where to hang my hat, and how he managed matters there. The rooms were whitewashed once a month; and this one, at least, was the whitest, most simply furnished, and probably neatest apartment in town. He naturally wanted to know where I came from, and what brought me there; and, when I had told him, I asked him in my turn how he came there, presuming him to be an honest man, of course; and as the world goes, I believe he was. "Why," said he, "they accuse me of burning a barn; but I never did it." As near as I could discover, he had probably gone to bed in a barn when drunk, and smoked his pipe there; and so a barn was burnt. He had the reputation of being a clever man, had been there some three months waiting for his trial to come on, and would have to wait as much longer; but he was quite domesticated and contented, since he got his board for nothing, and thought that he was well treated.

He occupied one window, and I the other; and I saw that if one stayed there long, his principal business would be to look out the window. I had soon read all the tracts that were left there, and examined where former prisoners had broken out, and where a grate had been sawed off, and heard the history of the various occupants of that room; for I found that even there there was a history and a gossip which never circulated beyond the walls of the jail. Probably this is the only house in the town where verses are composed, which are afterward printed in a circular form, but not published. I was shown quite a long list of young men who had been detected in an attempt to escape, who avenged themselves by singing them.

I pumped my fellow-prisoner as dry as I could, for fear I should never see him again; but at length he showed me which was my bed, and left me to blow out the lamp.

It was like travelling into a far country, such as I had never expected to behold, to lie there for one night. It seemed to me that I never had heard the town clock strike before, nor the evening sounds of the village; for we slept with the windows open, which were inside the grating. It was to see my native village in the light of the Middle Ages, and our Concord was turned into a Rhine stream, and visions of knights and castles passed before me. They were the voices of old burghers that I heard in the streets. I was an involuntary spectator and auditor of whatever was done and said in the kitchen of the adjacent village inn—a wholly new and rare experience to me. It was a closer view of my native town. I was fairly inside of it. I never had seen its institutions before. This is one of its peculiar institutions; for it is a shire town. I began to comprehend what its inhabitants were about.

In the morning, our breakfasts were put through the hole in the door, in small oblong-square tin pans, made to fit, and holding a pint of chocolate, with brown bread, and an iron spoon. When they called for the vessels again, I was green enough to return what bread I had left, but my comrade seized it, and said that I should lay that up for lunch or dinner. Soon after he was let out to work at haying in a neighboring field, whither he went every day, and would not be back till noon; so he bade me good day, saying that he doubted if he should see me again.

When I came out of prison—for some one interfered, and paid that tax—I did not perceive that great changes had taken place on the common, such as he observed who went in a youth and emerged a gray-headed man; and yet a change had come to my eyes come over the scene—the town, and State, and country, greater than any that mere time could effect. I saw yet more distinctly the State in which I lived. I saw to what extent the people among whom I lived could be trusted as good neighbors and friends; that their friendship was for summer weather only; that they did not greatly propose to do right; that they were a distinct race from me by their prejudices and superstitions, as the Chinamen and Malays are that in their sacrifices to humanity they ran no risks, not even to their property; that after all they were not so noble but they treated the thief as he had treated them, and hoped, by a certain outward observance and a few prayers, and by walking in a particular straight though useless path from time to time, to save their souls. This may be to judge my neighbors harshly; for I believe that many of them are not aware that they have such an institution as the jail in their village.

It was formerly the custom in our village, when a poor debtor came out of jail, for his acquaintances to salute him, looking through their fingers, which were crossed to represent the jail window, "How do ye do?" My neighbors did not thus salute me, but first looked at me, and then at one another, as if I had returned from a long journey. I was put into jail as I was going to the shoemaker's to get a shoe which was mended. When I was let out the next morning, I proceeded to finish my errand, and, having put on my mended shoe, joined a huckleberry party, who were impatient to put themselves under my conduct; and in half an hour—for the horse was soon tackled—was in the midst of a huckleberry field, on one of our highest hills, two miles off, and then the State was nowhere to be seen.

This is the whole history of "My Prisons."

I have never declined paying the highway tax, because I am as desirous of being a good neighbor as I am of being a bad subject; and as for supporting schools, I am doing my part to educate my fellow countrymen now. It is for no particular item in the tax bill that I refuse to pay it. I simply wish to refuse allegiance to the State, to withdraw and stand aloof from it effectually. I do not care to trace the course of my dollar, if I could, till it buys a man a musket to shoot one with—the dollar is innocent—but I am concerned to trace the effects of my allegiance. In fact, I quietly declare war with the State, after my fashion, though I will still make use and get what advantages of her I can, as is usual in such cases.

If others pay the tax which is demanded of me, from a sympathy with the State, they do but what they have already done in their own case, or rather they abet injustice to a greater extent than the State requires. If they pay the tax from a mistaken interest in the individual taxed, to save his property, or prevent his going to jail, it is because they have not considered wisely how far they let their private feelings interfere with the public good.

This, then is my position at present. But one cannot be too much on his guard in such a case, lest his actions be biased by obstinacy or an undue regard for the opinions of men. Let him see that he does only what belongs to himself and to the hour.

I think sometimes, Why, this people mean well, they are only ignorant; they would do better if they knew how: why give your neighbors this pain to treat you as they are not inclined to? But I think again, This is no reason why I should do as they do, or permit others to suffer much greater pain of a different kind. Again, I sometimes say to myself, When many millions of men, without heat, without ill will, without personal feelings of any kind, demand of you a few shillings only, without the possibility, such is their constitution, of retracting or altering their present demand, and without the possibility, on your side, of appeal to any other millions, why expose yourself to this overwhelming brute force? You do not resist cold and hunger, the winds and the waves, thus obstinately; you quietly submit to a thousand similar necessities. You do not put your head into the fire. But just in proportion as I regard this as not wholly a brute force, but partly a human force, and consider that I have relations to those millions as to so many millions of men, and not of mere brute or inanimate things, I see that appeal is possible, first and instantaneously, from them to the Maker of them, and, secondly, from them to themselves. But if I put my head deliberately into the fire, there is no appeal to fire or to the Maker for fire, and I have only myself to blame. If I could convince myself that I have any right to be satisfied with men as they are, and to treat them accordingly, and not according, in some respects, to my requisitions and expectations of what they and I ought to be, then, like a good Mussulman and fatalist, I should endeavor to be satisfied with things as they are, and say it is the will of God. And, above all, there is this difference between resisting this and a purely brute or natural force, that I can resist this with some effect; but I cannot expect, like Orpheus, to change the nature of the rocks and trees and beasts.

I do not wish to quarrel with any man or nation. I do not wish to split hairs, to make fine distinctions, or set myself up as better than my neighbors. I seek rather, I may say, even an excuse for conforming to the laws of the land. I am but too ready to conform to them. Indeed, I have reason to suspect myself on this head; and each year, as the tax-gatherer comes round, I find myself disposed to review the acts and position of the general and State governments, and the spirit of the people to discover a pretext for conformity.

> *"We must affect our country as our parents,*
> *And if at any time we alienate*
> *Our love or industry from doing it honor,*
> *We must respect effects and teach the soul*
> *Matter of conscience and religion,*
> *And not desire of rule or benefit."*

I believe that the State will soon be able to take all my work of this sort out of my hands, and then I shall be no better patriot than my fellow-countrymen. Seen from a lower point of view, the Constitution, with all its faults, is very good; the law and the courts are very respectable; even this State and this American government are, in many respects, very admirable, and rare things, to be thankful for, such as a great many have described them; but seen from a point of view a little higher, they are what I have described them; seen from a higher still, and the highest, who shall say what they are, or that they are worth looking at or thinking of at all?

However, the government does not concern me much, and I shall bestow the fewest possible thoughts on it. It is not many moments that I live under a government, even in this world. If a man is thought-free, fancy-free, imagination-free, that which is not never for a long time appearing to be to him, unwise rulers or reformers cannot fatally interrupt him.

I know that most men think differently from myself; but those whose lives are by profession devoted to the study of these or kindred subjects content me as little as any. Statesmen and legislators, standing so completely within the institution, never distinctly and nakedly behold it. They speak of moving society, but have no resting-place without it. They may be men of a certain experience and discrimination, and have no doubt invented ingenious and even useful systems, for which we sincerely thank them; but all their wit and usefulness lie within certain not very wide limits. They are wont to forget that the world is not governed by policy and expediency. [Daniel] Webster never goes behind government, and so cannot speak with authority about it. His words are wisdom to those legislators who contemplate no essential reform in the existing government; but for thinkers, and those who legislate for all time, he never once glances at the subject. I know of those whose serene and wise speculations on this theme would soon reveal the limits of his mind's range and hospitality. Yet, compared with the cheap professions of most reformers, and the still cheaper wisdom and eloquence of politicians in general, his are almost the only sensible and valuable words, and we thank Heaven for him. Comparatively, he is always strong, original, and, above all, practical. Still, his quality is not wisdom, but prudence. The lawyer's truth is not Truth, but consistency or a consistent expediency. Truth is always in harmony with herself, and is not concerned chiefly to reveal the justice that may consist with wrongdoing. He well deserves to be called, as he has been called, the Defender of the Constitution. There are really no blows to be given him but defensive ones. He is not a leader, but a follower. His leaders are the men of '87. "I have never made an effort," he says, "and never propose to make an effort; I have never countenanced an effort, and never mean to countenance an effort, to disturb the arrangement as originally made, by which various States came into the Union." Still thinking of the sanction which the Constitution gives to slavery, he says, "Because it was part of the original compact—let it stand." Notwithstanding his special acuteness and ability, he is unable to take a fact out of its merely political relations, and behold it as it lies absolutely to be disposed of by the intellect—what, for instance, it behooves a man to do here in America today with regard to slavery—but ventures, or is driven, to make some such desperate answer to the following, while professing to speak absolutely, and as a private man— from which what new and singular of social duties might be inferred? "The manner," says he, "in which the governments of the States where slavery exists are to regulate it is for their own consideration, under the responsibility to their constituents, to the general laws of propriety, humanity, and justice, and to God. Associations formed elsewhere, springing from a feeling of humanity, or any other cause, have nothing whatever to do with it. They have never received any encouragement from me and they never will. [These extracts have been inserted since the lecture was read -HDT]

They who know of no purer sources of truth, who have traced up its stream no higher, stand, and wisely stand, by the Bible and the Constitution, and drink at it there with reverence and humanity; but they who behold where it comes trickling into this lake or that pool, gird up their loins once more, and continue their pilgrimage toward its fountainhead.

No man with a genius for legislation has appeared in America. They are rare in the history of the world. There are orators, politicians, and eloquent men, by the thousand; but the speaker has not yet opened his mouth to speak who is capable of settling the much-vexed questions of the day. We love eloquence for its own sake, and not for any truth which it may utter, or any heroism it may inspire. Our legislators have not yet learned the comparative value of free trade and of freedom, of union, and of rectitude, to a nation. They have no genius or talent for comparatively humble questions of taxation and finance, commerce and manufactures and agriculture. If we were left solely to the wordy wit of legislators in Congress for our guidance, uncorrected by the seasonable experience and the effectual complaints of the people, America would not long retain her rank among the nations. For eighteen hundred years, though perchance I have no right to say it, the New Testament has been written; yet where is the legislator who has wisdom and practical talent enough to avail himself of the light which it sheds on the science of legislation.

The authority of government, even such as I am willing to submit to—for I will cheerfully obey those who know and can do better than I, and in many things even those who neither know nor can do so well—is still an impure one: to be strictly just, it must have the sanction and consent of the governed. It can have no pure right over my person and property but what I concede to it. The progress from an absolute to a limited monarchy, from a limited monarchy to a democracy, is a progress toward a true respect for the individual. Even the Chinese philosopher was wise enough to regard the individual as the basis of the empire. Is a democracy, such as we know it, the last improvement possible in government? Is it not possible to take a step further towards recognizing and organizing the rights of man? There will never be a really free and enlightened State until the State comes to recognize the individual as a higher and independent power, from which all its own power and authority are derived, and treats him accordingly. I please myself with imagining a State at last which can afford to be just to all men, and to treat the individual with respect as a neighbor; which even would not think it inconsistent with its own repose if a few were to live aloof from it, not meddling with it, nor embraced by it, who fulfilled all the duties of neighbors and fellow men. A State which bore this kind of fruit, and suffered it to drop off as fast as it ripened, would prepare the way for a still more perfect and glorious State, which I have also imagined, but not yet anywhere seen.

Lucy Stone (1818–1893)

A graduate of Oberlin College, Lucy Stone spent most of her life as an influential abolitionist and feminist. When she married Henry B. Blackwell in 1855, she not only kept her maiden name but also used the marriage ceremony to issue a protest statement in which she (and her husband) deplored the subjugation of women. What aspect of women's lives is most objectionable to Lucy Stone?

Statement on Marriage, 1855

While acknowledging our mutual affection by publicly assuming the relationship of husband and wife, yet in justice to ourselves and a great principle, we deem it a duty to declare that this act on our part implies no sanction of, nor promise of voluntary obedience to such of the present laws of marriage, as refuse to recognize the wife as an independent, rational being, while they confer upon the husband an injurious and unnatural superiority, investing him with legal powers which no honorable man would exercise, and which no man should possess. We protest especially against the laws which give to the husband:

SOURCE: Elizabeth Cady Stanton, Susan B. Anthony, and Matilda Joslyn Gage, eds., *History of Woman Suffrage,* vol. 1, (1881; New York: Arno Press and the New York Times, 1969), 260–261.

1. The custody of the wife's person.
2. The exclusive control and guardianship of their children.
3. The sole ownership of her personal, and use of her real estate, unless previ-ously settled upon her, or placed in the hands of trustees, as in the case of minors, lunatics, and idiots.
4. The absolute right to the product of her industry.
5. Also against laws which give to the widower so much larger and more perma-nent interest in the property of his deceased wife, than they give to the widow in that of the deceased husband.
6. Finally, against the whole system by which "the legal existence of the wife is suspended during marriage," so that in most States, she neither has a legal part in the choice of her residence, nor can she make a will, nor sue or be sued in her own name, nor inherit property.

We believe that personal independence and equal human rights can never be for-feited, except for crime; that marriage should be an equal and permanent partner-ship, and so recognized by law; that until it is so recognized, married partners should provide against the radical injustice of present laws, by every means in their power.

We believe that where domestic difficulties arise, no appeal should be made to legal tribunals under existing laws, but that all difficulties should be submitted to the equitable adjustment of arbitrators mutually chosen.

Thus reverencing law, we enter our protest against rules and customs which are unworthy of the name, since they violate justice, the essence of law.

[Signed]

Henry B. Blackwell

Lucy Stone

The Know-Nothings

As the issue of slavery was rapidly consuming party politics during the 1840s and 1850s, a growing number of people began to believe that the real threat to the United States was not slavery but immigration, especially the immigration of Roman Catholics from Ireland and Germany. Believing that the United States would be undermined by the influx of these immigrants, who would presumably put their loyalty to the pope over the Constitution, old-stock Americans began to espouse nativism and joined various secret antiforeigner organizations. Eventually, these nativist groups formed the American Party to keep "America for Americans" and to ensure that Protes-tantism remained the dominant religion. Popularly called the Know-Nothings (because they usually responded, "I know nothing" when outsiders ques-tioned them about the party), they met in Philadelphia in 1856, drew up a platform, and nominated former president Millard Fillmore as their candidate.

The party received 21 percent of the popular vote in the election, but by the election of 1860, the slavery issue so dominated the nation that the Know-Nothings' political influence had dissipated.

In protesting immigration, were the Know-Nothings really dissenting? Was their view a minority one, or were they expressing popular opinion? How did they propose to solve the problems caused by immigration?

American Party Platform, Philadelphia, February 21, 1856

1. An humble acknowledgement to the Supreme Being, for his protecting care vouchsafed to our fathers in their successful Revolutionary struggle, and hitherto manifested to us, their descendants, in the preservation of the liberties, the independence and the union of these States.

2. The perpetuation of the Federal Union and Constitution, as the palladium of our civil and religious liberties, and the only sure bulwarks of American Independence.

3. *Americans must rule America,* and to this end *native*-born citizens should be selected for all State, Federal, and municipal offices of government employment, in preference to all others. *Nevertheless,*

4. Persons born of American parents residing temporarily abroad, should be entitled to all the rights of native-born citizens.

5. No person should be selected for political station (whether of native or foreign birth), who recognizes any allegiance or obligation of any description to any foreign prince, potentate or power, or who refuses to recognize the Federal and State Constitution (each within its sphere) as paramount to all other laws, as rules of political action.

6. The unequalled recognition and maintenance of the reserved rights of the several States, and the cultivation of harmony and fraternal good will between the citizens of the several States, and to this end, non-interference by Congress with questions appertaining solely to the individual States, and non-intervention by each State with the affairs of any other State.

7. The recognition of the right of native-born and naturalized citizens of the United States, permanently residing in any Territory thereof, to frame their constitution and laws, and to regulate their domestic and social affairs in their own mode, subject only to the provisions of the Federal Constitution, with the privilege of admission into the Union whenever they have the requisite population for one Rep-

---

SOURCE: Thomas V. Cooper and Hector T. Fenton, *American Politics from the Beginning to Date* (Chicago: Charles R. Brodix, 1882), 35–36.

resentative in Congress: *Provided, always,* that none but those who are citizens of the United States, under the Constitution and laws thereof, and who have a fixed residence in any such territory, ought to participate in the formation of the Constitution, or in the enactment of laws for said Territory or State.

8. An enforcement of the principles that no State or Territory ought to admit others than citizens to the right of suffrage, or of holding political offices of the United States.

9. A change in the laws of naturalization, making a continued residence of twenty-one years, of all not heretofore provided for, an indispensable requisite for citizenship hereafter, and excluding all paupers, and persons convicted of crime, from landing upon our shores; but no interference with the vested rights of foreigners.

10. Opposition to any union between Church and State; no interference with religious faith or worship, and no test oaths for office.

11. Free and thorough investigation into any and all alleged abuses of public functionaries, and a strict economy in public expenditures.

12. The maintenance and enforcement of all laws constitutionally enacted until said laws shall be repealed, or shall be declared null and void by competent judicial authority.

13. Opposition to the reckless and unwise policy of the present Administration in the general management of our national affairs, and more especially as shown in removing "Americans" (by designation) and Conservatives in principle, from office, and placing foreigners and Ultraists in their places; as shown in a truckling subserviency to the stronger, and an insolent and cowardly bravado towards the weaker powers; as shown in re-opening sectional agitation; by the repeal of the Missouri Compromise; as shown in granting to unnaturalized foreigners the right of suffrage in Kansas and Nebraska question; as shown in the corruptions which pervade some of the Departments of the Government; as shown in disgracing meritorious naval officers through prejudice or caprice; and as shown in the blundering mismanagement of our foreign relations.

14. Therefore, to remedy existing evils, and prevent the disastrous consequences otherwise resulting therefrom, we would build up the "American Party" upon the principles hereinbefore stated.

15. That each State Council shall have authority to amend their several Constitutions, so as to abolish the several degrees and substitute a pledge of honor, instead of other obligations, for fellowship and admission into the party.

16. A free and open discussion of all political principles embraced in our platform.

John Brown (1800–1859)

One of the most famous and controversial figures in American history is the radical abolitionist John Brown. As with William Lloyd Garrison, there was very little "give" in John Brown. He held to his beliefs with a passion bordering on fanaticism. However, Brown was willing to go much further than Garrison, who had always held pacifist views. In 1856, he murdered five proslavery settlers in Pottawatomie, Kansas, by hacking them to death and thus plunged Bleeding Kansas into a guerrilla war that did not let up for more than a decade. On October 16, 1859, he led a band of 21 men (16 whites, 5 blacks) into Harpers Ferry, Virginia, where he hoped to seize the federal armory there. He intended to arm slaves and lead them into the Shenandoah Valley, where he believed other slaves would rally to the cause of armed insurrection. But the strategy failed. Enraged townspeople besieged Brown until several companies of U.S. marines and cavalry (one company under the command of Colonel Robert E. Lee) arrived. On October 18, Lee issued a demand for Brown to surrender. Brown rejected the offer, and in the ensuing shoot-out, 12 of Brown's men were killed and Brown himself, severely wounded, was captured. The event was regarded then—and is still so regarded by historians—as the final straw leading to the Civil War. To Northerners, the martyred Brown was a great hero. To Southerners, he was the devil incarnate, who would instigate the slaves to rise up and cut their masters' throats. The Southerners' conviction that Brown was representative of all Northerners led many slave states over the next several months to expand their state militias.

At his trial, Brown acknowledged that he was guilty of trying to free the slaves but not that he was guilty of a crime. Why does Brown claim that if he had "interfered on behalf of the rich," he would not have been brought to trial? Do his words hint that he was insane, as many historians have long claimed, or are they the words of a fully rational person? He was found guilty of treason, and on December 2, 1859, he was hanged. He handed a note to a soldier as he mounted the scaffold: "I, John Brown am now quite certain that the crimes of this guilty land will never be purged away, but with Blood. I had, as I now think vainly, flattered myself that without very much bloodshed, it might be done."

Address to the Virginia Court at Charles Town, Virginia, November 2, 1859

I have, may it please the court, a few words to say.

In the first place, I deny everything but what I have all along admitted,—the design on my part to free slaves. I intended certainly to have made a clean thing of

SOURCE: Louis Ruchames, ed., *A John Brown Reader* (London: Abelard-Schuman, 1959), 125–127.

that matter, as I did last winter, when I went into Missouri and took slaves without the snapping of a gun on either side, moved them through the country, and finally left them in Canada. I designed to do the same thing again, on a larger scale. That was all I intended. I never did intend murder, or treason, or the destruction of property, or to excite or incite slaves to rebellion, or to make insurrection.

I have another objection; and that is, it is unjust that I should suffer such a penalty. Had I interfered in the manner which I admit, and which I admit has been fairly proved (for I admire the truthfulness and candor of the greater portion of the witnesses who have testified in this case),—had I so interfered in behalf of the rich, the powerful, the intelligent, the so-called great, or in behalf of any of their friends—either father, mother, sister, wife, or children, or any of that class—and suffered and sacrificed what I have in this interference, it would have been all right; and every man in this court would have deemed it an act worthy of reward rather than punishment.

The court acknowledges, as I suppose, the validity of the law of God. I see a book kissed here which I suppose to be the Bible, or at least the New Testament. That teaches me that all things whatsoever I would that men should do to me, I should do even so to them. It teaches me further to "remember them that are in bonds, as bound with them." I endeavored to act up to that instruction. I say, I am too young to understand that God is any respecter of persons. I believe that to have interfered as I have done—as I have always freely admitted I have done—in behalf of His despised poor, was not wrong, but right. Now if it is deemed necessary that I should forfeit my life for the furtherance of the ends of justice, and mingle my blood further with the blood of my children and with the blood of millions in this slave country whose rights are disregarded by wicked, cruel, and unjust enactments.—I submit; so let it be done!

Let me say one word further.

I feel entirely satisfied with the treatment I have received on my trial. Considering all the circumstances, it has been more generous than I expected. I feel no consciousness of my guilt. I have stated from the first what was my intention, and what was not. I never had any design against the life of any person, nor any disposition to commit treason, or excite slaves to rebel, or make any general insurrection. I never encouraged any man to do so, but always discouraged any idea of any kind.

Let me say also, a word in regard to the statements made by some to those connected with me. I hear it has been said by some of them that I have induced them to join me. But the contrary is true. I do not say this to injure them, but as regretting their weakness. There is not one of them but joined me of his own accord, and the greater part of them at their own expense. A number of them I never saw, and never had a word of conversation with, till the day they came to me; and that was for the purpose I have stated.

Now I have done.

WEB RESOURCES FOR PART THREE

SITES FEATURING A NUMBER OF THE DISSENTERS IN PART THREE

The Cherokee, Indian Land Cessions, and the Trail of Tears
www.cherokee.org/
http://rosecity.net/tears/
www.tngenweb.org/cessions/cherokee.html

Labor Protest Documents of the 1820s and 1830s
www.oberlin.edu/history/GJK/H258S2000/LaborProtestList.html

Early Industrialization and Labor Organization
www.mvrhs.org/netsite/School/departments/social/johnson/apushistory/apushistory/
    WebPrimarySource/8.EarlyIndustrialization.htm

Lowell Mill Girls
http://wizard.hprtec.org/builder/worksheet.php3?ID=8316
http://womenshistory.about.com/cs/bagleysarah/

David Walker
www.africawithin.com/bios/david_walker.htm

William Lloyd Garrison
www.pbs.org/wgbh/aia/part4/4p1561.html
www.nps.gov/boaf/williamlloydgarrison.htm
www.state.il.us/hpa/lovejoy/abol.htm

Wendell Phillips
www.libertystory.net/LSACTIONPHILLIPS.htm

The Grimké Sisters
www.spartacus.schoolnet.co.uk/USASgrimkeS.htm
www.spartacus.schoolnet.co.uk/USASgrimke.htm

Sojourner Truth
www.lkwdpl.org/wihohio/trut-soj.htm

Frederick Douglass
http://memory.loc.gov/ammem/doughtml/doughome.html

Ralph Waldo Emerson
www.rwe.org

Margaret Fuller
www.arh.eku.edu/Eng/KOPACZ/fuller.html
www-english.tamu.edu/fuller/

Henry David Thoreau
www.vcu.edu/engweb/transcendentalism/index.html
www.thoreau.niu.edu/

Elizabeth Cady Stanton

Stanton and Anthony Papers Project:

http://ecssba.rutgers.edu/

Other sites for information on Stanton:

www.pbs.org/stantonanthony/
http://womenshistory.about.com/library/bio/blstanton.htm

Lucretia Mott

www.mott.pomona.edu/
http://womenshistory.about.com/library/bio/blmott.htm

Lucy Stone

www.oberlin.edu/external/EOG/OYTT-images/LucyStone.html
http://mama.essortment.com/lucystone_rdqf.htm

John Brown

www.pbs.org/wgbh/amex/brown/

OTHER DISSENTING VOICES OF THE TIME

Dorothea Dix

For information on the impact of Dorothea Dix on health reform, see:

www.webster.edu/~woolflm/dorotheadix.html

Frances Wright

Some information on British utopian, feminist, abolitionist Frances Wright and her emancipation experiment in Tennessee can be found here:

http://ww2.lafayette.edu/~library/special/specialexhibits/slaveryexhibit/onlineexhibit/
    franceswright.htm

John Humphrey Noyes, the Oneida Community

For the radical utopian community, see:

www.rouncefield.homestead.com/files/as_soc_family_27.htm
www.nyhistory.com/central/oneida.htm

George Henry Evans and the National Reform Union and the Workingmen's Party

Evans's Workingman's Advocate *was an important early labor newspaper. He worked for the rights of labor and for the establishment of public schools; see:*

www.geocities.com/CollegePark/Quad/6460/bio/E/vansGH.html

Juan Cortina

For information on the militant Mexican American who fought against racism in nineteenth-century Texas, see:

www.pbs.org/weta/thewest/people/a_c/cortina.htm

Harriet Tubman

For information on the famous abolitionist, see:

www.nyhistory.com/harriettubman/life.htm
www.pbs.org/wgbh/aia/part4/4p1535.html

Defenders of Slavery

For some examples of proslavery arguments leveled against abolitionists, see:

www.assumption.edu/users/lknoles/douglassproslaveryargs.html

PART FOUR

Civil War and Reconstruction, 1860–1877

Three musicians and two infantrymen from the Massachu-setts 54th Regiment, c. 1863. Soldiers from the Massachusetts 54th were among the many who protested their unequal pay.

Introduction: A Divided Nation

Abraham Lincoln's election in November 1860 precipitated the secession crisis. Before the year was out, South Carolina, convinced that the results of the election meant the death knell of slavery, seceded from the Union. By the time Lincoln took the presidential oath to preserve and protect the Union on Inauguration Day, March 4, 1861, Florida, Alabama, Mississippi, Louisiana, Georgia, and Texas had all followed suit. The Civil War broke out on April 12, when Confederate batteries opened fire on Fort Sumter in Charleston harbor. With Lincoln's call for troops to put down the rebellion, Virginia, Tennessee, Arkansas, and North Carolina seceded and joined the Confederacy. Although anger and rage led many Americans to march eagerly off to make war on one another, their opinions were not unanimous. Thousands of citizens in both sections of the country did not go along with the patriotic fervor permeating North and South, and, in varying degrees, many of these people raised their voices in protest against the war. The nation was divided, but in that divide were further divisions.

At the outset, one of President Lincoln's primary concerns was to prevent the four remaining slave states from joining the Confederacy. Lincoln felt that if Maryland, Delaware, Kentucky, and Missouri all seceded, the "game would be up" and he would be unable to fulfill his presidential oath. The Union would be dissolved. When the governor and legislature of Maryland made noises about seceding, Abraham Lincoln wasted little time. Under the "writ of habeas corpus," it is unconstitutional to keep defendants imprisoned without filing charges against them; nevertheless, Lincoln, suspending the writ, had the 31 Maryland legislators with secessionist leanings incarcerated. It was necessary, he explained, to bend the Constitution temporarily in order to preserve it. Naturally, this action met with a great deal of opposition, especially among "Peace Democrats," who opposed the war and were willing to let the South go if a compromise could not be negotiated. Ohio Congressman Clement L. Vallandigham was the most vocal member of the radical wing of the so-called Peace Democrats, the Copperheads.

In the South, too, there was opposition to the war. Southern dissenters were primarily those who lived in the mountain regions, where slavery had never been profitable, and who therefore did not own slaves. These mountain folk were not abolitionists (meaning they did not care one iota about black rights), but they deeply resented the economic and political power that slavery brought the lowland elite, and they were not willing to break up the Union to preserve slavery.

Both President Lincoln and President Davis were hampered by enormous opposition to their policies and military strategy. In the Confederacy, as in the United States, there were scores of congressmen and generals in the army who believed they knew far more than their commanders-in-chief. Lincoln and Davis faced a barrage of savage criticism not only from them but also from their own cabinets and from the press.

Laws establishing conscription were resented by citizens in both the North and the South. Especially infuriating to many was the clause that allowed conscripts to pay substitutes to take their places. Above and below the Mason-Dixon line, people cynically complained that it was a "rich man's war and a poor man's fight." Some were sufficiently incensed that they did everything they could to avoid being drafted; some even encouraged men in the army to desert. The New York City draft riots of July 11–15, 1863, were a vivid and violent testimony to the fact that the North was not fully unified behind the effort to save the Union. A Pennsylvania newspaper quoted one anticonscription protestor as saying he'd fight for Uncle Sam "but not for Uncle Sambo." Many Northern workers, fearing job competition from freed blacks, viewed the Civil War as a no-win situation. For them, it made no sense to fight and die to free blacks, who would then compete with them in the labor market. For several days, thousands of protesting workers, many of them Irish immigrants, took to the streets and targeted the homes of the rich as well as the black neighborhoods of New York City. When the frenzied rioting ended (quelled only after exhausted Union troops arrived from Gettysburg), 105 people lay dead—many of them free blacks who had been strung up on lampposts and burned to death.

There were, however, people who dissented nonviolently. Quakers like Cyrus Pringle refused to fight on grounds of conscience and moral principles. Black soldiers in the Union army challenged their unequal treatment, especially with respect to the War Department's policy of paying them less than white soldiers, by engaging in an effective protest campaign of refusing all money until their salaries equaled that of their white comrades in arms.

At the end of the war, as Congress began dealing with the problem of reconstructing the Union, many of those who had fought against slavery now took up the cause of the rights of the freedmen. Civil rights, citizenship, and suffrage all became significant issues. Women, who had championed abolition and black rights, began to lobby more vigorously for women's suffrage and engaged energetically in the debate over the Fifteenth Amendment. There were high hopes that the amendment guaranteeing the right to vote would include *all* citizens. But when the Fifteenth Amendment extended the suffrage only to black men, the women's movement split into moderates who supported the amendment and radicals who denounced it and heatedly agitated against its ratification. For the next 50 years, women like Susan B. Anthony and Elizabeth Cady Stanton, leading the National Woman's Suffrage Association; and Lucy Stone, leading the more moderate American Woman's Suffrage Association, carried on the struggle for suffrage.

During the 1870s, the issue of former slaves' civil and political rights began fading from public awareness. The fact that African American men now had the right to vote seemed to convince even the most ardent former abolitionists and advocates of civil rights that nothing more needed to be done to ease the transition of freedmen into the mainstream. Slaves were now free, black men could vote—what more was necessary? The nation's reply seemed to be "nothing." The presidential election of 1876 settled the issue. Although the Democratic candidate, New York Governor Samuel J. Tilden, won 51 percent of the popular vote, his 184 electoral votes were one shy of the majority he needed to be declared the victor. Twenty electoral votes from Florida, South Carolina, Louisiana, and Oregon were disputed, and those states submitted two sets of returns. From November 1876 to March 1877, an electoral commission debated how to resolve the issue. Democrats finally agreed, a few days before inauguration day, to acquiesce in granting all 20 of the disputed electoral votes to the Republican candidate, Rutherford B. Hayes. In return, Republicans agreed to several conditions, among which was the withdrawal of the remaining federal troops stationed in the South. This in effect ended Reconstruction. It removed the freedmen from the protection of the U.S. Army, put their fate into the hands of local politicians, and put conservative Southern Democrats back in power in the South. Southern state officials lost no time in establishing literacy tests and poll taxes to prevent freedmen from voting. They also set up Jim Crow apartheid, imposing the second-class citizenship on African Americans that would last for nearly a century.

In the aftermath of the Civil War, many Americans began moving west. The Homestead Act of 1862 and the completion of the Transcontinental Railroad in 1869 were two factors that made the West enormously attractive to many who sought to improve their lives after the tumult and dislocation of the Civil War. But as settlers poured into the Great Plains, erecting homesteads and wantonly killing the buffalo herds, the lives and livelihoods of Native Americans were so disrupted that Indian grievances and protests against white encroachment boiled over. In the Fort Laramie Treaty of 1868, the United States promised—in exchange for Sioux assurances not to attack whites traveling through the Great Plains—that the Black Hills would forever belong to the Sioux. Sitting Bull and Crazy Horse, believing that whites could not be trusted, refused to abide by any treaty. In 1873, Sioux warriors loyal to Sitting Bull and Crazy Horse violated the treaty by hunting on lands off the Sioux reservation and by attacking survey parties belonging to the Northern Pacific Railroad. Lieutenant Colonel George Armstrong Custer skirmished twice with these Indians while escorting Northern Pacific Railroad personnel, and because of this, the U.S. government sent him the following year to survey the Black Hills. The encroachment of Custer's Seventh Cavalry Regiment in the Black Hills deeply angered the Sioux, while simultaneously the Grant administration, eager to make the Black Hills safe for gold hunters, issued an ultimatum to all nontreaty Sioux to report to their agencies during the winter of 1875–1876. In March 1876, after a U.S. Army column attacked a Cheyenne camp, the Cheyenne joined up with Crazy Horse and Sitting Bull. The Arapaho also joined the Lakota and Cheyenne once the war had begun. The greatest Indian victory of the plains wars took place in June 1876 on the banks of the Greasy Grass in eastern Montana—whites called it the Little Big Horn—when Custer and his entire command were wiped out by Sitting Bull and Crazy Horse's confederation. But Custer's Last Stand was, in reality, one of the final blows for Indian hopes to maintain their way of life. Washington cracked down so severely that in spite of the Nez Perce's heroic run for freedom in 1877 and continued skirmishes with the Cheyenne and the Apache well into the 1880s, Indian resistance was effectively subdued.

Clement L. Vallandigham (1820–1871)

When the Civil War broke out, there was a great deal of antiwar dissent in the North. Northern Democrats divided into two factions: War Democrats favored a war (if necessary) to preserve the Union but not to abolish slavery. Peace Democrats were unwilling to go to war even if it meant the dissolution of the Union; if negotiations could save the Union, fine, but if not, then so be it. The most radical faction of the Peace Democrats, irrevocably opposed to war, were derisively labeled Copperheads by Republicans. By equating them with poisonous snakes, the Republicans were declaring that the Peace Democrat stance was unmistakably treasonous.

The most notorious Copperhead was Ohio Congressman Clement L. Vallandigham, who, from the moment Lincoln was inaugurated on March 4, opposed the administration's policies that, he was convinced, would lead only to war. Vallandigham wanted to preserve the Union but not through war. He argued that compromise and negotiation would work and that the Union would prevail. Once war broke out, he became particularly concerned with Lincoln's policies for stifling secessionist and antiwar sentiment, policies, Vallandigham believed, that would destroy the civil liberties guaranteed by the Constitution. Throughout the Civil War, Vallandigham was a thorn in the side of the Lincoln administration. In 1863, after Vallandigham declared in a fiery speech that Lincoln's agenda was not to save the Union but merely to free the blacks and enslave the whites, he was arrested, tried, and convicted by a military court. (Lincoln saw to it, however, that rather than serving his sentence, Vallandigham was deported to the Confederacy.) Soon thereafter, Vallandigham went to Canada and from there campaigned for governor of Ohio. He lost the election, but Lincoln, in order to defuse negative public opinion, shrewdly allowed the Copperhead to return the following year to Ohio, where, with the end of the war in sight, the furor around him subsided.

As a congressman, Vallandigham accused Lincoln of abusing his constitutional authority by issuing a call for recruits and proclaimed that the president was a tyrant. He was especially alarmed by Lincoln's disregard for free speech and civil liberties and by his suspension of habeas corpus—an act that Lincoln himself admitted was overstepping his constitutional authority. Lincoln's view was that he had to "bend" the Constitution temporarily in order to save it. How correct is Vallandigham in his criticism of Lincoln's acts? Was Lincoln justified in suspending habeas corpus? Should Vallandigham have remained silent? How important are civil liberties in a time of national crisis? How is this issue playing out in the United States today?

Response to Lincoln's Address to Congress, July 10, 1861

. . . Sir, the Constitution not only confines to Congress the right to declare war, but expressly provides that "Congress (not the President) shall have power to raise and support armies;" and to "provide and maintain a navy." In pursuance of this authority, Congress, years ago, had fixed the number of officers, and of the regiments, of the different kinds of service; and also, the number of ships, officers, marines, and seamen which should compose the navy. Not only that, but Congress has repeatedly, within the last five years, refused to increase the regular army. More than that still: in February and March last, the House, upon several test votes, repeatedly and expressly refused to authorize the President to accept the service of volunteers for the very purpose of protecting the public property, enforcing the laws, and collecting the revenue. And, yet, the President, of his own mere will and authority, and without the shadow of right, has proceeded to increase, and has increased, the standing army by twenty-five thousand men; the navy by eighteen thousand; and has called for, and accepted the services of, forty regiments of volunteers for three years, numbering forty-two thousand men, and making thus a grand army, or military force, raised by executive proclamation alone, without the sanction of Congress, without warrant of law, and in direct violation of the Constitution, and of his oath of office, of eighty-five thousand soldiers enlisted for three and five years, and already in the field. And, yet, the President now asks us to support the army which he has thus raised, to ratify his usurpations by a law ex post facto, and thus to make ourselves parties to our own degradation, and to his infractions of the Constitution. Meanwhile, however, he has taken good care not only to enlist the men, organize the regiments, and muster them into service, but to provide, in advance, for a horde of forlorn, worn-out, and broken-down politicians of his own party, by appointing, either by himself, or through the Governors of the States, major-generals, brigadier-generals, colonels, lieutenant-colonels, majors, captains, lieutenants, adjutants, quarter-masters, and surgeons, without any limit as to numbers, and without so much as once saying to Congress, "By your leave, gentlemen."

Beginning with this wide breach of the Constitution, this enormous usurpation of the most dangerous of all powers—the power of the sword—other infractions and assumptions were easy; and after public liberty, private right soon fell. The privacy of the telegraph was invaded in the search after treason and traitors; although it turns out, significantly enough, that the only victim, so far, is one of the appointees and especial pets of the Administration. The telegraphic dispatches, preserved under every pledge of secrecy for the protection and safety of the telegraph companies, were seized and carried away without search-warrant, without probable cause, without oath, and without description of the places to be searched, or of the things to be seized, and in plain violation of the right of the people to be secure in their houses, persons, papers, and effects, against unreasonable searches and seizures. One step more, sir, will bring upon us search and seizure of the public mails; and,

Source: Clement L. Vallandigham, *The Record of Hon. C. L. Vallandigham on Abolition, the Union, and the Civil War* (Cincinnati: J. Walter, 1863), passim.

finally, as in the worst days of English oppression—as in the times of the Russells and the Sydneys of English martyrdom—of the drawers and secretaries of the private citizen; though even then tyrants had the grace to look to the forms of the law, and the execution was judicial murder, not military slaughter. But who shall say that the future Tiberius of America shall have the modesty of his Roman predecessor, in extenuation of whose character it is written by the great historian, *avertit occulos, jussitque scelera non spectavit.*

Sir, the rights of property having been thus wantonly violated, it needed but a little stretch of usurpation to invade the sanctity of the person; and a victim was not long wanting. A private citizen of Maryland, not subject to the rules and articles of war—not in a case arising in the land or naval forces, nor in the militia, when in actual service—is seized in his own house, in the dead hour of the night, not by any civil officer, nor upon any civil process, but by a band of armed soldiers, under the verbal orders of a military chief, and is ruthlessly torn from his wife and his children, and hurried off to a fortress of the United States—and that fortress, as if in mockery, the very one over whose ramparts had floated that star-spangled banner immortalized in song by the patriot prisoner, who, "by dawn's early light," saw its folds gleaming amid the wreck of battle, and invoked the blessings of heaven upon it, and prayed that it might long wave "o'er the land of the free, and the home of the brave."

And, sir, when the highest judicial officer of the land, the Chief Justice of the Supreme Court, upon whose shoulders, "when the judicial ermine fell, it touched nothing not as spotless as itself," the aged, the venerable, the gentle, and pure-minded Taney, who, but a little while before, had administered to the President the oath to support the Constitution, and to execute the laws, issued, as by law it was his sworn duty to issue, the high prerogative writ of habeas corpus—that great writ of right, that main bulwark of personal liberty, commanding the body of the accused to be brought before him, that justice and right might be done by due course of law, and without denial or delay, the gates of the fortress, its cannon turned towards, and in plain sight of the city, where the court sat, and frowning from its ramparts, were closed against the officer of the law, and the answer returned that the officer in command has, by the authority of the President, suspended the writ of habeas corpus. And thus it is, sir, that the accused has ever since been held a prisoner without due process of law; without bail; without presentment by a grand jury; without speedy, or public trial by a petit jury, of his own State or district, or any trial at all; without information of the nature and cause of the accusation; without being confronted with the witnesses against him; without compulsory process to obtain witnesses in his favor; and without the assistance of counsel for his defense. And this is our boasted American liberty? And thus it is, too, sir, that here, here in America, in the seventy-third year of the Republic, that great writ and security of personal freedom, which it cost the patriots and freemen of England six hundred years of labor and toil and blood to extort and to hold fast from venal judges and tyrant kings; written in the great charter of Runnymede by the iron barons, who made the simple Latin and uncouth words of the times, *nullus liber homo,* in the language of Chatham, worth all the classics; recovered and confirmed a hundred times afterward, as often as violated and stolen away, and finally, and firmly secured at last by the great act of Charles II, and transferred thence to our own Constitution and laws, has been wantonly and ruthlessly trampled in the dust. Ay, sir, that great writ, bearing, by a special command of Parliament, those other uncouth, but magic words, *per statutum tricessimo primo Caroli secundi regis,* which no English judge, no English minister, no king or queen of England, dare disobey; that writ, brought over by our fathers, and cherished by them, as a priceless inheritance of liberty, an American President has contemptuously set at defiance. Nay, more, he has ordered his subordinate military chiefs to suspend it at their discretion! And, yet, after all this, he cooly comes before this House and the Senate and the country, and pleads that he is only preserving and protecting the Constitution; and demands and expects of this House and of the Senate and the country their thanks for his usurpations; while, outside of this capitol, his myrmidons are clamoring for impeachment of the Chief Justice, as engaged in a conspiracy to break down the Federal Government.

Sir, however much necessity—the tyrant's plea—may be urged in extenuation of the usurpations and infractions of the President in regard to public liberty, there can be no such apology or defense for his invasions of private right. What overruling necessity required the violation of the sanctity of private property and private confidence? What great public danger demanded the arrest and imprisonment, without trial by common law, of one single private citizen, for an act done weeks before, openly, and by authority of his State? If guilty of treason, was not the judicial power ample enough and strong enough for his conviction and punishment? What, then, was needed in his case, but the precedent under which other men, in other places, might become the victims of executive suspicion and displeasure?

As to the pretense, sir, that the President has the Constitutional right to suspend the writ of habeas corpus, I will not waste time in arguing it. The case is as plain as words can make it. It is a legislative power; it is found only in the legislative article; it belongs to Congress only to do it. Subordinate officers have disobeyed it; General Wilkinson disobeyed it, but he sent his prisoners on for judicial trial; General Jackson disobeyed it, and was reprimanded by James Madison; but no President, nobody but Congress, ever before assumed the right to suspend it. And, sir, that other pretense of necessity, I repeat, can not be allowed. It had no existence in fact. The Constitution can not be preserved by violating it. It is an offense to the intelligence of this House, and of the country, to pretend that all this, and the other gross and multiplied infractions of the Constitution and usurpations of power were done by the President and his advisors out of pure love and devotion to the Constitution. But if so, sir, then they have but one step further to take, and declare, in the language of Sir Boyle Roche, in the Irish House of Commons, that such is the depth of their attachment to it, that they are prepared to give up, not merely a part, but the whole of the Constitution, to preserve the remainder. And yet, if indeed this pretext of necessity be well founded, then let me say, that a cause which demands the sacrifice of the Constitution and of the dearest securities of property, liberty, and life, can not be just; at least, it is not worth the sacrifice.

Sir, I am obliged to pass by for want of time, other grave and dangerous infractions and usurpations of the President since the 4th of March. I only allude casually to the quartering of soldiers in private houses without the consent of the owners, and without any manner having been prescribed by law; to the subversion in a part, at least, of Maryland of her own State Government and of the authorities under it; to the censorship over the telegraph, and the infringement, repeatedly, in one or more of the States, of the right of the people to keep and to bear arms for their defense.

But if all these things, I ask, have been done in the first two months after the commencement of this war, and by men not military chieftains, and unused to arbitrary power, what may we not expect to see in three years, and by the successful heroes of the fight? Sir, the power and rights of the States and the people, and of their Representatives, have been usurped; the sanctity of the private house and of private property has been invaded; and the liberty of the person wantonly and wickedly stricken down; free speech, too, has been repeatedly denied; and all this under the plea of necessity. Sir, the right of petition will follow next—nay, it has already been shaken; the freedom of the press will soon fall after it; and let me whisper in your ear, that there will be few to mourn over its loss, unless, indeed, its ancient high and honorable character shall be rescued and redeemed from its present reckless mendacity and degradation. Freedom of religion will yield too, at last, amid the exultant shouts of millions, who have seen its holy temples defiled, and its white robes of a former innocency trampled now under the polluting hoofs of an ambitious and faithless or fanatical clergy. Meantime national banks, bankrupt laws, a vast and permanent public debt, high tariffs, heavy direct taxation, enormous expenditures, gigantic and stupendous peculation, anarchy first, and a strong government afterward—no more State lines, no more State governments, and a consolidated monarchy or vast centralized military despotism must all follow in the history of the future, as in the history of the past they have, centuries ago, been written. Sir, I have said nothing, and have time to say nothing now, of the immense indebtedness and the vast expenditures which have already accrued, nor of the folly and mismanagement of the war so far, nor of the atrocious and shameless peculations and frauds which have disgraced it in the State governments and the Federal Government from the beginning. The avenging hour for all these will come hereafter, and I pass by them now.

I have finished now, Mr. Chairman, what I proposed to say at this time upon the message of the President. As to my own position in regard to this most unhappy civil war, I have only to say that I stand to-day just where I stood upon the 4th of March last; where the whole Democratic party, and the whole Constitutional Union party, and a vast majority, as I believe, of the people of the United States stood too. I am for peace, speedy, immediate, honorable peace, with all its blessings. Others may have changed—I have not. I question not their motives nor quarrel with their course. It is vain and futile for them to question or to quarrel with me. My duty shall be discharged—calmly, firmly, quietly, and regardless of consequences. The approving voice of conscience void of offense, and the approving judgment which shall follow "after some time be past," these, God help me, are my trust and my support.

Sir, I have spoken freely and fearlessly to-day, as became an American Representative and an American citizen; one firmly resolved, come what may, not to lose his own Constitutional liberties, nor to surrender his own Constitutional rights in the vain effort to impose these rights and liberties upon ten millions of unwilling people. I have spoken earnestly, too, but yet not as one unmindful of the solemnity of the scenes which surround us upon every side to-day. Sir, when the Congress of the United States assembled here on the 3rd of December, 1860, just seven months ago, the Senate was composed of sixty-six Senators, representing the thirty-three States of the Union, and this House of two hundred and thirty-seven members— every State being present. It was a grand and solemn spectacle—the ambassadors of three and thirty sovereignties and thirty-one millions of people, the mightiest republic on earth, in general Congress assembled. In the Senate, too, and this House, were some of the ablest and most distinguished statesmen of the country; men whose names were familiar to the whole country—some of them destined to pass into history. The new wings of the capitol had then but just recently been finished, in all their gorgeous magnificence, and, except a hundred marines at the navy-yard, not a soldier was within forty miles of Washington.

Sir, the Congress of the United States meets here again to-day; but how changed the scene! Instead of thirty-four States, twenty-three only, one less than the number forty years ago, are here, or in the other wing of the capitol. Forty-six Senators and a hundred and seventy-three Representatives constitute the Congress of the now United States. And of these, eight Senators and twenty-four Representatives, from four States only, linger here yet as deputies from that great South which, from the beginning of the Government, contributed so much to mold its policy, to build up its greatness, and to control its destinies. All the other States of that South are gone. Twenty-two Senators and sixty-five Representatives no longer answer to their names. The vacant seats are, indeed, still here; and the escutcheons of their respective States look down now solemnly and sadly from these vaulted ceilings. But the Virginia of Washington and Henry and Madison, of Marshall and Jefferson, of Randolph and Monroe, the birthplace of Clay, the mother of States and of Presidents; the Carolinas of Pinckney and Sumter and Marion, of Calhoun and Macon; and Tennessee, the home and burial-place of Jackson; and other States, too, once most loyal and true, are no longer here. The voices and the footsteps of the great dead of the past two ages of the Republic linger still—it may be in echo—along the stately corridors of this capitol; but their descendants, from nearly one-half of the States of the Republic, will meet with us no more within these marble halls. But in the parks and lawns, and upon the broad avenues of this spacious city, seventy thousand soldiers have supplied their places; and the morning drum-beat from a score of encampments, within sight of this beleaguered capitol, give melancholy warning to the Representatives of the States and of the people, that amid arms the laws are silent.

Sir, some years hence—I would fain hope some months hence, if I dare—the present generation will demand to know the cause of all this; and, some ages hereafter, the grand and impartial tribunal of history will make solemn and diligent inquest of the authors of this terrible revolution.

William Brownlow (1805–1877)

Although he supported the institution of slavery, Tennessee newspaper publisher and Methodist preacher William G. ("Parson") Brownlow became one of the most outspoken and acerbic opponents of secession in the South. His influence in eastern Tennessee was so powerful that Union sentiment remained very high in that part of the state throughout the war. In May 1861, shortly before Tennessee seceded from the Union, Parson Brownlow published a statement in his paper, the Knoxville *Whig*, adamantly asserting his right to fly the American flag, even though his view was the minority opinion in secession-ist Tennessee. As a result, his newspaper was suppressed, his press was destroyed, and he was tried for treason against the Confederacy. Like Vallandigham in the North, he was eventually banished behind enemy lines. In a sense, he can be regarded as Jefferson Davis's Vallandigham.

As Tennessee "dissented" from the Union and voted to secede, would a man like Brownlow be regarded as a conservative remaining true to the Union or as a dissenter going against the majority opinion in his state? Does his stance on slavery negate his status as a dissenter? Is his position a moral one? Why does he refer to the Bible to support his proslavery argument? How would Angelina Grimké (p. 156–163) respond to this? According to Brownlow, what is the real cause of secession and the Civil War?

Knoxville *Whig* Antisecession Letters and Editorial, May 1861

Albany, N.Y., May 8, 1861

W. G. BROWNLOW, Esq.:

I send you by mail the Albany *Evening Journal,* containing Hon. Benj. Nott's speech on the crisis. Judge Nott is a life-long Democrat, of the Hard-Shell school, and an avowed advocate of the Dred Scott decision.

I read your paper with great interest, and your course is the subject of conversa-tion in every circle North, meeting the approval of all parties, for all parties here are for the Union. We understand you to be a pro-Slavery man, but for the Union, opposed to Secession—not even regarding the election of Lincoln as any just cause for dissolving the Union. Can't you give us a leading editorial on these points, and at the same time state the position of the Union men in the border Slave States in the event the Administration were to interfere in any way with the institution of slavery?

The masses of the Northern people have no feelings but the most friendly towards their brethren of the South, and are ready to concede to them all their rights. They are even for returning to them their slaves who have escaped, as the law requires. This Administration would protect Southern rights, and if it would not of choice, the public would require it to be done. And, in saying this, I assure you I am no Lincoln man. But this you very well know.

Hoping that you may be sustained, and live to see the Stars and Stripes float on every hill-top, and in every valley, from the St. Lawrence to the Rio Grande, I remain, very truly,

L. M. E.

SOURCE: Stephen V. Ash, ed., *Secessionists and Other Scoundrels: Selections from Parson Brown-low's Book* (Baton Rouge: Louisiana State University Press, 1999), 56–63.

Knoxville, May 14, 1861

To L. M. E.:

I have your letter of the 8th, and also the *Evening Journal.* I have perused the speech of Judge Nott: it is able, conservative, and eminently patriotic. Had you more Notts in the North, and fewer Slavery agitators, and had we fewer Rhetts, Yanceys, and Davises, in the South, none of these troubles would now be upon the country.

You correctly interpret the Union men of the border Slave States when you pro-nounce them "pro-Slavery men." I think I correctly represent them in my paper, as I shall do in this brief epistle, except, perhaps, that I am more *ultra* than most of them. I am a native of Virginia, and so were my parents before me, and, together with a numerous train of relatives, they were and are slave-holders. For thirty years I have lived in Tennessee, and my wife and children are native Tennesseans. My native State did more to form the old Confederacy and to form the Constitution of the United States than any other State; her soil is now the resting-place of the honored dead, the most ultra old Unionists dead or alive—Washington, Jefferson, Madison, Monroe, Marshall, Henry, and a host of others. I am sorry to have to record that it has, in the mysterious providence of God, been reserved to Virginia to do more towards overthrowing the [old] Confederacy and the Constitution than any other State, South Carolina not even excepted. It took the Virginia [Secession] Conven-tion of 1861 to overthrow her State Government—changing her organic political *status* contrary to the expressed direction of her people at the ballot-box when they elected the men who perpetrated the deed! Virginia, I am sorry to say, if I may be allowed to use an humble illustration, is like a *hill of potatoes*—the best part under ground: the part above ground reminds me but of *vines.* When citizens of other States are called upon to name their great statesmen, they point to *living men.* Make the call upon Virginians, and they ask you out into *a graveyard,* when they will point you to the tomb of Washington, the monument erected over Madison, or the grave of Jefferson!

I am a pro-Slavery man, and so are the Union men generally of the border Slave States. I have long since made up my mind upon the Slavery question, but not with-out studying it thoroughly. The result of my investigation is, that there is not a single passage in the New Testament, nor a single act in the records of the Church, during her early history even for centuries, containing any direct, professed, or *intended* censure of slavery. Christ and the apostles found the institution existing under the authority and sanction of law; and in their labors among the people, unlike *ultra* Abolitionists, *masters* and *slaves* bowed at the same altars, and were taken into the same Church, communing together around the same table—the Saviour and his apostles exhorting *owners* to treat *slaves* as became the gospel, and slaves to obedi-ence and honesty, that their religious profession might not be evil spoken of.

The original Church of Christ not only admitted the lawfulness of slavery, but in various ways, by her teachings and discipline, expressed her *approbation* of it, enforc-ing the observance of "Fugitive Slave Laws" which had been enacted by the State. God intended the relation of master and slave to exist, both *in* and *out* of his Church. Hence, when Christ and his apostles found slavery *incorporated with every department of society,* they went to work and adopted rules for the government of the

Church providing alike for the *rights* of slave-holders and the *wants* of slaves. Slavery in the days of the apostles had so penetrated society, and was so intimately interwoven with it, that a religion *preaching freedom to the slaves* would have arrayed against it the civil authorities, armed against it the whole power of the State, and destroyed the usefulness of its preachers.

Finally, I hold—and thirty years of observation and experience among slave-holders in the South have convinced me that I am not mistaken—that all the finer feelings of humanity may be cherished in the bosoms of slave-owners; that there are thousands of devout slave-owners and slaves in the South who are acceptable to God, through Christ. And, however much the bonds of the slaves of the South may provoke the wrath of the ultra Abolitionists of the North, the Redeemer of the world smiles alike upon the devout master and the pious slave!

Now, sir, allow me further to say that the Union men of the border Slave States are loyal to their Government, and do not regard the election of Lincoln as any just cause for dissolving this Union. We believe that slavery had very little to do with inaugurating armed secession, which commenced at Charleston, to overthrow the United States Government: it was the loss of the offices, power, and patronage of the Government by corrupt politicians and bad men in the South, who had long controlled the Government. Believing this, as we honestly do, we can never, like Mexico, inaugurate political conflicts and anarchy by armed secession. We can never agree to assist in the inauguration of a Government of conventions by armed secession. . . .

Whilst I say this, let me say, in all candor, that if we were once convinced in the border Slave States that the Administration at Washington, and the people of the North who are backing up the Administration with men and money, contemplated the *subjugation* of the South or the *abolishing* of slavery, there would not be a Union man among us in twenty-four hours. Come what might, sink or swim, survive or perish, we would fight you to the death, and we would unite our fortunes and destinies with even these demoralized seceded States, for whose leaders and laws we have no sort of respect. But we have not believed, nor do we yet believe, that the Administration has such purposes in view. Demagogues and designing men charge it here, and by this means enlist thousands under their banner who, otherwise, would never support their wicked schemes of Secession. We Union men believe that the blow was struck upon Fort Sumter to induce Virginia to go out, and to create sympathy elsewhere, and that the Administration at Washington is seeking to repossess its forts and property and to preserve its existence; and, as long as we believe this, we are for the Union and the Administration. I, of course, speak for Union men in the general. We are sustained in this by the Mobile *Advertiser,* which glories in the fact that the seven Confederated States *"struck the first blow in the conflict,"* and *"threw down the glove of mortal combat to their powerful foe."* The Mobile organ of Secession adds, "It was plucky in the seven Confederates: it was more—it was sublimely courageous and patriotic."

Allow me to say that the curse of the country has been that, for years, north of Mason & Dixon's line, you have kept pulpits open to the abuse of Southern slavery and of the Southern people.

In like manner, the clergy of the South—without distinction of sects—men of talents, learning, and influence—have raised the howl of Secession, and it falls like an

Indian war-cry upon our citizens from their prostituted pulpits every Sabbath. Many of them go so far as to petition their God, in their public prayers, to *blast* the people of the North! I have no idea that a God of peace will answer any such blasphemous supplications; but it shows the spirit of these minions of anarchy, who have sworn allegiance to the kingdom of Davis, and have been released from any further obligations to the kingdom of Jesus—at least during the war! Some of our clergy are officers in volunteer companies, with swords hung to their sides, and stripes on their pants. Others, having an eye to the loaves and fishes, are anxious to serve as chaplains.

We are in the midst of a reign of terror in Tennessee, and where it will end, and in what, I am not able to conjecture. We vote for or against the Ordinance of Secession on the 8th of June; and, although there is a majority of the voters of the State utterly and irreconcilably opposed to Secession, I can't promise you that it will not carry. Fraud and force, and all the other appliances of Secessionism, will be brought to bear in carrying the State out of the Union. When overpowered and voted down, we shall be forced to submit. When I surrender, it will be because I can no longer help myself; but it shall be under protest, claiming the right, as a Union man, to curse this whole movement in my heart of hearts! And, whether in or out of the Union, as long as I remember it was Washington who told us, *"The Constitution is sacredly obligatory upon all";* and that it was Jackson who told us, *"The Union, it must be preserved"*—I shall offer this prayer upon the altar of my country: Mania to the brain of him who would conceive, and palsy to the arm of him who would perpetrate, the dissolution of the Union!

And, whether my humble voice is hushed in death, or my press is muzzled by foul legislation, I beg you, and all into whose hands this letter may fall, to credit no Secession falsehood which may represent me as having changed.

W. G. BROWNLOW

EDITORIAL, MAY 25, 1861

It is known to this community and to the people of this county that I have had the Stars and Stripes, in the character of a small flag, floating over my dwelling, in East Knoxville, since February. This flag has become very offensive to certain leaders of the Secession party in this town, and to certain would-be leaders, and the more so as it is about the only one of the kind floating in the city. Squads of troops, from three to twenty, have come over to my house, within the last several days, cursing the flag in front of my house, and threatening to take it down, greatly to the annoyance of my wife and children. No attack has been made upon it, and consequently we have had no difficulty. It is due to the Tennessee troops to say that they have never made any such demonstrations. Other troops from the Southern States, passing on to Virginia, have been induced to do so, by certain cowardly, sneaking, white-livered scoundrels, residing here, who have not the *melt* to undertake what they urge strangers to do. One of the Louisiana squads proclaimed in front of my house, on Thursday, that they were told to take it down by citizens of Knoxville.

Now, I wish to say a few things to the public in connection with this subject. This flag is private property, upon a private dwelling, in a State that has *never voted herself out of the Union* or into the Southern Confederacy, and is therefore lawfully and constitutionally under these same Stars and Stripes I have floating over my house. Until the State, by her citizens, through the ballot-box, changes her Federal relations, her citizens have a right to fling this banner to the breeze. Those who are in rebellion against the Government represented by the Stars and Stripes have up the Rebel flag, and it is a high piece of work to deny loyal citizens of the Union the privilege of displaying their colors!

But there is one other feature of this tyranny and of these mobocratic assaults I wish to lay before the people, irrespective of parties. There are but a few of the leaders of this Secession movement in Knoxville—less than half a dozen—for whom I entertain any sort of respect, or whose good opinions I esteem. With one of these I had a free and full conversation, more than two weeks ago, in regard to this whole question. I told him that we Union men would make the best fight we could at the ballot-box, on the 8th of June, to keep the State in the Union; but that if we were overpowered, and a majority of the people of the State should say in this constitutional way that she must secede, we should have to come down, and bring our flags with us, bowing to the will of the majority with the best grace we could. I made the same statement to the colonel who got up a regiment here, and to one of his subordinate officers. I made the same statement to the president of the railroad, and I have repeatedly made the same statement through my paper. The whole Secession party here know this to be the position and purpose of the Union party; but a portion of them seek to bring about personal conflicts, and to engage strangers, under the influence of whiskey, to do a dirty and villainous work they have the meanness to do, without the courage.

If these God-forsaken scoundrels and hell-deserving assassins want satisfaction out of me for what I have said about them—and it has been no little—they can find me on these streets every day of my life but Sunday. I am at all times prepared to give them satisfaction. I take back nothing I have ever said against the corrupt and unprincipled villains, but reiterate all, cast it in their dastardly faces, and hurl down their lying throats their own infamous calumnies.

Finally, the destroying of my small flag or of my town-property is a small matter. The carrying out of the State upon the mad wave of Secession is also a small matter, compared with the great PRINCIPLE involved. Sink or swim, live or die, survive or perish, I am a Union man, and owe my allegiance to the Stars and Stripes of my country. Nor can I, in any possible contingency, have any respect for the Government of the Confederated States, originating as it did with, and being controlled by, the worst men in the South. And any man saying—whether of high or low degree—that I am an Abolitionist or a Black Republican, is a LIAR and a SCOUNDREL.

The Arkansas Peace Society, 1861

Just as there was antiwar sentiment in the North during the Civil War, a large number of Southerners resisted the war. Indeed, during the first year of the Civil War, Confederate authorities became aware of a secret antiwar organization in Arkansas. More than a thousand Unionists opposed to secession had formed the Arkansas Peace Society in 1861, vowing to resist the war effort. But Confederate authorities got wind of the society, and hundreds of people were arrested and forced either to stand trial for treason or to suffer conscription into the Confederate army. Many of those impressed into Confederate service wound up deserting to Union lines at the first opportunity.

The following documents were written by the Arkansas Peace Society. What is the peace society's chief objection to secession? Does the issue of slavery enter into their argument? What do these documents reveal about dissent in the Confederacy?

ARKANSAS PEACE SOCIETY DOCUMENTS, 1861

SAM LESLIE TO GOVERNOR H. M. RECTOR

Wiley's Cove, Arks Oct 21 1861 H. M. Rector Gov of Ark

Dear sir

Your Letter of the 16th Inst is now before me and contents notised. You say it has been reported to the Military Board there are One Hundred Good fighting men in Cove Township, Searcy Co that has not nor will not volunteer thir servicis In behalf of the South. What would prompt aney one to attempt to cast such a stigma upon the people of this Township I am not able to comprehend, ware your informant a citizen of Searcy Co I might have some Ida of the cause, this Township (Cove) has not turned out as many volunteers as she might have don, this county has about 300 men in service of the Confederate States though we are only represented by two companies the rest of our men Joined compained in the adjoining counties and those counties is receiving the credit. Cove Township has about 60 able bodied men subject to military duty all told only five out of that number single men and Eight volunteers which will leave 52 now subject to duty the Great bulk of our men now in service has been furnished by three Townships, there is other Townships in the County that has done but little better than Cove, and they pass unnoticed. I will say to you that the citizens of Cove Township is as Law abiding a people as lives and the records of out corts will bear me out in the assursion, which may account in some degree for their not being more ready to volunteer there is other causes, so many Misourians running off and leaving the state, has had its influence I know this county has had a bad name at a distance we have been called Black Republicans and Abolitionists &c but we have never had aney of thos characters amongst us. It is true that the citizens of this county war union men as long as there was aney hope of the Union and perhaps a little

---

Source: Ted R. Worley, ed., "Documents Relating to the Arkansas Peace Society of 1861," *The Arkansas Historical Quarterly,* Vol. 17, Spring 1958, No. 1. The original documents are located in the Kie Oldham Collection, at the Arkansas History Commission.

longer, but all Ida of the Union as it onst was is banished the time has passsed for the North and South to live to gether in pease and harmoney and we must be loyal to the government we live under this is the fealings of the people of this Co so fare as I have any knolledg and when you hear men call the pople of Searcy Co. by hard names rest assured they are willfully lying or uninformed with the character of our people. I write you this letter Gov. in order to plase the Good people of Searcy Co. write before you I feel it is a duty I owe to them to do so.

I hope Cove Township will yet give a Good account of hir self that you may have no reason to complain.

Respectfully your friend Sam Leslie. . . .

GOVERNOR H. M. RECTOR TO SAM LESLIE
Executive Office, Little Rock, Nov 28, 1861, Sam Leslie Col Commandant 45th Regt A.M.

Sir

Your letter of the 26 Inst has just reached me by couriers Melton and Griffin. I regret extremely that any of our citizens should prove disloyal to their government. But if they so conduct themselves the power of those in authority must be exercised to preserve peace, and enforce obedience to the Constitution and the Laws.

The people of the State Arkansas through their representatives in Convention have taken the State out of the Old Union and attached it to the Confederacy. And although there may be a minority against this action, yet ours is a government where a majority rules and the minority must submit.

I and my officers in the State are sworn to support and enforce the laws as they are and individuals, one or many, rebelling against those laws, must be looked after and if for the safety of the country, it becomes necessary to arrest and imprison them or to execute them for treason, that must and will be done promptly and certainly, if it is necessary to call out every man in the State to accomplish it.

Still, I deeply regret the necessity, but will not be deterred from doing my whole duty let the blow fall where it may. You will therefore proceed to arrest all men in your county who profess friendship for the Lincoln government or who harbor or support others arousing hostility to the Confederate States or the State of Arkansas. And when so arrested you will march them to this place, where they will be dealt with, as enemies of their country whose peace and safety is being endangered by their disloyal and treasonable acts.

To enable you to enforce this order you will call out such of the Militia as may be necessary and you will be careful also to afford protection to the loyal citizens and their property in your county, as occurring events may seem to require your interposition for their security.

Confiding in your intelligence and devotion to your state, and to the Confederacy of which you are a citizen, I entertain no opinion other than that you will do your whole duty, as a man and an officer.

Respectfully H. M. Rector Gov and Commander in Chief, A. M.

IZARD COUNTY COMMITTEE OF INVESTIGATION

To His Excellency H. M. Rector Govr. and Prest. Military Board of the State of Arkansas. . . .

Some ten days ago it became a matter of publicity in this county that a secret conspiracy against the laws and liberties of the people of this state was on foot extending from Fulton county this State quite through this and perhaps Searcy and Van Buren Counties.

Immediately the citizens of this county were in arms to quell the same. Scouting parties were sent out in every direction in search of those suspected of having connections with the organization; and a committee of investigation was elected to enquire into the existence, objects, and purposes of the aforesaid secret conspiracy which committee is composed of the undersigned, who have proceeded to examine and have examined all the persons apprehended and brought before us all of whose names are hereto attached.

And after a full and fair investigation of the matter with all the lights before us, we find that the persons above named together with others we have not found, had formed themselves into a secret organization having a constitution and by laws and secret signs a copy of which constitution is herewith submitted to your excellency and marked A. and we considered that the organization is a secret thing dangerous in its operations and subversive of the rights and liberties of the people of this State, and of the Confederate States; and if not treason itself, at least treasonable, and being acquainted with most if not all of the persons examined, and many of them being young, mere boys, who were doubtless led ignorantly into the society, that is led into it not being informed of its objects and purposes, and feeling willing in our minds that they should wipe out the foul stain, by enlisting in the service of the Confederate States for and during the war, we accordingly gave them an opportunity of so enlisting, whereupon the whole of them, that is to say forty seven the same whose names are hereunto attached immediately enrolled their names as volunteers in the Confederate Service for and during the war. This we think is a matter of lenity toward them and that they may possibly do good service to our country. They leave here as soon as transportation can be had, for Genl Borland's headquarters at Pocahontas Ark. Should it appear to your Excellency that we have not taken the proper steps in this matter we have reserved the right of your Excellency to do with them as you may deem proper, and have so informed Genl Borland with regard thereto. . . .

Sylamore Ark Nov 28 1861
W. B. F. Treat, Chairman Daniel Jeffery Wm. C. Dixon Simon E. Rosson Jesse Hinkle A. W. Harris R. B. Dicksen Moses Bishop G. W. Gray Henry Cole T. W. Edmundson A. P. Mix Secy

CONSTITUTION OF THE MILL CREEK PEACE ORGANIZATION SOCIETY

A

We the undersigned subscribers agree to form ourselves into an association call and known by the name and style of the Mill Creek peace organization society. Self preservation being an undisputed natural right, and the right of communities to combine together for the mutual protection of themselves their families and their property being well established. This being the sole purpose for which we met for this purpose alone we do adopt the following resolutions by which we expect to be governed in all our proceedings.

Resolved 1st. That each member before entering into this society shall take an oath as follows I do solemnly swear in the presence of Almighty God and these witnesses that I will well and truly keep all the secrets of this society that I will ever hail always conceal and never reveal anything. I will on the shortest notice go to the assistance of any other brother So help me God.

2nd As it is a matter of life or death with us any member of this society who shall betray to our enemies the existence of this society he shall forfeit his life and it shall be the duty of each member of this society having received knowledge of such betrayal to forthwith inform the brethren each of whose duty it shall be to follow such traitor and take his life at the price of their own. The manner of admitting members shall be in strict accordance with the foregoing preamble and resolutions and by such members as the society may select.

A true copy from the original furnished by a member of the society.

RECOMMENDATION FOR RELEASE OF WITNESSES AGAINST PEACE SOCIETY

Head Quarters Battalion Arkansas Cavalry Vounteers Camp Culloden, Carroll Co. Arks Decr. 6th, 1861

To the Governor, Military Board and Judicial Tribunals of the State of Arkansas Whereas this day John Christy and his two sons Joseph C. Christy and J. F. H. Christy and P. M. Hensly, Gilmore Smith and D. C. Baker Citizens of Searcy County Arkansas voluntarily came and appeared before Honbles Kelly Featherstone and William Owens associate justices sitting as a court of Enquiry and Investigation into certain secret treasonable and Insurrectionary movements believed to exist and formed into societies under various appellations held together by oaths, Signs, Tokens and pass words and made known to said court the existence of a society represented to them as a Peace Society organizations being a good thing and for the protection of their homes property and family against Robbers and thieves and that it was a neighborhood society and that the best men and oldest citizens of the County were members of it and by which representation they were induced to go into the same and took the oath as members and whereas from their testimony given before this court and to which your attention is particularly invited to, we are fully satisfied that these men were gulled and deceived into the same by false representations.

We would most respectfully Petition the Executive of the State for their release from confinement and that they may be used if necessary in behalf of the State as to what they know, that we believe them to be honest Respectable and unsuspecting men who have without design or intention of wrong to the State or Confederate States been induced by intriguing and designing men to become members of a society which they now believe had an evil design in it though so far as they were capable of judging at the time they were not capable of discovering although the said John

Christy, Joseph C. Christy, J. F. H. Christy, and Gilmore Smith said from their evidence which was taken separate and apart from each other and voluntarily given that they did not like the secret signs & tokens and while the oath was being given them and objected to that part at the time and that we are satisfied from the matter in which they came before the court and testified that they were anxious to ferret out all the wrong & evil if there was one in it.

Signed

We the undersigned cheerfully join in the recommendation for release of the parties above named and all others testifying voluntarily & making confessions as done by these parties and upon pledges of Fidelity and Support to the State of Arkansas and the Confederate States of America.

Signed. . . .

COMMITMENT OF PRISONERS IN CARROLL COUNTY JUSTICE OF PEACE COURT

Head Quarters Battalion Arkansas Cavalry Volunteers Camp Culloden Carroll County, Arks Dec 9, 1861

Now on this day it is ordered by Honbles Kelly Featherston and William Owens associate justices of this county of Carroll Arkansas, siting as a Court of Enquiry & Investigation into a certain secret Treasonable and Insurrectionary Society said to exist in this and the adjoining counties of the State of Arkansas and which society is said to be held together by secret oaths signed and pass words with the penalty of Death attached if revealed.

That the following named persons be committed for further trial and that Capt Jno R. H. Scott commanding Battalion Arks Cavalry Volunteers C.S.A be requested to convey them or have them conveyed under guard to Little Rock Arkansas and surrendered there to the Governor of the State of Arkansas Namely George Long, Solomon Branum, Joshua Reeves, David Curry, James Latterel, Samuel Thompson, Patrick L. Downey, James Thompson, James E. Curry, Charles W. Price, William Brown, George Hooten, Mike Tinkle, William Dugger, Luther Phillips, Thomas Dugger, William M. Will, James Hollis, Jasper Dugger, Mayfield Addison, William C. Singletary, and John M. Carithers.

And it is further ordered by the court that the following named persons enter in Bond the sum of Five Hundred dollars each for their appearance forthwith before the Governor of the State of Arkansas to testify in regard to certain matters voluntarily acknowledged before this court and not depart the order or decree of the Governor without leave therefrom, To Wit:

John Christy, Joseph Christy, J. F. H. Christy, P. M. Hensley, Gilmore Smith, Carroll Kilburn, E. L. Osborn, Carlton Keeling, George M. Hays, J. W. Kirkham, John McEntire, and John C. McNair.

Which is accordingly here done in open court, on this 9th day of Decr 1861. William Owens, J.P. Kelly Featherston J.P. . . .

HEAD QUARTERS BURROWSVILLE, 11ARK. DEC 9TH, [1861]
To His Excellency H. M. Rector Gov. of Ark.

Dear Sir:

I have this day ordered the prisoners under my care at this place to take up the line of march to Little Rock under a guard of one hundred Soldiers commanded by Lt. Brevet Lieut Col A. Ham, Maj John Bradshaw, and Agt Mager Jesse Cypert. I have no testimony only the testimony of the prisoners in their own confessions. You will call on Brev. Lieut. Col. Ham, Maj Bra[d]shaw, and Adj Maj Cypert, they can point out to you such other testimony as would become necessary, the most of the prisoners came in and surrendered, acknowledging their guilt and willing to Bide by the Law of their country, there is several men implicated in this seacret order skulking about in the woods and have not been arrested. I will do all I can to have then taken and brought to Justice. It seems as if the Whole Countrey have become ingaged in this matter to some Extent, and but for the timely discovery of it there is no telling what the can cequence would have been. Men who was considered to be amongest our best citizes has acknowledged them selves to be members of this secret order, said by some to be a home guard, by others home protection. I called on Capt Scott commanding Squadron at Camp Colodn Carroll Co. Capt Scott informs me that he would give me the aid ast fer and sent a portion of his command into this and Last Week arrested several men and carrying them to his head quarters and has them in his care and informed me that he would convey them to Little Rock. So soon as I think it safe to do so I will disband the men that I ordered into service. I have been sick for the last twelve [days] not able to attend to any kind of business and am just now able to sit up and write consequently I am not prepared any report at this time. Any instructions that you think [I] should have you will please Informe by Brevet Lieut Col Ham. I also send you a list of the names of the persons I have retained three prisoners here that could [not] travle on account of their health So soon as [I can] I will send them to Little Rock unless you see proper to order some other disposition made of them.

> Respectfully your Obt serv Sam Leslie Col Commanding 45th Reg Arkansas Militia

TESTIMONY OF PETER TYLER ON THE PEACE SOCIETY

Head Qrs Battalion Arks Cav Volunteers Camp Culloden Carroll Co. Arkansas Decr. 18th, 1861 The State of Arkansas Vs Knowledge of and identity with Secret Treasonable and Insurrectionary Society Peter Tyler and Isaiah Ezell

Before the Honble Kelly Featherston Justice of the Peace within and for the County of Carroll State of Arkansas

Personally came and appeared Peter A. Tyler party in the above action said to have a knowledge of and perhaps Identity with a certain secret society hold together by certain oaths signs Tokens pass word &c & the revelation of which subjected its members to the punishment of death and upon his own voluntary request makes the following acknowledgments in relations to the matter and things wherof he has knowledge.

I am a member of a certain secret society represented to me by Long and D. Jamison who initiated me into the society in company with Samuel Grinder and Josiah Lane all taking the oath & receiving the signs tokens and pass words from Jamison at one & the same time about three weeks ago more or less as a "home protection" society and that there was no harm in it but to protect our selves our families & property and that it came from the North and that it was all over the South. I told him I was no northern man what I have is here and he said it was for home protection & after he administered the oath to me & grinder & lane he then gave me and them the signs tokens and pass words, which as well as I remember are as follows. The first sign was placing the three fingers of the left hand angling across the nose the answer was carelessly feeling under the chin with one of the hands. The next sign was to place one finger in the shirt collar I believe left hand and the answer was to put the right hand on the left breast. The next was to raise the hat with one hand and place it back on the head the answer was turn the back to the person moving the hat.

A token was in meeting after night on speaking if anyone was with him you said "It was a very dark night" and the answer would be "Not so dark as it will be in the morning." One sign was to hang up in the front door of the house a piece of red ribbon, calico, or flannel. Another token was when they were separate to get together was to Hoot like and Owl, and the answer was to howl like a wolf I think. I heard somewhere after the noise commenced about it that it came from Washington City but Jamison did not tell me if I recollect right he said to me it was for protection when invaded by robbers, I gave the paper or obligation to David Curry & told him to take care of it for it might be of an advantage to them. I & Sam Grinder & Jo Lane were all sworn in by Jamison at the same time, and after that I rode around among the boys & swore in the following persons as members to wit Isaiah Ezell, David Curry, Peter Reeves, Joshua Reeves, Robert Grinder, David Barnett, John McEntire, Thomas Younger, Alexander Younger, George Hooten, John Brown, Robert Tinkle, Mike Tinkle, James Thompson, Thomas Thompson, Samuel Thompson, J. C. Mc Nair, Claiborn Maness, James Curry, Patrick L. Downly, A. J. Love, Green Adams, Spencer Adams, Joseph Adams, William Brown, Robert Grinder, Charles Price, Lindsay Price, Lindsay Bishop, John Ezell, Daniel Parks, & Austin Pierce I think is the name, then maybe some more but I do not now recollect them if there are. I told Jamison I was not no northern man all I had was here. I told him I did not like the oath he said there was nothing wrong about it & he did not want any thing said about it, wanted it secret not to tell any body of it although it was all over the South or something to this amount. All those named above & my self and Grinder & Lane all held up our right hands when the obligations recd by us and given to them by me, all of which I am ready [to] and here verify. P. A. Tyler

Sworn and subscribed to before me this 18th day of Decr. 1861 Kelly Featherston J P

It is ordered here by this court that the said P. A. Tyler above named be committed for further trial and that he be conveyed to the city of Little Rock and surrendered to the Governor of the State of Arkansas and that he be placed in the hands of Captn Jno R. H. Scott commanding Squadron Arks Cavalry Volunteers C. S. A. with a request that he send him under guard to the City of Little Rock with such number of means he may deem sufficient to prevent his escape from custody in accordance with this order. Given under my hand and seal this 18th day of December 1861 Kelly Featherston, J. P.

TESTIMONY OF ISAIAH EZELL ON THE PEACE SOCIETY

Arks Cav Vol Camp Culoden Carroll Co Arks Decr. 18 1861 State of Arks Vs Knowledge of and Identity with Secret Treasonable and Insurrectionary Society Peter Tyler and Isaiah Ezell

Before the Honble Kelly Featherston J. P. of Carroll Co. Arkansas Personally came & appeared Isaiah Ezell one of the parties above and on oath sayeth. That he belongs to a home guard or Home protection Society of a Secret nature held together by certain oaths Signs tokens & pass words the revelation of which was punishable by death that he was initiated into the same by Peter Tyler, of Tomahawk Township Searcy County Arkansas he presented me with a paper purporting to be an obligation to which I was sworn but to which I did not affix my name. I saw no other one taken into the society nor never initiated any one into it, myself, except seeing John Ezell initiated at another time by Peter Tyler. I do not know the wording of the oath. One of the signs given was to place one of the hands about the nose the answer was perhaps rubing the hand under the chin. There was a sign to be put up somewhere about the house a piece of Ribbon or calico dont recollect the color. I dont know the meaning of this sign. There was something about an owl but I don't recollect what or how it was represented to me to be for the protection of our homes and families against robbers &c and if it was for any other purpose I was deceived in it. his Isaiah X Ezell mark Sworn and subscribed to before me this 18th day of Decr. 1861 Kelly Featherston J P

COLONEL WILLIAM C. MITCHELL TO GOVERNOR RECTOR

Camp Madison, Ark. Decr. 23 1861
Hon. H. M. Rector Governor of the State of Arkansas

Sir

Three men enlisted by the name of George M. Hays Eli L. Osborn and John W. Kirkham from the countys of Marion and Carroll and from what I understand they are bound over to appear at Little Rock on a charge of Treason to the Confederate States. They belong to Captain R. E. Trimble Company in this Regt if you wish them conveyed to Little Rock a requisition for them you can make they are in safe hands and will be safely kept, subject to your demand.

> I am Yours Respectfully
> Wm C Mitchell
> Col. 14 Regt Arks Vol

Joseph E. Brown (1821–1894)

Not only in the North did concerned citizens protest their government's tendency to step on civil liberties during the wartime emergency. In the South, too, many people were critical of the Confederacy's disregard of civil liberties and its fondness for martial law. One of the ironies of the Civil War is that the Confederacy, in order to strengthen the war effort, which it claimed was to preserve and defend the principle of states' rights, was obliged to extend the power of the central government in Richmond. In this way, the Confederacy began to resemble the Union it was fighting against. In the first selection here, Georgia Governor Joseph E. Brown, in a letter to Alexander H. Stephens, vice-president of the Confederacy, attacks a policy that gives too much power to the military. In the second selection, an 1864 address delivered to the Georgia State Legislature, Brown takes on the issues of conscription and the suspension of the writ of habeas corpus. Brown was a Jacksonian Democrat who so staunchly defended states' rights that it could be argued that he was a hindrance to Jefferson Davis and the Confederate government, damaging the South's chances of winning the war. To Brown, martial law decreed by the Davis government infringed on both states' rights and individual rights.

What rights are jeopardized by the "dangerous usurpations of power" that the governor fears? How valid is Brown's argument? Why is conscription, according to Brown, unconstitutional? Was Brown's stance detrimental to the Confederate cause? What similarities do his views have with those of Lincoln's critics?

Letter to Alexander H. Stephens, 1862

Dear Sir:

I have the pleasure to acknowledge the receipt of your letter. . . . And am gratified that you take the view which you have expressed about the action of Genl. Bragg in his declaration of martial law over Atlanta and his appoint[ment], as the newspapers say, of a civil governor with aids, etc.

I have viewed this proceeding as I have others of our military authorities of late with painful apprehensiveness for the future. It seems military men are assuming the whole powers of government to themselves and setting at defiance constitution, laws, state rights, state sovereignty, and every other principle of civil liberty, and that our people engrossed in the struggle with the enemy are disposed to submit to these bold usurpations tending to military despotism without murmur, much less resis-

SOURCE: *Message of His Excellency Joseph E. Brown, to the Extra Session of the Legislature, Convened March 10th, 1864 . . .* (Milledgeville, GA: Boughton, Nisbet, Barnes & Moore, 1864), 11–21.

tance. I should have called this proceeding into question before this time but I was hopeful from the indications which I had noted that Congress would take such action as would check these dangerous usurpations of power, and for the further reasons that I have already come almost into conflict with the Confederate authorities in vindication of what I have considered the rights of the State and people of Georgia, and I was fearful, as no other governor seems to raise these questions, that I might be considered by good and true men in and out of Congress too refractory for the times. I had therefore concluded to take no notice of this matter till the meeting of the legislature when I expect to ask the representatives of the people to define the bounds to which they desire the Governor to go in the defense of the rights and sovereignty of the state. I confess I have apprehensions that our present General Assembly does not properly reflect the sentiments of our people upon this great question, but if the Executive goes beyond the bounds where he is sustained by the representatives of the people he exposes himself to censure without the moral power to do service to the great principles involved. I fear we have much more to apprehend from military despotism than from subjugation by the enemy. I trust our generals will improve well their time while we have the advantage and the enemy are organizing another army. Hoping that your health is good and begging that you will write me when your important duties are not too pressing to permit it. I am very truly your friend.

Message to the Legislature, March 10, 1864

THE NEW MILITIA ORGANIZATION AND CONSCRIPTION

Since your adjournment in December, the Adjutant and Inspector General, under my direction, has done all in his power to press forward the organization of the militia of the State, in conformity to the act passed for that purpose; and I have the pleasure to state, that the enrollments are generally made, except in a few localities, where proximity to the enemy has prevented it; and the organizations will soon be completed.

At this stage in our proceedings, we are met with formidable obstacles, thrown in our way by the late act of Congress, which subjects those between 17 and 50 to enrollment as Conscripts, for Confederate service. This act of Congress proposes to take from the State, as was done on a former occasion, her entire military force, who belong to the active list, and to leave her without a force, in the different counties, sufficient to execute her laws or suppress servile insurrection. Our Supreme Court has ruled, that the Confederate government has the power to raise armies by conscription, but it has not decided that it also has the power to enroll the whole population of the State who remain at home, so as to place the whole people under the military control of the Confederate government, and thereby take from the States all command over their own citizens, to execute their own laws, and place the internal police regulations of the States in the hands of the President. It is one thing to "raise armies", and another, and quite a different thing, to put the whole population at home under military law, and compel every man to obtain a military detail, upon such terms as the central government may dictate, and to carry a military pass in his pocket while he cultivates his farm, or attends to his other necessary avocations at home.

Neither a planter nor an overseer engaged upon the farm, nor a blacksmith making agricultural implements, nor a miller grinding for the people at home, belongs to, or constitutes any part of the armies of the Confederacy; and there is not the shadow of Constitutional power, vested in the Confederate government, for conscribing and putting these classes, and others engaged in home pursuits, under military rule, while they remain at home to discharge these duties. If conscription were constitutional as a means of raising armies by the Confederate government, it could not be constitutional to conscribe those not *actually* needed, and to be *employed* in the army, and the constitutional power to "raise armies", could never carry with it the power in Congress to conscribe the whole people, who are not needed for the armies, but are left at home, because more useful there, and place them under military government and compel them to get military details to plough in their fields, shoe their farm horses, or to go to mill.

Conscription carried to this extent, is the essence of military despotism; placing all civil rights in a state of subordination to military power, and putting the personal freedom of each individual, in civil life, at the will of the chief of the military power. But it may be said that conscription may act upon one class as legally as another, and that all classes are equally subject to it. This is undoubtedly true. If the government has a right to conscribe at all, it has a right to conscribe persons of all classes, till it has raised enough to supply its armies. But it has no right to go farther and conscribe all, who are, by its own consent, to remain at home to make supplies. If it considers supplies necessary, somebody must make them, and those who do it, being no part of the army, should be exempt from conscription, and the annoyance of military dictation, while engaged in civil, and not military pursuits.

If all between 17 and 50 are to be enrolled and placed in constant military service, we must conquer the enemy while we are consuming our present crop of provisions, or we are ruined; as it will be impossible for the old men over 50, and the boys under 17, to make supplies enough to feed our armies and people another year. I think every practical man in the Confederacy who knows anything about our agricultural interests and resources, will readily admit this. If, on the other hand, it is not the intention to put those between 17 and 18, and between 45 and 50, into service, as *soldiers,* but to leave them at home to produce supplies, and occasionally to do police and other duties, within the State, which properly belong to the militia of a State; or in other words, if it is the intention simply to take the control of them from the State, so as to deprive her of all power, and leave her without sufficient force to execute her own laws, or suppress servile insurrection, and place the whole militia of the State, not needed for constant service, in the Confederate armies, under the control of the President, while engaged in their civil pursuits, the act, is unconstitutional and oppressive, and ought not to be executed.

If the act is executed in this State, it deprives her of her whole *active* militia, as Congress has so shaped it as to include the identical persons embraced in the act passed at your late session, and to transfer the control of them all from the State to the Confederate government.

The State has already enrolled these persons under the solemn act of her Legislature, for her own defense, and it is a question for you to determine, whether the necessities of the State, her sovereignty and dignity, and justice to those who are to be affected by the act, do not forbid that she should permit her organization to be broken up, and her means of self-preservation to be taken out of her hands. If this is done, what will be our condition? I prefer to answer by adopting the language of the present able and patriotic Governor of Virginia: "A sovereign State without a soldier, and without the dignity of strength—stripped of all her men, and with only the form and pageantry of power—would indeed be nothing more than a wretched dependency, to which I should grieve to see our proud old Commonwealth reduced." . . .

CONFLICT WITH THE CONFEDERATE GOVERNMENT

But it may be said that an attempt to maintain the rights of the State will produce conflict with the Confederate Government. I am aware that there are those who, from motives not necessary to be here mentioned, are ever ready to raise the cry of *conflict,* and to criticise and condemn the action of Georgia, in every case where her constituted authorities protest against the encroachments of the central power, and seek to maintain her dignity and sovereignty as a State, and the constitutional rights and liberties of her people.

Those who are unfriendly to State sovereignty, and desire to consolidate all power in the hands of the Confederate Government, hoping to promote their undertaking by operating upon the fears of the timid, after each new aggression upon the constitutional rights of the States, fill the newspaper presses with the cry of *conflict,* and warn the people to beware of those who seek to maintain their constitutional rights, as *agitators* or *partisans* who may embarrass the Confederate Government in the prosecution of the war.

Let not the people be deceived by this false clamor. It is the same cry of *conflict* which the Lincoln Government raised against all who defended the rights of the Southern States against its tyranny. It is the cry which the usurpers of power have ever raised against those who rebuke their encroachments and refuse to yield to their aggressions. . . .

SUSPENSION OF THE HABEAS CORPUS

I cannot withhold the expression of the deep mortification I feel at the late action of Congress, in attempting to suspend the privilege of the writ of *Habeas Corpus,* and to confer upon the President powers expressly denied to him by the Constitution of the Confederate States. Under pretext of a *necessity* which our whole people know does not exist in this case whatever may have been the motives, our Congress, with the assent, and at the *request* of the Executive, has struck a fell blow at the liberties of these States.

The Constitution of the Confederate States declares that, "The privilege of the writ of *habeas corpus* shall not be suspended, unless when in cases of rebellion or invasion the public safety may require it." The power to suspend the *habeas corpus* at all, is derived, not from express and direct delegation, but from implication only, and an implication can never be raised in opposition to an express restriction. In case of any conflict between the two, an implied power must always yield to express restrictions upon its exercise. The power to suspend the privilege of the writ of *habeas corpus* derived by implication, must therefore be always limited by the *express* declaration in the Constitution that:

> "The right of the people to be secure in their *persons,* houses, papers, and effects, against unreasonable searches and seizures *shall not be violated;* and *no warrants shall issue* but upon probable cause, supported by *oath or affirmation,* and particularly describing the place to be searched, and the *persons* or things to be seized," and the further declaration that, "no person shall be deprived of life, *liberty* or property, without due process of law."

And that,

> "In all *criminal prosecutions* the accused shall enjoy the right of a *speedy* and public trial by an *impartial jury* of the State or District where the crime shall have been committed, which district shall have been previously ascertained by law, and to be informed of the nature and cause of the accusation; to be confronted with the witnesses against him; to have compulsory process for obtaining witnesses in his favor; and to have the assistance of counsel for his defense."

Thus it is an express guaranty of the Constitution, that the *"persons"* of the people shall be secure, and "*no warrants* shall issue," but upon probable cause, supported by *oath* or *affirmation,*" particularly describing "the *persons* to be seized;" that, "no *person* shall be deprived of *liberty,* without due process of law", and that, in "all criminal prosecutions the accused shall enjoy the right of a *speedy* and *public* trial, by an *impartial jury.*"

The Constitution also defines the *powers* of the Executive, which, are limited to those delegated, among which there is no one, authorizing him to issue *warrants* or *order arrests* of persons not in *actual* military service; or to sit as a judge in any case, to try any person for a criminal offense, or to appoint any *court* or *tribunal* to do it, not provided for in the Constitution, as part of the judiciary. The power to *issue warrants* and try persons under criminal accusations are *judicial* powers, which belong, under the Constitution, *exclusively* to the *judiciary* and not to the *Executive.* His power to order arrests, as Commander-in-Chief, is strictly a *military* power, and is confined to the arrest of *persons subject to military power,* as to the arrest of persons in the army or navy of the Confederate States; or in the Militia, when in the *actual* service of the Confederate States, and does not extend to any persons in civil life, unless they be followers of the camp, or within the lines of the army. This is clear from that provision of the Constitution which declares, that,

"No person shall be held to answer for a capital, or otherwise infamous crime, unless on a *presentment* or *indictment* of a *grand jury,* except in cases arising *in the land or naval forces,* or *in the militia,* when in *actual service* in time of war or public danger." But even here, the power of the President as Commander-in-Chief, is not absolute, as his powers and duties, in ordering arrests of persons, in the land or naval forces, or in the militia, when in *actual* service, are clearly defined by the rules and articles of war, prescribed by Congress. *Any warrant* issued by the President, or *any arrest* made by him, or under his order, of *any person* in civil life and not subject to military command, is *illegal* and in *plain violation of the Constitution;* as it is impossible for Congress, by implication, to confer upon the President the right to exercise powers of arrest, expressly forbidden to him by the Constitution. Any effort, on the part of Congress, to do this, is but an attempt to revive the odious practice of ordering political arrests, or issuing letters *de cachet* by royal prerogative, so long since renounced by our English ancestors; and the denial of the right of the constitutional judiciary to investigate such cases, and the provision for creating a court appointed by the Executive, and changeable at his will, to take jurisdiction of the same, are in violation of the great principles of *Magna Charta,* the Bill of Rights, the *habeas corpus* act, and the Constitution of the Confederate States, upon which both English and American liberty rest; and are but an attempt to revive the odious Star-Chamber court of England, which, in the hands of wicked kings, was used for tyrannical purposes, by the crown, until it was finally abolished by act of parliament, of 16th Charles the First, which went into operation on the first of August 1641. This act has ever since been regarded as one of the great bulwarks of English liberty; and as it was passed by the English Parliament to secure our English ancestors against the very same character of arbitrary arrests which the late act of Congress is intended to authorize the President to make, I append a copy of it to this message, with the same italics and small capital letters, which are used in the printed copy in the book from which it is taken. It will be seen that the court of "Star-Chamber," which was the instrument in the hands of the English king, for *investigating* his illegal arrests and carrying out his arbitrary decrees, was much more respectable, on account of the character, learning and ability of its members, than the Confederate Star-Chamber, or court of "proper officers," which the act of Congress gives the President power to appoint, to *investigate* his illegal arrests. . . .

The only suspension of the privilege of the writ of *habeas corpus,* known to our Constitution, and compatible with the provisions already stated, goes to the simple extent of preventing the release, under it, of persons whose arrests have been ordered under constitutional warrants from judicial authority. To this extent the Constitution allows the suspension, in case of rebellion or invasion, in order that the accused may be certainly and safely held for trial; but Congress has no right, under pretext of exercising this power, to authorize the President to make *illegal arrests,* prohibited by the Constitution; and when Congress has attempted to confer such powers on the President, if he should order such illegal arrests, it would be the imperative duty of the judges, who have solemnly sworn to support the Constitution, to disregard such unconstitutional legislation, and grant relief to persons so illegally imprisoned; and it would be the duty of the Legislative and Executive departments of the States to sustain and protect the judiciary in the discharge of this obligation.

By an examination of the act of Congress, now under consideration, it will be seen that it is not an act to suspend the privilege of the writ of *habeas corpus* in case of warrants issued by *judicial authority;* but the main purpose of the act seems to be to authorize the President to issue warrants, supported by neither *oath* nor *affirmation,* and to make arrests of persons not in military service, upon charges of a nature proper for investigation in the judicial tribunals only, and to prevent the Courts from inquiring into such arrests, or granting relief against such illegal usurpations of power, which are in direct and palpable violation of the Constitution. . . .

This then is not an act to suspend the privilege of the writ of *habeas corpus,* in the manner authorized by implication by the Constitution; but it is an act to authorize the President to make *illegal and unconstitutional arrests,* in cases which the Constitution gives to the judiciary, and denies to the Executive; and to prohibit all judicial interference for the relief of the citizen, when tyranized over by illegal arrest, under letters *de cachet* issued by Executive authority.

Instead of the legality of the arrest being examined in the judicial tribunals appointed by the Constitution, it is to be examined in the Confederate Star Chamber; that is, by *officers* appointed by the President. Why say that the "*President shall cause proper officers* to investigate" the legality of arrests ordered by him? Why not permit the Judges, whose constitutional right and duty it is to do it?

We are witnessing with too much indifference assumptions of power by the Confederate Government which in ordinary times would arouse the whole country to indignant rebuke and stern resistance. History teaches us that submission to one encroachment upon constitutional liberty is always followed by another; and we should not forget that important rights, yielded to those in power, without rebuke or protest, are never recovered by the people without revolution. . . .

When such bold strides towards military despotism and absolute authority, are taken, by those in whom we have confided, and who have been placed in high official position to guard and protect constitutional and personal liberty, it is the duty of every patriotic citizen to sound the alarm, and of the State Legislatures to say, in thunder tones, to those who assume to govern us by absolute power, that there is a point beyond which freemen will not permit encroachments to go.

The Legislatures of the respective States are looked to as the guardians of the rights of those whom they represent, and it is their duty to meet such dangerous encroachments upon the liberties of the people, promptly, and express their unqualified condemnation, and to instruct their Senators, and request their Representatives to repeal this most monstrous act, or resign a trust, which, by permitting it to remain on the statute book, they abuse, to the injury of those who have honored them with their confidence in this trying period of our history. I earnestly recommend that the Legislature of this State take prompt action upon this subject, and stamp the act with the seal of their indignant rebuke. . . .

Cyrus Pringle (1838–1911)

Throughout history, dissenters have opposed war for a variety of reasons. Often the reasons are political and connected to a specific war, such as Henry David Thoreau's opposition to the Mexican War. Thoreau was not necessarily a pacifist opposed to all wars. He was opposed to the war with Mexico because of its intention to extend slavery. There are individuals, however, who for moral or religious reasons are opposed to war in general. In both cases, whether the individual is a pacifist or a political dissenter, the antiwar stance is ultimately a question of conscience.

During the Civil War, Cyrus Pringle was drafted into the Union Army but, because of his Quaker convictions, refused to serve and even refused, when the option was offered to him, to pay for a substitute. His diary, discovered and published 50 years after the war, has been a source of inspiration for pacifists objecting to the First World War, the Second World War, and the Vietnam War in the twentieth century. Why didn't Pringle pay for a substitute to take his place in the army? Why would he refuse even to clean his gun?

The Record of a Quaker Conscience, 1863

At Burlington, Vt., on the 13th of the seventh month, 1863, I was drafted. Pleasant are my recollections of the 14th. Much of that rainy day I spent in my chamber, as yet unaware of my fate; in writing and reading and in reflecting to compose my mind for any event. The day and the exercise, by the blessing of the Father, brought me precious reconciliation to the will of Providence.

With ardent zeal for our Faith and the cause of our peaceable principles; and almost disgusted at the lukewarmness and unfaithfulness of very many who profess these; and considering how heavily slight crosses bore upon their shoulders, I felt to say, "Here am I, Father, for thy service. As thou will." May I trust it was He who called me and sent me forth with the consolation: "My grace is sufficient for thee." Deeply have I felt many times since that I am nothing without the companionship of the Spirit.

I was to report on the 27th. Then, loyal to our country, Wm. Lindley Dean and I appeared before the Provost Marshal with a statement of our cases. We were ordered for a hearing on the 29th. On the afternoon of that day W. L. D. was rejected upon examination of the Surgeon, but my case not coming up, he remained with me, much to my strength and comfort. Sweet was his converse and long to be remembered, as we lay together that warm summer night on the straw of the barracks. By his encouragement much was my mind strengthened; my desires for a pure life, and my resolutions for good. In him and those of whom he spoke I saw the abstract beauty of Quakerism. On the next morning came Joshua M. Dean to support me and plead my case before the Board of Enrollment. On the day after, the 31st, I came before the Board. Respectfully those men listened to the exposition of our principles; and, on our representing that we looked for some relief from the President, the marshal released me for twenty days. Meanwhile appeared Lindley M. Macomber and was likewise, by the kindness of the marshal, though they had received instructions from the Provost Marshal General to show such claims no partiality, released to appear on the 20th day of the eighth month.

SOURCE: Cyrus Pringle, *The Civil War Diary of Cyrus Pringle* (Wallingford, PA: Pendle Hill Pamphlet 122, 1962), 7–15, 27–39.

All these days we were urged by our acquaintances to pay our commutation money; by some through well-meant kindness and sympathy; by others through interest in the war; and by others still through a belief they entertained it was our duty. But we confess a higher duty than that to country; and, asking no military protection of our Government and grateful for none, deny any obligation to support so unlawful a system, as we hold a war to be even when waged in opposition to an evil and oppressive power and ostensibly in defence of liberty, virtue, and free institutions; and, though touched by the kind interest of friends, we could not relieve their distress by a means we held even more sinful than that of serving ourselves, as by supplying money to hire a substitute we would not only be responsible for the result, but be the agents in bringing others into evil. So looking to our Father alone for help, and remembering that "Whoso loseth his life for my sake shall find it; but whoso saveth it shall lose it," we presented ourselves again before the Board, as we had promised to do when released. Being offered four days more of time, we accepted it as affording opportunity to visit our friends; and moreover as there would be more probability of meeting Peter Dakin at Rutland.

Sweet was the comfort and sympathy of our friends as we visited them. There was a deep comfort, as we left them, in the thought that so many pure and pious people follow us with their love and prayers. Appearing finally before the marshal on the 24th, suits and uniforms were selected for us, and we were called upon to give receipts for them. L. M. M. was on his guard, and, being first called upon, declared he could not do so, as that would imply acceptance. Failing to come to any agreement, the matter was postponed till next morning, when we certified to the fact that the articles were "with us." Here I must make record of the kindness of the marshal, Rolla Gleason, who treated us with respect and kindness. He had spoken with respect of our Society; had given me furloughs to the amount of twenty four days, when the marshal at Rutland considered himself restricted by his oath and duty to six days; and here appeared in person to prevent any harsh treatment of us by his sergeants; and though much against his inclinations, assisted in putting on the uniform with his own hands. We bade him farewell with grateful feelings and expressions of fear that we should not fall into as tender hands again; and amid the rain in the early morning, as the town clock tolled the hour of seven, we were driven amongst the flock that was going forth to the slaughter, down the street and into the cars for Brattleboro. Dark was the day with murk and cloud and rain; and, as we rolled down through the narrow vales of eastern Vermont, somewhat of the shadow crept into our hearts and filled them with dark apprehensions of evil fortune ahead; of long, hopeless trials; of abuse from inferior officers; of contempt from common soldiers; of patient endurance (or an attempt at this), unto an end seen only by the eye of a strong faith.

Herded into a car by ourselves, we conscripts, substitutes, and the rest, through the greater part of the day, swept over the fertile meadows along the banks of the White River and the Connecticut, through pleasant scenes that had little of delight for us. At Woodstock we were joined by the conscripts from the 1st District—altogether an inferior company from those before with us, who were honest yeomen from the northern and mountainous towns, while these were many of them substitutes from the cities.

At Brattleboro we were marched up to the camp; our knapsacks and persons searched; and any articles of citizen's dress taken from us; and then shut up in a rough board building under a guard. . . .

Brattleboro, 26th, 8th month, 1863. Twenty-five or thirty caged lions roam lazily to and fro through this building hour after hour through the day. On every side without, sentries pace their slow beat, bearing loaded muskets. Men are ranging through the grounds or hanging in synods about the doors of the different buildings, apparently without a purpose. Aimless is military life, except betimes its aim is deadly. Idle life blends with violent death-struggles till the man is unmade a man; and henceforth there is little of manhood about him. Of a man he is made a soldier, which is a man-destroying machine in two senses,—a thing for the prosecuting or repelling an invasion like the block of stone in the fortress or the plate of iron on the side of the Monitor. They are alike. I have tried in vain to define a difference, and I see only this. The iron-clad with its gun is the bigger soldier: the more formidable in attack, the less liable to destruction in a given time; the block the most capable of resistance; both are equally obedient to officers. Or the more perfect is the soldier, the more nearly he approaches these in this respect.

Three times a day we are marched out to the mess houses for our rations. In our hands we carry a tin plate, whereon we bring back a piece of bread (sour and tough most likely), and a cup. Morning and noon a piece of meat, antique betimes, bears company with the bread. They who wish it receive in their cups two sorts of decoctions: in the morning burnt bread, or peas perhaps, steeped in water with some saccharine substance added (I dare not affirm it to be sugar). At night steeped tea extended by some other herbs probably and its pungency and acridity assuaged by the saccharine principle aforementioned. On this we have so far subsisted and, save some nauseating, comfortably. As we go out and return, on right and left and in front and rear go bayonets. Some substitutes heretofore have escaped and we are not to be neglected in our attendants. Hard beds are healthy, but I query cannot the result be defeated by the *degree*? Our mattresses are boards. Only the slight elasticity of our thin blankets breaks the fall of our flesh and bones thereon. Oh! now I praise the discipline I have received from uncarpeted floors through warm summer nights of my boyhood.

The building resounds with petty talk; jokes and laughter and swearing. Something more than that. Many of the caged lions are engaged with cards, and money changes hands freely. Some of the caged lions read, and some sleep, and so the weary day goes by.

L.M.M. and I addressed the following letter to Governor Holbrook and hired a corporal to forward it to him.

Brattleboro, Vt., 26th, 8th month, 1863.

Frederick Holbrook,

Governor of Vermont:—

We, the undersigned members of the Society of Friends, beg leave to represent to thee, that we were lately drafted in the 3d Dist. of Vermont, have been forced into the army and reached the camp near: this town yesterday.

That in the language of the elders of our New York Yearly Meeting, "We love our country and acknowledge with gratitude to our Heavenly Father the many blessings we have been favoured with under the government; and can feel no sympathy with any who seek its overthrow."

But that, true to well-known principles of our Society, we cannot violate our religious convictions either by complying with military requisitions or by the equivalents of this compliance, the furnishing of a substitute or payment of commutation money. That, therefore, we are brought into suffering and exposed to insult and contempt from those who have us in charge, as well as to the penalties of insubordination, though liberty of conscience is granted us by the Constitution of Vermont as well as that of the United States.

Therefore, we beg of thee as Governor of our State any assistance thou may be able to render, should it be no more than the influence of thy position interceding in our behalf.

Truly Thy Friend,

Cyrus G. Pringle.

P.S.—We are informed we are to be sent to the vicinity of Boston tomorrow.

27th. On board train to Boston. The long afternoon of yesterday passed slowly away. This morning passed by,—the time of our stay in Brattleboro, and we neither saw nor heard anything of our Governor. We suppose he could not or would not help us. So as we go down to our trial we have no arm to lean upon among all men; but why dost thou complain, oh, my Soul? Seek thou that faith that will prove a buckler to thy breast, and gain for thee the protection of an arm mightier than the arms of all men.

Camp Vermont: Long Island, Boston Harbour. 28th—In the early morning damp and cool we marched down off the heights of Brattleboro to take train for this place. Once in the car the dashing young cavalry officer, who had us in charge, gave notice he had placed men through the cars, with loaded revolvers, who had orders to shoot any person attempting to escape, or jump from the window, and that any one would be shot if he even put his head out of the window. Down the beautiful valley of the Connecticut, all through its broad intervals, heavy with its crops of corn or tobacco, or shaven smooth by the summer harvest; over the hard and stony counties of northern Massachusets, through its suburbs and under the shadow of Bunker Hill Monument we came into the City of Boston, "the Hub of the Universe." Out through street after street we were marched double guarded to the wharves, where we took a small steamer for the island some six miles out in the harbour. A circumstance connected with this march is worth mentioning for its singularity: at the head of this company, like convicts (and feeling very much like such), through the City of Boston walked, with heavy hearts and down-cast eyes, two Quakers.

Here on this dry and pleasant island in the midst of the beautiful Massachusetts Bay, we have the liberty of the camp, the privilege of air and sunshine and hay beds to sleep upon. So we went to bed last night with somewhat of gladness elevating our depressed spirits.

Here are many troops gathering daily from all the New England States except Connecticut and Rhode Island. Their white tents are dotting the green slopes and hilltops of the island and spreading wider and wider. This is the flow of military tide here just now. The ebb went out to sea in the shape of a great shipload just as we came in, and another load will be sent before many days. All is war here. We are surrounded by the pomp and circumstance of war, and enveloped in the cloud thereof. The cloud settles down over the minds and souls of all; they cannot see beyond, nor do they try; but with the clearer eye of Christian faith I try to look beyond all this error unto Truth and Holiness immaculate: and thanks to our Father, I am favoured with glimpses that are sweet consolation amid this darkness.

This is one gratification: the men with us give us their sympathy. They seem to look upon us tenderly and pitifully, and their expressions of kind wishes are warm. Although we are relieved from duty and from drill, and may lie in our tents during rain and at night, we have heard of no complaint. This is the more worthy of note as there are so few in our little (Vermont) camp. Each man comes on guard half the days. It would probably be otherwise were their hearts in the service; but I have yet to find the man in any of these camps or at any service who does not wish himself at home. Substitutes say if they knew all they know now before leaving home they would not have enlisted; and they have been but a week from their homes and have endured no hardships. Yesterday L. M. M. and I appeared before the Captain commanding this camp with a statement of our cases. He listened to us respectfully and promised to refer us to the General commanding here, General Devens; and in the meantime released us from duty. In a short time afterward he passed us in our tent, asking our names. We have not heard from him, but do not drill or stand guard; so, we suppose, his release was confirmed. At that interview a young lieutenant sneeringly told us he thought we had better throw away our scruples and fight in the service of the country; and as we told the Captain we could not accept pay, he laughed mockingly, and said he would not stay here for $13.00 per month. He gets more than a hundred, I suppose.

How beautiful seems the world on this glorious morning here by the seaside! Eastward and toward the sun, fair green isles with outlines of pure beauty are scattered over the blue bay. Along the far line of the mainland white hamlets and towns glisten in the morning sun; countless tiny waves dance in the wind that comes off shore and sparkle sunward like myriads of gems. Up the fair vault, flecked by scarcely a cloud, rolls the sun in glory. Though fair be the earth, it has come to be tainted and marred by him who was meant to be its crowning glory. Behind me on this island are crowded vile and wicked men, the murmur of whose ribaldry riseth continually like the smoke and fumes of a lower world. Oh! Father of Mercies, forgive the hard heartlessness and blindness and scarlet sins of my fellows, my brothers. . . .

Regimental Hospital, 4th Vermont. 29th—On the evening of the 26th the Colonel came to us apologizing for the roughness with which he treated us at first, which was, as he insisted, through ignorance of our real character and position. He told us if we persisted in our course, death would probably follow; though at another time he confessed to P. D. that this would only be the extreme sentence of court-martial. He urged us to go into the hospital, stating that this course was advised by Friends about New York. We were too well aware of such a fact to make any denial, though it was a subject of surprise to us that he should be informed of it. He pleaded with us long and earnestly, urging us with many promises of indulgence and favour and attentions we found afterwards to be untrue. He gave us till the next morning to consider the question and report our decision. In our discussion of the subject among ourselves, we were very much perplexed. If all his statements concerning the ground taken by our Society were true, we seemed to be liable, if we persisted in the course which alone seemed to us to be in accordance with Truth, to be exposed to the charge of over-zeal and fanaticism even among our own brethren. Regarding the work to be done in hospital as one of mercy and benevolence, we asked if we had any right to refuse its performance; and questioned whether we could do more good by deavouring to bear to the end a clear testimony against war, than by labouring by word and deed among the needy in the hospitals and camps. We saw around us a rich field for usefulness in which there were scarce any labourers and toward whose work our hands had often started involuntarily and unbidden. At last we consented to a trial, at least till we could make inquiries concerning the Colonel's allegations, and ask the counsel of our friends, reserving the privilege of returning to our former position.

At first a great load seemed rolled away from us; we rejoiced in the prospect of life again. But soon there prevailed a feeling of condemnation, as though we had sold Our Master. And that first day was one of the bitterest I ever experienced. It was a time of stern conflict of soul. The voice that seemed to say, "Follow me," as I sought guidance the night before, kept pleading with me, convincing of sin, till I knew of a truth my feet had strayed from His path. The Scriptures, which the day before I could scarcely open without finding words of strength and comfort, seemed closed against me, till after a severe struggle alone in the wood to which I had retired, I consented to give up and retrace my steps in faith. But it was too late. L.M.M. wishing to make a fair, honest trial, we were brought here—P.D. being already here unwell. We feel we are erring; but scarce anything is required of us and we wait to hear from Friends.

Of these days of going down into sin, I wish to make little mention. I would that my record of such degradation be brief. We wish to come to an understanding with our friends and the Society before we move, but it does not seem that we can repress the up-heavings of Truth in our hearts. We are bruised by sin.

It is with pleasure I record we have just waited upon the Colonel with an explanation of our distress of mind, requesting him to proceed with court-martial. We were kindly and tenderly received. "If you want a trial I can give it to you," he answered. The brigade has just marched out to join with the division for inspection. After that we are to have attention to our case.

P.M. There is particular cause for congratulation in the consideration that we took this step this morning, when now we received a letter from H. D. charging us to faithfulness.

When lately I have seen dear L. M. M. in the thoroughness and patience of his trial to perform service in hospital, his uneasiness and the intensity of his struggle as manifested by his silence and disposition to avoid the company of his friends, and seen him fail and declare to us, "I cannot stay here," I have received a new proof, and to me a strong one, because it is from the experimental knowledge of an honest man, that no Friend, who is really such, desiring to keep himself clear of complicity with this system of war and to bear a perfect testimony against it, can lawfully perform service in the hospitals of the Army in lieu of bearing arms.

3rd, 10th month—Today dawned fair and our Camp is dry again. I was asked to clean the gun I brought, and declining, was tied some two hours upon the ground.

At Washington. 6th—At first, after being informed of our declining to serve in his hospital, Colonel Foster did not appear altered in his kind regard for us. But his spleen soon became evident. At the time we asked for a trial by court-martial, and it was his duty to place us under arrest and proceed with the preferring of his charges against us. For a while he seemed to hesitate and consult his inferior officers, and among them his Chaplain. The result of the conference was our being ordered into our companies, that, separated, and with the force of the officers of a company bearing upon us, we might the more likely be subdued. Yet the Colonel assured L.M.M., interceding in my behalf, when the lieutenant commanding my company threatened force upon me, that he should not allow any personal injury. When we marched next day I was compelled to bear a gun and equipments. My associates were more fortunate, for, being asked if they would carry their guns, declined and saw no more trouble from them. The captain of the company in which P.D. was placed told him he did not believe he was ugly about it, and that he could only put him under arrest and prefer charges against him. He accordingly was taken under guard, where he lay till we left for here.

The next morning the men were busy in burnishing their arms. When I looked toward the one I had borne, yellow with rust, I trembled in the weakness of the flesh at the trial I felt impending over me. Before the Colonel was up I knocked at his tent, but was told he was asleep, though, through the opening, I saw him lying gazing at me. Although I felt I should gain no relief from him, I applied again soon after. He admitted me and, lying on his bed, inquired with cold heartlessness what I wanted. I stated to him, that I could never consent to serve, and, being under the war-power, was resigned to suffer instead all the just penalties of the law. I begged of him release from the attempts by violence to compel my obedience and service, and a trial, though likely to be made by those having no sympathy with me, yet probably in a manner comfortable to law.

He replied that he had shown us all the favour he should; that he had, now, turned us over to the military power and was going to let that take its course; that is, henceforth we were to be at the mercy of the inferior officers, without appeal to law, justice, or mercy. He said he had placed us in a pleasant position, against which we could have no reasonable objection, and that we had failed to perform our agreement. He wished to deny that our consent was only temporary and conditional. He declared, furthermore, his belief, that a man who would not fight for his country did not deserve to live. I was glad to withdraw from his presence as soon as I could.

I went back to my tent and lay down for a season of retirement, endeavouring to gain resignation to any event. I dreaded torture and desired strength of flesh and spirit. My trial soon came. The lieutenant called me out, and pointing to the gun that lay near by, asked if I was going to clean it. I replied to him, that I could not comply with military requisitions, and felt resigned to the consequences. "I do not ask about your feelings; I want to know if you are going to clean that gun?" "I cannot do it," was my answer. He went away, saying, "Very well," and I crawled into the tent again. Two sergeants soon called for me, and taking me a little aside, bid me lie down on my back, and stretching my limbs apart tied cords to my wrists and ankles and these to four stakes driven in the ground somewhat in the form of an X.

I was very quiet in my mind as I lay there on the ground with the rain of the previous day, exposed to the heat of the sun, and suffering keenly from the cords binding my wrists and straining my muscles. And, if I dared the presumption, I should say that I caught a glimpse of heavenly pity. I wept, not so much from my own suffering as from sorrow that such things should be in our own country, where Justice and Freedom and Liberty of Conscience have been the annual boast of Fourth-of-July orators so many years. It seemed that our forefathers in the faith had wrought and suffered in vain, when the privileges they so dearly bought were so soon set aside. And I was sad, that one endeavouring to follow our dear Master should be so generally regarded as a despicable and stubborn culprit.

After something like an hour had passed, the lieutenant came with his orderly to ask me if I was ready to clean the gun. I replied to the orderly asking the question, that it could but give me pain to be asked or required to do anything I believed wrong. He repeated it to the lieutenant just behind him, who advanced and addressed me. I was favoured to improve the opportunity to say to him a few things I wished. He said little; and, when I had finished, he withdrew with the others who had gathered around. About the end of another hour his orderly came and released me.

I arose and sat on the ground. I did not rise to go away. I had not where to go, nothing to do. As I sat there my heart swelled with joy from above. The consolation and sweet fruit of tribulation patiently endured. But I also grieved, that the world was so far gone astray, so cruel and blind. It seemed as if the gospel of Christ had never been preached upon earth, and the beautiful example of his life had been utterly lost sight of.

Some of the men came about me, advising me to yield, and among them one of those who had tied me down, telling me what I had already suffered was nothing to what I must yet suffer unless I yielded; that human flesh could not endure what they would put upon me. I wondered if it, could be that they could force me to obedience by torture, and examined myself closely to see if they had advanced as yet one step toward the accomplishment of their purposes. Though weaker in body, I believed I found myself, through divine strength, as firm in my resolution to maintain my allegiance to my Master.

The relaxation of my nerves and muscles after having been so tensely strained left me that afternoon so weak that I could hardly walk or perform any mental exertion.

I had not yet eaten the mean and scanty breakfast I had prepared, when I was ordered to pack up my things and report myself at the lieutenant's tent. I was accustomed to such orders and complied, little moved.

The lieutenant received me politely with, "Good-morning, Mr. Pringle," and desiring me to be seated, proceeded with the writing with which he was engaged. I sat down in some wonderment and sought to be quiet and prepared for any event.

"You are ordered to report to Washington," said he; "I do not know what it is for." I assured him that neither did I know. We were gathered before the Major's tent for preparation for departure. The regimental officers were there manifesting surprise and chagrin; for they could not but show both as they looked upon us, whom the day before they were threatening to crush into submission, and attempting also to execute their threats that morning, standing out of their power and under orders from one superior to their Major Commanding E.M. As the bird uncaged, so were our hearts that morning. Short and uncertain at first were the flights of Hope. As the slave many times before us, leaving his yoke behind him, turned from the plantations of Virginia and set his face toward the far North, so we from out a grasp as close and as abundant in suffering and severity, and from without the line of bayonets that had so many weeks surrounded us, turned our backs upon the camp of the 4th Vermont and took our way over the turnpike that ran through the tented fields of Culpeper.

At the War Office we were soon admitted to an audience with the Adjutant General, Colonel Townsend, whom we found to be a very fine man, mild and kind. He referred our cases to the Secretary of War, Stanton, by whom we were ordered to report for service to Surgeon General Hammond. Here we met Isaac Newton, Commissioner of Agriculture, waiting for our arrival, and James Austin of Nantucket, expecting his son, Charles L. Austin, and Edward W. Holway of Sandwich, Mass., conscripted Friends like ourselves, and ordered here from the 22nd Massachusetts.

We understand it is through the influence of Isaac Newton that Friends have been able to approach the heads of Government in our behalf and to prevail with them to so great an extent. He explained to us the circumstance in which we are placed. That the Secretary of War and President sympathized with Friends in their present suffering, and would grant them full release, but that they felt themselves bound by their oaths that they would execute the laws, to carry out to its full extent the Conscription Act. That there appeared but one door of relief open, that was to parole us and allow us to go home, but subjected to their call again ostensibly, though this they neither wished nor proposed to do. That the fact of Friends in the Army and refusing service had attracted public attention so that it was not expedient to parole us at present. That, therefore, we were to be sent to one of the hospitals for a short time, where it was hoped and expressly requested that we would consent to remain quiet and acquiesce, if possible, in whatever might be required of us. That our work there would be quite free from objection, being for the direct relief of the sick; and that there we would release none for active service in the field, as the nurses were hired civilians.

These requirements being so much less objectionable than we had feared, we felt relief, and consented to them. I.N. went with us himself to the Surgeon General's office, where he procured peculiar favours for us: that we should be sent to a hospital in the city, where he could see us often; and that orders should be given that nothing should interfere with our comfort, or our enjoyment of our consciences.

Thence we were sent to Medical Purveyor Abbot, who assigned us to the best hospital in the city, the Douglas Hospital.

The next day after our coming here Isaac Newton and James Austin came to add to our number E.W.H. and C.L.A., so now there are five of us instead of three. We are pleasantly situated in a room by ourselves in the upper or fourth story, and are enjoying our advantages of good quarters and tolerable food as no one can except he has been deprived of them.

8th—Today we have a pass to go out to see the city.

9th—We all went, thinking to do the whole city in a day, but before the time of our passes expired, we were glad to drag ourselves back to the rest and quiet of D.H. During the day we called upon our friend I. N. in the Patent Office. When he came to see us on the 7th, he stated he had called upon the President that afternoon to request him to release us and let us go home to our friends. The President promised to consider it over-night. Accordingly yesterday morning, as I.N. told us, he waited upon him again. He found there a woman in the greatest distress. Her son, only a boy of fifteen years and four months, having been enticed into the Army, had deserted and been sentenced to be shot the next day. As the clerks were telling her, the President was in the War Office and could not be seen, nor did they think he could attend to her case that day. I.N. found her almost wild with grief. "Do not despair, my good woman," said he, "I guess the President can be seen after a bit." He soon presented her case to the President, who exclaimed at once, "That must not be, I must look into that case, before they shoot that boy"; and telegraphed at once to have the order suspended.

I.N. judged it was not a fit time to urge our case. We feel we can afford to wait, that a life may be saved. But we long for release. We do not feel easy to remain here.

11th—Today we attended meeting held in the house of a Friend, Asa Arnold, living near here. There were but four persons beside ourselves. E.W.H. and C.L.A. showed their copy of the charges about to have been preferred against them in courtmartial before they left their regiment, to a lawyer who attended the meeting. He laughed at the Specification of Mutiny, declaring such a charge could not have been lawfully sustained against them.

The experiences of our new friends were similar to ours, except they fell among officers who usually showed them favour and rejoiced with them in their release.

13th—L. M. M. had quite an adventure yesterday. He being fireman with another was in the furnace room among three or four others, when the officer of the day, one of the surgeons, passed around on inspection. "Stand up," he ordered them, wishing to be saluted. The others arose; but by no means L. The order was repeated for his benefit, but he sat with his cap on, telling the surgeon he had supposed he was excused from such things as he was one of the Friends. Thereat the officer flew at him, exclaiming, he would take the Quaker out of him. He snatched off his cap and seizing him by the collar tried to raise him to his feet; but finding his strength insufficient and that L. was not to be frightened, he changed his purpose in his wrath and calling for the corporal of the guard had him taken to the guard-house. This was about eleven A.M. and he lay there till about six P.M., when the surgeon in charge, arriving home and hearing of it, ordered the officer of the day to go and take him out, telling him never to put another man into the guard-house while he was in charge here without consulting him. The manner of his release was very satisfactory to us, and we waited for this rather than effect it by our own efforts. We are all getting uneasy about remaining here, and if our release do not come soon, we feel we must intercede with the authorities, even if the alternative be imprisonment.

The privations I have endured since leaving home, the great tax upon my nervous strength, and my mind as well, since I have had charge of our extensive correspondence, are beginning to tell upon my health and I long for rest.

20th—We begin to feel we shall have to decline service as heretofore, unless our position is changed. I shall not say but we submit too much in not declining at once, but it has seemed most prudent at least to make suit with Government rather than provoke the hostility of their subalterns. We were ordered here with little understanding of the true state of things as they really exist here; and were advised by Friends to come and make no objections, being assured it was but for a very brief time and only a matter of form. It might not have been wrong; but as we find we do too much fill the places of soldiers (L.M.M.'s fellow fireman has just left for the field, and I am to take his place, for instance), and are clearly doing military service, we are continually oppressed by a sense of guilt, that makes our struggles earnest.

21st—I.N. has not called yet; our situation is becoming almost intolerable. I query if patience is justified under the circumstances. My distress of mind may be enhanced by my feeble condition of health, for today I am confined to my bed, almost too weak to get downstairs. This is owing to exposure after being heated over the furnaces.

26th—Though a week has gone by, and my cold has left me, I find I am no better, and that I am reduced very low in strength and flesh by the sickness and pain I am experiencing. Yet I still persist in going below once a day. The food I am able to get is not such as is proper.

5th 11th month—I spend most of my time on my bed, much of it alone. And very precious to me is the nearness unto the Master I am favoured to attain to. Notwithstanding my situation and state, I am happy in the enjoyment of His consolations. Lately my confidence has been strong, and I think I begin to feel that our patience is soon to be rewarded with relief; insomuch that a little while ago, when dear P.D. was almost overcome With sorrow, I felt bold to comfort him with the assurance of my belief, that it would not be long so. My mind is too weak to allow of my reading much; and, though I enjoy the company of my companions a part of the time, especially in the evening, I am much alone; which affords me abundant time for meditation and waiting upon God. The fruits of this are sweet, and a recompense for affliction.

6th—Last evening E.W. H. saw I.N. particularly on my behalf, I suppose. He left at once for the President. This morning he called to inform us of his interview at the White House. The President was moved to sympathy in my behalf, when I.N. gave him a letter from one of our Friends in New York. After its perusal he exclaimed to our friend, "I want you to go and tell Stanton that it is my wish all those young men be sent home at once." He was on his way to the Secretary this morning as he called.

Later—I.N. has just called again informing us in joy that we are free. At the War Office he was urging the Secretary to consent to our paroles, when the President entered. "It is my urgent wish," said he. The Secretary yielded; the order was given; and we were released. What we had waited for so many weeks was accomplished in a few moments by a Providential ordering of circumstances.

7th—I.N. came again last evening bringing our paroles. The preliminary arrangements are being made, and we are to start this afternoon for New York.

Note. Rising from my sick-bed to undertake this journey, which lasted through the night, its fatigues overcame me, and upon my arrival, in New York I was seized with delirium from which I only recovered after many weeks, through the mercy and favour of Him, who in all this trial had been our guide and strength and comfort.

African American Soldiers of the Union Army

Because of the prevalent racist beliefs that blacks would not make good soldiers, there was considerable resistance to the idea of forming black Civil War regiments. But after more than a year of fighting and the administration's extreme frustration that the war seemed to be going nowhere, President Lincoln began to support the idea of "colored regiments." More than 200,000 African Americans served in the Union army during the Civil War. The first black regiments were mustered in the autumn of 1862, and after the Emancipation Proclamation went into effect on January 1, 1863, Lincoln authorized the formation of black regiments in Massachusetts, Connecticut, and Rhode Island. The most famous of these was the Massachusetts 54th, which, in July 1863, led a valiant yet futile attack on Fort Wagner in South Carolina.

Although African American troops were demonstrating that they could fight as well and as heroically as any white regiment, they still faced prejudicial treatment. One of the most passionate grievances that swept through their ranks was that they received about half the pay of white troops—only $7 a month. A number of black soldiers refused their duties in an effort to gain equal pay. Some were court-martialed and shot for treason. But most protestors adopted the tactic of continuing to perform their soldierly duties while refusing any pay at all. This tactic finally achieved some success in August 1864, when blacks who were already free before enlisting were granted equal pay. Eventually, in March 1865, all black soldiers were given equal pay, backdated to their enlistment.

During their fight for equal pay, many soldiers wrote letters to newspapers, friends, and relatives to make the case for their position. In the first letter, George E. Stephens, a sergeant in the 54th Massachusetts Infantry, several weeks after his regiment's assault on Fort Wagner, criticizes the federal government for overruling Governor John A. Andrews's announcement that black troops would receive equal pay. In the second letter, another soldier in the 54th argues that the equal pay issue is not merely an economic issue. In the third, a soldier from the 55th Massachusetts Infantry demands "liberty and equality." In the next letter, a soldier from the 6th Pennsylvania Infantry regiment does press the economic issue. In the fifth letter, another member of the 54th (E. W. D.) eloquently questions the justness of a government that will keep a gallant regiment in the field without remuneration. In the sixth letter, H. I. W. of the 54th argues that if they cannot be paid equally, then they should be given an honorable discharge. In the seventh, Sergeant John H. W. N. Collins of the 54th complains that, nearly a year after the battle at Fort Wagner, their pay has still not been forthcoming. And in the final letter, J. H. Hall of the 54th wants to know why the soldiers are not recognized as lawful citizens and brave soldiers but instead are disparaged "as an inferior sort of laborer" paid $7 a month.

What do these letters say about African American soldiers' patriotism? What do they reveal about the wisdom of the soldiers' assessment of their situation? What do they reveal about their courage and fighting ability?

Correspondence Protesting Unequal Pay, 1863–1864

A LETTER FROM GEORGE E. STEPHENS

. . . The question of our pay continues to be the topic of conversation and correspondence. Numerous letters have reached us from distinguished friends in the State of Massachusetts, all expressing the utmost confidence that we will receive all of our pay, and have secured to us every right that other Massachusetts soldiers enjoy. His Excellency Gov. Andrew, in a letter dated, "Executive Department, Boston, August 24th," and addressed to Mr. Frederick Johnson, an officer in the regiment, says:

"I have this day received your letter of the 10th of August, and in reply desire, in the first place, to express to you the lively interest with which I have watched every step of the fifty-fourth Regiment since it left Massachusetts, and the feelings of pride and admiration with which I have learned and read of the accounts of the heroic conduct of the regiment in the attack upon Fort Wagner, when you and your brave soldiers so well proved their manhood, and showed themselves to be true soldiers of Massachusetts. As to the matter inquired about in your letter, you may rest assured that I shall not rest until you have secured all of your rights, and that I have no doubt whatever of ultimate success. I have no doubt, by law, you are entitled to the same pay as other soldiers, and on the authority of the Secretary of War, I promised that you should be paid and treated in all respects like other soldiers of Massachusetts. Till this is done I feel that my promise is dishonored by the government. The whole difficulty arises from a misapprehension, the correction of which will no doubt be made as soon as I can get the subject fully examined by the Secretary of War. I have the honor to be your obedient servant,

JOHN A. ANDREW, Governor of Massachusetts."

The trouble seems to be something like this: The Paymaster General, whoever that may be, has directed the paymasters to pay all negro troops of African descent, $10 per month, the pay allowed to contrabands by statute when employed in the Commissary or Quartermaster's Department. There seems to have been no provision made to pay colored soldiers. There may be some reason for making a distinction between armed and unarmed men in the service of the government, but when the nationality of a man takes away his title to pay it become another thing. Suppose a regiment of Spaniards should be mustered into the service of the United States, would Congress have to pass a special law to pay Spaniards? Or, suppose, a regiment of Sandwich Islanders should do duty as soldiers of the United States, would it be necessary to pass a law to pay Sandwich Islanders? Does not the deed of muster secure the services and even life of the man mustered into the service to the government? And does not this same deed of muster give a man title to all pay and bounties awarded to soldiers bearing arms? I believe that, "by law, we are entitled to the same pay as other soldiers," and "misapprehension arises" from this: The Paymaster General will not have the colored soldiers paid under the law which pay[s] white soldiers, and virtually creates in his own mind the necessity for the passage of a special law authorizing them to be paid. Is there a special law on the statute books of the National Legislature touching the payment of colored men employed in the naval service? . . .

SOURCE: *The Weekly Anglo African* (September 19, 1863).

A LETTER FROM A MASSACHUSETTS SOLDIER

A strange misapprehension . . . exists as to the matter of pay; and it pains us deeply. We came forward at the call of Gov. Andrew, in which call he distinctly told us that we were to be subsisted, *clothed, paid,* and treated in *all* respects the same as other Massachusetts soldiers. Again, on the presentation of flags to the regiment, at Camp Meigs, the Governor reiterated this promise, on the strength of which we marched through Boston, holding our heads high, as men and as soldiers. Nor did we grumble because we were not paid the portion of United States bounty paid to other volunteer regiments in advance.

Now that we have gained some reputation as soldiers, we claim the right to be heard.

Three times have we been mustered in for pay. Twice have we swallowed the insult offered us by the United States paymaster, contenting ourselves with a simple refusal to acknowledge ourselves, in this matter, different from other Massachusetts soldiers. Once, in the face of insult and intimidation, such as no body of men and soldiers were ever subjected to before, we quietly refused, and continued to do our duty.

For four months we've been steadily working, night and day, under fire. And such work! Up to our knees in mud half the time—causing the tearing and wearing out of more than the volunteer's yearly allowance of clothing—denied time to repair and wash (what we might by that means have saved), denied time to drill and perfect ourselves in soldierly quality, denied the privilege of burying our dead decently! All this we've borne patiently, waiting for justice.

Imagine our surprise and disappointment, on the receipt by the last mail of the Governor's Address to the General Court, to find him making a proposition to them to pay this regiment the difference between what the United States Government offers us and what they are legally bound to pay us, which, in effect, advertises us to the world as holding out for *money* and not from *principle*—that we sink our manhood in consideration of a few more dollars. How has this come about? What false friend has been misrepresenting us to the Governor, to make him think that our necessities outweigh our self-respect? I am sure no representation of *ours* ever impelled him to this action.

A LETTER FROM A SOLDIER OF THE 55TH MASSACHUSETTS REGIMENT

. . . We don't wish you to look upon us as being inclined to be a little stubborn; we were told that we would be accepted by the U.S. Government on the same terms as her other Regiments, and do you call the same terms reducing pay, and receiving part pay from Mass., and a part from the government of the same? If you look at it in that way, you don't look at it as we do. Massachusetts has always been first to open

SOURCE: *The Boston Journal* (c. December 15, 1863).
SOURCE: *The Christian Recorder,* Philadelphia (January 2, 1864).

the door to the poor colored man; was first to send two colored regiments in the field to extinguish the last spark of a most infamous rebellion—one that will figure largely in the annals of history for centuries to come. You sit at your firesides and just study a little what the poor soldier is suffering. You have no idea, and just you fight and slay the rebels that are at our backs, or we will fight them that are in front of us, or fight in Congress for our rights, and we will fight here for yours. I feel proud, and so does every other man that belongs to the 55th, to think that they stand so well upon the principles which they came here to fight for. Our pride has won us a name amongst the white regiments around us; they call us the Independent Colored Regiment, and say to us, You do the work that we ought to share in, and they don't want to pay you anything for it. Do you want to break that spirit of pride! I hope not; and as you say that we have proved ourselves worthy of approbation, don't put our principle upon the grindstone. We love this government, and will sacrifice our lives to maintain it. Just think for a moment, reflect deeply, that there is good for you to gain by it; our lives we value just as highly as you do yours; but without a stimulant, our exertions would not be worth anything. Let our faces be black, but our hearts be true, you will find us true and loyal and obedient, and all qualities pertaining to a soldier. A true and rather singular idea for a colored man to wish to be placed on equal footing with a white man! Why not? Can't we fight just as well? We showed our qualities at Port Gibson and Wagner. Now, if there is not pluck, just fall in some big hole, and we will guarantee to pull you out without blacking your hands; fall down and we will pick you up; we won't pass by and perhaps give you a kick or a cuff, but pick you up, carry you home to your good wife, and won't ask of you your daughter for compensation; all the compensation that we ask is to give us our rights, and don't be dodging around every corner as if you owed us something, and your conscience is getting the upper hand of you. . . . Our motto: "Liberty and Equality."

A LETTER FROM A SOLDIER OF THE 6TH PENNSYLVANIA REGIMENT

I am a soldier, or at least that is what I was drafted for in the 6th USCT; have been in the service since Aug., last. I could not afford to get a substitute, or I would not be here now and my poor wife at home almost starving. When I was at home I could make a living for her and my two little ones; but now that I am a soldier they must do the best they can or starve. It almost tempts me to desert and run a chance of getting shot, when I read her letters, hoping that I would come to her relief. But what am I to do? It is a shame the way they treat us; our officers tell me now that we are not soldiers; that if we were we would get the same pay as the white men; that the government just called us out to dig and drudge, that we are to get but $7.00 per month. Really I thought I was a soldier, and it made me feel somewhat proud to think that I had a right to fight for Uncle Sam. When I was at Chelton Hill I felt very patriotic;

SOURCE: *The Christian Recorder,* Philadelphia (February 20, 1864).

but my wife's letters have brought my patriotism down to the freezing point, and I don't think it will ever rise again; and it is the case all through the regiment. Men having families at home, and they looking to them for support, and they not being able to send them one penny. . . .

ARMY CORRESPONDENCE

Morris Island, S. C., June 9, 1864.

Mr. Editor:

It is with pleasure I write these few lines concerning things here at present. We have had a few shells fired from Sullivan's Island on our fleet, though no damage was done, and the old ram came down to Sumpter and was fired on by our batteries on the 7th of this month.

The Fifty-fourth Regiment Massachusetts Volunteers is still in the field without pay, and the Government shows no disposition to pay us. We have declined doing active field service, except in cases of the greatest emergency, and we are, therefore, divided into four departments, doing garrison duty, we have served our country manfully for over twelve months without receiving one cent from the Government, and all that we have for our bravery is the credit of fighting well, but we are deprived of our wages and the rights of soldiers. We are glad to see the success of our regiment, and feel thankful that so many have escaped the soldier's grave, through the instrumentality of God, who is the giver of all good. God has fought our battles for us, and in His own good time He will avenge our wrongs. We still do the duty assigned us, and trust to God for future events; but, if our merits will not warrant our acknowledgment as men, veterans and soldiers, the hand of God may send forth His destroying angel and slay our enemies. No nation has ever risen to dignity without self-sacrifice, none has ever triumphed in victory without undergoing great hardships and long forbearance; but we still abide in faith, and look forward to the time when Ethiopia shall stretch forth her hand and rise from obscurity with healing in her wings.

If the Fifty-fourth must be as the leaders of Israel, let us suffer in the wilderness until a second Moses shall rise up and smite the rock, that we may drink of the spring of freedom, and the spring of learning.

We all cry, "Union!" and shout for the battle. It is a question whether we can call this a Union Government—a free Government—that will keep a regiment in the field fifteen or sixteen months without pay because they are black. Will you call it an honorable and just Government that gives for a reason that there has been no act passed of Congress to pay negro soldiers? If we understand the Declaration of Independence, it asserts the freedom and equality of all men. We ask nothing more. Give

---

SOURCE: *The Christian Recorder,* Philadelphia (June 25, 1864).

us equality and acknowledge us as men, and we are willing to stand by the flag of our Union and support the leaders of this great Government until every traitor shall be banished from our shore, out of the North as well as the South.

Look at our families, reduced to the necessities of the alms-house for want of the support of their wounded and bleeding husbands, who have fallen before the enemy! We hope that our liberal Government will not be guilty of such atrocious robbery. When we enlisted, it was not for a large bounty nor great salary. We thought that we could help to put down the rebellion. We anticipated future benefits. We intended to distinguish ourselves as heroes and supporters of the Government, and to share alike their rights and privileges, to have the same opportunity for promotion as our freely and ability would warrant. But our bravery is always in vain, our heroism discountenanced, our patriotism disregarded, and we are offered the paltry sum of seven dollars per month, and are given the insulting reason, that the negro is not worth as much as the white man. They cannot tell us that we do not fight as well nor die as freely as the white man, but they can tell us they are a majority, and, therefore, assume presumption of their power, and intend to compel us to involuntary servitude, or, in other words, compel us to work for half pay, which is involuntary servitude. Under such wrongs no nation can prosper. If a strong power crush the weak and deprive them of the blessings which God has ordained for them, it must fall. God's supreme power will break them into pieces that will not obey His righteous laws. Let the hand of Justice have the ruling power, and his omniscience will ever guide our path and direct us in the establishment of the most pure Government.

Let the rulers of our country consult the God of nations and reconsider His instructions with the dictates of their consciences, and every soldier will receive equal compensation according to his merits. If those at the White House were compelled to encounter what the Fifty-fourth have undergone, they would not only allow the negro his rights and acknowledge his citizenship, but, in my humble opinion, they would acknowledge the independence of the Southern Confederacy. But it is not so with many brave negro troops that are in the field. We do not allow a traitor one inch of ground. Give us our rights—acknowledge us as men and citizens— and we are willing to flood the rebellious cities with pools of our blood, and never lay down our arms until every vestige of rebellion is driven from our land.

E.W.D.,

Co. B, 54th Mass. Vols.

A LETTER FROM A SOLDIER

Morris Island, South Carolina, June 8, 1864.

Mr. Editor:

What do you think of this? We rally to the defence of our imperilled country; we freely offer our lives in its defence. The Government acknowledges the value of our

SOURCE: *The Christian Recorder,* Philadelphia (July 23, 1864).

services, and yet they permit our brave men to be treated in a shameful manner. When I enlisted at Boston, Mass., Feb. 21st, 1863, I enlisted on the same terms as other soldiers—clothing, rations, and pay. But all their promises are false and untrue. We have been serving nearly sixteen months, faithfully and truely, the Government of the United States, yet not received one cent of pay. No! they come with woe-stricken face and say they can pay us but $10 a month, and $3 deducted for clothing, which leaves us but $7 a month. Just let them think of Fort Wagner, James' Island, and Olustee, Florida! The men of the 54th have suffered terribly, and still they have the cheek to wrest these brave men of color out of their rights. When the 54th left Boston for the South, they left many white men at home. Therefore, if we are good enough to fill up white men's places and fight, we should be treated then, in all respects, the same as the white man. We have families as well as the white man. The State of Massachusetts has given our people nothing. We, that came out of other States to fill up her regiment, the 54th, for the sake of the service, for the sake of the country, for the sake of justice, and the rights of our gallant regiment, we call upon the authorities of Mass., in behalf of this noble regiment; and, if not, we should like to have an honorable discharge. This regiment has, for many a day, mourned the loss of their gallant Colonel Shaw. The contrabands are better off to-day than the men of the 54th. If there are any slaves, the men of the 54th are as much slaves as any. But the day will soon come when God Almighty will drop the weight on their own shoulders that they are pressing on the black man.

Your humble servant,
H. I. W.

A LETTER FROM A SOLDIER OF THE 54TH MASSACHUSETTS REGIMENT

Black Island, South Carolina,
Co. H, 54th Regt. Mass. Vols, Inf.
July 7th, 1864.

Mr. Editor:

What a great change there has taken place since I penned my last letter to you, from this little post of duty, written on the 1st of this month. There was another Expedition left this vicinity for James Island, on which occasion the gallant 54th must have a hand in the matter, as in almost every other movement of any interest transpiring within the Department's limits.

On the second day nothing of importance was done. Everything was as still as death. The 3d comes upon us, and as the bright rosy beams break gently forth, comes the sharp and rolling reverberation of the deadly "Enfields," mingled with the loud and deep-toned booming of cannon. Once more has the 54th got her foot upon that soil which was the instigation of many of the brave members of her regiment

---

Source: *The Christian Recorder*, Philadelphia (July 23, 1864).

to sink to the earth, never to rise again until the last trump of God shall sound on the dawning of the resurrection morn to call each and every one to give a true and just account of the deeds done here below in the body.

For the first time since we have been in the field, we have been allowed the pleasure of the company of our sister regiment, the 55th, who has many features noticeable in the 54th, for both regiments have stood side by side and fought, never yielding an inch of ground to the stubborn foeman.

Sir, in view of such a noble and generous display of patriotism and courage, it is a disgrace to the name of this great and glorious Union, that these brave fellows should be compelled to fight and toil without receiving their stipulated remuneration. Why is it? Is the laborer not worthy of his hire? Never was such ingratitude heard of before or since the world commenced. Here we are, toiling and sweating beneath the burning rays of the sun, for nothing. We receive nothing but our hard tack and salt pork, and a constant attendance of the blues. All that we get in return for our services are such hackneyed expressions as these: "Why, boys, you are good fighters; don't want any better; white men could not do better, should they try; your bravery cannot be excelled by any troops in the field."

Day after day we await the arrival of each mail in anxious expectancy, to see whether Congress has taken any steps to pay us off, for you know that men cannot live without something to nourish them at times. We should particularly like to have such things as little eatables for our dessert.

We still hold the Island. To-day, even as I write, the booming of the distant cannon can be plainly heard.

Dear sir, before this letter shall have reached you, I may be called away to appear before the great Tribunal of my God. Should I fall in this fearful conflict, I trust that I may, by the assistance and grace of God, be enabled to shake hands with you and all dear friends together in my Father's kingdom, where partings and sorrows are unknown.

Yours in Christ,
JOHN H. W. N. COLLINS,
Orderly Sergeant Co. H, 54 Regt. Mass. Vols.

LETTER FROM THE 54TH MASSACHUSETTS REGIMENT

Morris Island, South Carolina,
August 3, 1864.

Dear Editor:

I now, in making my first attempt at correspondence with you and your paper, write you a few lines concerning things in general that have transpired of late under my own observation in this department of military affairs.

SOURCE: *The Christian Recorder,* Philadelphia (August 27, 1864).

We returned from the James Island Expedition. It was indeed a most perilous undertaking; and the prompt performance of the duty assigned us necessarily involved much hazard and difficulty, as the numerical strength of our troops was much inferior to that of the rebels; but although inferior in numbers, we were vastly superior in point of courage and discipline. We had a great advantage in acting under the guidance of brave and skilful officers, who well knew how to dispose and handle the heroic band under their command.

Our forces were advanced in a most judicious and cautious manner. Heavy lines of skirmishers were thrown forward and across the entire Island, intending to present the appearance of a strong force, and succeeded in keeping the rebs at bay until we were reinforced by seven additional regiments.

We were securely intrenched, and our boys had been anticipating an attack every hour, but the rebs failed to make a general attack on our lines. Nevertheless, General Hatch succeeded in completely surprising them on John's Island. The astonished rebels at that place were rudely awakened from their morning slumbers by a loud salute from our artillery men in the shape of a perfect shower of singeing shot and screaming shell! With true cordiality and feeling the rebs returned our warm greeting, but they were soon compelled to fall back beneath the furious assault and impetuosity of our troops. In the attack, General Hatch was most nobly supported from our right. Having effected the design of the expedition, our brave General withdrew his trusty forces.

I shall now endeavor to make a few remarks in reference to the condition of the 54th. It has been sixteen months since we were mustered in as a regiment, and fourteen months of that time have been spent in active service. We have been on a great many arduous and dangerous expeditions, fought three hard battles, and yet after all this, we have not received one cent of remuneration from the Government. We now would ask the Christian and law-abiding citizen, and all dignitaries in authority, if we have not performed our duty as soldiers, and maintained our dignity and honour as citizens? And have we not borne a patriotic part in every campaign, and ranked in discipline, bravery and heroism with the first regiments in the Southern department? Why, then, is it that we are not recognised as true and lawful citizens, and receive our pay as soldiers? Why are we insulted and told by the paymaster that the negro is not considered as a soldier, but rather as an inferior sort of laborer, to whom he is to pay at most not more than seven dollars per month? I would respectfully ask the question, gentlemen of the city of Boston and Commonwealth of Massachusetts, if this is fit treatment for a brave and gallant regiment of men. Will the vast city of Boston, and the generous and sympathizing State of Massachusetts stand by unmoved, and with unpitying eye permit this foul opprobrium and scorn to be cast upon them? Or will they stand in our defence, even if that derision be heaped upon them which was cast upon that stern old patriot, Andrew Jackson, when he acknowledged the negroes as soldiers, as brethren, and as fellow-citizens—to incur the same dangers and share the same glory alike with their white fellow-citizens? The city of Boston has made the same kind of promises, guarantying that every colored recruit shall have all the rights and privileges, and receive the same pay, bounty, clothing, etc., as the white troops—but, alas! like Andrew Jackson, they too have promised the negroes every thing pertaining to a citizenship, in order to get them into the field, and then they keep them there, without pay, without the stipu-lated bounty, and not even deigning to treat them in a Christian and civil manner. No promise has been regarded by them.

Now, Boston and Massachusetts want to shift the responsibility of this inhuman-ity from their door, and cast it on the shoulders of the general Government. They now say that there has been no law passed in reference to the pay of colored troops.

The educated negro does not enter into contracts without knowing what rec-ompense he is to receive or is promised for his services. The State of Massachusetts has agents in the county of Suffolk, and some one of these parties is responsible.

We are fully satisfied that our debtors are solvent, and we are determined to get all we have enlisted for, when we get back to prosecute the matter, those of us, at least, who may live to come back.

Twenty thousand dollars, over and above our three years, will be sacrificed by this regiment, in order that we may test the law upon this matter. We will have all or nothing. We will not tamely submit to the infliction of wrongs most foul, as did our forefathers, and go back to despondency and submission without even a single struggle.

We have sacrificed our homes and comforts, and even our lives, for the frivolous promise of the unprincipled recruiting officers of Boston and vicinity that we should have all the rights of citizens.

If I had not thought that there might be some truth or veracity in owl-leaders in cities, states, &c., I would have staid in England when I last visited that place—but God will avenge the wrongs of him who is oppressed—and no Government can prosper that is deceptive and false at its very foundation and rules of doing things. The Governor of the Commonwealth of Massachusetts and the Boston authorities need not think that the negro, with his present greatly increased share of learning and wealth, will be satisfied with the easy, palm-off and shut-your-eye-up style of Andrew Jackson assurance, nor be content with any thing less than their just rights and privileges. If we fight to maintain a Republican Government, we want Republi-can privileges; if a monarchical Government, monarchical privileges.

If we are to be recognized as citizens, we want the rights of citizens! Have we lost ground or receded any in the advanced stage of this nineteenth century, or has our race degenerated on account of living in this enlightened and free country?

If we are less worthy as soldiers, as brothers, or as citizens, which has so nobly been set forth by Washington, Madison, Jefferson and Jackson, acknowledging our dignity, honor, bravery and love of country, if we have become so degenerated in this enlightened country that our ability is less worthy our acknowledgment as citi-zens than they were at the time of the Revolutionary War against Great Britain, it would be better if we had been left in the States of Barbary or on the coast of Niger. Much better would it have been.

But, gentlemen, I am gratified to know that the descendants of Africa, and the so-called adopted sons of America have more than kept pace with the Anglo-Saxon. We do not claim that we are more intelligent than our so-called superior race, but we are nearly equal in intelligence, and have acquired a knowledge of science and liter-ature that would surprise the world, if they only knew of the difficulties we have had to encounter to acquire it for ourselves and for our children.

The Anglo-Saxon in America claims that if we are acknowledged citizens, we will covet their wives, daughters and sisters—but it is to the contrary. The respectable part of the colored race consider that their own kind would make the most affectionate companions, and in the case of the so-called aristocracy, if any were known to thus sinfully amalgamate, or should cause their race to be degenerated, the same should be cut off from his inheritance. We do not covet your wives nor your daughters, nor the position of the political orator. All we ask is the proper enjoyment of the rights of citizenship, and a free title and acknowledged share in our own noble birthplace, which we are ready and willing to defend while a single drop of blood courses through our veins.

The negro has a mind susceptible and alive to improvement, and a manly spirit that aspires to dignity and refinement, and is well competent to discern when his services or society are depreciated. These are true facts which cannot be denied.

We, as a regiment, have bound ourselves together with one accord and as one man to protect our own rights: those rights which are now denied us should be given us. There is but one course left for us to pursue. If we are still persistently held and treated as aliens, we must, as a necessary and inevitable consequence, apply to aliens for redress!

And now, Mr. Editor, in conclusion, let me say that I shall correspond with you again, with your permission.

I will give you the whole particulars in reference to matters on the Island when next I write.

We have some good news to tell you. By the exchange of prisoners the following names were brought to light that were thought killed in the assault made upon Fort Wagner some time ago. General Seymour and some others were only exchanged:

Corporal Charles Hardy, Lemuel Blakes, Geo. Conneill, George Grant, Samuel Wilson, Jesse Brown, William Rigby, Solomon Anderson, Alf. Green, Daniel States.

All these have been in the city of Charleston, and were engaged while there in waiting upon officers. They were all from the city of Philadelphia, and State of Pennsylvania. It will indeed be a joyful meeting when they all get home once more.

Yours, &c.,
J.H. HALL, Co. B.,
Fifty-fourth Mass. Col. Troops.

Frederick Douglass (1818–1895)

At the close of the Civil War, Frederick Douglass was no less restrained in his political activism on behalf of African Americans than he was when he traveled throughout the country calling for the abolition of slavery. To be sure, slavery would no longer be legal in the United States, but he was quite aware that there would still be a struggle for equal rights, economic opportunity, and suffrage. Douglass dove into this struggle with the same fervor he displayed for the abolitionist crusade. He delivered this persuasive demand for the rights and privileges of full citizenship for the freedmen at the 1865 annual meeting of the Massachusetts Anti-Slavery Society.

Why should blacks, according to Douglass, have the right to vote immediately? What does he say about women's suffrage? How effective is his use of irony in this speech?

What the Black Man Wants, April 1865

. . . I have had but one idea for the last three years to present to the American people, and the phraseology in which I clothe it is the old abolition phraseology. I am for the "immediate, unconditional, and universal" enfranchisement of the black man, in every State in the Union. Without this, his liberty is a mockery; without this, you might as well almost retain the old name of slavery for his condition; for in fact, if he is not the slave of the individual master, he is the slave of society, and holds his liberty as a privilege, not as a right. He is at the mercy of the mob, and has no means of protecting himself.

It may be objected, however, that this pressing of the Negro's right to suffrage is premature. Let us have slavery abolished, it may be said, let us have labor organized, and then, in the natural course of events, the right of suffrage will be extended to the Negro. I do not agree with this. The constitution of the human mind is such, that if it once disregards the conviction forced upon it by a revelation of truth, it requires the exercise of a higher power to produce the same conviction afterwards. The American people are now in tears. The Shenandoah has run blood—the best blood of the North. All around Richmond, the blood of New England and of the North has been shed—of your sons, your brothers and your fathers. We all feel, in the existence of this Rebellion, that judgments terrible, wide-spread, far-reaching, overwhelming, are abroad in the land; and we feel, in view of these judgments, just now, a disposition to learn righteousness. This is the hour. Our streets are in mourning, tears are falling at every fireside, and under the chastisement of this Rebellion we have almost come up to the point of conceding this great, this all-important right of suffrage. I fear that if we fail to do it now, if abolitionists fail to press it now, we may not see, for centuries to come, the same disposition that exists at this moment. Hence, I say, now is the time to press this right.

It may be asked, "Why do you want it? Some men have got along very well without it. Women have not this right." Shall we justify one wrong by another? This is the sufficient answer. Shall we at this moment justify the deprivation of the Negro of the right to vote, because some one else is deprived of that privilege? I hold that women, as well as men, have the right to vote, and my heart and voice go with the movement to extend suffrage to woman; but that question rests upon another basis than which

SOURCE: Philip S. Foner, *The Life and Writings of Frederick Douglass* (New York: International Publishers, 1950), vol. 4, 157–165.

our right rests. We may be asked, I say, why we want it. I will tell you why we want it. We want it because it is our right, first of all. No class of men can, without insulting their own nature, be content with any deprivation of their rights. We want it again, as a means for educating our race. Men are so constituted that they derive their conviction of their own possibilities largely by the estimate formed of them by others. If nothing is expected of a people, that people will find it difficult to contradict that expectation. By depriving us of suffrage, you affirm our incapacity to form an intelligent judgment respecting public men and public measures; you declare before the world that we are unfit to exercise the elective franchise, and by this means lead us to undervalue ourselves, to put a low estimate upon ourselves, and to feel that we have no possibilities like other men. Again, I want the elective franchise, for one, as a colored man, because ours is a peculiar government, based upon a peculiar idea, and that idea is universal suffrage. If I were in a monarchial government, or an autocratic or aristocratic government, where the few bore rule and the many were subject, there would be no special stigma resting upon me, because I did not exercise the elective franchise. It would do me no great violence. Mingling with the mass I should partake of the strength of the mass; I should be supported by the mass, and I should have the same incentives to endeavor with the mass of my fellow-men; it would be no particular burden, no particular deprivation; but here where universal suffrage is the rule, where that is the fundamental idea of the Government, to rule us out is to make us an exception, to brand us with the stigma of inferiority, and to invite to our heads the missiles of those about us; therefore, I want the franchise for the black man. . . .

I know that we are inferior to you in some things—virtually inferior. We walk about you like dwarfs among giants. Our heads are scarcely seen above the great sea of humanity. The Germans are superior to us; the Irish are superior to us; the Yankees are superior to us; they can do what we cannot, that is, what we have not hitherto been allowed to do. But while I make this admission, I utterly deny, that we are originally, or naturally, or practically, or in any way, or in any important sense, inferior to anybody on this globe. This charge of inferiority is an old dodge. It has been made available for oppression on many occasions. It is only about six centuries since the blue-eyed and fair-haired Anglo-Saxons were considered inferior by the haughty Normans, who once trampled upon them. If you read the history of the Norman Conquest, you will find that this proud Anglo-Saxon was once looked upon as of coarser clay than his Norman master, and might be found in the highways and byways of Old England laboring with a brass collar on his neck, and the name of his master marked upon it. You were down then! You are up now. I am glad you are up, and I want you to be glad to help us up also.

The story of our inferiority is an old dodge, as I have said; for wherever men oppress their fellows, wherever they enslave them, they will endeavor to find the needed apology for such enslavement and oppression in the character of the people oppressed and enslaved. When we wanted, a few years ago, a slice of Mexico, it was hinted that the Mexicans were an inferior race, that the old Castilian blood had become so weak that it would scarcely run down hill, and that Mexico needed the long, strong and beneficent arm of the Anglo-Saxon care extended over it. We said that it was necessary to its salvation, and a part of the "manifest destiny" of this

Republic, to extend our arm over that dilapidated government. So, too, when Russia wanted to take possession of a part of the Ottoman Empire, the Turks were an "inferior race." So, too, when England wants to set the heel of her power more firmly in the quivering heart of old Ireland, the Celts are an "inferior race." So, too, the Negro, when he is to be robbed of any right which is justly his, is an "inferior man." It is said that we are ignorant; I admit it. But if we know enough to be hung, we know enough to vote. If the Negro knows enough to pay taxes to support the government, he knows enough to vote; taxation and representation should go together. If he knows enough to shoulder a musket and fight for the flag, fight for the government, he knows enough to vote. If he knows as much when he is sober as an Irishman knows when drunk, he knows enough to vote, on good American principles.

But I was saying that you needed a counterpoise in the persons of the slaves to the enmity that would exist at the South after the Rebellion is put down. I hold that the American people are bound, not only in self-defence, to extend this right to the freedmen of the South, but they are bound by their love of country, and by all their regard for the future safety of those Southern States, to do this—to do it as a measure essential to the preservation of peace there. But I will not dwell upon this. I put it to the American sense of honor. The honor of a nation is an important thing. It is said in the Scriptures, "What doth it profit a man if he gain the whole world, and lose his own soul?" It may be said, also, What doth it profit a nation if it gain the whole world, but lose its honor? I hold that the American government has taken upon itself a solemn obligation of honor, to see that this war—let it be long or short, let it cost much or let it cost little—that this war shall not cease until every freedman at the South has the right to vote. It has bound itself to it. What have you asked the black men of the South, the black men of the whole country to do? Why, you have asked them to incure the enmity of their masters, in order to befriend you and to befriend this Government. You have asked us to call down, not only upon ourselves, but upon our children's children, the deadly hate of the entire Southern people. You have called upon us to turn our backs upon our masters, to abandon their cause and espouse yours; to turn against the South and in favor of the North; to shoot down the Confederacy and uphold the flag—the American flag. You have called upon us to expose ourselves to all the subtle machinations of their malignity for all time. And now, what do you propose to do when you come to make peace? To reward your enemies, and trample in the dust your friends? Do you intend to sacrifice the very men who have come to the rescue of your banner in the South, and incurred the lasting displeasure of their masters thereby? Do you intend to sacrifice them and reward your enemies? Do you mean to give your enemies the right to vote, and take it away from your friends? Is that wise policy? Is that honorable? Could American honor withstand such a blow? I do not believe you will do it. I think you will see to it that we have the right to vote. There is something too mean in looking upon the Negro, when you are in trouble, as a citizen, and when you are free from trouble, as an alien. When this nation was in trouble, in its early struggles, it looked upon the Negro as a citizen. In 1776 he was a citizen. At the time of the formation of the Constitution the Negro had the right to vote in eleven States out of the old thirteen. In your trouble you have made us citizens. In 1812 Gen. Jackson addressed us as citizens—"fellow-citizens." He wanted us to fight. We were citizens then! And now, when you come to frame a conscription bill, the Negro is a citizen again. He has been a citizen just three times in the history of this government, and it has always been in time of trouble. In time of trouble we are citizens. Shall we be citizens in war, and aliens in peace? Would that be just?

I ask my friends who are apologizing for not insisting upon this right, where can the black man look, in this country, for the assertion of his right, if he may not look to the Massachusetts Anti-Slavery Society? Where under the whole heavens can he look for sympathy, in asserting this right, if he may not look to this platform? Have you lifted us up to a certain height to see that we are men, and then are any disposed to leave us there, without seeing that we are put in possession of all our rights? We look naturally to this platform for the assertion of all our rights, and for this one especially. I understand the anti-slavery societies of this country to be based on two principles,—first, the freedom of the blacks of this country; and, second, the elevation of them. Let me not be misunderstood here. I am not asking for sympathy at the hands of abolitionists, sympathy at the hands of any. I think the American people are disposed often to be generous rather than just. I look over this country at the present time, and I see Educational Societies, Sanitary Commissions, Freedmen's Associations, and the like,—all very good: but in regard to the colored people there is always more that is benevolent, I perceive, than just, manifested towards us. What I ask for the Negro is not benevolence, not pity, not sympathy, but simply justice. The American people have always been anxious to know what they shall do with us. Gen. Banks was distressed with solicitude as to what he should do with the Negro. Everybody has asked the question, and they learned to ask it early of the abolitionists, "What shall we do with the Negro?" I have had but one answer from the beginning. Do nothing with us! Your doing with us has already played the mischief with us. Do nothing with us! If the apples will not remain on the tree of their own strength, if they are wormeaten at the core, if they are early ripe and disposed to fall, let them fall! I am not for tying or fastening them on the tree in any way, except by nature's plan, and if they will not stay there, let them fall. And if the Negro cannot stand on his own legs, let him fall also. All I ask is, give him a chance to stand on his own legs! Let him alone! If you see him on his way to school, let him alone, don't disturb him! If you see him going to the dinner table at a hotel, let him go! If you see him going to the ballot-box, let him alone, don't disturb him! If you see him going into a work-shop, just let him alone,—your interference is doing him a positive injury. Gen. Banks' "preparation" is of a piece with this attempt to prop up the Negro. Let him fall if he cannot stand alone! If the Negro cannot live by the line of eternal justice, so beautifully pictured to you in the illustration used by Mr. Phillips, the fault will not be yours, it will be his who made the Negro, and established that line for his government. Let him live or die by that. If you will only untie his hands, and give him a chance, I think he will live. He will work as readily for himself as the white man. A great many delusions have been swept away by this war. One was, that the Negro would not work; he has proved his ability to work. Another was, that the Negro would not fight; that he possessed only the most sheepish attributes of humanity; was a perfect lamb, or an "Uncle Tom;" disposed to take off his coat whenever required, fold his hands, and be whipped by anybody who wanted to whip him. But the war has proved that there is a great deal of human nature in the Negro, and that "he will fight," as Mr. Quincy, our President, said, in earlier days than these, "when there is reasonable probability of his whipping anybody."

Zion Presbyterian Church

The African American Zion Presbyterian Church of Charleston, South Carolina, submitted a petition to Congress several months after the end of the Civil War, in which the parishioners demanded that the black people of South Carolina be accorded all the rights and privileges of U.S. citizens.

Upon what documents do the church members base their argument? What does this petition imply about circumstances for African Americans in the South at a time when the Confederacy had been utterly destroyed? Why are they so concerned with the Constitutional right to bear arms?

Petition to the United States Congress, November 24, 1865

Gentlemen:

We, the colored people of the State of South Carolina, in Convention assembled, respectfully present for your attention some prominent facts in relation to our present condition, and make a modest yet earnest appeal to your considerate judgment. . . .

Conscious of the difficulties that surround our position we would ask for no rights or privileges but such as rest upon the strong basis of justice and expediency, in view of the best interests of our entire country.

We ask first, that the strong arm of law and order be placed alike over the entire people of this State; that life and property be secured, and the laborer free to sell his labor as the merchant his goods.

We ask that a fair and impartial instruction be given to the pledges of the government to us concerning the land question.

We ask that the three great agents of civilized society—the school, the pulpit, the press—be as secure in South Carolina as in Massachusetts or Vermont.

Source: James S. Allen, *Reconstruction: The Battle for Democracy, 1865–1876* (New York: International Publishers, 1937), 228–229.

We ask that equal suffrage be conferred upon us, in common with the white men of this State. This we ask, because "all free governments derive their just powers from the consent of the governed"; and we are largely in the majority in this State, bearing for a long period the burden of onerous taxation, without a just representation. We ask for equal suffrage as a protection for the hostility evoked by our known faithfulness to our country and flag under all circumstances.

We ask that colored men shall not in every instance be tried by white men; and that neither by custom nor enactment shall we be excluded from the jury box.

We ask that, inasmuch as the Constitution of the United States explicitly declares that the right to keep and bear arms shall not be infringed and the Constitution is the Supreme law of the land—that the late efforts of the Legislature of this State to pass an act to deprive us of arms be forbidden, as a plain violation of the Constitution, and unjust to many of us in the highest degree, who have been soldiers, and purchased our muskets from the United States Government when mustered out of service.

We protest against any code of black laws the Legislature of this State may enact, and pray to be governed by the same laws that control other men. The right to assemble in peaceful convention, to discuss the political questions of the day; the right to enter upon all the avenues of agriculture, commerce, trade; to amass wealth by thrift and industry; the right to develop our whole being by all the appliances that belong to civilized society, cannot be questioned by any class of intelligent legislators.

We solemnly affirm and desire to live orderly and peacefully with all the people of this State; and commending this memorial to your considerate judgment.

Thus we ever pray.

Charleston, S.C. November 24, 1865
Zion Presbyterian Church

American Equal Rights Association

During congressional debates on the proposed Fifteenth Amendment, many people who had been involved in the abolitionist and feminist crusades argued fervently that the suffrage amendment should include women. The American Equal Rights Association (founded in 1866) issued the following resolution arguing its position on the topic. Although such influential people as Frederick Douglass, Susan B. Anthony, and Elizabeth Cady Stanton signed the resolution, the amendment approved by Congress in 1869 granted the suffrage to only African American men: "The right of citizens of the United States to vote shall not be denied or abridged by the United States or any State on account of race, color, or previous condition of servitude." In a bitter aftermath, the ratification process wound up splitting the feminist movement into those who supported the amendment with the intention of continuing the struggle for women's suffrage and those more radical women (and men) who fought energetically against ratification until women were included. The Fifteenth Amendment was ratified in 1870. It would be another 50 years before the Nineteenth Amendment opened the suffrage to women.

What is the basis for the claim that "republican institutions are based on individual rights"? Why do the writers of the resolution bring up the issue of taxes? Why are men reluctant to grant women suffrage?

National Convention Resolutions, New York, May 1867

RESOLVED, That as republican institutions are based on individual rights, and not on the rights of races or sexes, the first question for the American people to settle in the reconstruction of the government, is the RIGHTS OF INDIVIDUALS.

RESOLVED, That the present claim for "manhood suffrage," marked with the words "equal," "impartial," "universal," is a cruel abandonment of the slave women of the South, a fraud on the tax paying women of the North, and an insult to the civilization of the nineteenth century.

RESOLVED, That the [Republican Party] proposal to reconstruct our government on the basis of manhood suffrage . . . [which] has received the recent sanction of the American Anti-Slavery Society, is but a continuation of the old system of class and caste legislation, always cruel and proscriptive in itself, and ending in all ages in national degradation and revolution.

MEMORIAL OF THE AMERICAN EQUAL RIGHTS ASSOCIATION TO CONGRESS

The undersigned . . . respectfully but earnestly protest against any change in the Constitution of the United States, or legislation by Congress, which shall longer violate the principle of Republican Government, by proscriptive distinctions in rights of suffrage or citizenship, on account of color or sex. Your Memorialists would respectfully represent, that neither the colored man's loyalty, bravery on the battle field and general good conduct, nor woman's heroic devotion to liberty and her country, in peace and war, have yet availed to admit them to equal citizenship. . . .

We believe that humanity is one in all those intellectual, moral and spiritual attributes, out of which grow human responsibilities. The Scripture declaration is, "so God created man in his own image: male and female created he them." And all divine legislation throughout the realm of nature recognizes the perfect equality of

SOURCE: Retrieved on 3/11/2003 from the 19th-Century American Women Writers Web Etext Library at http://womenshistory.about.com/gi/dynamic/offsite.htm?site=http://www.unl.edu/legacy/19cwww/books/elibe/documents/suffrage/PURITAN6.HTM

the two conditions. For male and female are but different conditions. neither color nor sex is ever discharged from obedience to law, natural or moral; written or unwritten. The commands, thou shalt not steal, nor kill, nor commit adultery, know nothing of sex in their demands; nothing in their penalty. And hence we believe that all human legislation which is at variance with the divine code, is essentially unrighteous and unjust. Woman and the colored man are taxed. . . . Woman has been fined, whipped, branded with red-hot irons, imprisoned and hung; but when was woman ever tried by a jury of her peers? . . .

Woman and the colored man are loyal, patriotic, property-holding, tax-paying, liberty-loving citizens; and we can not believe that sex or complexion should be any ground for civil or political degradation. In our government, one-half the citizens are disfranchised by their sex, and about one-eighth by the color of their skin; and thus a large majority have no voice in enacting or executing the laws they are taxed to support and compelled to obey. . . . Against such outrages on the very name of republican freedoms, your memorialists do and must ever protest. And is not our protest pre-eminently as just against the tyranny of "taxation without representation," as was that thundered from Bunker Hill . . . ?

And your Memorialists especially remember . . . that our country is still reeling [from] . . . a terrible civil war. . . . [I]n restoring the foundations of our nationality, [we] . . . pray that all discriminations on account of sex or race may be removed; and that our Government may be republican in fact as well as form; A GOVERN-MENT BY THE PEOPLE, AND THE WHOLE PEOPLE; FOR THE PEOPLE, AND THE WHOLE PEOPLE. . . .

[Signed by Theodore Tilton, Frederick Douglass, Elizabeth Cady Stanton, Lucretia Mott, and Susan B. Anthony].

Susan B. Anthony (1820–1906)

Susan B. Anthony fought for temperance, abolition, labor reform, educational reform, and most notably women's rights. A close friend of Elizabeth Cady Stanton, she became by mid-century a driving force in nineteenth-century feminism and perhaps the most important person in the struggle for women's suffrage. At the end of the Civil War, she cofounded with Stanton the American Equal Rights Association and campaigned vigorously for women to be included in the amendment that would give black men the vote. In 1870, after the Fifteenth Amendment was ratified, indignant that women had been excluded, Anthony stepped up her campaign. In 1872, she was arrested in Rochester, New York, when she voted in the presidential election. She was tried and fined $100 in June 1873. When she refused to pay the fine, the judge, not wanting to create more publicity for her cause, shrewdly chose not to sentence her to a jail term. It was Susan B. Anthony who wrote the women's suffrage constitutional amendment that was introduced in Congress, where it was repeatedly debated, tabled, defeated, reintroduced, rejected, and eventually, more than a decade after her death, approved and ratified as the Nineteenth Amendment to the Constitution.

There is no accurate account of her comments at the trial. The first document here is an excerpt from one of three separate accounts reported after the event. The second document is a speech she gave on more than 20 occasions between her arrest and her trial. Is Susan B. Anthony's argument that women have the right to vote based on moral, political, or legal grounds? How effective is her tactic of citing passages of the federal and state constitutions? Does the evidence she uses support her case? What is the basis for her contention that there is no difference between being a woman in the United States and being a slave?

From an Account of the Trial of Susan B. Anthony, July 3, 1873

As a matter of outward form the defendant was asked if she had anything to say why the sentence of the court should not be pronounced upon her.

"Yes, your honor," replied Miss Anthony, "I have many things to say. My every right, constitutional, civil, political and judicial has been tramped upon. I have not only had no jury of my peers, but I have had no jury at all."

Court— "Sit down Miss Anthony. I cannot allow you to argue the question."

Miss Anthony— "I shall not sit down. I will not lose my only chance to speak."

Court— "You have been tried, Miss Anthony, by the forms of law, and my decision has been rendered by law."

Miss Anthony— "Yes, but laws made by men, under a government of men, interpreted by men and for the benefit of men. The only chance women have for justice in this country is to violate the law, as I have done, and as I shall *continue* to do," and she struck her hand heavily on the table in emphasis of what she said. "Does your honor suppose that we obeyed the infamous fugitive slave law which forbade to give a cup of cold water to a slave fleeing from his master? I tell you we did not obey it; we fed him and clothed him, and sent him on his way to Canada. *So shall we trample all unjust laws* under foot. I do not ask the clemency of the court. I came into it to get justice, having failed in this, I demand the full rigors of the law."

Court— "The sentence of the court is $100 fine and the costs of the prosecution."

Miss Anthony— "I have no money to pay with, but am $10,000 in debt."

Court— "You are not ordered to stand committed till it is paid."

Source: Matilda Joslyn Gage to Editor, 20 June 1873, Kansas *Leavenworth Times*, 3 July 1873, SBA scrapbook 6, Rare Books, DLC.

Is It a Crime for a U.S. Citizen to Vote?, 1873

Friends and Fellow-citizens: I stand before you to-night, under indictment for the alleged crime of having voted at the last Presidential election, without having a lawful right to vote. It shall be my work this evening to prove to you that in thus voting, I not only committed no crime, but, instead, simply exercised my citizen's right, guaranteed to me and all United States citizens by the National Constitution, beyond the power of any State to deny.

Our democratic-republican government is based on the idea of the natural right of every individual member thereof to a voice and a vote in making and executing the laws. We assert the province of government to be to secure the people in the enjoyment of their unalienable rights. We throw to the winds the old dogma that governments can give rights. Before governments were organized, no one denies that each individual possessed the right to protect his own life, liberty and property. And when 100 or 1,000,000 people enter into a free government, they do not barter away their natural rights; they simply pledge themselves to protect each other in the enjoyment of them, through prescribed judicial and legislative tribunals. They agree to abandon the methods of brute force in the adjustment of their differences, and adopt those of civilization.

Nor can you find a word in any of the grand documents left us by the fathers that assumes for government the power to create or to confer rights. The Declaration of Independence, the United States Constitution, the constitutions of the several states and the organic laws of the territories, all alike propose to protect the people in the exercise of their God-given rights. Not one of them pretends to bestow rights.

"All men are created equal, and endowed by their Creator with certain unalienable rights. Among these are life, liberty and the pursuit of happiness. That to secure these, governments are instituted among men, deriving their just powers from the consent of the governed."

Here is no shadow of government authority over rights, nor exclusion of any from their full and equal enjoyment. Here is pronounced the right of all men, and "consequently," as the Quaker preacher said, "of all women," to a voice in the government. And here, in this very first paragraph of the declaration, is the assertion of the natural right of all to the ballot; for, how can "the consent of the governed" be given, if the right to vote be denied? Again: "That whenever any form of government becomes destructive of these ends, it is the right of the people to alter or abolish it, and to institute a new government, laying its foundations on such principles, and organizing its powers in such forms as to them shall seem most likely to effect their safety and happiness."

Source: Retrieved on 10/19/2003 from www.pbs.org/stantonanthony/resources/index.html?body=crime_to_vote.html. For the full text of another copy of this address, see Ann D. Gordon, ed., *The Selected Papers of Elizabeth Cady Stanton and Susan B. Anthony* (New Brunswick, NJ: Rutgers University Press, 2000), vol. 2, 554–583.

Surely, the right of the whole people to vote is here clearly implied. For however destructive in their happiness this government might become, a disfranchised class could neither alter nor abolish it, nor institute a new one, except by the old brute force method of insurrection and rebellion. One-half of the people of this nation to-day are utterly powerless to blot from the statute books an unjust law, or to write there a new and a just one. The women, dissatisfied as they are with this form of government, that enforces taxation without representation, that compels them to obey laws to which they have never given their consent, that imprisons and hangs them without a trial by a jury of their peers, that robs them, in marriage, of the custody of their own persons, wages and children, are this half of the people left wholly at the mercy of the other half, in direct violation of the spirit and letter of the declarations of the framers of this government, every one of which was based on the immutable principle of equal rights to all. By those declarations, kings, priests, popes, aristocrats, were all alike dethroned, and placed on a common level politically, with the lowliest born subject or serf. By them, too, men, as such, were deprived of their divine right to rule, and placed on a political level with women. By the practice of those declarations all class and caste distinction will be abolished; and slave, serf, plebeian, wife, woman, all alike, bound from their subject position to the proud platform of equality.

The preamble of the federal constitution says: "We, the people of the United States, in order to form a more perfect union, establish justice, insure domestic tranquility, provide for the common defense, promote the general welfare and secure the blessings of liberty to ourselves and our posterity, do ordain and established this constitution for the United States of America."

It was we, the people, not we, the white male citizens, nor yet we, the male citizens; but we, the whole people, who formed this Union. And we formed it, not to give the blessings of liberty, but to secure them; not to the half of ourselves and the half of our posterity, but to the whole people—women as well as men. And it is downright mockery to talk to women of their enjoyment of the blessings of liberty while they are denied the use of the only means of securing them provided by this democratic-republican government—the ballot.

The early journals of Congress show that when the committee reported to that body the original articles of confederation, the very first article which became the subject of discussion was that respecting equality of suffrage. Article 4th said: "The better to secure and perpetuate mutual friendship and intercourse between the people of the different States of this Union, the free inhabitants of each of the States, (paupers, vagabonds and fugitives from justice excepted,) shall be entitled to all the privileges and immunities of the free citizens of the several States."

Thus, at the very beginning, did the fathers see the necessity of the universal application of the great principle of equal rights to all—in order to produce the desired result—a harmonious union and a homogeneous people. . . .

The preamble of the Constitution of the State of New York declares. . . : "We, the people of the State of New York, grateful to Almighty God for our freedom, in order to secure its blessings, do establish this Constitution."

Here is not the slightest intimation either of receiving freedom from the United States Constitution, or of the State conferring the blessings of liberty upon the people; and the same is true of every one of the thirty-six State Constitutions. Each and all, alike declare rights God-given, and that to secure the people in the enjoyment of their inalienable rights, is their one and only object in ordaining and establishing government. And all of the State Constitutions are equally emphatic in their recognition of the ballot as the means of securing the people in the enjoyment of these rights.

Article 1 of the New York State Constitution says: "No member of this State shall be disfranchised or deprived of the rights or privileges secured to any citizen thereof, unless by the law of the land, or the judgement of his peers."

And so carefully guarded is the citizen's right to vote, that the Constitution makes special mention of all who may be excluded. It says: "Laws may be passed excluding from the right of suffrage all persons who have been or may be convicted of bribery, larceny or any infamous crime."

In naming the various employments that shall not affect the residence of voters the 3d section of article 2d says "that being kept at any alms house, or other asylum, at public expense, nor being confined at any public prison, shall deprive a person of his residence," and hence his vote. Thus is the right of voting most sacredly hedged about. The only seeming permission in the New York State Constitution for the disfranchisement of women is in section 1st of article 2d, which says "Every male citizen of the age of twenty-one years, shall be entitled to vote."

But I submit that in view of the explicit assertions of the equal right of the whole people, both in the preamble and previous article of the constitution, this omission of the adjective "female" in the second, should not be construed into a denial; but, instead, counted as of no effect. Mark the direct prohibition: "No member of this State shall be disfranchised, unless by the law of the land, or the judgment of his peers." "The law of the land," is the United States Constitution: and there is no provision in that document that can be fairly construed into a permission to the States to deprive any class of their citizens of their right to vote. Hence New York can get no power from that source to disfranchise one entire half of her members. Nor has "the judgment of their peers" been pronounced against women exercising their right to vote; no disfranchised person is allowed to be judge or juror and none but disfranchised persons can be women's peers; nor has the legislature passed laws excluding them on account of idiocy of lunacy; nor yet the courts convicted them of bribery, larceny, or any infamous crime. Clearly, then, there is no constitutional ground for the exclusion of women from the ballot-box in the State of New York. No barriers whatever stand to-day between women and the exercise of their right to vote save those of precedent and prejudice. . . .

The only question left to be settled, now, is: Are women persons? And I hardly believe any of our opponents will have the hardihood to say they are not. Being persons, then, women are citizens, and no state has a right to make any new law, or to enforce any old law, that shall abridge their privileges or immunities. Hence, every discrimination against women in the constitutions and laws of the several states, is to-day null and void, precisely as is every one against negroes. Is the right to vote one of the privileges or immunities of citizens? I think the disfranchised ex-rebels, and the ex-state prisoners will agree with me, that it is not only one of them, but the one without which all the others are nothing. Seek first the kingdom of the ballot, and all things else shall be given thee, is the political injunction.

Webster, Worcester and Bouvier all define citizen to be a person, in the United States, entitled to vote and hold office.

Prior to the adoption of the thirteenth amendment, by which slavery was forever abolished, and black men transformed from property to persons, the judicial opinions of the country had always been in harmony with these definitions. To be a person was to be a citizen, and to be a citizen was to be a voter. . . .

If we once establish the false principle, that United States citizenship does not carry with it the right to vote in every state in this Union, there is no end to the petty freaks and cunning devices, that will be resorted to, to exclude one and another class of citizens from the right of suffrage. It will not always be men combining to disfranchise all women; native born men combining to abridge the rights of all naturalized citizens, as in Rhode Island. It will not always be the rich and educated who may combine to cut off the poor and ignorant; but we may live to see the poor, hardworking, uncultivated day laborers, foreign and native born, learning the power of the ballot and their vast majority of numbers, combine and amend state constitutions so as to disfranchise the Vanderbilts and A. T. Stewarts, the Conklings and Fentons. It is poor rule that won't work more ways than one. Establish this precedent, admit the right to deny suffrage to the states, and there is no power to foresee the confusion, discord and disruption that may await us. There is, and can be, but one safe principle of government—equal rights to all. And any and every discrimination against any class, whether on account of color, race, nativity, sex, property, culture, can but embitter and disaffect that class, and thereby endanger the safety of the whole people.

Clearly, then, the national government must not only define the rights of citizens, but it must stretch out its powerful hand and protect them in every state in this Union.

But if you will insist that the fifteenth amendment's emphatic interdiction against robbing United States citizens of their right to vote, "on account of race, color, or previous condition of servitude," is a recognition of the right, either of the United States, or any state, to rob citizens of that right, for any or all other reason, I will prove to you that the class of citizens for which I now plead, and to which I belong, may be, by all the principles of our government, and many of the laws of the states, included under the term "previous condition of servitude."

First.—The married women and their legal status. What is servitude? "The condition of a slave." What is a slave? "A person who is robbed of the proceeds of his labor; a person who is subject to the will of another."

By the law of Georgia, South Carolina, and all the states of the South, the negro had no right to the custody and control of his person. He belonged to his master. If he was disobedient, the master had the right to use correction. If the negro didn't like the correction, and attempted to run away, the master had a right to use coercion to bring him back.

By the law of every state in this Union to-day, North as well as South, the married woman has no right to the custody and control of her person. The wife belongs to her husband; and if she refuses obedience to his will, he may use moderate correction, and if she doesn't like his moderate correction, and attempts to leave his "bed and board," the husband may use moderate coercion to bring her back. The little word "moderate," you see, is the saving clause for the wife, and would doubtless be overstepped should offended husband administer his correction with the "cat-o'-nine-tails," or accomplish his coercion with blood-hounds.

Again, the slave had no right to the earnings of his hands, they belonged to his master; no right to the custody of his children, they belonged to his master; no right to sue or be sued, or testify in the courts. If he committed a crime, it was the master who must sue or be sued.

In many of the states there has been special legislation, giving to married women the right to property inherited, or received by bequest, or earned by the pursuit of any avocation outside of the home; also, giving her the right to sue and be sued in matters pertaining to such separate property; but not a single state of this Union has ever secured the wife in the enjoyment of her right to the joint ownership of the joint earnings of the marriage copartnership. And since, in the nature of things, the vast majority of married women never earn a dollar, by work outside of their families, nor inherit a dollar from their fathers, it follows that from the day of their marriage to the day of the death of their husbands, not one of them ever has a dollar, except it shall please her husband to let her have it.

In some of the states, also, there have been laws passed giving to the mother a joint right with the father in the guardianship of the children. But twenty years ago, when our woman's rights movement commenced, by the laws of the State of New York, and all the states, the father had the sole custody and control of the children. No matter if he were a brutal, drunken libertine, he had the legal right, without the mother's consent, to apprentice her sons to rumsellers, or her daughters to brothel keepers. He could even will away an unborn child, to some other person than the mother. And in many of the states the law still prevails, and the mothers are still utterly powerless under the common law. . . .

There is an old saying that "a rose by any other name would smell as sweet," and I submit it the deprivation by law of the ownership of one's own person, wages, property, children, the denial of the right as an individual, to sue and be sued, and to testify in the courts, is not a condition of servitude most bitter and absolute, though under the sacred name of marriage?

Does any lawyer doubt my statement of the legal status of married women? I will remind him of the fact that the old common law of England prevails in every State in this Union, except where the Legislature has enacted special laws annulling it. And I am ashamed that not one State has yet blotted from its statute books the old common law of marriage, by which Blackstone, summed up in the fewest words possible, is made to say, "husband and wife are one, and that one is the husband."

Thus may all married women, wives and widows, by the laws of the several States, be technically included in the fifteenth amendment's specification of "condition of servitude," present or previous. And not only married women, but I will also prove to you that by all the great fundamental principles of our free government, the entire womanhood of the nation is in a "condition of servitude" as surely as were our revolutionary fathers, when they rebelled against old King George. Women are taxed without representation, governed without their consent, tried, convicted and punished without a jury of their peers. And is all this tyranny any less humiliating and degrading to women under our democratic-republican government to-day than it was to men under their aristocratic, monarchical government one hundred years ago? There is not an utterance of old John Adams, John Hancock or Patrick Henry, but finds a living response in the soul of every intelligent, patriotic woman of the nation. Bring to me a common-sense woman property holder, and I will show you one whose soul is fired with all the indignation of 1776 every time the tax-gatherer presents himself at her door. You will not find one such but feels her condition of servitude as galling as did James Otis when he said: "The very act of taxing exercised over those who are not represented appears to me to be depriving them of one of their most essential rights, and if continued, seems to be in effect an entire disfranchisement of every civil right. For, what one civil right is worth a rush after a man's property is subject to be taken from him at pleasure without his consent? If a man is not his own assessor in person, or by deputy, his liberty is gone, or he is wholly at the mercy of others." . . .

That liberty or freedom consists in having an actual share in the appointment of those who are to frame the laws, and who are to be the guardians of every man's life, property and peace. For the all of one man is as dear to him as the all of another; and the poor man has an equal right, but more need to have representatives in the Legislature than the rich one. That they who have no voice or vote in the electing of representatives, do not enjoy liberty, but are absolutely enslaved to those who have votes and their representatives; for to be enslaved is to have governors whom other men have set over us, and to be subject to laws made by the representatives of others, without having had representatives of our own to give consent in our behalf."

Suppose I read it with the feminine gender: "That women who have no voice nor vote in the electing of representatives, do not enjoy liberty, but are absolutely enslaved to men who have votes and their representatives; for to be enslaved is to have governors whom men have set over us, and to be subject to the laws made by the representatives of men, without having representatives of our own to give consent in our behalf."

And yet one more authority; that of Thomas Paine, than whom not one of the Revolutionary patriots more ably vindicated the principles upon which our government is founded: "The right of voting for representatives is the primary right by which other rights are protected. To take away this right is to reduce man to a state of slavery; for slavery consists in being subject to the will of another; and he that has not a vote in the election of representatives is in this case. The proposal, therefore, to disfranchise any class of men is as criminal as the proposal to take away property."

Is anything further needed to prove woman's condition of servitude sufficiently orthodox to entitle her to the guaranties of the fifteenth amendment?

Is there a man who will not agree with me, that to talk of freedom without the ballot, is mockery—is slavery—to the women of this Republic, precisely as New England's orator Wendell Phillips, at the close of the late war, declared it to be to the newly emancipated black men? . . .

We no longer petition Legislature or Congress to give us the right to vote. We appeal to the women everywhere to exercise their too long neglected "citizen's right to vote." We appeal to the inspectors of election everywhere to receive the votes of all United States citizens as it is their duty to do. We appeal to United States commissioners and marshals to arrest the inspectors who reject the names and votes of United States citizens, as it is their duty to do, and leave those alone who, like our eighth ward inspectors, perform their duties faithfully and well.

We ask the juries to fail to return verdicts of "guilty" against honest, law-abiding, tax-paying United States citizens for offering their votes at our elections. Or against intelligent, worthy young men, inspectors of elections, for receiving and counting such citizens votes.

We ask the judges to render true and unprejudiced opinions of the law, and wherever there is room for a doubt to give its benefit on the side of liberty and equal rights to women, remembering that "the true rule of interpretation under our national constitution, especially since its amendments, is that anything for human rights is constitutional, everything against human right unconstitutional."

And it is on this line that we propose to fight our battle for the ballot—all peaceably, but nevertheless persistently through to complete triumph, when all United States citizens shall be recognized as equals before the law.

Robert B. Elliott (1842–1884)

Born and reared in England, Robert B. Elliott moved to South Carolina in the aftermath of the Civil War, where in 1869 he became the first black commander of the state's national guard. From 1871 to 1874 he served in the U.S. House of Representatives. He became an active participant in the congressional debates on the civil rights bill that was eventually passed in 1875.

What would happen, according to Elliott, if the government respected states' rights above individual rights? How did blacks prove their patriotism and therefore their rights to citizenship and suffrage? Why is the civil rights bill necessary?

Speech in Congress on the Civil Rights Bill, January 6, 1874

. . . While I am sincerely grateful for this high mark of courtesy that has been accorded to me by this House, it is a matter of regret to me that it is necessary at this day that I should rise in the presence of an American Congress to advocate a bill which simply asserts equal rights and equal public privileges for all classes of American citizens. I

SOURCE: Retrieved on 3/11/2003 from www.law.nyu.edu/davisp/neglectedvoices/Elliot Jan061874.html

regret, sir, that the dark hue of my skin may lend a color to the imputation that I am controlled by motives personal to myself in my advocacy of this great measure of national justice. Sir, the motive that impels me is restricted by no such narrow boundary, but is as broad as your Constitution. I advocate it, sir, because it is right. The bill, however, not only appeals to your justice, but it demands a response from your gratitude.

In the events that led to the achievement of American Independence the negro was not an inactive or unconcerned spectator. He bore his part bravely upon many battle-fields, although uncheered by that certain hope of political elevation which victory would secure to the white man. The tall granite shaft, which a grateful State has reared above its sons who fell in defending Fort Griswold against the attack of Benedict Arnold, bears the name of Jordan, Freeman, and other brave men of the African race who there cemented with their blood the corner-stone of the Republic. In the State which I have the honor in part to represent the rifle of the black man rang out against the troops of the British crown in the darkest days of the American revolution. Said General Greene, who has been justly termed the Washington of the North, in a letter written by him to Alexander Hamilton, on the 10th day of January, 1781, from the vicinity of Camden, South Carolina: There is no such thing as national character or national sentiment. The inhabitants are numerous, but they would be rather formidable abroad than at home. There is a great spirit of enterprise among the black people, and those that come out as volunteers are not a little formidable to the enemy.

At the battle of New Orleans, under the immortal Jackson, a colored regiment held the extreme right of the American line unflinchingly, and drove back the British column that pressed upon them, at the point of the bayonet. So marked was their valor on that occasion that it evoked from their great commander the warmest encomiums, as will be seen from his dispatch announcing the brilliant victory.

As the gentleman from Kentucky, [Mr. Beck,] who seems to be the leading exponent on this floor of the party that is arrayed against the principle of this bill; has been pleased, in season and out of season, to cast odium upon the negro and to vaunt the chivalry of his state, I may be pardoned for calling attention to another portion of the same dispatch. Referring to the various regiments under his command, and their conduct on that field which terminated the second war of American Independence, General Jackson says: At the very moment when the entire discomfiture of the enemy was looked for with a confidence amounting to certainty, the Kentucky reinforcements, in whom so much reliance had been placed, ingloriously fled.

In quoting this indisputable piece of history, I do so only by way of admonition and not to question the well-attested gallantry of the true Kentuckian, and to suggest to the gentleman that it would be well that he should not flaunt his heraldry so proudly while he bears this scar—sinister on the military escutcheon of his State—a State which answered the call of the Republic in 1861, when treason thundered at the very gates of the capital by coldly declaring her neutrality in the impending struggle. The negro, true to that patriotism and love of country that have ever characterized and marked his history on this continent, came to the aid of the Government in its efforts to maintain the Constitution. To that Government he now appeals; that Constitution he now invokes for protection against outrage and unjust prejudices founded upon caste.

But, sir, we are told by the distinguished gentleman from Georgia [Mr. Stephens] that Congress has no power under the Constitution to pass such a law, and that the passage of such an act is in direct contravention of the rights of the States. I cannot assent to any such proposition. The constitution of a free government ought always to be construed in favor of human rights. Indeed, the thirteenth, fourteenth, and fifteenth amendments, in positive words, invest Congress with the power to protect the citizen in his civil and political rights. Now, sir, what are civil rights: Rights natural, modified by civil society. . . .

Is it the interest of the Government to sacrifice individual rights to the preservation of the rights of an artificial being called States? There can be no truer principle than this, that every individual of the community at large has an equal right to the protection of Government. Can this be a free Government if partial distinctions are tolerated or maintained? . . .

The process of restoring to their proper relations with the Federal Government and with the other States those which had sided with the rebellion, undertaken under the proclamation of President Johnson in 1865, and before the assembling of Congress, developed the fact that, notwithstanding the formal recognition by those states of the abolition of slavery, the condition of the slave race would, without further protection of the Federal Government, be almost as bad as it was before. Among the first acts of legislation adopted by several of the states in the legislative bodies which claimed to be in their normal relations with the Federal government, were laws which imposed upon the colored race onerous disabilities and burdens, and curtailed their rights in the pursuit of life, liberty, and property to such an extent that their freedom was of little value, while they had lost the protection which they had received from their former owners from motives both of interest and humanity.

They were in some States forbidden to appear in the towns in any other character than menial servants. They were required to reside on and cultivate the soil, without the right to purchase or own it. They were excluded from any occupations of gain, and were not permitted to give testimony in the courts in any case where a white man was a party. It was said that their lives were at the mercy of bad men, either because the laws for their protection were insufficient or were not enforced.

These circumstances, whatever of falsehood or misconception may have been mingled with their presentation forced upon the statesmen who had conducted the Federal government in safety through the crisis of the rebellion, and who supposed that by the thirteenth article of amendment they had secured the result of their labors, the conviction that something more was necessary in the way of constitutional protection to the unfortunate race who had suffered so much. They accordingly passed through Congress the proposition for the fourteenth amendment, and they declined to treat as restored to their full participation in the Government of the Union the States which had been in insurrection until they ratified that article by a formal vote of their legislative bodies.

Before we proceed to examine more critically the provisions of this amendment, on which the plaintiffs in error rely, let us complete and dismiss the history of the recent amendments, as that history relates to the general purpose which pervades them all. A few years' experience satisfied the thoughtful men who had been the authors of the other two amendments that, notwithstanding the restraints of those articles on the States and the laws passed under the additional powers granted to Congress, these were inadequate for the protection of life, liberty, and property, without which freedom to the slave was no boon. They were in all those States denied the right of suffrage. The laws were administered by the white man alone. It was urged that a race of men distinctively marked as was the negro, living in the midst of another and dominant race, could never be fully secured in their person and their property without the right of suffrage.

Hence the fifteenth amendment, which declares that "the right of a citizen of the United States to vote shall not be denied or abridged by any state on account of race, color, or previous condition of servitude." The negro having, by the fourteenth amendment, been declared to be a citizen of the United states, is thus made a voter in every State of the Union.

We repeat, then, in the light of this recapitulation of events almost too recent to be called history, but which are familiar to us all, and on the most casual examination of the language of these amendments, no one can fail to be impressed with the one pervading purpose found in them all, lying at the foundation of each, and without which none of them would have been even suggested: we mean the freedom of the slave race, the security and firm establishment of that freedom and the protection of the newly-made freeman and citizen from the oppressions of those who had formerly exercised unlimited dominion over him. It is true that only the fifteenth amendment in terms mentions the negro by speaking of his color and his slavery. But it is just as true that each of the other articles was addressed to the grievances of that race, and designed to remedy them, as the fifteenth.

These amendments, one and all, are thus declared to have as their all-pervading design and end the security to the recently enslaved race, not only their nominal freedom, but their complete protection from those who had formerly exercised unlimited dominion over them. It is in this broad light that all these amendments must be read, the purpose to secure the perfect equality before the law of all citizens of the United states. What you give to one class you must give to all; what you deny to one class you shall deny to all, unless in the exercise of the common and universal police power of the state you find it needful to confer exclusive privileges on certain citizens, to be held and exercised still for the common good of all. . . .

Sir, it is scarcely twelve years since that gentleman [Alexander H. Stephens] shocked the civilized world by announcing the birth of a government which rested on human slavery as its corner-stone. The progress of events has swept away that *pseudo*-government which rested on greed, pride, and tyranny; and the race whom he then ruthlessly spurned and trampled on are here to meet him in debate, and to demand that the rights which are enjoyed by their former oppressors—who vainly sought to overthrow a Government which they could not prostitute to the base uses of slavery—shall be accorded to those who even in the darkness of slavery kept their allegiance true to freedom and the Union. Sir, the gentleman from Georgia has learned much since 1861; but he is still a laggard. Let him put away entirely the false and fatal theories which have so greatly marred an otherwise enviable record. Let him accept, in its fullness and beneficence, the great doctrine that American citizenship carries with it every civil and political right which manhood can confer. Let him lend his influence, with all his masterly ability, to complete the proud structure of legislation which makes his nation worthy of the great declaration which heralded its birth, and he will have done that which will most nearly redeem his reputation in the eyes of the world, and best vindicate the wisdom of that policy which has permitted him to regain his seat upon this floor.

To the diatribe of the gentleman from Virginia, [Mr. Harris,] who spoke on yesterday, and who so far transcended the limits of decency and propriety as to announce upon this floor that his remarks were addressed to white men alone, I shall have no word of reply. Let him feel that a negro was not only too magnanimous to smite him in his weakness, but was even charitable enough to grant him the mercy of his silence. [Laughter and applause on the floor and in the galleries.] I shall, sir, leave to others less charitable the unenviable and fatiguing task of sifting out of that mass of chaff the few grains of sense that may, perchance, deserve notice. Assuring the gentleman that the negro in this country aims at a higher degree of intellect than that exhibited by him in this debate, I cheerfully commend him to the commiseration of all intelligent men the world over—black men as well as white men.

Sir, equality before the law is now the broad, universal, glorious rule and mandate of the Republic. No State can violate that. Kentucky and Georgia may crowd their statute-books with retrograde and barbarous legislation; they may rejoice in the odious eminence of their consistent hostility to all the great steps of human progress which have marked our national history since slavery tore down the stars and stripes on Fort Sumter; but, if Congress shall do its duty, if Congress shall enforce the great guarantees which the Supreme Court has declared to be the one pervading purpose of all the recent amendments, then their unwise and unenlightened conduct will fall with the same weight upon the gentlemen from those States who now lend their influence to defeat this bill, as upon the poorest slave who once had no rights which the honorable gentlemen were bound to respect.

But, sir, not only does the decision in the Slaughter-house[1] cases contain nothing which suggests a doubt of the power of Congress to pass the pending bill, but it contains an express recognition and affirmance of such power. I quote now from page 81 of the volume:

> "Nor shall any State deny to any person within its jurisdiction the equal protection of the laws."
>
> In the light of the history of these amendments, and the pervading purpose of them, which we have already discussed, it is not difficult to give a meaning to this clause. The existence of laws in the States where the newly emancipated negroes resided, which discriminated with gross injustice and hardship against them as a class, was the evil to be remedied by this clause, and by it such laws are forbidden.
>
> If, however, the States did not conform their laws to its requirements, then, by the fifth section of the article of amendment, Congress was authorized to enforce it by suitable legislation. We doubt very much whether any action of a State not

[1]When the city of New Orleans granted a monopoly to a slaughterhouse, other slaughterhouse companies sued that the monopoly was depriving them of their livelihood in violation of the 14th Amendment's due process of law clause. The Supreme Court ruled, in 1873, that the 14th Amendment was written to guarantee the rights of former slaves and did not apply to these companies' grievances. However, the court also affirmed that the amendment did not deny a state's right of jurisdiction over its citizens' civil rights.

directed by way of discrimination against the negroes as a class, or on account of their race, will ever be held to come within the purview of this provision. It is so clearly a provision for that race and that emergency, that a strong case would be necessary for its application to any other. But as it is a State that is to be dealt with, and not alone the validity of its laws, we may safely leave that matter until Congress shall have exercised its power, or some case of State oppression, by denial of equal justice in its courts shall, have claimed a decision at our hands.

No language could convey a more complete assertion of the power of Congress over the subject embraced in the present bill than is here expressed. If the States do not conform to the requirements of this clause, if they continue to deny to any person within their jurisdiction the equal protection of the laws, or as the Supreme Court had said, "deny equal justice in its courts," then Congress is here said to have power to enforce the constitutional guarantee by appropriate legislation. That is the power which this bill now seeks to put in exercise. It proposes to enforce the constitutional guarantee against inequality and discrimination by appropriate legislation. It does not seek to confer new rights, nor to place rights conferred by State citizenship under the protection of the United States, but simply to prevent and forbid inequality and discrimination on account of race, color, or previous condition of servitude. Never was there a bill more completely within the constitutional power of Congress. Never was there a bill which appealed for support more strongly to that sense of justice and fair-play which has been said, and in the main with justice, to be a characteristic of the Anglo-Saxon race. The Constitution warrants it; the Supreme Court sanctions it; justice demands it.

Sir, I have replied to the extent of my ability to the arguments which have been presented by the opponents of this measure. I have replied also to some of the legal propositions advanced by gentlemen on the other side; and now that I am about to conclude, I am deeply sensible of the imperfect manner in which I have preformed the task. Technically, this bill is to decide upon the civil status of the colored American citizen: a point disputed at the very formation of our present Government, when by a short-sighted policy, a policy repugnant to true republican government, one negro counted as three-fifths of a man. The logical result of this mistake of the framers of the Constitution strengthened the cancer of slavery, which finally spread its poisonous tentacles over the southern portion of the body-politic. To arrest its growth and save the nation we have passed through the harrowing operation of internecine war, dreaded at all times, resorted to at the last extremity, like the surgeon's knife, but absolutely necessary to extirpate the disease which threatened with the life of the nation the overthrow of civil and political liberty on this continent. In that dire extremity the members of the race which I have the honor in part to represent—the race which pleads for justice at your hands today, forgetful of their inhuman and brutalizing servitude at the South, their degradation and ostracism at the North—flew willingly and gallantly to the support of the national Government. Their sufferings, assistance, privations, and trials in the swamps and in the rice-fields, their valor on the land and on the sea, is a part of the ever-glorious record which makes up the history of a nation preserved, and might, should I urge the claim, incline you to respect and guarantee their rights and privileges as citizens of our common Republic. But I remember that valor, devotion, and loyalty are not always rewarded according to their just deserts, and that after the battle some who have borne the brunt of the fray may, through neglect or contempt, be assigned to a subordinate place, while the enemies in war may be preferred to the sufferers.

The results of the war, as seen in reconstruction, have settled forever the political status of my race. The passage of this bill will determine the civil status, not only of the negro, but of any other class of citizens who may feel themselves discriminated against. It will form the cap-stone of that temple of liberty, begun on this continent under discouraging circumstances, carried on in spite of the sneers of monarchists and the cavils of pretended friends of freedom, until at last it stands in all its beautiful symmetry and proportions, a building the grandest which the world has ever seen, realizing the most sanguine expectations and the highest hopes of those who, in the name of equal, impartial, and universal liberty, laid the foundation stones. . . .

WEB RESOURCES FOR PART FOUR

SITES FEATURING A NUMBER OF THE DISSENTERS IN PART FOUR

Clement L. Vallandigham

www.ehistory.com/world/peopleview.cfm?PID=332
www.civilwarhome.com/vallandighambio.htm

William Brownlow

www.lib.utk.edu/~outreach/utkpubs/infoissues/civilwar.html
www.adena.com/adena/usa/cw/cw174.htm

Joseph E. Brown

http://ngeorgia.com/people/brown.html

Cyrus Pringle

www.qhpress.org/quakerpages/qwhp/q19b.htm

African American Soldiers

http://academicinfo.net/africanamcw.html

Susan B. Anthony

www.law.umkc.edu/faculty/projects/ftrials/anthony/sbahome.html
http://mep.cla.sc.edu/sa/sa-table.html
http://ecssba.rutgers.edu/

Robert B. Elliott

There is very little information online about Robert B. Elliott. A brief biographical sketch is located here:

www.aaregistry.com/african_american_history/490/Robert_B_Elliott_a_talented_
     political_force

OTHER DISSENTING VOICES OF THE TIME

1863 Draft Riots

There are many sites furnishing information about the 1863 draft protests in New York City. Among them are:

www.civilwarhome.com/draftriots.htm
www.press.uchicago.edu/Misc/Chicago/317749.html
www.nyhistory.org/draftriots.html

Ku Klux Klan

Although Klansmen wanted to turn back the clock and prevent African Americans from attaining their rights, it is possible to consider the Ku Klux Klan as a dissenting organization. Though they were reactionary, members undoubtedly saw themselves as legitimate dissenters, resisting the new reality of the postwar world. For information on the early Klan, see:

www.pointsouth.com/csanet/kkk.htm
www.tngenweb.org/giles/afro-amer/history/kkk5.html

George Perkins Marsh

For information on nineteenth-century environmentalist George Perkins Marsh, see:

http://bailey.uvm.edu/specialcollections/gpmorc.html

The 1872 Prohibition Party Platform

The Prohibition Party, as its name implies, sought to outlaw alcoholic beverages. Their platform can be found at this site:

www.prohibitionists.org/Background/background.html